CATHOLIC SCHOOLS *STILL* MAKE A DIFFERENCE:

TEN YEARS OF RESEARCH 1991-2000

Edited by

**Thomas C. Hunt
Ellis A. Joseph
Ronald J. Nuzzi**

**NATIONAL CATHOLIC
EDUCATIONAL ASSOCIATION**

Published in the United States of America by

The National Catholic Educational Association
1077 30th Street, NW, Suite 100
Washington, DC 20007-3852
Copyright 2002
ISBN 1-55833-278-2

Production by Phyllis Kokus
Design by Beatriz Ruiz

Printed in the United States of America

CONTENTS

PREFACE

In 1992, Dr. John Convey, then of the Department of Education and currently Provost at The Catholic University of America, authored *Catholic Schools Make A Difference*. Not only did this extensive work provide an overview and syntheses of Catholic school research between 1965 and 1991 but it also included indicators of the effectiveness of Catholic schools. Another important component of Dr. Convey's work was the identification of future research studies on Catholic schools, which you see reflected in this publication

Catholic Schools Still Make A Difference, 1991-2000 edited by Dr. Thomas C. Hunt, Dr. Ellis A. Joseph and Father Ronald Nuzzi, Ph.D, provides the latest research on many of the same issues included in Dr. Convey's earlier work. Several new areas of Catholic school research are included in this new publication. I extend deep appreciation to these three editors for their unwavering efforts to bring this important publication to Catholic educators and others interested in Catholic education.

Specifically, this book is a valuable resource for a number of groups who are responsible for making decisions for Catholic schools: national and diocesan leaders, pastors, Catholic school principals, teachers and staff members and school board, commission or council members. In a special way, it provides an invaluable resource for the general public on the effectiveness of Catholic schools

In addition to the three editors, a number of authors contributed in a significant way to the book's publication. I am grateful to: Linda J. Bufkin, James B. Carroll, Maria J. Ciriello, OP, Timothy J. Cook, William F. Davis, OSFS, James M. Frabutt, Jeanne Hagelskamp, SP, Richard M. Jacobs, OSA, Ellis A. Joseph, Patricia M. Kelleher, Mary F. Landers, Richard J. McGrath, OSA, Elizabeth A. Meegan, OP, Dorothy D. Miles, Ronald J. Nuzzi, Leslie S. Rebhorn, Ann M. Rule, Frank X. Savage, Theodore J. Wallace and H. Roberta Weaver.

Let me also express gratitude to a number of individuals for their professional services in bringing this work to publication: Colleen Wildenhaus of the University of Dayton, Timothy Dwyer, CACE Assistant Executive Director, as well as Phyllis Kokus and Beatriz Ruiz of the NCEA staff.

Catholic schools continue to be one of the greatest gifts of the Catholic Church. As the new millennium begins, there is a renewed spirit and dedication to Catholic school education. This renewed focus on the outstanding success and effectiveness of Catholic schools has never been greater than in recent years as the topic of parental choice in education is discussed in many arenas. I am confident that *Catholic Schools Still Make A Difference, 1991 – 2000* will provide a significant contribution to these and other discussions and to the impact of Catholic schools in service to the Church and the nation.

DANIEL F. CURTIN
Executive Director
Chief Administrators of Catholic Education

FOREWORD

This edited volume presents a review of the research on Catholic schools during the past decade and, as such, represents an update of *Catholic Schools Make A Difference: Twenty-five Years of Research*. I am grateful to Tom Hunt for inviting me to write this Foreword. My administrative responsibilities at The Catholic University of America have prevented me from undertaking the considerable effort of updating *Catholic Schools Make A Difference*, which provided a summary of the research on Catholic schools from approximately 1965 to 1990. Tom, Ellis, Ron, and the contributors to this volume have done an admirable job in producing a comprehensive account of the past decade of Catholic school research that will be helpful to everyone with an interest in Catholic schools.

When I set out to write *Catholic Schools Make A Difference*, I discovered that no comprehensive review of the research on Catholic schools had ever been compiled, although a number of significant studies concerning Catholic schools had been conducted. Prior to 1980, the best-known studies were those by Andrew Greeley, who was often identified as the preeminent Catholic school researcher. Following 1980, Catholic school research moved more to the forefront of the attention of the Catholic school community and the public, helped by the initiatives sponsored by two key organizations: the United States Department of Education and the National Catholic Educational Association. In designing the extensive longitudinal study *High School and Beyond*, the National Center for Educational Statistics decided to include a number of Catholic schools in the database. The first major publication from *High School and Beyond* was the controversial research by James Coleman and his associates, *High School Achievement: Public, Private, and Catholic Schools Compared*. Known in some circles as the Second Coleman Report, a reference to Coleman's controversial *Equality of Educational Opportunity* in 1966, its principal finding, that Catholic schools were more effective than public schools in producing educational outcomes, unleashed a firestorm of controversy and a cottage industry of reanalysis. The finding, however, was largely upheld and later confirmed in Coleman's sequel, *Public and Private High Schools: The Impact of Communities*.

Also during the 1980s, the National Catholic Educational Association launched a series of studies on Catholic schools. These studies on Catholic high schools, their teachers and their outcomes enriched the research literature on Catholic schools and provided a complement to the research from *High School and Beyond*.

The decade of the 1990s continued to see important research on Catholic schools. I believe at least three factors contributed to researchers' continued interest in Catholic schools: (1) the support of Catholic schools by families, as evidenced by gains in Catholic school enrollment, (2) the increased publicity about Catholic schools and their effectiveness, particularly for disadvantaged students, and (3) the political climate, which generated increased attention on issues such as school vouchers and parental choice. In 1991, the enrollment in Catholic schools began to increase after decades of decline. Although slow, the gains were widespread, with 38 states reporting increases in enrollment by 1995. The resurgence of interest in Catholic schools, both from parents who sent their children to Catholic schools and from the general public because of issues concerning school choice and the effectiveness of Catholic schools for disadvantaged children, led to additional strands of research.

I will point to just a few of the resulting research initiatives and trends. The first was the publication in 1993 of Anthony Bryk, Valerie Lee, and Peter Holland's *Catholic Schools and the Common Good*, an influential work that portrayed Catholic schools as the real common schools in the United States, more integrated than the public schools and more likely to benefit disadvantaged students. The second was the increased number of significant doctoral dissertations on Catholic schools, many of which are cited in this volume and at least one of which, Paul Galetto's *Building the Foundations of Faith*, appeared also in book form. The third was the renewed interest in supporting Catholic schools in urban areas and the related issues of school choice. The fourth was the sponsorship by the Lilly Foundation of a significant research initiative on the future of Catholic schools that resulted in the publication of two books, *Catholic Schools at the Crossroads* and *The Catholic Character of Catholic Schools*.

At a research symposium at the University of Dayton in 1994, I identified 10 priority areas for research on Catholic schools: Catholic elementary schools, religious outcomes of Catholic schools, school as community, leadership values, parents and school choice, Catholic school teachers, Catholic school governance, development, and Catholic school finances. This present volume summarizes the advances made in many of these areas during the past decade and adds other topics, including students with special needs, gifted and talented students, the use of technology in Catholic schools, and new learning theories and individual learning styles.

I believe that the research reviewed in this volume will help to corroborate what many Catholics believe and which continues to draw families to Catholic schools—that is, Catholic schools do make a difference.

JOHN J. CONVEY
Provost
The Catholic University of America

INTRODUCTION

In 1992, the National Catholic Educational Association (NCEA) published John Convey's *Catholic Schools Make A Difference: Twenty-five Years of Research*. Convey's book proved to be a most worthwhile contribution to Catholic education. It was thorough, well-researched, and dealt with topics that were both critical and interesting to Catholic education and educators. His "References" alone were worth the price of the book.

The editors of this book were honored when they were given the opportunity to do a sequel to Convey's groundbreaking effort. First, we decided to seek out qualified authors for a number of chapters in order to present the research on a given topic through the pens of established scholars. Second, we determined to follow, to the extent possible, the model employed by Professor Convey. The reader will note that some of the chapters deal with the same topics (e.g., "Demography") as did Convey's original work. Other chapters address topics in which there was scant, if any, research within the years 1965 to 1990 covered by Convey. Even in those chapters, we asked the authors to be cognizant of Convey's work as a model.

We have divided this volume into five sections. The first is CATHOLIC SCHOOLS AND THE BROADER CHURCH, which contains two chapters: "Faith Leadership," authored by co-editor Ellis Joseph, and "Catholic Identity," written by co-editor Ronald Nuzzi. INTERNAL AND EXTERNAL FACTORS is the title of the second section. Richard Jacobs, OSA wrote on "Environment," while Maria Ciriello, OP, James Carroll, and Elizabeth Meegan, OP, combined to write "Outcomes." Chapters on "Teachers" by Timothy Cook, "Parents" by James Frabutt, and "Students" by Richard McGrath, OSA, constitute the third section, which we have called HUMAN RESOURCES. The fourth section, TEACHING AND LEARNING, contains four chapters. Leslie Rebhorn penned "Gifted Education in Catholic Schools," Mary Frances Landers and Roberta Weaver addressed "Special Needs," Dorothy Miles, Ann Rule, and Linda Bufkin composed the chapter on "Learning Styles," and Jeanne Hagelskamp, SP, authored the "Technology" chapter. The final section is entitled SOCIAL, FISCAL, AND POLITICAL CAPITAL. Frank Savage authored the "Demographics" chapter, Patricia Kelleher wrote on "Governance and Administration," William Davis, OSFS, drafted the chapter on "School Choice and Vouchers," and Theodore Wallace was responsible for the "Finance and Development" chapter.

We present this work to the Catholic educational community through the NCEA with the hope that it will be of use to researchers, teachers, administrators, bishops, pastors, and policymakers. We appreciate the opportunity that the NCEA gave us to put this work together. In that spirit we dedicate this volume to all those whose God-given vocation has been to minister in the fruitful vineyard that is Catholic education. We are happy to report and proud to claim that Catholic schools *still* make a difference.

THOMAS C. HUNT
ELLIS A. JOSEPH
RONALD J. NUZZI

CATHOLIC SCHOOLS
AND THE
BROADER CHURCH

CHAPTER 1
FAITH LEADERSHIP

ELLIS A. JOSEPH

Massucci's (1993) study of the unique identity of Catholic high schools indicated that witnessing the gospel by school personnel is the *most important characteristic* of the Catholic school's mission. In addition to Massucci's study, many dissertations have emerged in the last decade treating the topic (with the use of various terms) of spiritual leadership, faith leadership, or ministerial leadership (Anastasio, 1996; Carr, 1995; Compagnone, 1999; Diamond, 1997; Moore, 1999; Wallace, 1995). The principal concern appears to be whether the Catholic identity of Catholic schools will receive proper attention given the rapid shift from religious to lay leadership.

Fifty-three percent of Catholic elementary school and 38% of Catholic high school principals in the United States are lay (Archer, 1997a). Wallace (1995) found approximately 50% of Catholic high school principals are lay. Drahmann (1984) and Ryan (1964), among many others, predicted this increase in lay leadership as early as approximately four decades ago. Drahmann indicated that religious orders would be increasingly unable to prepare their members for administration. Ryan wondered whether Catholic schools would survive without religious staffs. Vaughan (1978) was concerned about public acceptance of the laity in Catholic schools. In 1960, 27% of Catholic school teachers were lay persons; in 1990, 85% of teachers in Catholic elementary and high schools were lay (Buetow, 1985). Administrative and teaching personnel, then, are increasingly lay.

It is relevant, given this change in personnel, to consider two important topics: (1) terminology which is juxtaposed to leadership and whether all terminology employed has the same meaning in relation to the unique identity of Catholic schooling; and (2) the concern over the performance of lay leadership.

Terminology and Unique Identity

In Wallace's (1995) study, 324 lay Catholic high school principals responded to a questionnaire seeking to determine the effectiveness of their preparation to serve as faith leaders. Wallace utilized the term faith leadership. He defined faith leadership as "Competencies needed to provide staff development and school experiences that reinforce the primary Catholic mission of the school" (p. 10). Wallace made a distinction between faith leadership and pastoral leadership. He considers a pastoral leader to be "One with responsibilities to develop the spiritual direction of the members of a particular community" (p. 10). Elsewhere in his study Wallace uses the terms "spiritual/faith leader" as if they were synonymous (p. 13). He also avers "The 'faith formation' role of the principal is particularly crucial given the increasingly lay teaching staff" (pp. 15-16).

Heft (1991a) is specific in describing what he expects of a Catholic school leader who is attempting to foster Catholic identity: "institutionalizing Catholic traditions and doctrinal emphases" (p. 5). One may assume spiritual leader, faith formation, faith leader, spiritual leadership, ministerial leadership, pastoral, and moral leadership all are encompassed within institutionalizing Catholic traditions and doctrinal emphases. Some studies use terms such as: benefit students spiritually (Payne, 1989), modeling gospel values in the classroom (Dorsey, 1992), and "create favorable conditions for a formation process" (Congregation for Catholic Education,

1988, p. 12). Some of these terms are more specific than others; many of them encompass others. All of them perhaps are included within Heft's terminology: institutionalizing Catholic traditions and doctrinal emphases.

If a Catholic school principal is wondering what actions should be taken in regard to the specifics of doctrinal emphases and institutionalizing Catholic traditions, then reference may be made to what Manno (1985) calls pastoral competencies of the principal. Wallace (1995), even though he uses the term faith leader, acknowledges Manno's preference for designating specific competencies. Manno designates certain pastoral competencies which are unique to the Catholic school principal:

> Is familiar with and creates an environment where the process of faith and moral development as it relates to working with youth and adults can be applied
>
> Is familiar with and creates an environment where the contents and methods of religious education can be applied
>
> Knows and applies Church documents and other religious resources that relate to schools
>
> Is capable of providing opportunities which foster the spiritual growth of faculty, students and other members of the school community
>
> Is capable of leading the school community in prayer
>
> Is capable of linking the school and the local school community
>
> Is capable of integrating gospel values and Christian social principles into the curriculum and the life of the school
>
> Is capable of articulating the Catholic educational vision and directing its accomplishments
>
> Is sensitive to the demands of justice in making financial decisions, especially as they relate to the Church's social teachings. (pp. 11, 12)

Manno (1985) also elaborates some professional educational and managerial competencies which may be unique to Catholic school leaders and at the same time common to any school leader:

> Is capable of working collaboratively with a variety of parish and/or diocesan groups, especially governance groups
>
> Is capable of promoting staff morale and a sense of Christian community among teachers
>
> Is capable of providing leadership in curriculum development in general, including the integration of Christian values
>
> Is capable of shaping, sharing, and implementing a school philosophy which reflects the unique character of the school
>
> Is capable of initiating and conducting appropriate staff development activities
>
> Recognizes, respects, and is capable of facilitating the primary role of parents as educators
>
> Is capable of providing effective instructional leadership and supervision of staff and programs which reflect the unique Catholic character of the school
>
> Is capable of providing leadership for long range planning and development activities
>
> Knows current school law as it applies to the Catholic school. (p. 12)

Two closely related elements listed by Manno appear in his "unique to the Catholic school" list which is classified as pastoral *and* also in his list of professional educational and managerial competencies. Both of these elements are concerned with: (1) integrating gospel values and Christian social principles into the curriculum and (2) providing leadership in the kind of curriculum development which includes the integration of Christian values. Since Catholic schools *are* educational institutions and not merely religious institutes, it seems that the most challenging task for the Catholic school leader is to focus upon, in an intellectually defensible and sophisticated manner, that unique Catholic identity as it permeates the subjects in the curriculum. The Church's magisterium is counter cultural. It demands faith, discipline, and sacrifice, and it demands that Catholic school students are expected to hold different views from others. The daunting task of integration is made arduous by both contextual and intellectual factors.

Gleason (1994) addresses the contextual by referring to young Catholics who came of age after World War II. They wondered why they had to have their own separate institutions, why they were expected to hold views different from their wider culture (to which they had been assimilated) on matters such as divorce, birth control, abortion, the meaning of natural law doctrine, premarital sex, and so on.

One searches in vain for research evidence of a sustained, formal, and systematic effort to achieve integration of Catholic identity in actual school subjects. Schuttloffel (2000) hints at the importance of the effort. This is an intellectual task requiring broad as well as in-depth intellectual capacity in Catholic school leaders. There is confusion in the literature about the distinction between instructional leadership and intellectual leadership. There is no scarcity of sources stressing the importance of instructional leadership (Ciriello, 1993; Indrisano, 1989; Perri, 1989; Ristau, 1991; Rogus, 1991; Wallace, 1995). However, intellectual leadership is rarely discussed. Simon (1997) perhaps, although only partially addressing Catholic schools, supports the notion that broad and in-depth intellectual capacity is required for intellectual leadership.

There are few, if any, models in research literature on Catholic schools that would discuss the distinction between intellectual leadership and instructional leadership. Some sources (Feynman, 1998; Swinburne, 1996) not directed at Catholic education are excellent examples of the depth and breadth of knowledge required should Catholic school *intellectual* (as contrasted to *instructional*) leaders decide to treat the issue of integrating unique Catholic identity in the subjects of the school's curriculum. These two sources explore the relationship of science to religion.

Manno (1985) quite rightly identifies capability of integrating gospel values and Christian social principles into the curriculum of the school as a principal competency. Many documents stress this capability on the *level of principle*. While this is necessary, Manno and these documents (Canon Law Society, 1983; Congregation for Catholic Education, 1988; National Conference, 1984; Paul VI, 1975, 1977; Sacred Congregation, 1972, 1982; Second Vatican Council, 1965/1996; United States Catholic Conference, 1983b) did not intend to provide the kind of scholarship which specifically examines how integration occurs in the given disciplines taught.

In literature, for example, Edgar Allen Poe (1948) asked himself: "Of all melancholy topics, what, according to the *universal* understanding of mankind, is the *most* melancholy? Death was the obvious reply" (p. 478). The Catholic school student has to be prompted to wonder further about Poe's statement. Death in relation to what? To merely intra temporal phenomena? Extra temporal phenomena? Why is it "according to the universal understanding of mankind"? Poe did not raise these questions and neither do those who teach about him in secular schools.

Dudley and Faricy (1951), in their influential work, *The Humanities*, gazed upon the entire history of art and made the statement, with little fear of contradiction, that the greatest single source and subject of art in any country is religion. For them, this statement is de facto, what, as a matter of fact, is. The Catholic school student should be encouraged to search for an elaboration of why religion has been such a recurring subject of art. Could it be that, through religion as source and subject, art may long have had a profound influence upon human beings? Could it be that something besides color mixtures and line relationships have had and should have content value for humans? While Dudley and Faricy may be reluctant to extend themselves beyond de facto concerns, they identify some hierarchical domains when discussing emotions in the arts. They assert "some emotions are admittedly of a nobler kind than others. Love is higher than hate; forgiveness is higher than revenge. The positive emotions are higher than the negative; the constructive are higher than the destructive" (Dudley & Faricy, 1951, p. 473). They do approach a non de facto concern by actually including a rather lengthy treatment of judgment in the arts. They indicate that if one speaks of judgment in the arts, one must consider "magnitude," or the worth of an artist's idea. For them, differences in worth (or magnitude) "may be traced to differences in the kind and the degree of emotions involved" (p. 473). When treating the intensity of feeling, they state "the greatest magnitude occurs when we have a great emotion felt greatly" (p. 473). The Catholic school student should be encouraged to wonder about the ultimate source of such normative words as "higher" and "greatest."

When line in art is discussed, the average non artist seldom internalizes such a formalism as being something which deserves to dwell within one's breast. However, in rare instances we are told "line is probably the earliest and simplest element in the visual arts" (Dudley & Faricy, 1951, p. 207). We are told "probably because of its force, the vertical line stands for moral probity, exaltation, and inspiration. When we speak of...'upright' we mean...moral worth" (p. 207). This power of the vertical has often been recognized: for example, "the vertical line is found in the *Castelfranco Madonna*"; and "a great deal of the sense of majesty in the painting derives from the repeated verticals" (p. 208). Secular formalism would have us merely study the intricacies of line in the *Castelfranco Madonna*. The Catholic school would encourage students to gaze upon it for a sense of majesty, exaltation, uprightness, and moral worth.

Let us use history as another example. How is Josef Pieper's (1954) assertion that history must be viewed as extra temporal, beyond time, and not merely within time to be incorporated? This is a distinctively Catholic view of history as contrasted to those who view history merely chronologically or conceptually or as existing for some sort of secular self-understanding. A student in a Catholic school progressing through a history text mindful of Pieper's assertion does so with an altogether different mindset than merely covering the material chronologically or conceptually or with a view of secular self-understanding. These approaches to history are *intellectual* issues, not merely *instructional* concerns. Each discipline contains intellectual issues particular to its methodology of inquiry. Principals, while they cannot be experts in every discipline, *should* and *can* be acquainted with the intellectual issues in each discipline. The manner in which the Catholic school makes choices when considering these issues is of immense *practical* importance. In history, for example, it affects the kinds of texts selected and the method and content of teaching. Instructional leadership which, by definition, deals with ability grouping, team teaching, educational technology, and so on, does not address intellectual issues.

Wallace (1995), Massucci (1993), Moore (1999), Compagnone (1999), and Reichel (1999) have conducted excellent studies on Catholic school administrators as "faith leaders." Neither these studies nor Manno's (1985) list of competencies indicate that the Catholic school principal should be an intellectual or a scholar. Such an indication was not within their purposes. In all the research literature on the Catholic school principalship one is hard pressed to find an advocate for the notion that leadership belongs to intellectuals or scholars. It seems probable that this omission will perpetuate the situation, which finds unique Catholic identity averred on the level of principal and neglected at the point of permeating the academic subjects of the curriculum. Mass, prayer, religious symbols, and rituals are all necessary. However, the Catholic school is first and foremost about education. Good persons of faith are required to lead in the former; good persons of faith and broad intellect are needed for the latter. It may be hypothesized that so much is written about unique Catholic identity not because it is difficult to grasp, but because of anxiety over how to achieve its presence in the curriculum.

As Porath (2000) has stated, the Catholic school is more than an institute of religious formation. It has an academic character that is devoted to imparting a specific concept of the world, of human beings, and of history. It includes all forms of knowing and strives for the unity of knowledge.

The Performance of Lay Leadership

Wallace (1995) has conducted the most massive study that sought to assess the preparedness of lay Catholic high school principals to be faith leaders. Wallace determined there were 1,249 Catholic high schools in the United States. Lay principals led 619 of these high schools. Wallace's survey yielded 324 responses. All six regions of the country as defined by the National Catholic Educational Association were represented. Three hundred twenty-four questionnaires were returned followed by selected interviews. Wallace's results indicated:

Of the 324 questionnaires returned, 70% rated their formal course work as inadequate in the area of faith leadership.
More than half indicated they had taken no courses or seminars beyond their bachelor's degrees related to the faith leadership role. (p. ii)

Even though principals in the study indicated inadequate preparation, 69% believed that "today's Catholic schools are as successful as schools in the 1950's in establishing and maintaining Catholic identity even though those 1950's schools were predominantly staffed by vowed religious" (Wallace, 1995, p. ii). Prior experiences in Catholic schools, experiences as practicing Catholics, mentors, and the charisms of sponsoring religious orders were factors listed by principals to explain the difference between inadequate preparation and success in establishing and maintaining Catholic identity. Wallace offers three recommendations:

Bishops and Catholic school central office personnel need to be proactive in assuring that principals have the necessary combination of formal coursework and personal faith development experiences to serve effectively as faith leaders in their schools. Catholic colleges and universities must work with Church leaders to create and deliver programs of faith development. Programs currently in operation and those yet to be established must provide a balance between formal education and personal faith development experiences including mentoring. (p. iii)

Moore (1999) studied elementary school principals in a large midwestern diocese. Her survey, the Catholic Elementary School Survey developed by Carr (1995), was administered to all 112 elementary school principals in the diocese and was followed by personal focused interviews. Ninety-four surveys (84%) were returned and used. Approximately 72% of the population are lay principals, 20% religious, and 8% former religious. Moore's study focused on mission motivation, spiritual satisfaction, and spiritual efficacy. Selected findings from Moore's study are as follows:

All Catholic school principals in the study reported high mean scores for mission motivation, spiritual satisfaction, and spiritual efficacy.
Vowed religious principals reported being the most satisfied of all three groups with their roles as spiritual leaders in Catholic schools.
Lay principals reported the lowest scores in spiritual satisfaction among the three groups.
Those principals who reported the highest scores in mission motivation, spiritual satisfaction, and spiritual efficacy engage in a greater degree of spiritual formation activities than persons who report lower mean scores.
Principals who have received at least some formal training (graduate or undergraduate course work) in Catholic school philosophy, theology, or history reported higher combined mean scores for mission motivation, spiritual satisfaction, and spiritual efficacy than those who received no formal training in those areas...Religious and former religious reported more formal training...in the purposes of Catholic schools than did lay principals.
Religious and former religious principals reported higher religiosity scores than their lay counterparts.
Religiosity appears to be related to mean scores for mission motivation, spiritual satisfaction, and spiritual efficacy. (pp. 149-151)

Moore's (1999) study also indicated principals, lay and religious, reported strong mission motivation regarding their work in a Catholic school. All interviewees spoke of the importance of significant persons for principals' spiritual formation. All principals place a high value on religion in their lives.

Carr's (1995) study, which greatly influenced Moore, was national in scope. It proved to be of great value for those interested in appropriate instrumentation for surveying elementary school principals. In addition to developing the Catholic Elementary School Principal Survey, she brought some precision to the use of terminology such as mission motivation, spiritual leadership satisfaction, spiritual leadership efficacy, and religiosity. Moore's findings were congruent with Carr's in the areas of mission motivation and spiritual efficacy and religiosity. Moore's results were consistent with Carr's conclusion that spiritual leadership satisfaction of religious principals dominates all other dimensions for both lay and religious principals.

Carr's study was also important methodologically to Compagnone's (1999) research on the self-perceptions of lay Catholic elementary school principals in Kansas in the areas of spiritual leadership and ministerial roles. All 101 religious and lay principals of Catholic elementary schools in Kansas were surveyed. Responses were received from approximately 74% or 75 principals. Compagnone modified Carr's instrument for purposes of his study. Of the 101 participants in his study, 91 are lay.

Compagnone (1999) concluded that participants in his study have strong positive perceptions of themselves as spiritual and ministerial leaders. Even though not required, 95% of principals achieved certified status as catechists, providing an example for faculty and staff. Sixty-nine percent of lay principals indicated that assuming leadership in a Catholic school was God's choice for their life; 73% indicated it was their commitment to Catholic education that attracted them to the ministerial aspects of Catholic schools; 90% reported frequently attending Eucharistic services; and 55% frequently attend retreats other than those sponsored by their dioceses. In organizing prayer or liturgical services, principals are not as strong in their confidence level as they were in other areas. Ninety-five percent of lay principals indicated a moderate to high priority to lead in the spiritual formation of faculty. Ninety-seven percent rate as *very important* or *extremely important* to have opportunities to reflect upon and contemplate their role as principals in a Catholic school. Thirty-two lay principal respondents in this study had not attended a Catholic school. Compagnone concluded that these respondents have lower priorities for implementing the spiritual dimensions of Catholic schools than those who did attend.

As Wallace (1995) emphasized, Compagnone calls for collaboration and leadership on the diocesan level in assisting principals and potential principals in professional development and preparation, and he agrees with Wallace on encouraging university-diocesan partnerships.

CHAPTER 2
CATHOLIC IDENTITY

RONALD J. NUZZI

What does it mean in the third millennium of Christianity to call oneself Catholic? Does the uppercase, capitalized version of Catholic explicitly connect one to the institutional Church, headquartered in Rome, with dioceses, parishes, and schools spread throughout the world? Can a person claim to be a Catholic without affiliation and participation in one of the local Catholic institutions? Moreover, when the word Catholic is used as an adjective, for example, as in Catholic school or Catholic hospital, what is it that makes such an institution Catholic? What are the constitutive elements of Catholic identity?

The decade 1990-2000 has witnessed a soaring interest in this question, especially as it relates to the Catholic identity of institutions of higher learning-colleges and universities-in light of Pope John Paul II's Apostolic Constitution, *Ex Corde Ecclesiae* (1990). On June 5, 2001, the United States bishops accepted a set of guidelines for implementing a process for granting the *mandatum* to professors in the theological disciplines as required by *Ex Corde Ecclesiae* as well as Canon #812 of the *Code of Canon Law* (Canon Law Society, 1983). While the theological and juridical prudence of both *Ex Corde Ecclesiae* and the U.S. bishops' implementation plan are still intensely debated issues (Breslin, 2000; Dosen, 2000; George, 2000; Iozzio, 2000), a significant number of the questions under consideration could be assumed under one, pointed question: What makes a Catholic university Catholic?

A similar version of this question is being asked at the elementary and secondary levels in Catholic education. Catholic educators, including teachers, bishops, administrators, diocesan central office staff, and university professors are asking, "What makes a Catholic school Catholic?" In recent years, the question has been asked repeatedly (Groome, 1996; Pilarczyk, 1982, 1998; Quirin, 2001; Trafford, 1993; Veverka, 1993). This chapter presents a review of the various responses that have been proffered to this vital question and contextualizes those responses in framework that attempts to organize the many answers that have been proposed.

Responses From Theologians

Seasoned educators might wonder how theological disciplines can inform the Catholic identity question at the elementary and secondary levels in ways that are helpful to K-12 educators. While one would expect theologians to influence the shape of Catholic identity at the university level, Catholic educators in typical parish elementary schools and diocesan and private high schools are unaccustomed to professional theological discourse in relation to the conduct of K-12 education. This is regrettable. Some scholars believe that theological issues are at the heart of the identity question:

> What makes Catholic schools Catholic are the theological truths which govern and give guidance to both philosophy and to persons of Catholic faith. These truths have made the Catholic church a countercultural church....The failure on the part of Catholic schools to understand that their guidance emanates from theology, and not solely from philosophy, may account for their problems with identity and distinctiveness. (Joseph, 2001, pp. 31-32)

Two important theological works have shaped the general nature of responses to the question during the 1990s. The first and most important is an issue of the theological journal *Concilium* dedicated to the question of Catholic identity (Provost & Walf, 1994). Containing more than a dozen scholarly essays on different aspects of Catholic identity, one volume of this distinguished publication has made a significant contribution to the Church's growing understanding of the identity question. *Concilium*, founded in 1965 in the midst of the Second Vatican Council, is an international journal of theology dedicated to the spirit of Vatican II. As if to answer the question of Catholic identity, *Concilium* says in its own promotional literature that it "is a catholic journal in the widest sense: rooted firmly in the Catholic heritage, open to other Christian traditions and the world's faiths" (1994, p. 152). Tellingly, "each issue focuses on a theme of crucial importance and the widest possible concern for our time" (1994, p. 152). Catholic identity, it would appear, is not simply a concern for American Catholic schools. It is an issue for the universal church.

The second major theological work is an essay by Charles E. Curran (1997) in the prestigious journal, *Theological Studies*. Curran, a moral theologian and professor of Human Values at Southern Methodist University in Dallas, analyzed the question of Catholic identity by discussing the very possibility of Catholic institutions in our modern age.

Provost and Walf (1994) anticipated that the question of Catholic identity for institutions and individuals might become polemical. A danger in naming or listing essential elements to any identity is that such a list can easily become a litmus test used in the public forum to welcome some and exclude others. Moreover, the question is given critical urgency today because there appears to be open and honest debate about what were once commonly accepted standards. "Criteria which once seemed so clear are now in crisis. Practical measures, such as the visible presence of clergy or religious, are becoming less reliable as laity take on a rightful and increasingly visible role in church life" (Provost & Walf, 1994, p. vii). A generation ago, this question of Catholic identity arguably did not exist in its present form. Today, we not only have to ask the question of schools, hospitals, and social service agencies, but of an increasing variety of services and products that call themselves Catholic, including investments (http://moneycentral.msn.com/articles/invest/funds/6659.asp) and Catholic Internet providers (http://www.justcatholic.com).

Greinacher (1994) connected the current identity question with the conflict experienced at Vatican II between two Catholic identities. Arguing that the Council precipitated an identity crisis about the very meaning of church, Greinacher pointed to the lack of clarity around the identity question that may be traced to the Council.

> Identity means agreement over certain issues and persons. There has never been a Catholic identity that transcends history, nor can there be. Nevertheless, before the Council there was an amazingly comprehensive, at least implicit, agreement among *all* Catholics, men and women, clergy and laity, Magisterium and believers, on what was Catholic. (1994, p. 6)

This firmness in pre-concil
iar Catholic identity differed considerably from the attitude of many Catholics after the Council. One author characterized this new understanding by relating: "People in Rome can decide what they like, but I'm remaining Catholic" (Greinacher, 1994, p. 6).

The basic tenet of pre-conciliar Catholicism concerning Catholic identity was the doctrine of the Church as the *societas perfectas*, or the perfect society. The Catholic Church was understood to be the means of salvation for all, and salvation necessitated identification with this Church. Vatican II moved away from this emphasis on the institutional church and offered a new conceptualization of the Church as the People of God. The current age's question about the constitutive elements of contemporary Catholic identity has its roots in the conciliar development about the nature of the Church. Working out the significance of this identity development has touched every aspect of church life, including the Catholicity of the institutions that the Church sponsors, to questions like the relationship between priests and their bishop, bishops and the Pope, parishioners and their pastor.

Greinacher (1994) delineated four important elements of Catholic identity according to the Second Vatican Council: 1) belief in the Christian faith in loyalty to the Scriptures and to the tradition of the Church as proclaimed by the Magisterium; 2) being an active part of God's beloved people; 3) being bound in familial ties with Catholics throughout the world; and 4) believing that God is active in both the Church and throughout the world. Acknowledging that the teaching of the Council had given rise to a new focus on Catholic identity, Greinacher concluded:

> Catholic identity has become more difficult to live out since the Second Vatican Council. For first of all it has to be *sought*, certainly within the Christian community, but in the last resort individually, and it must be sought again and again. People were not aware of this before the Council. Being Catholic means being questioned by the world. But in the end-and it is this that constitutes identity-being Catholic can and must also be an enquiry [sic] to the world. Being Catholic has become more demanding as a result of the Second Vatican Council, but also more liberating and enriching. (pp. 12-13)

Canon law has also been consulted as a vehicle for assisting in the decision about individual Catholic identity. Borras (1994) claimed that as the People of God, built on faith in Jesus Christ, the Church was a society *sui generis*, like no other. And because the Church is still on its way to the kingdom and has an element of ongoing growth and development, it is decidedly unrealistic to expect individual believers to be perfect, or even close to it. "The Church is an extremely heterogeneous reality…sinners form part of the Church" (Borras, 1994, pp. 47-48). Borras enumerated six conditions that have created a problematical situation for individual Catholics regarding their Catholic identity: 1) Catholics in a state of manifest grave sin; 2) Catholics under penal sanction; 3) Catholics who have become apostates, heretics, or formal schismatics; 4) Catholics who have defected from the faith or the Church in a public or notorious way; 5) Catholics who have defected from the Church by a formal act; and 6) Catholics in an irregular matrimonial situation. After an analysis of the relevant canon laws, Borras (1994) concluded that only two of the above problematical situations bring about the loss of one's Catholic identity:

> Of all the problematical situations from a canonical point of view relating to Catholic identity, only Catholics who have become apostates, heretics, and schismatics and those who have left the Church by a formal act must be considered as no longer taking part in *visible* communion with the Catholic Church (Canon 205). The other categories continue in general to live in *visible* communion even if their incorporation is *less full* and their participation in the life of the church is reduced or at least limited by the law. (p. 58)

The struggle for clarity in relation to the question of Catholic identity occurs at the institutional level as well as the individual level. Curran (1997) examined the question of Catholic identity at it relates to three kinds of Catholic organizations: health care, education, and social service. While it may appear that hospitals, schools, universities, and Catholic Charities have little in common, Curran argued that these institutions share a similar historical development in the United States. Each of them was created to meet a perceived need in the context of a Catholic subculture. As all grew and developed, they gradually became more professionalized and opened structured and official lines of communication with state agencies, licensing organizations, and voluntary associations of similar professionals. All three experienced remarkable growth during the post-World War II period. All experienced dramatic staffing changes, especially in leadership positions, in response to the declining numbers of available priests, clergy, and vowed religious.

Curran (1997) openly wondered whether it was even possible to have such organizations exist today as identifiably Catholic. Observing that much of the literature generated around the question of Catholic identity comes out of these very institutions, Curran rightly pointed out that the possibility and desirability of such Catholic institutions is simply taken for granted in contemporary Catholic discourse.

Many outsiders would be amazed at the basic assumption that such institutions can be Catholic. How can one be a Catholic institution while at the same time serving the general public, having non-Catholics on staff and on one's board of trustees, and even receiving government aid of various types? Why do Catholics so readily assume that such institutions can be Catholic? (Curran, 1997, p. 92)

Whatever Catholic identity is becoming, Curran maintained that it cannot be defined in purely sectarian terms. "Catholic always includes catholic with a small c" (Curran, 1997, p. 92).

Are Catholic institutions desirable today? Scholars agree that such institutions are good not only for the Church, but for the general public. Nearly all such Catholic institutions, in addition to providing high quality professional services, open their doors to non-Catholics and indeed to all who enter. In short, Catholic institutions such as hospitals, schools, colleges and universities, and social service agencies, promote the common good as well as incarnate the mission of the Church (Bryk, Lee, & Holland, 1993; Catholic Health Association, 1987; Fahey & Lewis, 1992; Schindler, 1995).

Responses from Educators

Classroom teachers, religious educators, school administrators, and university professors involved in Catholic school leadership programs have each attempted, from their own vantage point, to answer the question, "what makes a Catholic school Catholic?" Several of their responses are summarized below.

Thomas Groome (1996), perhaps the leading scholar of religious education in the United States today, tackled the issue in an essay, "What Makes A School Catholic?" Admitting a somewhat circular argument, Groome introduced a proposal for Catholic identity, stating "that the distinctiveness of Catholic education is prompted by the distinctive characteristics of Catholicism itself, and these characteristics should be reflected in the whole curriculum of Catholic schools" (1996, p. 107). Following this logic, a Catholic school takes its identity from the Catholic Church, so the characteristics unique to a school—its entire curriculum—must be rooted in and configured to the faith of the Church.

Building on the work of American theologian Langdon Gilkey, Groome (1996) articulated a collage of eight characteristics of an education that is Catholic. Five of these characteristics are theological in that they have their roots in a Catholic worldview and are widely held convictions within the theological community. The five theological characteristics are: 1) Catholicism is committed to tradition, and therefore honors the weight of history, human experience, and the growth and development of knowledge; 2) Catholicism has a positive anthropology, acknowledges sin, but believes in the basic goodness of all people; 3) Catholicism has a sense of sacramentality, believing that the world and life's experiences are enduring channels of God's grace; 4) Catholicism has a communal emphasis, calling believers into a shared responsibility for the common good and for building the kingdom; and 5) Catholicism has an appreciation of rationality and learning, convinced that the human mind and spirit can come to know and love God.

In addition to these theological insights found in Catholicism, three additional themes can be found in the tradition that have relevance for Catholic education. Groome termed these themes "cardinal characteristics" (1996, p. 109), for they are the hinges that hold the five theological characteristics together. The cardinal characteristics are: 1) Catholicism is committed to individual personhood and to the quality of person that each of us becomes; 2) Catholicism is committed to justice at all levels; and 3) Catholicism is committed to catholicity, in its broadest, etymological, universal sense.

Groome (1996) maintained that these eight characteristics provide a helpful structure or model in which to understand all the activities and efforts of the school. These characteristics are also what constitute the distinctiveness of the Catholic school, for many, if not most, would not be readily manifest in public education or even in other private schools.

Another response to the question of Catholic identity addressed the role of teachers in Catholic schools. What makes a school Catholic? One answer is clearly "its faculty." Catholic teacher identity is thus one way of examining the constitutive elements of Catholic identity for a school.

Shimabukuro (1998) addressed the nature of Catholic teacher identity through an examination of Church documents during and since the Second Vatican Council. After probing the relevant Church documents for emerging and repeated themes, Shimabukuro identified five themes that comprise the Catholic identity of teachers. The themes were presented as commitments that the ideal Catholic school teacher would possess. They are commitments to: 1) "community building"; 2) "lifelong spiritual growth"; 3) "lifelong professional development"; 4) "students' spiritual formation"; and 5) "students' human development" (Shimabukuro, 1998, p. 1).

Such a focus on identity broadens the question to include not simply the components of curriculum that are presented in the Catholic school, but also the faith, temperament, spirituality, professionalism, and life goals of the faculty. Clarifying what we mean by Catholic identity today is thus a significant part of staff development and faculty faith formation for the Catholic school. Left unattended, the lack of clarity about identity can thwart the overall mission of the school.

> Clarification of Catholic identity among Catholic school teachers is one of the greatest challenges facing Catholic schools today. It is an issue of critical importance, affecting the future of Catholic education globally. Confusion on behalf of its members divides a school and creates areas of "hidden" curricula that sabotage Gospel-driven educational goals. (Shimabukuro, 1998, p. 1)

This is a critical insight for those who exercise leadership responsibilities for Catholic schools, especially principals and central office and diocesan personnel. Plans to strengthen Catholic identity in any school should consider the important role of the faculty, not only in carrying out the school-wide plan, but also in terms of their own spiritual development and lifelong learning. "Total focus on student formation without ongoing teacher formation...potentially cripples this holistic approach to education" (Shimabukuro, 1998, p. 7).

The crucial role of teachers in creating and sustaining a Catholic ethos in the school is echoed by the Congregation for Catholic Education (1997), the Vatican office dedicated to school oversight, in its document, *The Catholic School on the Threshold of the Third Millennium*:

> In the Catholic school, prime responsibility for creating this unique Christian school climate rests with the teachers as individuals and as a community. Teaching has an extraordinary moral depth and is one of man's most excellent and creative activities, for the teacher does not write on inanimate materials, but on the very spirits of human beings. The personal relations between the teachers and students, therefore, assume an enormous importance and are not limited simply to giving and taking.

> Moreover, we must remember that teachers and educators fulfill a specific Christian vocation and share an equally specific participation in the mission of the church, to the extent that it depends chiefly on them whether the Catholic school achieves its purpose. (#19)

Kelly (1991) provided a sampling of answers to the question of the Catholicity in schools through the publication of conference papers from a June 1988 gathering at the University of Dayton. Sponsored by the Departments of Religious Education and Secondary Schools of the National Catholic Educational Association

(NCEA), the conference consisted of 180 Catholic school educators reflecting for a week together on the question, "What Makes A School Catholic?" (Kelly, 1991).

William J. O'Malley, S.J. (1991), a widely published high school teacher from New York, approached the issue by a series of questions, providing pointed indicators of a school's Catholic identity. O'Malley asked:

> Are there as many students in your service programs as there are on your varsity teams? Is your retreat budget as large as your athletic budget? Are all the faculty and staff, without exception, genuine Christian apostles? (p. 8)

Other authors proffered answers to the question along more traditional lines. Francis Keating (1991) spoke of the need for prayer and contemplation, extolling the value of spiritual reading and reflection. James Heft, S.M., pointed to the marks of the Church (one, holy, catholic, apostolic) as a way that identity might be brought into clearer focus (Heft, 1991b). Tom Zanzig (1991), a nationally known author and speaker in the field of youth ministry and religious education, focused on the centrality of the religion curriculum in the quest for Catholic identity, calling for clarity of goals and attention to the silent or hidden curriculum in Catholic schools, for it often is antithetical to gospel values. Mark Link, S.J., (1991) advocated for more attention to students' self-image as a way to appreciate fully our being created in God's image, and Loretta Carey, R.D.C., (1991) argued for a clear commitment on the part of schools to the social teaching of the Church in the areas of peace and justice.

In papers commissioned for the *National Congress on Catholic Schools for the 21st Century*, convened by the National Catholic Educational Association, November 6-10, 1991, two scholars addressed the theme: *The Catholic Identity of Catholic Schools*. Heft (1991c) addressed the theological components of Catholic identity, while Carleen Reck, SSND (1991), situated the mission of Catholic schools in their broader civic and national purposes.

Heft (1991c) presented a brief history of Catholic schools in the United States, arguing persuasively that there has been a major shift in support by all Catholics for their schools. This shift is evident in parents who no longer choose Catholic schools for their children, in pastors who prefer parishes without schools, and in bishops who would rather not build schools in the first place. Citing the legacy of Mary Perkins Ryan, Heft concluded that American Catholics are at best ambivalent about Catholic schools. And in a final section of speculation about four possible future scenarios, Heft correctly predicted the collaboration of Catholic universities and colleges in the formation and preparation of teachers for Catholic schools.

Reck (1991) took a different approach and encouraged school leaders to "find ways to broaden the school's potential for community and service, thereby strengthening its identity with the parish" (p. 32). While acknowledging that the school is intimately related to the parish and local church, Reck also challenged educators to be mindful of the Catholic school's relationship to the civic community and its participation in the promotion of the common good. This relationship with the general public is often neglected because Catholic school administrators typically have their hands full with internal affairs, administration, and fundraising. Prefiguring what we would today call a school-community relations plan, Reck offered four facts that schools need to communicate more clearly in the public domain: 1) The founders and leaders of the United States expressed the need for religion and morality; 2) The interpretation of the Constitution's "establishment" clause has changed from the intent of its writers; 3) The United States has been the only major free nation that, in practice, excludes religious elements from education and limits government education to the secular; and 4) Catholic schools are more effective in offering equal opportunities to minority groups than the government schools (Reck, 1991, pp. 34-35). Reck believed that the general public would be surprised to learn how much more closely the Catholic school embodies the ideals, vision, and values of the nation's founders than does the typical public school.

A comprehensive and helpful handbook for discussion about Catholic school identity was published by the proverbial grandfather of Catholic school leadership programs, Edwin, J. McDermott, S.J., (1997) of the University of San Francisco. McDermott surveyed a wide spectrum of Church documents, Scripture, NCEA publications, educational research, and Catholic school data in compiling a practitioner-oriented handbook for the study and discussion of Catholic identity. *Distinctive Qualities of the Catholic School* offers ample resources and references, discussion questions, and possible formats and plans for using the text for a faculty inservice, retreat presentation, or individual reflection. A one-volume compendium written in easily accessible language, this text is clearly the best resource available to the uninitiated and to newcomers to Catholic education.

A number of doctoral dissertations addressed the question of Catholic identity from various points of inquiry (Hunt, 1998). Blecksmith (1996) used official Church documents on education as a basis for a 64-item survey delineating various aspects of Catholic identity at the elementary level. The survey was used to measure agreement between principals and teachers on the various components of Catholic identity as expressed in the documents. The study found a significant degree of congruence between the beliefs of educators and the teachings of the Church as found in the documents, leading Blecksmith to argue for ongoing inservice on the education documents for all those involved in Catholic schools.

Another study targeted the elementary level, but with a different angle on the identity question. Using the descriptors of *To Teach As Jesus Did* (Sacred Congregation, 1972), Gross (1994) examined whether the attributes of message, community, and service were present in teachers working in the Catholic elementary schools of the Archdiocese of Omaha. While the study is not an effort to define or describe Catholic identity, it is a clear attempt to measure identity, given a set of descriptors.

Three studies gave special attention to Catholic identity at the high school level. Tomasiello (1993) pointed to the paradigm shift within the Church about its very purpose since the Second Vatican Council and the ensuing confusion this created for school leaders. If it is unclear what the Church is or what the Church does, Tomasiello stated, it is all the more difficult for the Catholic school principal to help prepare students for adult membership in the Church. This is especially significant at the secondary level, placing new demands on the Catholic high school principal. Thus, Catholic high schools and their principals face the challenge of educating their students for adult life and mature faith in a Church whose identity is in flux.

Both Massucci (1993) and Greenlee (1995) studied the communication and transmission of Catholic values, attitudes, and mission at the secondary level and found, to varying degrees, that Catholic high schools were successful in establishing an all-encompassing ethos that was tangible to students and staff. While different groups within individual schools frequently had different beliefs and interpretations of experiences within the school community, there was a general agreement about the unique identity of a Catholic high school and ample indicators of students and staff witnessing to the gospel.

Kelty (1993) looked to H. Richard Niebuhr for a template with which to analyze the changing nature of Catholic education since the Second Vatican Council. Niebuhr (1951) had offered a once popular typology for clarifying the relationship between Christ and culture. Niebuhr presented four possible scenarios for understanding how a Christian might strive to be Christ-like: Christ against culture, Christ of culture, Christ above culture, and Christ and culture in paradox. Kelty argued that the changing character of Catholic education could be understood by drawing attention to four themes that were in flux in the wider culture: the nature of the person, the role of knowledge, the view of human history, especially the destiny of humanity, and the nature of society.

Stabile (2000) invited nearly two dozen Catholic school administrators, representative of schools throughout the United States, to reflect on the need to ensure Catholic identity in Catholic elementary schools. While not offering a template for replication everywhere, the essays point out a consistent set of approaches that are now common in schools to ensure Catholic identity. Among these approaches are: embracing the goals of worship, community, and service as enunciated in Church documents, a pervasive interest in school climate, a focus on academic achievement as a response to God's goodness, an effort to maintain high parental communication and involvement, and a holistic approach to education. Moreover, the administrators concurred that Catholic identity, in order to be a lived dynamic of school life, must become institutionalized. "It is an essential ingredient in the schools' programs, culture, staff, and students and parents. It is not something that has been added on to the school; rather it is integral to the very concept of the school" (Kealey & Brennan, 2000, pp. v-vi).

One principal delineated three key areas where Catholic identity "surfaces" in the school: 1) the Catholic school is a place of evangelization where the Gospel message is proclaimed; 2) the Catholic school forms a faith community inviting its members to pray and to worship; 3) the Catholic school provides opportunities for its members to transform the world through works of justice and service (Jenkins, 2000, pp. 77-79).

Responses from Bishops

During the 1990s, the most developed and nuanced answer from an episcopal pen to the question, "what makes a Catholic school Catholic?" came from Daniel Pilarczyk, Archbishop of Cincinnati, occasioned by an invited keynote address at the annual meeting of the Chief Administrators of Catholic Education (CACE). Pilarczyk (1998) presented a comprehensive view of Catholic identity, articulating many of the elements already discussed in this chapter: the witness of faculty, a focus on the teachings of Jesus, the universal call to holiness, and participation in the sacramental life of the Church. Pilarczyk began, however, with an insight this reviewer found peculiar to bishops: "The Code of Canon Law (Canons 803.3 and 808) says that no school or university can call itself Catholic without the consent of the competent ecclesiastical authority. A school is Catholic only if the bishop says it's Catholic" (Pilarczyk, 1998, p. 405).

This canonically precise understanding serves to highlight a facet of Catholic schooling heretofore unmentioned in the literature; namely, that Catholic schools have a juridical relationship with the local bishop. While this relationship may be different depending on the nature, structure, and ownership of the school, all schools that claim to be Catholic may do so only with the blessing and permission of the local bishop.

A Catholic high school owned and operated by a religious community, for example, relates to the local bishop in a different way than we might expect from a parish elementary school. Parish elementary schools and diocesan high schools have a direct and immediate relationship to the local bishop, a relationship that is protected in law and frequently the subject of in-service days for principals and administrators. It is not uncommon for such administrators to be reminded that, at the parish level, the pastor—the canonical delegate of the bishop— has ultimate responsibility for the school. With private high schools and those operated by religious communities, the chain of command and control is somewhat distinct, for such a school is technically not a part of the diocesan system. However, in issues concerning the religious education of students and the Catholicity of the school, and in all matters pertaining to the faith, all Catholic schools, parish, diocesan, and private, can call themselves Catholic only if the local bishop agrees.

Like Groome (1996), Pilarczyk (1998) placed the Catholic school community within the broader ecclesial community and offered this definition of a Catholic school:

> A Catholic school is a community of persons gathered for the purpose of learning secular and religious matters, which learning is directed toward a deeper acceptance of holiness from God, all in affiliation with the sacraments, the doctrines and the structures of the Catholic Church. (Pilarczyk, 1998, p. 407)

For Pilarczyk, and indeed in the view of many bishops, the question of Catholic identity involves a relationship to the universal church, and this relationship is embodied in a relationship with the local bishop. Or, said negatively, one may not simply ignore the presence, teaching, and authority of the local bishop in the administration of a Catholic school and claim, for example, that the institution's Catholicity emanates directly from Rome, because the administration and faculty are loyal to the Holy Father. "There is no such thing as a free-standing, totally independent Catholic school…no person or institution can lay claim to Catholic identity unless there is some kind of clear relationship with the local bishop" (Pilarczyk, 1998, p. 407).

In an official document intended for the universal Church, the Congregation for Catholic Education (1997) published *The Catholic School on the Threshold of the Third Millennium*. Though the Congregation as a whole takes responsibility for authorship, it is commonly understood that such documents are accepted as official church teaching and worthy of special attention and consideration. While Catholic identity is not a major theme of the document, the question of identity does come into play during consideration of the place of the Catholic school in the overall educational mission of the Church. The Congregation (1997) stated:

> The Catholic school participates in the evangelizing mission of the church and is the privileged environment in which Christian education is carried out…. The complexity of the modern world makes it all the more necessary to increase awareness of the ecclesial identity of the Catholic school. It is from its Catholic identity that the school derives its original characteristics and its "structure" as a genuine instrument of the church, a place of real and specific pastoral ministry. (#11)

By connecting the identity of the Catholic school to the broader mission of the Church, the Congregation is clearly offering strong support to Catholic educators and affirming the conviction that schools are an essential part of the Church's ministry. By stating that Catholic schools participate in the Church's mission and ministry as genuine instruments in a privileged environment, the Congregation makes clear that schools are not some inconsequential afterthought or expensive luxury that the Church could do without. On the contrary, given the Congregation's strong conviction, it would seem inaccurate to speak of parishes or dioceses as subsidizing schools because they fiscally support them. As an authentic part of the educational mission of the Church, the Catholic school has a rightful claim of support, both fiscal and moral.

In subtle contrast to other documents, especially those on Catholic higher education, *The Catholic School on the Threshold of the Third Millennium* places the school "at the heart of the Church" (Congregation for Catholic Education, 1997, #11). *Ex Corde Ecclesiae*, John Paul II's (1990) Apostolic Constitution on Catholic universities, stated repeatedly that the Catholic university is born *ex corde ecclesiae*, out of the heart of the church. Introducing a paragraph on Catholic identity and the ecclesial nature of the Catholic school, *The Catholic School on the Threshold of the Third Millennium* described Catholic schools as "at the heart of the Church" (Congregation for Catholic Education, 1997, #11). One might imagine a metaphorical Church, the body of Christ. Emanating from the heart, *ex corde*, we find Catholic universities. But at the heart, we find Catholic schools. Working in the Catholic school, therefore, is a privileged opportunity for it entails ministry in the very heart of the Church.

International Responses

Catholic educators in other countries have been addressing the question of Catholic identity (Conroy, 1999; Duignan & d'Arbon, 1998; Keane & Riley, 1997). Australia, with a vibrant Catholic school system, has been wrestling with the question of the Catholicity of its schools. Treston (1997) framed the question of identity as a matter of ethos.

The ethos of a Catholic school is rooted in a 2000 year old tradition of being Catholic Christian. The Catholicism of the school is not an optional appendium to the identity of the school but a fundamental reference point for its ethos and the shape of its education. (p. 16)

Treston, like most scholars in the United States, affirmed the Catholic school's participation in the local and universal Church, and pointed to the importance of the principle of sacramentality and the need for schools to be places where Christ is incarnated in day-to-day experiences. More importantly, the identity of the school is friendly, not hostile.

The Catholic identity of the school should not be relegated [sic] into oblivion because of any overreaction to the wide array of religious positions of its staff, parents, and students. The Catholic character of a school grounds the school in its essential story. It is not a club of indoctrination to beat Catholicism into the heads of unwilling school members. The Catholic paradigm is a lens to experience education as well as a commitment to work in partnership with other agencies of schooling in the community. (Treston, 1997, p. 17)

Duncan (1998) suggested that the responsibility for Catholic culture in a school rests on the leaders of that school. Arguing that much of behavior is learned through modeling, Duncan challenged Catholic educators in Australia to be sensitive to the political ramifications, both internal and external, of leadership behaviors that move to strengthen Catholic identity:

Leaders must negotiate Catholic ideals through the process of cultural politics because it is suggested cultural politics are at the heart of political "battles" over competing ideologies and commitments, e.g., secularism of the wider society with its emphasis on materialism and consumerism as against the gospel way of life with its emphasis on sharing and respect for the dignity of the individual. (p. 56)

Barry Dwyer (1993), perhaps the most widely published scholar of Australian Catholic education with decades of experience in a variety of schools, opined that a cultural shift was going on in Australia relative to the Catholic identity of schools. Reflecting on the conscious effort that many educational leaders have made recently to develop vision and mission statements, Dwyer believed that patterns were beginning to emerge. Specifically, most school mission statements seem to share a commitment to four foundational activities: 1) evangelization, 2) an explicit and deep respect for the individual and for individualized learning, 3) the building of Christian community, and 4) service. While analyzing the tremendous good found in these mission statements, Dwyer also expressed hope that four additional elements might grow in prominence. Dwyer called for a Catholic school culture that would be: 1) more reflective—recognizing the need for ongoing evaluation and review; 2) more generative—focusing on growth and development; 3) more communal—celebrating connectedness and interdependence; and 4) more prophetic—proclaiming the gospel clearly in an often unfriendly culture.

Terence McLaughlin (1999) of St. Edmund's College, Cambridge, considered the question of the distinctiveness of the Catholic school and counseled school leaders about elements currently threatening that distinctiveness: a lack of a balanced judgment in matters of the Catholic faith and the temptations of commonality, what we might call in the United States, "the lowest common denominator."

Balanced judgment is required because matters of faith are increasingly complex today, and school leaders themselves need to be perennial learners in matters of science and technology as well as morality and history. McLaughlin (1999) argues that school personnel can never settle for a superficial understanding of the faith, nor be content with their own spiritual development, for the life of faith is a journey undertaken daily, not a harbor forever enjoyed once one arrived. Ongoing faith formation for faculty is the best assurance the Church can have that educators are fully prepared to integrate their own life of faith into the daily discipline of the school.

The attractions of commonality are those temptations that move us to articulate the distinctive elements of the Catholic school in ways that might be predicated on other schools, whether Catholic or not. McLaughlin related the story of a research effort focused on a Catholic high school sponsored by a religious order. While the research indicated that there were many clear instances of the founders' charisms present in the school, these charisms were described in a way that expressed values commonly recognized in society as a whole. Thus, the founders' personal virtues were replicated in the school, but their spiritual, and indeed their Catholic purposes, were not (McLaughlin, 1998).

SUMMARY AND CONCLUSION

It is evident from the abundant writing on the question of Catholic identity that the issue is still very much an open question (Hunt, Joseph, Nuzzi, 2001). The fact that there is such a scholarly interest in the question bodes well for Catholic institutions, for the constant examination of the question provides a vigilance that can often strengthen Catholic identity. In examining the responses offered from theologians, bishops, educators, and scholars in Australia and Ireland on the matter of Catholic identity, some clear patterns do emerge. In general, three distinct categories serve to contain all that has been said about the Catholic identity of Catholic schools. To be sure, Catholic identity means all three of these things at once, and never one over the other or in place of the other. But there appear to be three types of responses to the question, "what makes a Catholic school Catholic?" First, there is the canonical response, clarified by Pilarczyk (1998) that maintains that Catholic schools are those which a bishop says are Catholic. These types of responses point out the juridical relationships that sustain the school and give clarity to the chain of command. Whatever else may be going on in a school, for good or for ill, its legal and canonical identity as a Catholic school is dependent upon a relationship with a local bishop. In short, bishops make schools Catholic. This first category of responses may appear overstated to some and so obvious to others as not to merit mention. But it serves as a caveat to those who, for whatever reason, would attempt to circumvent, contradict, or ignore the local bishop in the unfolding of a Catholic institution.

Second is the sacramental response. These responses appeal to the sacramental life of the Church and point us to the person of Christ. Catholic schools make Christ present and are places where the example and life of Christ are incarnated daily. More importantly, they are places where the Sacraments of the Church are celebrated. Catholic schools are thus sacramental places and participate in the Church's overall ministry of sanctification. In other words, it is Christ who makes schools Catholic, for no school can claim Catholicity apart from Jesus Christ. Theologically speaking, this is the central purpose of the Catholic school as well the existential reality that would lead a bishop to proclaim a school a Catholic school. In the absence of a manifest commitment to Christ, juridical proclamations of Catholicity might go unheeded.

Third is the ecclesial response, which places the Catholic school in the larger contexts of the universal Church and civic society. These responses point out that schools are not freestanding, unrelated entities, advancing their own, self-chosen mission. Rather, Catholic schools are part and parcel of the educational mission of the Church and enjoy a privileged position, for they embody the most effective and successful effort anywhere to educate children in the faith and to prepare responsible and faithful citizens for Christian witness and action in the world. Simply stated, it is the Church that makes a school Catholic, for when any school community embraces the faith, celebrates the sacraments, struggles to be like Jesus, and lives and works in the world for peace and justice, it truly becomes a Catholic school. No school can be Catholic, therefore, by serving itself and remaining focused on its own existence. Part of what it means to be Catholic is to be catholic, to be in union with the rest of the Church and with all of humanity.

One final caveat is in order. It seems clear that the question of Catholic identity is going to remain a challenge for Catholic schools at the beginning of the third millennium of Christianity. Responses come from many divergent disciplines and in qualitatively different tones. Theologians, educators, members of the hierarchy, and Catholic school leaders everywhere grapple with the question, "what makes a Catholic school Catholic?" The nature and purpose of Catholicism often seems in question. Some argue that liberal, pro-change Catholics are re-shaping the Church (Dillon, 1999). Others maintain that the answer to the so-called identity crisis is to be found in religious education, specifically, a faithful presentation of Catholic doctrines as found, for example, in the *Catechism of the Catholic Church* (Phan, 1998). Experienced Catholic educators understand that the question of Catholic identity is a complex phenomenon, requiring careful analysis and consideration, and not admitting of a singular, satisfying response. Indeed, one of the most popular recent books on Catholicism (Leach & Borchard, 2000) did not address the issue of identity or dogma directly, but appealed more to the imagination as a way to understand what it means to be Catholic. Its title is a fitting conclusion to this examination of Catholic identity, for it expresses the sentiment of thousands of Catholic educators: "I Like Being Catholic."

INTERNAL AND EXTERNAL FACTORS

CHAPTER 3
ENVIRONMENT

RICHARD M. JACOBS, OSA

The concept of "environment" has received rather scant scholarly attention. Much of this neglect can be attributed to the concept itself. "Environment" denotes the external factors that influence organizational effectiveness (Drucker, 1980; Emery & Trist, 1965; Lawrence & Lorsch, 1967; Pfeffer & Salancik, 1978). But, as the subject shifted to the internal factors alleged to promote school effectiveness, two other concepts captivated researchers. Increasingly, they turned to "culture" (Schein, 1992; Trice & Beyer, 1993) and "climate" (Anderson, 1982, 1985) to isolate which, if any, internal factors contributed to school effectiveness.

This is not to say the concept of environment became irrelevant. The concept was significant, if only because the internal factors purported to promote school effectiveness were influenced by external factors (Burns & Stalker, 1961; Lawrence & Lorsch, 1967; Miles & Snow, 1978; Woodward, 1965). And, as researchers recognized how both sets of factors interact to influence school effectiveness, a more balanced, though more complex, concept of school environment emerged during the 1990s.

For educators, who direct their focus upon what transpires inside of schools, this research provides a comprehensive view about the dynamic environment of schooling, one challenging educators to consider three changes that may increase school effectiveness. First, educators must engage in the substantive personal and professional change so that they can collaborate as colleagues to improve curriculum, teaching, and learning. Second, educators must deal directly with and respond inside of schools to the external environment. Third, educators must utilize the external reform infrastructure to build support for and to sustain change inside of schools. In sum, research indicated that the environment was rapidly changing. Failure to attend to this condition could translate into school ineffectiveness.

The literature also challenges educators in Catholic schools to think progressively about Catholic schooling and what this implies for Catholic school effectiveness. While personal and professional change may secure the foundation for improved school effectiveness, educators in Catholic schools must extend that foundation to include a deeper and continuing conversion to the adult requirements of the Catholic faith if they are to witness effectively to the school's distinctive purpose. In addition, if school effectiveness hinges upon educators forming professional learning communities, educators in Catholic schools must also form faith formation communities if Catholic schools are to be more effectively Catholic. Lastly, educators in Catholic schools need to be mindful about how their schools function within larger systems and need to exploit the resources available in these systems to build a broader base of support for and to sustain Catholic school reform as distinctively Catholic. Once again, failure to attend to these challenges may well translate into Catholic school ineffectiveness.

To unify the trajectory of research interest in the concept of environment during the closing three decades of the 20th century, in general, and the 1990s, in particular, this chapter defines "environment" as "the internal and external factors purported to impact school effectiveness." Using Fullan's (2000) three stories of education reform, this chapter sorts and summarizes the factors that researchers alleged to promote school effectiveness. This chapter closes with a discussion concerning the methodological groundwork researchers put into place during the 1990s for their successors to examine the moral dimensions of schooling and how these influence school effectiveness.

The "Inside" Story

The subject of this story is "how schools change for the better in terms of their internal dynamics" (Fullan, 2000, p. 581). This narrative focuses upon how educators in effective schools use their time inside of schools to overcome any obstacles to the personal and professional self-change purported to enhance school effectiveness.

Inquiry into school effectiveness extends back to the 1970s as scholars examined the conditions enabling students to perform better than socioeconomic factors would predict. Edmonds blazed this trail, promoting the study of school effectiveness in a speech delivered to the National Conference of the Teacher Corps in 1978. Edmonds (1979b, 1981) focused on school culture, citing five characteristics evidencing themselves in effective schools, including: strong leadership, a clear emphasis on learning, a positive school climate, regular and appropriate monitoring of student progress, and high expectation of both students and staff. Later, Coleman and his colleagues (Coleman & Hoffer, 1987; Coleman, Hoffer, & Kilgore, 1982) focused on standardized testing, using data from large national samples to study school effectiveness. The conclusion that inner city Catholic high schools were more effective than public schools in promoting academic achievement ignited a firestorm that continued unabated through the 1990s. Concurrently, politicians seized upon Coleman and his colleagues' conclusion to assert a new educational policy agenda. While much of the scholarly debate focused upon theoretical and methodological grounds (Alexander & Pallas, 1983), the educational policy debate—and especially the arguments posed by the proponents of educational vouchers and tuition tax credit schemes—asserted the alleged effectiveness of private (and particularly, Catholic) schools. Meanwhile, researchers developed more highly complex models to measure school effectiveness (Uline, Miller, & Tschannen-Moran, 1998). At the close of the 1990s, Hoffer (2000) reined in any excessive rhetoric with his assertion:

> I take as a point of departure a range of empirical evidence from national surveys showing that Catholic school students score significantly higher on standardized achievement tests than their public school counterparts. These data do not, however, necessarily indicate that Catholic schools are more effective than public schools, for that is an issue that must be resolved through analysis of the overall sector differences. (p. 88)

For him, the data indicate that "some, perhaps all, of the achievement differences may be due to social background differences between public and Catholic school students" (p. 92).

What is of consequence for the inside story of school reform is that during the 1980s and 1990s scholars appropriated Coleman and his colleagues' conclusions to inquire into what principals and, in turn, teachers and students do inside of schools and how that may contribute to school effectiveness.

Early on, Rosenholtz (1985) argued that principals in effective schools carefully hire and socialize new teachers, buffer teachers from unwarranted intrusions on instructional time, provide substantive feedback about teaching, and create a culture of continuous improvement. One decade later, Louis and Kruse (1995) extended this line of inquiry, identifying the effects principals in effective urban schools had upon student learning outcomes. Not only did they develop "professional learning communities" (Fine, 1994; Louis, Marks, & Kruse, 1996; Talbert, 1996) inside of these schools; in addition, these principals engaged in two particular activities: attending to individual teacher development as well as creating and sustaining networks of discourse among teachers that focus upon curriculum, teaching, and learning. The authors suggested that restructuring schools as professional learning communities improved the quality of teaching and raised student achievement in urban schools. The researchers also cautiously asserted that creating professional learning communities may be a strategy to make non-urban schools more effective.

As researchers examined the purported relationship between school effectiveness and instructional leadership, the former appeared to hinge upon supportive, facilitative, or catalytic instructional leaders (Leithwood,

1994; Murphy & Louis, 1994). In effective schools, instructional leaders, and principals in particular, engaged in a myriad of activities. They established goals, obtained resources, stimulated new understandings, changed structures, and promoted instructional practices that improved learning experiences and outcomes for students (Duke & Leithwood, 1994; Hallinger & McCary, 1990; Leithwood & Duke, 1999). Research in the sociology of education replicated these findings, correlating effective instructional leadership with curriculum, teaching, and learning effectiveness. For example, the organizational factors that instructional leaders influenced (e.g., school and class size, ability groups and tracking, curriculum differentiation) impacted the teaching and learning process and, hence, school effectiveness (Gamoran, 1996; Lee & Smith, 1997; Lee, Smith, & Croninger, 1997).

Leithwood and his colleagues exemplified the prevailing view of the 1990s. Their research indicated that principals in effective schools "determine the direction of improvements in the school and who influences the nature and extent of efforts by school members to learn how to bring about these improvements" (Leithwood, Leonard, & Sharratt, 1998, p. 249). These individuals identify and articulate a vision, foster the acceptance of group goals, and convey high performance expectations. They also provide appropriate models, individual support, and intellectual stimulation. Others suggested that principals in effective schools build vibrant school cultures with flexible structures that enhance teacher participation in the decision-making process (Barth, 1990; Deal & Peterson, 1994; Duke, 1996; Duke & Leithwood, 1994; Fullan, 1991; Heck & Hallinger, 1999; Murphy & Beck, 1995; Sergiovanni, 1992, 1994, 1996). In short, principals in effective schools foster the conditions enabling teachers to become self-governing professional communities (Louis & Kruse, 1995). Lastly, Hart and Bredeson (1996) argued that school effectiveness hinged upon principals who, like teachers in classrooms, engaged in learning from professional practice.

By decade's end, Hughes (1999) surveyed this mélange of administrator activities purported to promote school effectiveness, and asked "Is the principal an artist, architect, or commissar?" Indeed, research into the principal's role in orchestrating school effectiveness during the 1990s culminated in a smorgasbord of competing and conflicting expectations which Copland (2001) termed "the myth of the superprincipal."

Dillard (1995), however, contested these assessments, arguing that the school effectiveness literature promoted an overly rigid model and undemocratic notion of leadership, one predicated upon a principal's "absolute and rational activity." Some theorists also expressed doubts that principals can lead schools to achieve the outcomes promised. One critic argued that principals are not oriented toward change because of the role and its traditions, the training they receive, as well as the context of schooling. In addition, the structural-functionalist model of school administration gives undue emphasis to managing schools rather than leading them (Sarason, 1993, 1996). The net result? Principals are ill-prepared to lead school communities capable of engaging in the "reculturing" (Fullan, 2000) that is the focus of the second story of school reform.

A growing body of scholars also argued that these findings, because they focus almost exclusively upon administrators, in general, and principals, in particular, are more troubling than helpful in understanding the factors inside of schools that make it possible to change them for the better.

From a deconstructionist perspective, Dantley (1990) argued that, if schools are to be effective, administrators would have to engage teachers in dialogue that encourages critical analysis of practice and promotes school cultures which foster the articulation of hope. For his part, Giroux opined that educators must become "engaged and transformative critics" (1992, p. 242) who combine the discourse of hope with social and self criticism to challenge the practices of privilege that make schools reproducers of privilege and oppression. Fairclough (1995) noted that if professional practice in schools is to be connected to enhancing the identity of the professionals serving in them—which, it is assumed, will make schools more effective—then school administrators need to become more critically aware of their language. Anderson and Grinberg noted, however, that school administrators are incapable of asking critical questions because these individuals are "trapped within a discourse of efficiency, productivity, and effectiveness that make problematization or critical reflection difficult" (1998, p. 344).

The substance of this critique introduces another strand of research identifying one factor purported to influence school effectiveness. During the 1990s, researchers focused upon collaboration among educators—what Fullan (2000) calls the "black box" of schooling (pp. 581-582)—as a crucial element in making schools change for the better.

In general, researchers suggested that it is not enough for outsiders to mandate that educators collaborate inside of schools. Instead, if educators are to collaborate together in an effort to improve a school's effectiveness, they must learn to direct their attention away from external factors and focus instead upon internal factors, becoming assessment literate (Hargreaves & Fullan, 1998). The operative notion is that, as educators collaborate to hone their individual and collective abilities to interpret achievement data and then to formulate action plans designed to improve curriculum, teaching, and learning, then student learning outcomes will improve.

Data substantiate this assertion, indicating how educators in effective schools achieve better learning outcomes with their students than do their peers in other schools where collaboration is not normative. Two studies found educators in effective schools engaging in substantive personal and professional self-change (Louis & Kruse, 1995; Newmann & Wehlage, 1995). This endeavor formed the foundation for administrators and teachers to focus upon and improve curriculum, teaching, and learning. In addition, these educators continuously reconstructed their achievements to attain ever-increasing levels of effectiveness as they focused their individual and collective energies upon student learning and engaged in assessing what students actually learn. These educators then expanded collaboration to include incorporating instructional practices that would provide data-driven feedback indicating what they could do to improve student learning outcomes as well as to enhance teacher satisfaction.

Theoretically, the investment of time in professional discourse and the formation of professional learning communities should yield greater academic achievement on the students' part than does expanding instructional time (Darling-Hammond, 1997a; Lieberman, 1990; Little, 1993; Louis, Kruse, & Marks, 1996). Zigarelli (1996) issued one caveat; namely, that principals must protect instructional time from unwarranted intrusions, disruptions, and low expectations. One often neglected assumption, however, is that teachers will spend less time directly engaged in teaching.

As the inside story concerns teachers and their interactions, Lave and Wenger's (1991) ethnographic study provided a typology for thinking about professional discourse and collaboration inside of schools. This typology, elsewhere articulated by Schön (1991), requires non-masters to engage with masters in sustained conversation aimed at learning, developing, and evolving the non-master's skills to the point that the apprentice becomes capable of making independent decisions with regard to what excellence demands. Lave and Wenger differentiated expert and non-expert communication from communication patterns predominating workers' conversations in sweatshops, wondering whether the latter predominate in and typify communication inside of schools. For Sarason (1999), this is the case and one of many reasons that schools are ineffective.

While critics may argue that "craft-oriented" conversations waste time, some research suggested otherwise. Greeno, Collins, and Resnick (1996) argued that professional discourse does not hinder a common project such as educating youth from proceeding efficiently even though there may be extensive disagreement within the professional community concerning the best way to proceed. Instead, craft-oriented conversations provide "cognitive apprenticeships" wherein non-masters practice and acquire crucial skills. In addition, these conversations enable non-masters to assume the identity of the master practitioner within the community of master craftsmen. Cognitive apprenticeships differ from craft apprenticeships in two important ways: 1) learning is valued in its own right and not as a means to acquire marketable skills, and 2) variation and creativity are valued rather than imitation and uniform repetition of skills.

An array of researchers—spanning from the empirical to the normative and critical traditions—refocused upon a perennial theme during the 1990s, namely, utilizing democratic discourse inside of schools to promote a collaboration and, hence, to increase school effectiveness. Taken at face value, the argument is steeped in the belief that, by engaging teachers in more democratic discourse about their profession, principals can foster new understandings and beliefs about diversity and more inclusive practices in school management (Corson, 1995; Perry & Fraser, 1993; Rusch, 1998).

The most often invoked concept used to identify this discursive process, "empowerment," is grounded in the assumption that teachers are the crucial players in promoting school effectiveness (Conley & Bacharach, 1990; Midgley & Wood, 1993; Rinehart, Short, Short, & Eckley, 1998). As a management strategy, then, principals use empowerment to delegate instructional leadership responsibility to teachers. In turn, they engage in decision making ranging from matters pertaining to teaching and learning (Rinehart & Short, 1994; Rinehart, Short, & Johnson, 1997; Schermerhorn, Hunt, & Osborn, 1994; Wall & Rinehart, 1998) to curriculum development, personnel, student life, and school financial matters (Rinehart & Short, 1991). Other researchers offered more complex definitions of empowerment, which included multiple dimensions (e.g., decision making, professional growth, status, self-efficacy, autonomy, and impact) (Rinehart, Short, Short, & Eckley, 1998) and domains (e.g., school operations and management, students' school experiences, teachers' work lives, and control of classroom instruction) (Marks & Louis, 1997).

Much of this talk about empowerment, however, coalesced around the notion of forming professional learning communities. Inside of these schools, people

> share a way of knowing, a set of practices, and the shared value of the knowledge that these procedures generate. There are ways for novices and experts to work in the same system to accomplish similar goals. Community members are recognized for what they know as well as what they need to learn. Leadership comes from people who can inspire others to work better to accomplish shared goals. Evaluation is based on the work of the group, in which the individual is expected to contribute his or her own part. Cooperation rather than competition is stressed. (Reil & Fulton, 2001, p. 519)

Once again, personal and professional self-change, as these result from the interaction of administrator support, teacher cognition, and school culture, appeared to be at the core of school effectiveness. In professional learning communities, then, the culture promotes skills' development through increased administrator and teacher interaction and joint decision making. This outcome emerges, however, not as a consequence of isolated in-service programs and workshops but through forming professional learning communities inside of schools. This appears to offer the greatest promise of increasing school effectiveness (Cohen, McLaughlin, & Talbert, 1993; Louis & Kruse, 1995; Perez, 1997).

Reviews concerning the relationship between teacher empowerment and school effectiveness are mixed (Conley, 1991; Marks & Louis, 1997; Smylie, 1994). For his part, Popkewitz (1996) was not sanguine, taking direct aim at those who propagated empowering teachers as a means to promote democratic discourse and freedom in schools. He noted that "constructivist strategies are intended to enable teachers to have the 'correct' dispositions and capabilities for effecting school reform…[and] constructivist pedagogies are not neutral strategies to teach problem solving" (pp. 39-40). Instead, Popkewitz argued, empowerment may be yet another covert attempt to exert control over others, one that assumed increasingly sinister proportions in the 1990s because efforts to promote collaboration and democracy in schools may actually have been more invasive, controlling, and dominating than were previous attempts. How? Empowerment became a tool for principals to direct the teachers' internal processes of creativity and self-motivation, all in an effort to achieve other goals.

Schaub (2000) offers data that give reason to pause and reconsider carefully whether school effectiveness is a consequence of forming professional learning communities, collaborating, and teacher empowerment inside of schools. Examining the U.S. Department of Education's "Schools and Staffing Survey" for the 1993-1994 academic year, Schaub (2000) found that teachers in Catholic schools reported their principals exercising a higher degree of significant influence in the decision-making process than teachers in public schools reported with regard to their principals. In particular, Catholic school principals figured more prominently in decisions about curriculum, teacher hiring, student discipline, budget expenditures, content of in-service programs, and teacher evaluations. Although this more centralized approach to organizational decision making may diminish the teachers' ability to influence these matters, teachers in Catholic schools report being more satisfied with their working conditions and jobs than do their counterparts in public schools. Forming professional learning communities, encouraging greater collaboration, and empowering teachers may not be quite as significant in improving school effectiveness as many researchers asserted during the 1990s.

The decade of the 1990s also offered empirical evidence that it is the teacher-student relationship that contributes most to school effectiveness, especially in urban schools. Three studies indicated that classrooms in effective schools promoted and expected high academic achievement (Katz, 1999; Miron, 1997; Parker & Shapiro, 1993). Several studies also indicated that, as teachers personalized instruction and treated students as individuals rather than as members of groups, classroom instruction was more effective (Katz, 1999; Sather, 1999; Winfield, Johnson, & Manning, 1993). Deering's (1996) ethnographic study of a multiethnic urban middle school indicated that, when teachers create a caring environment in classrooms, student achievement improved. Likewise, when teachers provided appropriate support to non-achieving students, even to the point of working directly with parents (e.g., meeting in their homes or at work, providing translators, developing parent competencies to assist in the education of their children), academic achievement improved.

Researchers in the 1990s unearthed yet another factor of the inside story possibly impacting school effectiveness, one that requires careful reconsideration. That factor is how the size of the student body impacts school effectiveness.

Since the 1950s, small schools, and especially high schools, were consolidated into large schools through district reorganization efforts fueled by the vision of large comprehensive schools. These would provide for the academic and social needs of every student (Conant, 1959; Keller, 1955). Although several states launched class size reduction efforts for the early elementary grades in the 1990s (Egleson, Harman, & Achilles, 1996; Viadero, 1998), large high schools continued to be normative with more than 70% of high school students attending schools in which more than 1,000 students are enrolled (Cotton, 1996). The 1990s also evidenced a growing body of research indicating that small schools correlate with higher academic and social achievement and, hence, school effectiveness (Grissmer, 1999).

Commenting on the research conducted in the mid- to late-1990s, Lee and Loeb (2000) noted that teachers in small elementary schools took more individual and collective responsibility for student academic and social achievement, but more importantly, school size impacted student achievement independent of the collective responsibility for achievement that teachers expressed. Lee and Loeb (2000) asserted:

> The findings are straightforward and consistent. Small elementary schools work better on the outcomes we examine. In schools with fewer than 400 students, teachers report that they and their colleagues assume more responsibility for student learning. Students attending small schools also learn more mathematics over a year. (p. 23)

However, Lee and Loeb suggest, the quality and character of the more intimate and personal social relations among teachers and students may be the likely mechanism through which the size of the student body affected student learning.

Likewise, small high schools appeared to influence academic and social achievement. For example, students enrolled in 90 small high schools (e.g., "schools within a school") in Chicago exhibited significant improvements in academic and social achievement when compared to their peers in the host schools. Students in the small schools also reported feeling safer, more connected with the adults, and more engaged in peer critique and analysis of their learning experiences (Wasley et al., 2000). Furthermore, small schools appeared to be more effective with respect to student behavior, attitude, and satisfaction, as well as with respect to safety, parental involvement, and dropout prevention (Raywid, 1999). There is some additional evidence that small schools exhibit less violent behavior on the students' part (Franklin & Crone, 1992; National Center for Education Statistics, 1998; Zane, 1994). Teachers in small schools reported a greater sense of personal efficacy and professional satisfaction. They collaborated with their colleagues primarily in building more coherent educational programs and in experimenting with and expanding their pedagogical repertoires. In addition, these teachers interacted more with parents than their colleagues in large high schools (Wasley et al., 2000). In sum, the great majority of studies conducted during the 1990s asserted net positive academic outcomes for small schools (Achilles & Finn, 2000; Bryk & Driscoll, 1988; Fine, 1994; Lee & Smith, 1994, 1997; Lee et al., 1997; Molnar, Smith, Zahorik, Palmer, Halbach, & Ehrle, 1999a, 1999b; Raywid, 1997-1998; Sares, 1992).

The federal government took note of this research, investing heavily in class-size reduction programs. In 1999, Congress appropriated $1.2 billion—and an additional $1.3 billion in 2000—for public school districts to hire new teachers in order to drive elementary school class size to 18 or fewer students (United States Department of Education, 2000a). However, much of the research about school size is fraught with methodological problems. Identifying what constitutes a small school—for example, is its student population less than 500, 1000, or 1500—is one such problem. The sample size used in many studies also presents problems. For example, while the effects evident in 264 elementary schools (Lee & Loeb, 2000) and nine high schools (Lee et al., 1997) may provide insight into how school size impacted student academic and social achievement, findings based upon this limited number of schools cannot be generalized to the universe of schools.

As researchers examined the inside story of Catholic schooling, the most substantive and influential study published in the 1990s was *Catholic Schools and the Common Good* (Bryk, Lee, & Holland, 1993). In this volume, the authors identified the distinctive features of effective Catholic high schools and the ways in which these inside factors combined to form a supportive environment promoting academic achievement for a broad cross section of students. Using both quantitative and qualitative methods, the authors maintained that post-Vatican II Catholic high schools have an independent effect upon student achievement, especially in reducing disparities between disadvantaged and privileged students. These positive outcomes appeared to be a consequence of four factors: a delimited technical core; a communal organization; decentralized governance; and, an inspirational ideology. At decade's end, there is no empirical evidence to identify which of these four inside factors influence Catholic school effectiveness, although two studies did indicate that Catholic high schools may present a more challenging academic climate than do public schools (Witte, 1992, 1996).

Academic achievement is important but, in terms of Catholic school effectiveness, one cannot overlook student moral achievement. That is to say, Catholic schools exist to provide students an "integral formation" (Congregation for Catholic Education, 1988), one that unites the school's program of intellectual formation with its program of moral formation. In the late 1990s several researchers raised the obvious, yet potentially devastating question of great importance to anyone concerned about Catholic education: Just how effective are Catholic schools in achieving generally desired moral outcomes in their graduates (Baker & Riordan, 1998; Greeley, 1998, 1999; Youniss & McLellan, 1999)? There is very little published research that responds directly to this question and some of it is nearly two decades old.

The National Opinion Research Center (NORC), for example, surveyed the moral attitudes of students enrolled in Catholic schools in 1981 to determine how effective Catholic schools were with regard to their programs of moral formation (as cited in Walch, 1996, p. 232). The NORC study indicated that Catholic schools were effective in shaping student morals, albeit in rather limited ways. Students who attended Catholic schools were more likely to go to Mass, to consider a religious vocation, and to oppose abortion. This was good news. In other significant ways, the news was not so good. Assuming that attitudes toward prayer and sexual morality are the most crucial dimensions of a Catholic school's program of moral formation, the data revealed Catholic schools to be ineffective. That is, students who attended Catholic schools exhibited no significant difference in their attitudes toward prayer and sexual morality than did their peers enrolled in other schools.

Educational Testing Service (ETS) conducted a study in the early 1990s that generally replicated the 1981 NORC findings. That is, depending how one defines effectiveness—and, for the most part, this has denoted scores on tests of knowledge of the content of the Catholic faith—out-of-school religious education programs were almost as effective as parochial school programs in handing on the faith to the next generation (Sommerfeld, 1994). Elford's (2000) data indicated otherwise. But, he argued, Catholic schools may not be as effective as they could be due to the quality of catechists: "some Catholic school students at grades 10-12 scored above the average of beginning catechists and within the middle two-thirds of the certified catechists" (p. 152). In light of this very important finding, it is unfortunate that Elford's sample included students from only 20 dioceses and, thus, lacks generalizability. The question also remains whether these higher scores are significant differences, given the substantial financial and personnel commitments that parishes have made to enable students in Catholic schools to achieve those higher scores.

To date, the number and quality of the studies, and hence the conclusions that can be drawn, are too few to warrant broad generalizations. One can only hope that future research will unearth data providing insight into the effects of Catholic schools upon students' attitudes when it comes to other significant areas of Catholic life beyond the knowledge of religious concepts and their permanence following graduation. There is much more to discover, including how Catholic schools enable students to witness to the faith, to engage in the new evangelization, and to model Catholic leadership within the school as a faith formation community.

What about the people who administer and teach in Catholic schools? How effective are they in fostering the moral formation of their students?

Harkins' (1993) study of Catholic school principals provides evidence of four important beliefs that shaped how principals defined the concept of "Catholic" when applied to hiring teachers for Catholic schools. For example, 22.1% of the principals believed that if a job applicant stated that abortion is a woman's right, that fact should not be a factor in the decision to hire. In addition, 36.3% believed that if a job applicant stated that his or her sexual orientation is homosexual, that too should not negatively impact a hiring decision. Furthermore, 52.3% believed that if a job applicant stated that he or she sees nothing wrong with using birth control pills or devices, the applicant could still be hired. Lastly, 61.5% believed that the Catholic Church should ordain women. Although this study possesses methodological limitations, it offered an indication that the way Catholic school principals defined "Catholic" could influence the type of person hired to teach and, ultimately, impact life inside of Catholic schools and their programs of moral formation.

In 1995, Carr (2000) sampled 887 Catholic elementary school principals, 56% of whom were laypersons representing 156 dioceses. Pertinent to the inside story of Catholic schooling, both lay and religious principals valued equally the Catholic school's program of moral formation (what they identify as cultivating the students' "religious-spiritual development"). In addition, the longer one served as a principal in the Catholic school system, the more he or she experienced a sense of satisfaction, feelings of self-efficacy, and motivation. However, "religious principals are apt to have significantly higher levels of a mission-related motivation orientation and spiritual leadership satisfaction than their Catholic school lay principal counterparts" (p. 72). Left unchecked, lowered motivation and satisfaction could lead to a diminution of the school's identity as Catholic, especially if lay principals in Catholic schools are motivated by and experience greater satisfaction from the school's academic achievements than from fulfilling its moral purpose.

With regard to teachers in Catholic schools, Galetto's (2000) national sample boasted more than 2,000 Catholic elementary school religion teachers. Not surprisingly, veteran educators possessed more formal instruction in the content of the Catholic faith and more orthodox personal beliefs than did non-veterans. In addition, there is a high turnover rate for teachers of religion, many of whom are young and not necessarily products of Catholic schooling.

More substantively, the Galetto (2000) data evidenced a dichotomy existing inside of Catholic schools. That is, what Catholic elementary school religion teachers identified correctly as the Church's position on several fundamental theological and moral issues differed from their personal position. With regard to fundamental theological issues: 86.5% correctly identified the Church's position on Real Presence while 63.4% did not identify that position as their own; 88.8% correctly identified the Church's position on the indissolubility of marriage while 54.4% did not identify that position as their own; and, although 71.6% correctly identified the Church's position concerning male priesthood while 32.5% did not identify that as their personal position. With regard to fundamental moral issues: 30.7% identified the Church's moral teaching while 27.6% did not identify that position as their own; 77.2% correctly identified the Church's position on elective abortion while 26.3% did not identify that as their personal position; and, while 99% correctly identified the Church's position on premarital sex, 60.5% did not identify that position as their own.

Although there is no analysis indicating which if any differences are statistically significant, the differences are noteworthy. As these differences possibly impact the formal and informal teaching of religion in Catholic school classrooms, the question emerges concerning how teachers can faithfully transmit the content of the Catholic religion—what John Paul II has called the "essential criterion" (1992, p. 179)—if they do not personally believe it. Viewing these data alongside the NORC and ETS data, one can legitimately question whether students in Catholic schools during the 1990s did receive the content of the Catholic religion faithfully.

Kushner and Helbling's (1995) study of Catholic elementary school teachers lent credence to the data Galetto collected in 1994. In this study, 21.7% of the teachers reported believing that abortion is a woman's right. In addition, 55.1% believed it inappropriate that a constitutional amendment banning abortions be approved. Moreover, 29.6% believed that a teacher should not be fired if that teacher tells students that there is nothing wrong with using birth control pills or devices. Lastly, 59% believed the Catholic Church should ordain women.

These studies represented an initial foray into researching the effectiveness of the programs of moral formation found inside of the nation's Catholic schools and the educators charged with translating these programs into educational experiences. In summary, Catholic school principals and teachers differed very little from one another as well as the larger U.S. Catholic community when it came to beliefs about fundamental theological and moral issues (D'Antonio, Davidson, Hoge, & Wallace, 1996; Kosmin & Lachman, 1993). Whether the divergence of attitudes and beliefs about the Catholic faith held by lay educators in Catholic schools during the 1990s from official Church teaching is greater than their religious forebears in previous generations and, hence a threat to a school's identity as *Catholic*, remains an open question. What is profoundly significant for the future of schooling as identifiably *Catholic* is how these personal beliefs impact the hiring of lay teachers and their subsequent catechetical efforts inside of Catholic schools. Ultimately, these are the women and men who define and communicate the content of the program of moral formation that students in Catholic schools experience.

Thus, although Catholic schools may not have been exemplary in communicating the content of the Catholic faith, they appeared to be effective in transmitting a Catholic ethos (Bryk et al., 1993). Much work remains, however, if the inside story of Catholic schooling is to be characterized by a professional educational community that is also a faith formation community wherein the faith and practice of the Catholic Church permeate every aspect of life in every Catholic school. One challenge this limited body of research presents to educators in Catholic schools is the need to reculture them—the subject of the second story of school reform (Fullan, 2000)—so that these schools will be as effective in fulfilling their moral purpose in the 21st century as they were in fulfilling their intellectual purpose during the 20th century.

To conclude this section, the subject of the inside story is "how schools change for the better in terms of their internal dynamics" (Fullan, 2000, p. 581). As one of three factors directly impacting school effectiveness, research provided ample evidence that the working relationships among principals and faculty members impact school effectiveness. The major challenge concerns how educators will improve the quality and character of their professional discourse to overcome the obstacles that negatively impact school effectiveness. To this end, researchers suggested that leadership inside of schools become more decentralized or "distributed" (Neuman & Simmons, 2000). Teachers, then, will need to provide more instructional leadership, particularly in matters relating to curriculum, teaching, and learning.

Research conducted during the 1990s also indicated that Catholic schools might not be all that much different from their private and public counterparts in terms of academic achievement. However, there is an added dimension that educators in Catholic schools must also attend to; namely, the school's effectiveness in providing equally effective programs of moral formation to students. Some of the research evidenced that, as the laity accepted almost complete responsibility for the Church's educational apostolate, Catholic schools transmitted a Catholic ethos to students. However, a limited number of studies indicated that Catholic schools may not be as effective in communicating the content of the Catholic faith. Part of this may be explained by how educators in Catholic schools operationalized the concept "Catholic" in actual practice. There is an urgent need to study this matter, if only to the degree to which educators in Catholic schools envision their profession as a ministry.

Life inside of schools is dynamic, ever fluctuating, and hectic. Perhaps this aspect of the environment explains why educators are so preoccupied with it. This aspect of the environment may also explain why researchers in the 1990s studied the time educators spent inside of effective schools, their patterns of relation-ships, and how this has the potential to improve curriculum, teaching, and learning. However, the inside story is only one of three stories of school reform (Fullan, 2000). Researchers in the 1990s also examined other environmental factors influencing school effectiveness.

The "Inside-Out" Story

The subject of Fullan's (2000) second story of school reform is school reculturing. This narrative challenges educators to recognize that efforts to change their patterns of interactions in order to form professional learning communities—the subject of the inside story—requires dealing directly with a new environment—the subject of the outside story.

The environment of schooling at the conclusion of the 1990s was "more complex, turbulent, contra-dictory, relentless, uncertain, and transparent. At the same time, it has increased demands for better performance and greater accountability" (Fullan, 2000, p. 582). In addition, it was predicted that 10 "seismic societal shifts" would exert a profound impact on schooling early in the 21st century (Marx, 2000). These shifts, portending dramatic and sweeping changes in the school's external environment, would require educating children for a profoundly different future. To do so effectively, educators would have to be proactive by forging resilient school cultures capable of contending with fundamental change.

Echoing the contingency theorists of the 1960s and 1970s (Burns & Stalker, 1961; Lawrence & Lorsch, 1967; Miles & Snow, 1978; Woodward, 1965), researchers in the 1990s asserted that the environmental turbulence outside of schools mandated that educators could no longer ensconce themselves inside of schools while keeping parents and community members locked out. While external groups can legislate internal school restructuring, the reculturing that appears necessary if educators inside of schools are to make schools more effective is a matter that cannot be mandated by legislative fiat. What transpired inside of schools that dealt effectively with these challenges is that educators contended with and turned five potentially external menacing forces to their advantage. These included: parents and the community; technology; corporate connections; government policy, and, the wider teaching profession (Hargreaves & Fullan, 1998). For his part, Fullan notes: "These external forces…do not come in helpful packages; they are an amalgam of complex and uncoordinated phenomenon. The work of the school is to figure out how to make its relationship with them a productive one" (2000, p. 583). In contrast to their colleagues in ineffective schools, educators in effective schools realized that they needed these external forces (where they were present) to engage in the reculturing necessary to get the job inside of schools completed.

Researchers also examined how principals in effective schools influenced what events meant to stake-holders both inside and outside of schools (Rallis, 1990). Anderson (1990) specified three strategies: managing the day-to-day meanings of events; mediating conflict as contention emerges; and, resolving contradictions in one's ideological perspective. Strike (1993) also asserted that effective principals used multiple rhetorical and dialogical strategies to identify what events meant to people, for example, by crafting language to promote new meanings at official ceremonies, public relations events, as well as at meetings.

However, efforts to manage what things mean and to build consensus among various stakeholders both inside and outside of schools may not make schools more effective if principals fail to recognize that meaning is a socially negotiated phenomenon (Miron, 1997). Two studies sustain this assertion. In one study, a well-intentioned principal—committed to detracking—implemented several strategies to support this change (Cooper, 1996). Yet, among important stakeholders, this principal failed to generate new, shared meaning about detracking. In particular, the principal did not deal effectively with some veteran teachers as well as the parents of some students enrolled in the upper-track classes. In the end, the principal resigned and the detracking initiative was abandoned. In a second study, Robinson (1995) observed a group discussing a school's policy regarding uniforms and coming to the conclusion that the principal had exercised legitimate power. However, the group believed the principal compromised that power by failing to be open about the uniform policy in the beginning and to test the idea in the public arena. The lesson of these two studies is clear: negotiating meaning is a shared process. Efforts to reculture schools, then, must engage principals and internal stakeholders.

Another factor purported to influence the inside-out story was the increasingly heterogeneous population of students who attended schools in the 1990s and yet even more heterogeneous population predicted to be attending schools in the decades beyond the 1990s. As with any demographic change, the increasing diversity of the student population made reculturing schools more difficult. For example, Hodgkinson (1988) predicted that demographic changes would greatly transform schooling in the 1990s, estimating that 40% of the high school graduating class of 2000 would be culturally different from English-speaking, White European Americans. In addition, he estimated that 24% of these children would be born into poverty. Hodgkinson may have overestimated because 1998 data suggested that somewhat more than 10% of the school-aged population—nearly six million students—were served by Chapter 1 and IDEA funds for students with disabilities (United States Department of Education, 1998).

Several other demographic changes further complicated the challenges educators confronted inside of schools. For example, two studies indicated that the growth rate among African American and Hispanic populations outpaced the White population. In addition, these studies suggested that children born into these groups would much more likely be born into poverty (Baptiste, 1999; Natriello, McDill, & Pallas, 1990). For their part, Natriello et al. projected that by the year 2020, 26% of all children would be living in poverty and 8% would not speak English as a primary language. Only 49% of the school-age population would be White.

The notion that educators inside of schools must deal with the increasing cultural diversity outside of schools is not new (Grubb, 1995). However, during the 1990s, the dual notions that schools exist to assimilate non-majority youth into the dominant culture and that schools should homogenize youth waned as the goal of multiculturalism moved to the fore (Adams, 1997; Baptiste, 1999). Further increasing the pressure that changing demographics had upon life inside of schools was the "diversity of diversities" present in the school-aged population. Not only were race and ethnicity becoming increasingly diverse, so were a host of other factors, including: disability, primary language, social class, gender, and sexual orientation. Polite also included the increasing number of students affected by the human immunodeficiency virus as well as students living in households where abuse is present (2000, p. 145). Moreover, groups that had formerly appeared to be cohesive— at least to outsiders—were not (Lee, 1996). One impact of this lack of cultural cohesion was that consensus about educational goals and strategies inside of schools became increasingly difficult to achieve (Marshall, 1993). This is a matter of particular import if educators are to reculture schools in ways that foster greater school effectiveness in increasingly diverse settings.

During the 1990s, a handful of theorists continued to assert the proposition that public education is the best antidote for intolerance (Barber, 1997; Goodlad & McMannon, 1997; Larabee, 1997). Yet, a significant study by Godwin, Ausbrooks, and Martinez found that "none of the key research that concerns either the development of tolerance or the effects of public schools has examined empirically whether public schools are more effective in teaching political tolerance" (2001, p. 543). Testing the notion that experience with diversity is the key to teaching tolerance, Godwin et al. discovered that students enrolled in nonevangelical private schools had statistically significantly higher scores on the democratic norms scale. In addition, these students perceived less threat from their least-liked groups and scored higher on the tolerance scale from those of public school students, although these differences were not statistically significant. It may be that reculturing schools to emphasize diversity and inclusion increases neither tolerance nor school effectiveness.

Lastly, one cannot overlook the effect that the increase of single-parent households and those where two adults are employed full-time had upon educators' efforts to reculture schools. Without doubt, this particular demographic change expanded the inside story of schooling, albeit mostly by expanding after-school programs. And so, during the 1990s, various interests examined the estimated 30% of discretionary or free time students have each week of the academic year (Asmussen & Larson, 1991; Bianchi & Robinson, 1997). Most research focused upon how students spent that time and whether and how this affected school effectiveness and, in particular, student academic and social achievement (Eccles & Barber, 1999; Miller, 1995; Miller, O'Connor, Sirignano, & Joshi, 1996).

One study provided evidence that after-school programs positively impact academic outcomes (e.g., higher grades and test scores), especially for low-income students (Hamilton & Klein, 1998). Three additional studies suggested that after-school programs impact important attitudes toward schooling, in particular, raising expectations about academic achievement, work habits, and attendance rates, especially for low-income students (Brooks, Mojica, & Land, 1995; Posner & Vandell, 1994; Witt & Baker, 1997). Four other studies indicated that after-school programs significantly lower student involvement in undesirable behavior, in particular, drinking, smoking, drug use, sexual activity, and violence. Concurrently, students involved in after-school programs demonstrated increased social and behavioral adjustment, improved peer relations, and more effective strategies for dealing with conflict. In addition, several studies concluded that parental involvement increased when students were enrolled in after-school programs (Beuhring, Blum, & Rinehart, 2000; Miller, 1995; Pierce, Hamm, & Vandell, 1994; Zill, Nord, & Loomis, 1995).

While after-school programs normally do not impact school structure and instructional practice during the school day, most programs are immensely popular not only with parents, but also with the public and private agencies. For its part, the federal government increased Department of Education funding for three-year grants to schools for after-school programs from $1 million in 1997 to more than $800 million in 2001. In addition,

26 states now fund—or are in the process of funding—after-school learning programs as have numerous cities (including New York and San Diego) and various intermediary organizations (including the National Academy of Sciences and an amalgam of private foundations) (Miller, 2001). While all of this research points to some positive outcomes, researchers need to examine the precise outcomes after-school programs have upon school effectiveness, especially as after-school programs expand into non-academic areas, including clubs and activities (Schinke, Cole, & Poulin, 1998).

The movement away from a unitary vision of schooling as well as purpose for educating youth uncovers yet another external factor—normative theory—which impacted the inside story of schooling during the 1990s.

Amidst all of this turbulence and as educators engaged in reculturing efforts to deal with it during the 1990s, normative theorists indicated that there no longer existed a unitary way to think about schooling. For example, Baptiste (1999) advocated cultural pluralism as a social and educational ideal. Once marginal goals of schooling—for example, promoting cultural differences and social justice inside of schools—also moved front and center (Asante, 1991; Cummins, 1997; Delpit, 1995; Foster, 1995; Ladson-Billings, 1994; Sears, 1993). These scholars influenced more centrist researchers who acknowledged that educators must make provisions inside of schools so that every student, regardless of personal characteristics or social background, would succeed in school (Darling-Hammond, 1997a; O'Day & Smith, 1993; Rossi, 1994). The scholarly rhetoric did not escape the notice of politicians. "Leave no student behind," was the mantra then-candidate for President, George W. Bush, espoused on the campaign trail and again when he unveiled his educational agenda one week after being sworn into office.

In addition, postmodern and post-structural thought (Derrida, 1984; Foucault, 1984; Habermas, 1987, 1990) extended its influence upon the academic community, beginning in the 1980s. Then, during the 1990s, postmodern and post-structural thought wielded influence upon educational theorists and, by extension, administrators and teachers enrolled in certification programs. Educators were exposed, for example, to arguments—like Butler's (1997) or some variant—that society has entered a "post-liberatory" era. For these theorists, there no longer exists a coherent sense about what constitutes the "authentic" self that education is supposed to release from the fetters of oppression, as Freìre (1970) asserted three decades ago. In addition, educators learned that there is no universal theory of progress and that it is extremely difficult to know or assert with any confidence whatsoever what "better" or "worse" might mean. This presented quite a dilemma. How are educators to reculture schools if they do not have confidence that the goal of school improvement is an improvement?

Whether one agrees with postmodern and post-structural thought, it does remind educators that they should pause before jumping headfirst into school reculturing. Oftentimes, innovations that appear to be progressive when introduced (e.g., tracking or detracking, phonics or whole language, competitive or collaborative learning) express regressive and undemocratic power systems operating both inside and outside of schools. These "regimes of truth" are aimed solely at regulating human activity (Foucault, 1977). For example, in schools and classrooms, a dominant elite—whether it be administrators or teachers—exerts power over a powerless and disenfranchised majority—in the former case, teachers, and in the latter case, the students. Trapped in this situation, the disenfranchised must cower and accept this condition as the permanent status quo. All is not lost, however, because teachers and students possess an array of political strategies and can direct institutional dynamics to subvert and dismantle efforts aimed at change by any dominant élite (Cooper, 1996; Wells & Oakes, 1996; Wells & Serna, 1996). This should remind those both inside and outside of schools that regulating human activity does not prevent the regime from being undone (Anderson & Grinberg, 1998).

Of considerable importance is the effect that all of this had upon schools, the challenges presented to educators as they responded by reculturing schools, and, therefore, the impact all of this had upon school effectiveness.

Take, for example, the principalship. Increased diversity and the need for more inclusive practices complicated decision making as principals now had to deal with several new challenges simultaneously, namely: how best to organize schools and classrooms; forging relationships between families, communities, and the school; and, how to provide professional development for teachers that would enable them to determine how best to respond to demographic changes. Some administrators turned a blind eye to the full extent of these demographic changes inside of their schools and other administrators, while they promoted practices sensitive to the issues of inclusion and diversity, did not tightly couple these practices to the school's programs, especially curriculum, teaching, and learning (Capper, 1993). Furthermore, if principals were to engage teachers in reculturing efforts so that schools better served a more diverse body of students and were more fully inclusive, research indicated that principals had better be prepared for and capable of dealing with conflict (Parker & Shapiro, 1993). Interestingly, at least part of this conflict can be attributed to the expectation on the part of some stakeholders that principals should maintain a traditional model of school organization. But, this is a model of organization that many principals already know does not promote the goals of greater diversity and inclusion.

As these external forces impacted the inside story of Catholic schooling and the reculturing efforts on the part of educators in Catholic schools to respond to these forces, research provided evidence that Catholic schools of the 1990s dealt these challenges in creative ways that did not detract from school effectiveness.

Contrary to popular caricatures, demographic data indicated that the Catholic schools of the 1990s resembled more of a "patchwork quilt" than a "seamless garment," exhibiting diversity in structure, student population, and curriculum. One reason is structural diversity. There are diocesan parish elementary and secondary schools, those owned and operated or sponsored by religious communities, as well as a growing number of independent Catholic schools (Mueller, 2000; Nelson, 2000). Because of this structural diversity and the differing legal status each possesses, there really was no Catholic school "system."

In addition, even though enrollments have decreased substantially since the early 1970s, the nation's Catholic schools served a more diverse (i.e., increasingly non-Catholic, non-White, and even nonreligious) student population than many imagined (McDonald, 2000b). In terms of religious diversity, a study of 31 predominantly African American Catholic high schools in 1996-1997 indicated that a majority of the students (54%) described themselves as non-Catholic Christians while a minority (46%) identified themselves as Roman Catholic (Polite, 2000). A 1997 study of 18 dioceses (15 of which rank among the largest 20 dioceses nationwide) found that smaller immigrant groups have enrolled children in Catholic schools, in some cases, at a rate that is much higher than for Whites or Blacks (Lawrence, 2000). There are regional differences, but the pattern of increasing diversity is clear. For example, Cubans now account for 50-60% of Miami's annual Catholic school enrollment. Hispanic groups constitute between 20 and 40% of total enrollment in the northeast and southwest dioceses. Lastly, Filipinos account for more than 10% of the total Catholic school enrollment in Los Angeles and San Jose (Polite, 2000).

In terms of socio-economic diversity, a study of Catholic secondary schools in the early 1990s indicated that minority students come from more economically élite families. As Riordan (2000) notes, "Quite remarkably, the percentage of non-White students in Catholic secondary schools has increased dramatically over the past 20 years to a point where the racial demography of Catholic and public schools is now virtually the same" (p. 39). Yet, at the same time, "Catholic schools on average have become more selective and are no longer serving primarily the disadvantaged or even the working class, despite the fact that a goodly number of minority students now attend Catholic schools" (p. 40). Polite's sample of 33 inner city Catholic high schools portrays a different picture. "Nearly half of the schools report that they are serving increasing numbers of students who are living in poverty, indicating that upper-middle-income African American parents are not likely to select predominantly African American Catholic schools for their children" (Polite, 2000, p. 144). It appears that, when upper-middle-income African American parents identify a Catholic high school as serving children of marginalized and lower middle income folk, African American parents do not send a child to that school. Possessing greater economic means, it may be that they send a child to another, integrated Catholic school.

Diversity also typifies Catholic school curricula. A survey of 18 dioceses and archdioceses indicated that a "Catholic elementary school curriculum *does not exist*" (Schuttloffel, 2000, p. 107). It may be that the practice of many dioceses to "provide only direction to the local school through a broad curriculum framework" (p. 108), in combination with the relative independence of many schools—especially high schools sponsored by religious congregations—would yield similar results in dioceses not included in Schuttloffel's sample.

In sum, structural, socio-economic, and curricular diversity suggests that there probably was no "generic" Catholic school during the 1990s even though many Catholic schools appeared to be similar. Furthermore, educators inside of these schools dealt effectively with the challenges that increased diversity presented. In contrast to caricatures of Catholic schools, which emphasized conformity (McLaren, 1986), the data indicate that educators in Catholic schools of the 1990s constructed cultures which incorporated greater diversity and did not adversely impact student achievement. For Greeley (1998, 1999), the data proved to be exactly the opposite of what many believed (or perhaps, hoped). In sum, the 1990s offered evidence contradicting any criticism that Catholic schools inculcated in students a sheltered, defensive, ghetto mentality. In fact, educators in Catholic schools throughout the three decades of the post-Vatican II era inculcated rather tolerant attitudes in students about a wide array of social issues (Bryk et al., 1993).

The "Outside-In" Story

Fullan's (2000) first two stories of education reform focus upon efforts to improve school effectiveness at the local level by examining the internal and external factors impacting educators and their functioning inside of schools, what might be called the "micro" level of analysis (i.e., the local school). In contrast, the "outside-in" story examines phenomena at the "macro" level of analysis, looking at schools and their functioning within larger systems, (e.g., district, state, or the host of other intermediate agencies), all of which exist to promote school effectiveness. The subject of this story, then, is the "external reform infrastructure" (p. 583) organized to support school effectiveness.

During the 1990s, perhaps the primary external reform infrastructure to support school effectiveness was state-mandated testing and the concurrent movement toward the establishment of national standards. Enormous pressure was brought to bear upon educators to get students to meet and surpass the minimum standards set for various grade levels.

Testing would appear to make schools and teachers more accountable and perhaps more effective. But, Popham (2000) asserted that teachers responded to these initiatives during the 1990s with two strategies. First: "teaching to the test," including "item teaching" (instruction organized around actual items found on a test or around a set of similar items). Second: "curriculum teaching" (instruction directed toward a specific body of content knowledge or a specific set of cognitive skills included in a specific test). Popham's primary concern was the net effect these strategies had upon testing, that is, the threat posed to validity.

Teaching to the test also involves professional ethics. Why would teachers succumb to the pressure to improve test scores by engaging in unethical behavior? And, why did administrators not stop teachers from teaching to the test? Ackroyd and Thompson (1999) have argued that administrative efforts to detect and deter misbehavior only increase the probability of more sinister misbehavior. As this concerns teaching to the test, as administrators would attempt to decrease teaching to the test, teachers would become more inventive about how to increase student achievement. In the end, achievement test data would demonstrate increased student achievement but students actually would not be as knowledgeable as the results indicated. Furthermore, educators would have sullied themselves in a deeper ethical morass.

A second external reform infrastructure to support school effectiveness—and perhaps the most hotly-contested educational policy debate of the 1990s—concerned educational vouchers (Chubb & Moe, 1990;

Cookson, 1994; Fuller, Elmore, & Orfield, 1996; Ladd, 1996; Moe, 1995; Peterson & Hassel, 1998; Wells, 1993). Supporters asserted that vouchers would increase inter-school competition and, hence, positively impact school effectiveness. Various schemes were proposed and some were implemented. Initiatives differed in scope and approach (Levin, 1991).

Of particular significance to the topic of school environment is that the proponents' allegations of inefficiency and ineffectiveness in the nation's public schools and the purported effectiveness of private schools, in general, and Catholic schools, in particular, fueled much of this debate (Hanushek, 1996).

Examining the proponents' assertion, Schiller (1994) discovered significant effects in mathematics achievement for Catholic school students between the tenth- and twelfth- grade years. Sander's (1996) study of Catholic grade schools indicated that eight years in a Catholic grade school are associated with higher vocabulary, mathematics, and reading test scores with no effect evident on science test scores. However, this effect may be driven by the non-Catholic students who attend Catholic grade schools because, by eliminating non-Catholics from the sample, the Catholic school effect is zero. Lending credence to this assertion, Gamoran (1996) found no significant Catholic school effects upon student achievement in reading, science, or social studies when compared to public school students. There was evidence, however, of a meager positive effect on mathematics achievement of about .03 per year. Goldhaber's (1996) research contested even this minimal effect, arguing that the data indicate no private school effects. For his part, Neal (1997a) found gains from Catholic schooling to be modest for urban Whites and negligible for suburban students. In addition, while urban minorities seemed to benefit most from access to Catholic schooling, most of the benefit could be attributed to the poor quality of the local public schools. In contrast, a handful of non-experimental studies indicated that attending Catholic school increased the probability of completing high school or attending college, especially for students enrolled in urban schools and for minority students (Evans & Schwab, 1995; Figlio & Stone, 1999; Sander & Krautmann, 1995). Rouse (1998a, 1998b) contested this assertion for data-related and methodological reasons while other researchers cited inefficacious statistical testing (Murnane, Newstead, & Olsen, 1985), inappropriate instrumentation (Neal, 1997a), and poor sets of instrumental variables (Figlio & Stone, 1999).

By decade's end, there was no convincing resolution to the debate. Furthermore, interpretations about Catholic school effectiveness vis-à-vis public school inefficiency and ineffectiveness are tenuous, if not entirely speculative, because student academic achievement in private schools may not have been as high as previously believed (Levin, 1998; Neal, 1998; Witte, 1992). Jencks (1985) was most likely accurate when he suggested that any differences be regarded as suggestive rather than conclusive. The worst news for Catholic and private school proponents, then, is that there may really be no statistical difference in terms of academic achievement. However, this body of research, utilizing non-experimental data from the High School and Beyond and National Education Longitudinal Study 1988 survey, did not address other, non-quantitative variables that may help to explain school effectiveness in more qualitative terms, as did Bryk et al. (1993).

A third external reform infrastructure of the 1990s intended to support effectiveness was the increased external pressure being brought to bear upon schools to be more diverse and inclusive. In this context, "diversity" and "inclusion" denoted external constituents (and oftentimes, non-educators) participating in school gover-nance and daily operations, what advocates termed "increasing local control of schools." This reform infrastruc-ture re-introduced into educational policy discourse Horace Mann's arguments about "common schools" and the need for broad-based local support if they are to survive (Cremin, 1957).

Principals—and, in particular, elementary school principals—responded by creating or expanding the role of school councils, parent committees, and community volunteers (Cohen, 1990; Epps, 1994; Malen, Ogawa, & Kranz, 1990). Others formed coalitions, partnerships, and networks to support various educational reform initiatives (Cibulka & Kritek, 1996). Rollow and Bryk's (1993) research into school reform practices in Chicago's public schools indicated that effective schools that supported greater inclusion and diversity were "marked by sustained debate over the key ideas that vie for moral authority and what these ideas mean in terms of specific school improvement plans" (p. 102). For his part, Coleman asserted that "achievement-oriented schools" required educators who would reculture schools by involving parents more meaningfully in the education of their children (Coleman, 1995).

Arguably, wider participation can enhance the principal's role (Hess, 1993) and yet, democratic discourse aimed at transforming what goes on inside of schools is not present in many, if not most schools (Keyes, Hanley-Maxwell, & Capper, 1999). Perhaps this reticence can be attributed to principals who fear expanding opportunities for outsiders to participate in the social construction of meaning (Miron, 1997), especially in local communities where trust is low, as Cibulka (1978) and Watson (1978) asserted more than two decades ago. This reticence may also be attributable to the perceived need on the part of educators in general to control other people and their discourse, that is, if educators are to achieve the goals they prefer to identify and set for themselves.

Researchers in the 1990s also scrutinized the neighborhoods and communities where effective schools were located. One early study (Crowson & Boyd, 1992) focused upon Chicago's school reforms that were consciously designed to involve community members in the decision-making process inside of schools. Early evidence indicated that a new model for a neighborhood-based politics of education, constructed upon a school's responsiveness to the community whose children the school serves, correlated positively with improved school effectiveness. Other research suggested that, by coordinating various social agencies and their programs with schools, schools could better serve their students as well as effect social change beyond the schoolyard. In addition, partnerships between schools and other institutions could serve as a foundation for educational renewal and community regeneration (Kretzmann & McKnight, 1993). Successful collaborative efforts demonstrated that community development projects should target schools as a locus for community development or, at least, as catalysts for developing other community institutions and neighborhoods (Miron, 1997). Unfortunately, the terrain was littered with many more failed efforts than successes (Capper, 1996; Crowson & Boyd, 1996; Kahne & Kelley, 1993; Langman & McLaughlin, 1993; Smrekar & Mawhiney, 1999; White & Wehlage, 1995; Yowell, 1996).

Greater diversity and inclusion did not come without cost. Increased participation in school governance and daily operations by outsiders made leading a school an increasingly more complex, tenuous, and uncertain matter. Hallinger (1992), Hart (1995), and Hess (1999) argued that, by expanding the number of outsiders involved inside of schools, principals had to attend to an increasing number of demands and conflicts as well as to forge alliances and agreements between contending parties. Thus, to make schools more diverse and inclusive, principals had to re-envision their role. For example, principals could no longer busy themselves protecting teachers from change and outside distractions. Instead, principals attended directly to building the networks, coalitions, and partnerships that provided the external resources teachers needed to implement school reform and to make it work. What is the cost of this role change? As principals spent more time dealing with external constituents, principals spent less time attending to their instructional leadership responsibilities.

Researchers during the 1990s also raised the question concerning how these external reform infrastructure initiatives impacted teachers. While much of the research described teachers as critical actors in educational reform efforts (Elmore, 1996), research offered no singular pattern describing how teachers responded to reform initiatives emanating from outside of schools.

For example, Sikes (1992) found that teachers rejected externally mandated change, carrying on much as they did before. In schools where the faculty was split into old guard-new guard factions, "grumbling cliques" emerged. And, in some instances, teachers left the profession while others seized upon reform mandates as opportunities to pursue new career prospects in the educational system. Datnow's (1998) study indicated that some teachers pushed or sustained reform efforts, while others passively resisted or actively subverted efforts directed at changing teachers' functioning inside of schools. Valenzuela (1999) and McNeil (2000) confirmed

Datnow's findings. Moreover, Blackmore (1998) found that externally mandated reforms created a "culture of compliance." Thus, when principals announced yet another externally mandated reform initiative, "all [teachers] want[ed] to know [is] how to do it as painlessly as possible" (p. 472). Complicating matters further, several researchers discovered that many teachers felt bound to respond to their students' needs and, hence, adapted rather than adopted new policies (Helsby, 1999; McLaughlin & Talbert, 1993; Tyack & Cuban, 1995). What research into teachers' responses to externally mandated reforms indicated is that the social, historical, and economic context in which schools are located directly impacted how teachers responded to externally mandated reform efforts (Little, 1990; Louis, 1990; McLaughlin, Talbert, & Bascia, 1990; Siskin, 1994b). For example, budget changes, new testing and curriculum guidelines, and elections of new board members and other education officials disrupted or derailed even the best reform plans (Siskin, 1994a). Lastly, Bailey (2000) noted that, if the rhetoric of reform did not match the reality of the teacher's classroom experience, teachers would actively resist reforms.

Thus, externally mandated change rarely played out in a linear trajectory inside of schools. The change process was transformational, emerging gradually as teachers implemented "the innovation as developed in the classroom" (Snyder, Bolin, & Zumwalt, 1992, p. 404). It is easy to see how many of the external reform infrastructures' initiatives intended to support school effectiveness, "seemingly straightforward policies—content requirements for specific grade levels, for example, —are often implemented very differently across localities, school, and classrooms" (Elmore & Sykes, 1992, p. 186). In light of this finding, Healey and DeStefano (1997) cautioned policymakers to craft new policies so that they can be locally developed and to clear away old policies that block school-based reform.

In sum, research examining how external reform infrastructure initiatives during the 1990s increased school effectiveness clarified four salient factors. These included: implementing decentralization, building and expanding school capacity, engaging in rigorous accountability to external agencies and constituencies, and, stimulating innovation (Bryk, Bekrig, Kerbow, & Rollow, 1998). The research also indicated that there is a synergy of effects through which external forces can increase school capacity and accountability (Dolan, 1994; Epstein, 1995). At the decade's end, however, more systematic research is required if we are to understand better just how external reform infrastructure increases school effectiveness.

The emergence of new external reform infrastructures also impacted life inside Catholic schools. While Catholic schools exist within public school districts, counties, states, regions, and the nation, they also exist within dioceses, ecclesiastical provinces, and national conferences. But, because secular external reform infrastructures are intended primarily to promote Catholic school effectiveness as secular entities, ecclesiastical offices developed external reform infrastructures that focus primarily upon Catholic school effectiveness as a religious entity, namely, the school's identity as distinctively *Catholic*. For a variety of reasons, this matter became increasingly important during the 1990s.

To appreciate this infrastructure and its impact upon school effectiveness, one must grapple with the complicated juridical relationship between the Church's organizational levels. For example, the structural diversity of Catholic schools represents one dimension of complexity (Mueller, 2000; Nelson, 2000). The concept of subsidiarity complicates matters further. Theoretically at least, decision making about how to implement Church policy takes place at the lowest possible level of organizational responsibility. Catholic elementary school curricula provide a snapshot demonstrating precisely how subsidiarity works in actual practice (Schuttloffel, 2000). Moreover, financing Catholic schools is mostly a local matter as there is no direct federal, state, or district government funding of Catholic schools. Thus, the external reform infrastructure intended to promote identifiably *Catholic* school reform during the 1990s consisted not of financial or professional resources that educators in Catholic schools could use to implement reform policies. Instead, external players issued policy statements and exhortations challenging educators to use their personal, professional, and spiritual resources to perfect Catholic schools, especially through catechesis.

The "outside-in" story of school reform examines phenomena at the "macro" level of analysis, focusing upon schools and their functioning within the larger systems intended to promote school effectiveness. The subject of this story is the "external reform infrastructure" (Fullan, 2000, p. 583) organized to support school effectiveness. During the 1990s, effectiveness appears to have increased in some schools as a consequence of several external reform structures; namely, decentralization, building and expanding school capacity, increasing accountability, and stimulating innovation (Bryk, Bekrig, Kerbow, & Rollow, 1998).

It is clear that much more systematic research is necessary to better understand how external reform infrastructure initiatives have increased both public and Catholic school effectiveness.

Some Lessons and a Research Challenge

The concept of "environment," a concept given little scholarly attention during the 1990s, subsumes many of the topics that have predominated discourse about school effectiveness during the decade. In this chapter, Fullan's (2000) three stories of educational reform made it possible to classify the sets of internal and external environmental factors researchers suggested influence school effectiveness. While each story casts light upon different factors, it is the synergy of effects—when stakeholders weave these three stories into a "grand narrative" of school reform—that appears to have made it possible for some schools during the 1990s to be more effective in accomplishing their educative purpose than other schools whose stakeholders have focused only upon one or two of the stories of school reform. Fullan notes:

> What happens as the three stories coalesce is that there is a fusion of three powerful forces— the spiritual, the political, and the intellectual. The spiritual dimension has to do with the purpose and meaning of reform. Indeed, the moral purpose of reform is to make a difference in the lives of students....The purposeful interactions that occur within and across learning communities serve to mobilize moral commitments and energies. Second, such mobilization is power, so that the political capacity to overcome obstacles and to persist despite setbacks is also enhanced. Third, good ideas in the market place—hitherto not noticed or not implemented—become more accessible as schools and school systems increase their capacity to find out about, select, integrate, and use new ideas effectively. (p. 584)

Readers should take note of the author's use of normative rather than descriptive language to describe school reform efforts in the 1990s. In the 1980s, inquiry into school effectiveness utilized data from large national databases and quantitative measures to describe differences in academic achievement between students enrolled in public, private, and Catholic schools (Coleman & Hoffer, 1987; Coleman, et al., 1982). In the 1990s, researchers utilized qualitative measures to examine the experiences of the people inside of schools in order to identify factors influencing the quantitative differences previously described (Bryk et al., 1993). A substantial body of research indicates that an emphasis upon academic achievement, high expectations for students, and a well-developed sense of community contribute to school effectiveness (Anderson, 1982, 1985; Brookover, Beady, Flood, Schweitzer, & Wisenbaker, 1979; Bryk & Driscoll, 1988; Chubb & Moe, 1988, 1990; Edmonds, 1979a, 1979b; Lightfoot, 1983; Purkey & Smith, 1983, 1985; Rutter, Maughan, Mortimore, Ouston, & Smith, 1979; Wynne, 1980).

While this methodological turn should be of significance to historians, what is of paramount importance for the purposes of both researchers and practitioners is not the turn to qualitative methods per se, but the language this turn afforded researchers when writing about the internal and external factors impacting school effectiveness. Earlier, quantitative models enabled researchers to use secular concepts like "social capital" and "human capital" to describe school effectiveness (Coleman, 1987a, 1987b, 1988, 1991). But, in the 1990s, qualitative models enabled researchers to re-introduce normative terminology—concepts from philosophy and religion—long absent from scholarly discourse about school effectiveness. For example, researchers wrote about improving school effectiveness by attending to the moral dimensions of schooling (Carr, 1991; Sergiovanni, 1994; Starratt, 1994), of educational administration (Beck, 1994; Greenfield, 1991; Hodgkinson, 1991; Sergiovanni, 1992; Smith & Blase, 1991) and of teaching as well (Beyer, 1991; Goodlad, Soder, & Sirotnik, 1991).

It may be that the nation's Catholic schools can provide researchers in the next decade a fertile loam for deeper inquiry into and analysis of school effectiveness from a normative vantage. Utilizing both quantitative and qualitative methods to elucidate additional environmental factors that potentially impact school effectiveness, the focus need not be solely upon sterile academic effects exclusively. In addition, and perhaps more substantively, research might be able to identify more specifically the moral purpose that motivates administrators and teachers in schools, one that coalesces in educative experiences which promote the moral and intellectual development of youth. Perhaps this research will vindicate the wisdom of the U.S. Catholic community in the late-1800s. Would it not be ironic were researchers to discover that Baltimore III did have it right? Is "an education devoid of [a moral purpose] ...no education at all"?

CHAPTER 4
OUTCOMES

ELIZABETH A. MEEGAN, OP
JAMES B. CARROLL
MARIA J. CIRIELLO, OP

Research on school effectiveness in the last 10 years has continued to focus on academic outcomes of students. The outcomes include standardized test scores, graduation rates, post-secondary aspirations, and college attendance.

Catholic schools, while they aspire to academic success, include among their primary objectives, "the understanding of the Catholic faith, a commitment to the practice of religion, and a set of values that will influence the students' present and future lives" (Convey, 1992, p. 59). These objectives, as well as the academic outcomes, are important components of the Catholic school's effectiveness.

ACADEMIC OUTCOMES

Academic Achievement

The strong emphasis of research on Catholic schools' student academic outcomes has been driven by several factors. Much of the debate arguing in favor of school choice has emphasized the effectiveness of the Catholic schools in educating its students, particularly among disadvantaged students. The U.S. Department of Education has been the largest collector of data on education and the federal government's focus has, of course, been principally on academic achievement. The National Assessment of Educational Progress (NAEP) has been the largest group of studies to date on student achievement. It may be that only the federal government has the resources to maintain this broad a data collection and allow for some analysis of achievement over time. The cost of huge national studies at regular intervals will always be prohibitive for single school systems. Studies have abounded in the past 30 years, which indicate higher achievement of Catholic school students than of students in public schools. Recent national testing, particularly the NAEP 1992-2000, (NCES), while showing some variation in both Catholic and public school scores, continues to indicate higher average scores among Catholic school students. Some of the differences are significant. Disagreement continues on the reasons for the differences in test scores. One extensive examination of data on Catholic school student achievement is that of Thomas B. Hoffer (2000). Though using older data (e.g., *High School and Beyond*, (HS&B), the *National Education Longitudinal Study of 1988* (NELS:88) and *National Assessment of Educational Progress* (NAEP)) found in Convey's *Catholic Schools Make a Difference* (CSMD), he also includes the 1992 NAEP data.

Table 1 represents one year's results of the NAEP. It suggests that the effect size in mathematics and writing skills increases with grade level. Though the mean differences in reading get progressively large, the effect size does not (Hoffer, 2000).

TABLE 1: Average NAEP Test Scores for Public and Catholic School Students, 1992*

Test, grade level, and full sample SD	Public	Catholic	Difference#	Effect size**
Mathematics				
Grade 4 (SD=33.1)	217.3 (0.8)	226.6 (1.2)	9.3 (1.4)	.28
Grade 8 (SD=30.9)	266.1 (1.0)	277.2 (2.1)	11.1 (2.3)	.36
Grade 12 (SD=30.1)	296.6 (1.0)	310.4 (2.5)	13.8 (2.7)	.46
Reading comprehension				
Grade 4 (SD=40.3)	215.9 (1.1)	230.2 (2.2)	14.3 (2.5)	.35
Grade 8 (SD=39.4)	258.1 (1.0)	275.4 (1.9)	17.3 (2.1)	.44
Grade 12 (SD=43.0)	288.7 (0.7)	306.3 (1.5)	17.6 (1.7)	.41
Writing skills				
Grade 4 (SD=38.2)	220.1 (1.3)	233.5 (2.3)	13.5 (2.6)	.35
Grade 8 (SD=36.3)	259.9 (1.2)	274.4 (2.4)	14.5 (2.7)	.40
Grade 12 (SD=32.0)	283.3 (1.0)	304.8 (1.6)	21.5 (1.9)	.67

*Hoffer (2000): National Center for Education Statistics (1994), NAEP *Data on Disk: 1992 Almanac Viewer* (Washington, DC: US Department of Education). Full sample standard deviations are taken from the Data Appendix of Campbell, Reese, O'Sullivan, and Dossey (1996). *Note:* Numbers in parentheses are standard errors.

#Catholic-minus-public differences. Standard errors of the differences are calculated by taking the square root of the sum of squared errors for the separate public and Catholic means.

**Effect sizes are calculated by dividing the Catholic-minus-public difference by the total sample standard deviation. These estimates are not adjusted for social background or other differences among public and Catholic school students.

The research by Hoffer (2000) is included as a sample of published comparisons of core subject achievement during a particular year. The comparison between Catholic and public schools, which this table suggests, is not meant to infer that Catholic schools are merely a private replacement for public schools, but do provide a frame of reference in basic academic areas. As Youniss and McLellan (1999) stress, Catholic schools are essentially complementary options for parents who desire a religious value based academic program. As such, academic quality is an essential component.

Hoffer (2000) describes the explanations that have been offered for the differences in Catholic and public school achievement. Some writers maintain that there is no effect of Catholic school attendance on achievement. According to this theory, differences in Catholic school students are the result of their being higher achieving students to begin with or other sociological differences, such as having more interested parents, for instance. In other words, the differences are explained by factors other than the effect of attending a Catholic school. When most of the suggested factors accounting for the differences are held constant, there remains a "Catholic school effect" in at least some subjects in specific grade levels. The size and reasons for this effect continue to be debated.

A New York University study (Hartocollis, 2001) comparing Catholic and public school students in New York City on state reading and math tests found that, though student scores in the lower elementary grades are similar, by 8th grade the public school students test considerably behind on these tests. These results are achieved despite fewer resources, as indicated by one teacher for every 21 students in the Catholic schools compared with one teacher for every 16 students in the New York City public schools.

America (*Harvard Study,* 2000) reported that a Washington DC study of 81 African American students selected at random by lottery to receive Washington Scholarship Funds (tuition vouchers) compared children in grades 2 through 5 with those students not chosen who remained in public schools. After six to seven months, students in private schools scored higher in math and reading than their public school peers. Approximately 70% of the students receiving Washington Scholarship Fund vouchers attend Catholic schools.

In another Washington DC study, Johnson (1999) analyzes 1996 NAEP scores of African American 4th and 8th graders in the Washington, DC public and Catholic schools. Fourth and eighth grades in Catholic schools outperformed their peers in public schools. The difference widens from 4th (6.5%) to 8th grade (8.2%). When similar statistics are quoted, a common response is that Catholic school students enjoy certain advantages that account for their higher achievement, (e.g. family stability, parent education, etc.). This Heritage Foundation Study specifically holds other relevant factors constant. Johnson (1999) asserts that

> for fourth grade students in the nation's capital, attending a Catholic school has almost four times the effect on standardized math scores than living in an intact, two-parent home and ten times the effect of attending a slightly more affluent public school. (p. 7)

NAEP Data

NAEP has generated extensive data that have not yet been subjected to analysis by other researchers. It is included to give some insight on current test results and perhaps suggest areas of research that could be pursued. The achievement level definitions used throughout NAEP assessments are the following:

Achievement Level Policy Definitions

Basic	*Partial mastery* of prerequisite knowledge and skills that are fundamental for proficient work at each grade.
Proficient	*Solid academic performance* for each grade assessed. Students reaching this level have demonstrated competency over challenging subject matter, including subject-matter knowledge, application of such knowledge to real-world situations, and analytical skills appropriate to the subject matter.
Advanced	*Superior performance.*

The data given for Tables 2-7 list percentages of students who tested at the advanced, proficient, and basic levels or above and those who failed to achieve what the researchers deemed a basic level score.

Writing test scores over the past decade are one example of these data. NAEP writing summary data for 1998 for grades 4, 8, and 12 are given in Table 2. This test, given in the same year for all three grades tested, allows comparison of recent scores in writing. It indicates that significant differences between public and Catholic schools are fairly consistent in grades 4, 8, and 12.

TABLE 2: NAEP 1998 National Writing Summary Data Tables for Grades 4, 8, and 12 Achievement Level Results (Standard Errors in Parentheses) Percentage of Students At or Above Each Achievement Level

	N	WTD %	MEAN	ADV.	PRFCIENT	BASIC	<BASIC
Total							
Grade 4	19816	100(0.0)	150(0.7)	1(0.2)	23(0.8)	84 (0.4)	16(0.4)
Grade 8	20586	100(0.0)	150(0.6)	1(0.1)	27(0.7)	84(0.5)	16(0.5)
Grade 12	19505	100(0.0)	150(0.7)	1(0.1)	22(0.7)	78(0.7)	22(0.7)
Public							
Grade 4	16330	89(0.7)	148(0.8)	1(0.2)	22(0.9)	83(0.5)	17(0.5)
Grade 8	17005	89(1.1)	148(0.6)	1(0.1)	24(0.8)	83(0.5)	17(0.5)
Grade 12	16221	88(1.0)	148(0.7)	1(0.1)	20(0.8)	77(0.7)	23(0.7)
Catholic Only							
Grade 4	2346	7(0.6)	163(1.3)	2(0.3)	34(1.7)	94(0.8)	6(0.8)
Grade 8	2193	7(0.9)	169(1.2)	2(0.6)	46(1.9)	97(0.6)	3(0.6)
Grade 12	2304	8(0.9)	167(1.9)	2(0.4)	37(2.7)	91(1.5)	9(1.5)

Source: Donahue, Voelkl, Campbell, & Mazzeo, 1999; Greenwald, Persky, Campbell, & Mazzeo, 1999; National Center for Education Statistics, National Assessment of Educational Progress (NAEP); 1998 Writing Assessment.

During the 1990s the *National Assessment of Education Progress* (NAEP) continued to show that Catholic elementary school students consistently outperformed public school students in reading. Table 3 shows data at the 4th, 8th, and 12th grade levels for 1992, 1994, 1998, and 2000.

TABLE 3: NAEP 1992, 1994, 1998, and 2000 National Reading Summary Tables for Grades 4, 8, and 12 (Non Accommodated) Percentage of Students At or Above Each Achievement Level (Standard Errors in Parenthesis)

Grade 4	Year	N	WTD %	MEAN	ADV.	PRFCIENT	BASIC	<BASIC)
Total	1992	6314	100 (0.0)	217 (0.9)	6 (0.6)	29 (1.2)	62 (1.1)	38 (1.1)
	1994	7382	100 (0.0)	214 (1.0)	7 (0.7)	30 (1.1)	60 (1.0)	40 (1.0)
	1998	7672	100 (0.0)	217 (0.8)	7 (0.5)	31 (0.9)	62 (0.9)	38 (0.9)
	2000	7914	100 (0.0)	217 (0.8)	8 (0.5)	32 (0.9)	63 (0.8)	37 (0.8)
Public	1992	5045	89 (1.0)	215 (1.0)	6 (0.6)	27 (1.3)	60 (1.1)	40 (1.1)
	1994	6030	90 (0.9)	212 (1.1)	7 (0.7)	28 (1.2)	59 (1.1)	41 (1.1)
	1998	6300	89 (1.2)	215 (0.8)	6 (0.5)	29 (0.9)	61 (1.0)	39 (1.0)
	2000	5945	89 (0.7)	215 (0.9)	7 (0.6)	30 (1.0)	60 (0.9)	40 (0.9)
Catholic	1992	914	8 (0.8)	229 (2.2)	10 (1.5)	41 (2.7)	76 (2.7)	24 (2.7)
	1994	910	7 (0.8)	229 (3.3)	12 (2.2)	42 (3.9)	76 (3.2)	24 (3.2)
	1998	876	7 (1.0)	233 (2.5)	13 (1.7)	46 (3.3)	79 (2.9)	21 (2.9)
	2000	1063	6 (0.5)	231 (2.6)	11 (1.9)	44 (3.1)	78 (2.9)	22 (2.9)

Grade 8	Year	N	WTD %	MEAN	ADV.	PRFCIENT	BASIC	<BASIC
Total	1992	9464	100 (0.0)	260 (0.9)	3 (0.3)	29 (1.1)	69 (1.0)	31 (1.0)
	1994	10135	100 (0.0)	260 (0.8)	3 (0.3)	30 (0.9)	70 (0.9)	30 (0.9)
	1998	11051	100 (0.0)	264 (0.8) ab	3 (0.4)	33 (0.9) ab	74 (0.9) ab	26 (0.9) ab
Public	1992	7656	89 (0.8)	258 (1.0)	2 (0.3)	27 (1.1)	67 (1.1)	33 (1.1)
	1994	8327	89 (1.0)	257 (0.8)	2 (0.3)	27 (0.9)	67 (0.9)	33 (0.9)
	1998	9091	89 (1.5)	261 (0.8) ab	2 (0.4)	31 (0.9) ab	72 (0.9) ab	28 (0.9) ab
Catholic	1992	1187	6 (0.6)	275 (1.9)	6 (1.0)	45 (2.8)	84 (1.6)	16 (1.6)
	1994	1136	7 (0.6)	279 (1.3)	6 (1.1)	49 (2.1)	88 (1.3)	12 (1.3)
	1998	1214	7 (1.3)	281 (1.6) b	5 (1.1)	53 (2.6)	91 (1.2) b	9 (1.2) b

Grade 12	Year	N	WTD %	MEAN	ADV.	PRFCIENT	BASIC	<BASIC
Total	1992	9856	100 (0.0)	292 (0.6)	4 (0.3)	40 (0.8)	80 (0.6)	20 (0.6)
	1994	9935	100 (0.0)	287 (0.7)	4 (0.5)	36 (1.0)	75 (0.7)	25 (0.7)
	1998	12675	100 (0.0)	291 (0.7) a	6 (0.4)ab	40 (0.9) a	77 (0.9) ab	23 (0.9) ab
Public	1992	7766	87 (1.2)	290 (0.7)	3 (0.3)	37 (0.9)	78 (0.7)	22 (0.7)
	1994	8044	90 (1.1)	286 (0.7)	4 (0.5)	35 (1.0)	73 (0.7)	27 (0.7)
	1998	10664	89 (1.0)	289 (0.8)	5 (0.4) b	39 (1.1)	76 (1.0)	24 (1.0)
Catholic	1992	1447	9 (1.2)	307 (1.5)	8 (0.7)	59 (2.6)	93 (0.9)	7 (0.9)
	1994	1164	6 (1.0)	298 (2.4)	6 (1.1)	47 (3.7)	85 (2.2)	15 (2.2)
	1998	1423	8 (0.8)	303 (2.0)	8 (1.3)	54 (2.8)	87 (2.0)	13 (2.0)

a   Significantly different from 1994
b   Significantly different from 1992
Source: Donahue, Finnegan, Lutkus, Allen, & Campbell, 2001; National Center for Education Statistics, National Assessment of Educational Progress (NAEP), 1994, 1998, 1999 and for Grade 4, 2000 Reading Assessments.

Table 4 shows differences in percentages of students reaching achievement levels in mathematics in grades 4, 8, and 12 in 1990, 1992, and 1996. Though both Catholic and public school scores are increasing over time, for Catholic schools at the proficient level, the increase is greater.

Table 4: NAEP 1996, 1992 and 1990 National Mathematics Summary Tables for Grades 4, 8, and 12 Percentages of Students At or Above Each Achievement Level

	Advanced	At or About Proficient	At or Above Basic	<Basic
Grade 4				
All Students				
1990	1	13	50	50
1992	2	18*	59*	41*
1996	2	21*#	64*#	36*#
Public Schools				
1990	1	12	48	52
1992	2	17*	57*	43*
1996	2	20*	62*	38*
Catholic Schools				
1990	1	15	59	41
1992	2	22	70	30
1996	2	26*	76*	24*
Grade 8				
All Students				
1990	2	15	52	48
1992	3	21*	58*	42*
1996	4*	24*	62*#	38*#
Public Schools				
1990	2	15	51	49
1992	3	20*	56	44
1996	4	23*	61*#	39*#
Catholic Schools				
1990	1	16	63	37
1992	3	27*	70	30
1996	4	32*	75	25
Grade 12				
All Students				
1990	1	12	58	42
1992	2	15	64*	36*
1996	2	16*	69*#	31*#
Public Schools				
1990	1	12	57	43
1992	3	20*	56	44
1996	2	15	68*#	32*#
Catholic Schools				
1990	1!	14!	67!	33!
1992	2	21	79	21
1996	2	20	79	21

* Indicates a significant difference in 1990.

\# Indicates a significant difference in 1992.

! Statistical tests involving this value should be interpreted with caution. Standard error estimates may not be accurately determined and/or the sampling distribution of the statistics does not match statistical test assumptions.

Source: National Center for Education Statistics, National Assessment of Education Progress (NAEP), 1990, 1992 and 1996 Mathematics Assessments; Reese, Miller, Mazzeo, & Dossey, 1997.

Table 5: NAEP 1994 National U.S. History Summary Data Table for Grades 4, 8, and 12 Achievement Level Results (Standard Errors in Parenthesis) Percentage of Students At or Above Achievement Level

| | | | Percentage of Students | | |
	Percentage of All Students	At Advanced	At or Above Proficient	At or Above Basic	Below Basic
Grade 4					
Nation	100	2(0.3)	17(1.0)	64(1.1)	36(1.1)
Public Schools	90(0.8)	2(0.3)	16(1.1)	62(1.2)	38(1.2)
Catholic Schools	6(0.7)	2(0.7)	24(2.3)	81(2.6)	19(2.6)
Grade 8					
Nation	100	1(0.1)	14(0.6)	61(0.9)	39(0.9)
Public Schools	90(0.9)	1(0.1)	12(0.6)	59(1.0)	41(1.0)
Catholic Schools	6(0.6)	2(0.8)	29(2.3)	85(1.7)	15(1.7)
Grade 12					
Nation	100	1(0.8)	11(0.7)	43(1.1)	57(1.1)
Public Schools	89(1.1)	1(0.2)	10(0.7)	41(1.2)	59(1.2)
Catholic Schools	6(0.9)	1(0.4)	18(2.0)	57(3.8)	43(3.8)

Differences between the groups may be partially explained by other factors not included in this table.

The standard errors of the estimated percentages appear in parenthesis. It can be said with 95% certainty that, for each population of interest, the value for the whole population is within plus or minus two standard errors of the estimate for the sample.

Source: National Center for Education Statistics, National Assessment of Educational Progress (NAEP), Beatty, Reese, Persky, & Carr, 1996.

TABLE 6: **NAEP 1994 National Geography Summary Data Table for Grades 4, 8, and 12 Achievement Level Results (Standard Errors in Parenthesis) Percentage of Students At or Above Achievement Level**

	Percentage of All Students	At Advanced	Percentage of Students At or Above Proficient	At or Above Basic	Below Basic
Grade 4					
Nation	100	3(0.4)	22(1.2)	70(1.1)	30(1.1)
Public Schools	90(0.8)	3(0.5)	21(1.3)	68(1.2)	32(1.2)
Catholic Schools	6(0.7)	5(1.9)	30(3.0)	85(2.8)	15(2.8)
Grade 8					
Nation	100	4(0.4)	28(1.0)	71(1.0)	29(1.0)
Public Schools	90(0.8)	4(0.4)	26(1.0)	69(1.0)	31(1.0)
Catholic Schools	6(0.6)	8(1.6)	44(2.6)	89(1.8)	11(1.8)
Grade 12					
Nation	100	2(0.5)	27(1.2)	70(0.9)	30(0.9)
Public Schools	89(1.0)	1(0.5)	26(1.3)	68(1.0)	32(1.0)
Catholic Schools	6(0.9)	1(0.5)	33(3.8)	80(3.9)	20(3.9)

Differences between the groups may be partially explained by other factors not included in this table.

The standard errors of the estimated percentages appear in parenthesis. It can be said with 95% certainty that, for each population of interest, the value for the whole population is within plus or minus two standard errors of the estimate for the sample.

Percentages for students in the two types of nonpublic schools may not total the percentage in nonpublic schools only due to rounding.

Source: National Center for Education Statistics, National Assessment of Educational Progress (NAEP), Persky et al., 1996.

TABLE 7:   NAEP 1998 National Civics Summary Data Table for Grades 4, 8, and 12 Achievement Level Results (Standard Errors in Parenthesis) Percentage of Students At or Above Achievement Level

	Below Basic	At or Above Basic	At or Above Proficient	Advanced
Grade 4				
Nation	31	69	23	2
Public Schools	33	67	21	1
Catholic Schools	14	86	35	4
Grade 8				
Nation	30	70	22	2
Public Schools	32	68	20	1
Catholic Schools	10	90	40	3
Grade 12				
Nation	35	65	26	4
Public Schools	37	63	25	4
Catholic Schools	17	83	39	7

Source: Lutkus, Weiss, Campbell, Mazzeo, and Lazer, 1999; National Center for Education Statistics, National Assessment of Educational Progress (NAEP), 1998 Civics Assessment.

The NAEP 1996 Science Assessment, instead of using the levels of proficiency as in Tables 2-7, uses average scores and selected percentiles.

TABLE 8:   NAEP 1996 National Science Summary Data Table for Grades 4, 8, and 12 Achievement Level Results (Standard Errors in Parenthesis) Percentage of Students At or Above Achievement Level

	Percentage of Students	Average Scale Score	10th	25th	50th	75th	90th
Grade 4							
All Students	100	150	105	130	153	173	190
Public Schools	88	148	103	127	151	172	188
Catholic Schools	8	163	127	146	165	182	197
Grade 8							
All Students	100	150	104	128	153	174	192
Public Schools	89	148	102	126	151	172	191
Catholic Schools	7	163	125	144	165	182	199
Grade 12							
All Students	100	150	104	128	152	174	192
Public Schools	88	149	103	126	151	174	192
Catholic Schools	8	154	116	136	155	174	190

NAEP science scales were developed independently for each grade assessed; therefore, results are not comparable across grades. Scale scores for all grades range from 0 to 300.

Percentages of students attending Catholic Schools and Other Private Schools may not total the percentage for Nonpublic Schools due to rounding.

Source: National Center for Education Statistics, National Assessment of Educational Progress (NAEP), O'Sullivan, Reese, & Mazzeo, 1997.

Although the questions related to the exact causes of the higher achievement apparent from Catholic school students may never be answered, a growing body of evidence demonstrates that the differences between Catholic school and public school students have remained over a considerable period of time, through substantial changes in the economy, education, and society as a whole.

High School Graduation Rates and Post Secondary Aspirations and Attendance

Neal (1997b) does additional analysis of data from the National Longitudinal Survey of Youth (NLSY). Dividing students into four groups: urban minorities, urban Whites, non-urban minorities, and non-urban Whites, he compared students from public schools with students from Catholic schools. For a minority student in an urban public high school the predicted probability of graduating is 62%. For a minority student in an urban Catholic high school with the same observed characteristics (education of parents, parents' occupation, family structure, and reading materials in the home) the predicted probability of graduating is 88%, a striking difference.

For urban White students in public schools, the probability of graduating from high school is 75%. Catholic school students more likely to finish high school are, as a result, also more likely to attend and complete college. Neal (1997b) asserts that this is the case "even when the effects of family background and home environment are removed" (p. 84).

Educational aspirations of high school seniors follow in Table 9. The growth in percent of seniors intending to go to college is presented for both public and Catholic high school seniors. The percent of Catholic high school seniors who plan to attend post secondary school was 93% in 1992. That same year less than 1% of Catholic school students aspired to a high school diploma or less. The curriculum in Catholic high schools, which emphasizes college preparatory classes and general education, most likely contributes to the high number who plan to attend postsecondary institutions.

TABLE 9: Educational Aspirations Percent of Seniors Who Plan to Go to College After Graduation and Educational Aspirations, By Selected Characteristics: 1982 and 1992

Student and School Characteristics	Planned Timing of Postsecondary Attendance			Level of Educational Aspirations			
	Right after high school	A year or more after graduation	No or don't know	High school diploma or less	Two years or less of college or vocational school	College graduate	Post graduate degree
	1982 1992	1982 1992	1982 1992	1982 1992	1982 1992	1982 1992	1982 1992
All seniors	58.3 76.6	11.0 14.8	30.6 8.6	24.6 5.3	36.6 25.3	21.3 36.1	17.5 33.3
Public school	56.0 74.8	11.4 15.9	32.5 9.3	26.1 5.8	37.7 27.1	20.2 35.3	16.1 31.9
Catholic sch.	80.0 93.0	6.5 5.0	13.6 2.1	12.0 0.7	26.7 10.1	32.5 47.7	28.8 41.5

Source: U.S. Department of Education, National Center for Education Statistics, "High School and Beyond," First Followup survey; and "National Education Longitudinal Study of 1988," Second Followup survey.

In its private school profile, the United States Department of Education (USDE, 1997) indicates that, in 1993-94, 90% of 12th grade students in Catholic schools, 75% of 12th grade students in private schools, and 50% of 12th grade students in public schools, actually apply to college.

RELIGIOUS OUTCOMES

Little research regarding religious outcomes of Catholic schools has been done in the past decade. One major recent study examining Catholic religious education is that of Convey and Thompson (1999). Though they have done a detailed assessment, they have avoided almost all comparisons between Catholic schools and other Catholic religious education programs. They note only that attending a Catholic school is the greatest predictor of strong religious knowledge.

The absence of ongoing and current research regarding religious outcomes of Catholic schools is a serious concern; particularly as student populations shift and school programs change. Recent concern with the Catholic identity of Catholic schools would suggest that solid research would provide a base from which to evaluate programs and efforts in this area. Most importantly, ongoing research would allow all involved in Catholic education to assess student outcomes in religion that are central to the mission of Catholic schools.

Summary:

As noted in Convey (1992), the major data yielding evidence concerning academic outcomes in Catholic schools continue to come from studies based on the national databases, particularly the *National Assessment of Educational Progress and the National Longitudinal Survey of Youth*. Indicators continue to suggest that Catholic elementary and secondary school students, on average, outperform their public school counterparts. Catholic schools endure in sending a higher percentage of their students to college than do public schools and are more successful in preventing dropouts than are public schools. Catholic schools remain effective for minorities and disadvantaged youth as well.

Despite the fact that various studies control for family background and other socio-economic factors, there still exist no definitive data to conclude that Catholic schools, in and of themselves, are the major reason yielding these favorable outcomes for youth, particularly disadvantaged youth.

Historically, Catholic schools are entering into a new era because the face and educational background of leadership are rapidly changing (Traviss, 2001). Because many of the new administrators have had less personal and professional exposure to Catholic education, there are some concerns about maintaining the Catholic identity of schools (Cook, 2001a). Ongoing research incorporating leadership factors while carefully tracking academic outcomes will be important in the future.

It is equally unfortunate that more research on religious outcomes has not been pursued. Just as the face of Catholic school leadership is changing, so is that of the teaching workforce. As younger teachers replace those who received their education before Vatican II, religious education programs both in schools and in other venues are impacted (Galetto, 1996). Because religious education is central to the mission of the Catholic school, ongoing efforts toward tracking student outcomes in religion needs a high priority

Discovering relevant studies on academic and religious outcomes was arduous work; very few recent studies were found. Even more disheartening is that no studies using qualitative methods were found. As Convey (1992) noted, qualitative studies allow for deeper investigation of specific issues. Such research could enrich our understanding many aspects of Catholic school outcomes.

HUMAN RESOURCES

CHAPTER 5
TEACHERS

TIMOTHY J. COOK

Teachers are the backbone of a school. The quality of a school is only as good as the quality of its teachers. Correspondingly, the faith-based mission of a Catholic school is only as effective as its teachers determine. Church documents related to education have consistently affirmed the central importance of the teacher in the Catholic educational project (Congregation for Catholic Education, 1977, 1997; National Conference of Catholic Bishops, 1972, 1976, 1979,1990; Sacred Congregation, 1982; Second Vatican Council, 1965/ 1996). In *Declaration on Christian Education*, Second Vatican Council (1965/1996) asserts: "Teachers must remember that it depends chiefly on them whether the Catholic school achieves its purpose" (#8).

This chapter reviews research and scholarship on Catholic school teachers that was conducted during the 1990s. The major topics include recent Church documents, demographic characteristics, professional preparation and experience, distinctive qualities and roles, goal consensus, work conditions, commitment and satisfaction, and teacher shortage issues.

RECENT CHURCH DOCUMENTS

During the 1990s, Church officials issued two statements related to Catholic education: *The Catholic School on the Threshold of the Third Millennium* (Congregation, 1997) and *In Support of Catholic Elementary and Secondary Schools* (National Conference, 1990). These two documents reinforced three themes relative to the importance of teachers in Catholic schools. In *The Catholic School on the Threshold of the Third Millennium*, the Congregation for Catholic Education (1997) focuses on the student-teacher relationship:

Teaching has an extraordinary moral depth and is one of man's most excellent and creative activities, for the teacher does not write on inanimate material, but on the very spirits of human beings. The personal relations between the teacher and the students, therefore, assume an enormous importance and are not limited simply to giving and taking. (#19)

The Congregation reinforces the belief that Catholic education is relational on several levels. Catholic schools provide the setting for students to cultivate their relationships with God, self, others, and the local and world community. Catholic schools also strive to help students see the relationships between faith and culture, faith and reason, and faith and life (Cook, 2001a).

The second theme that finds support in *The Catholic School on the Threshold of the Third Millennium* is the belief that teaching in a Catholic school is a legitimate vocation within the Church. As the authors of the document remind us, "Moreover, we must remember that teachers and educators fulfill a specific Christian vocation and share an equally specific participation in the mission of the Church" (#19). In this document, The Congregation for Catholic Education again confirms that Catholic school teaching is an apostolate, a public ministry that advances the evangelizing mission of the Church.

In a 1990 statement entitled *In Support of Catholic Elementary and Secondary Schools*, American bishops illuminate a third theme relative to Catholic school teachers. This latest installment about Catholic education was written in anticipation of the 25th anniversary of *To Teach as Jesus Did* (Sacred Congregation, 1972). As they looked to 1997, the National Conference of Catholic Bishops (1990) enumerated four unequivocal goals. The goal pertaining to teachers reads: "That the salaries and benefits of Catholic school teachers and administrators will reflect our teaching as expressed in *Economic Justice for All*" (p. 6). This pledge that the bishops made in *In Support of Catholic Elementary and Secondary Schools* acknowledges the fact that, in the years since *To Teach as Jesus Did* was promulgated, salary issues in Catholic schools have become even more critical, becoming a matter of social justice.

Demographic Characteristics of Catholic School Teachers

Among religious-affiliated private schools, Catholic schools have the highest percentage of full-time teachers (Catholic = 85%; other religious schools = 77%). Catholic schools come nearest the public school percentage of almost 90% (Schaub, 2000). Historically speaking, Catholic schools had more faculty and staff in 2000 than they did in 1960 when they had twice the enrollment.

During the 1990s, the rate of school closures declined and enrollments grew steadily. Even though there were 575 fewer schools in 2000 than in 1990, overall student enrollment grew by 2.5%. During the same period, the number of full-time teachers employed in the nation's Catholic schools grew by 15%, increasing from 136,000 to 157,134. Because teacher growth exceeded student growth during the 1990s, the overall student-teacher ratio in Catholic schools improved from $18^1/_2$:1 to 17:1.

A comparison of elementary and secondary schools yields interesting findings. Elementary school closures accounted for 82% of the total decrease in Catholic schools, while secondary closures accounted for 18%. Each level accounted for approximately half of the enrollment growth for the decade (elementary = 47%; secondary = 53%), yet elementary faculty increases accounted for three-fourths (75%) of the faculty growth in the nation's Catholic schools. In sum, despite the fact that elementary schools accounted for more school closures and slightly less enrollment increases than secondary schools, their increase in teachers far exceeded secondary schools. Because the number of teachers increased more than students on both levels, student-teacher ratios improved as well. The elementary student-teacher ratio improved from 20:1 to 18:1 and the secondary student-faculty ratio improved from 14:1 to 13:1 (Brigham, 1990; McDonald, 2000b).

Religious and Lay Teachers

The 1990s saw a continuation of the shift in composition of Catholic school faculties that began in the 1950s. In 1960, vowed religious and clergy comprised 73.8% of Catholic school faculties. By 1980, the situation reversed itself, and lay teachers constituted 71% of Catholic school educators. The percentage of vowed religious and clergy was halved during each of the most recent two decades. During the 1980s their percentage dropped from 29% to 14.6%, and, during the 1990s, their percentage dropped from 14.6% to 7.0%. Correspondingly, the percentage of lay teachers increased to 85.4% in 1990 and 93% in 2000.

Among vowed religious and clergy, women religious experienced the sharpest drop in number of teachers during the 1990s. In schools overall, the percentage of teaching sisters fell from 12% to 5.5%, representing a decline of 54%, whereas the percentage of teaching brothers and priests fell from 2.6 to 1.5, representing a decline of 42%. Although their percentages were never high to begin with, brothers and priests on the elementary level saw the smallest (25%) drop, decreasing from .4% to .3% during the decade.

Although the experience of elementary and secondary schools reflects overall trends, there are some differences between the two levels. For instance, in 1990 vowed religious and clergy comprised a larger percentage of high school faculties (17.6%) than grade school ones (13.3%). In 2000, this was still the case (8.7% versus 6.3%). Furthermore, unlike elementary schools where sisters (5.9%) far outnumber brothers and priests (.3%), secondary schools now have equal representation between sisters (4.5%) and brothers and priests (4.3%) (Brigham, 1990; McDonald, 2000b).

On the secondary level, even though vowed religious and clergy comprised 8.7% of the overall faculty in 2000, they still maintained a substantial presence in administration and the religion department. *CHS 2000: A First Look* (Guerra, 1998) reported that although lay leadership in secondary schools grew from 27% in 1983 to 52% in 1997, religious and clergy still accounted for 48% of secondary school chief administrators. Most of the decrease occurred among vowed religious women and men. By contrast, chief administrators who were diocesan clergy actually increased from 9% to 10% (Guerra, 1998).

Data from *CHS 2000* (Guerra, 1998) also reveal that a sizable minority (24%) of high school religion teachers are sisters, brothers, and priests. Given that 1 in 2 high school chief administrators and 1 in 4 high school religion teachers are vowed religious and clergy, their presence and influence in these two areas of Catholic secondary education form a nucleus that is still numerically significant.

Gender

In comparison to other schools during the 1993-1994 school year, Catholic elementary schools had more female teachers than public schools or other private schools (91%; 84%; 83%, respectively). At the secondary level, about half of the teachers at Catholic (53%) and public (54%) high schools are women, in comparison to nearly two-thirds at other private (65%) high schools (Schaub, 2000).

The gender composition of Catholic school faculties as a whole did not change between 1990 and 2000. In both years, women comprised 80% of all Catholic school teachers and men comprised 20%. The 6.5% drop in women religious and the 1.2% drop in men religious and clergy that occurred during the decade were matched by identical increases in lay women and men respectively (Brigham, 1991; McDonald, 2000b).

Women account for 9 out of 10 Catholic elementary teachers (women = 90.7%; men = 9.3%). Again, the figures for 2000 are identical to those for 1990. On the high school level, the genders are more evenly represented (54.7% women and 45.4% men). In fact, male high school teachers increased by 1% between 1990 and 2000. In other words, as positions once held by women and men religious and clergy became available during the 1990s, the likelihood that male lay teachers would fill these positions increased.

Race and Ethnicity

Compared to public and other private schools, Catholic schools have fewer minority teachers. For the 1993-1994 school year, minority teachers in Catholic schools comprised 7.7%, compared to 8.1% for all private schools and 13.5% for public schools. The percentages are similar for minority principals in Catholic (7.2%), private (7.5%), and public (15.7%) schools (McLaughlin, 1997).

The percentage of minority teachers in Catholic schools increased during the 1990s. When NCEA began publishing racial and ethnic breakdowns in 1998, minority teachers had risen to 8.5% of all teachers reporting their ethnic and racial background. The two minority groups with the highest percentage of teachers were Hispanics (3.7%) and Blacks (2.4%) (McDonald, 1998c). It is worth noting that in the late 1990s, NCEA altered the categories for ethnic and racial reporting. By 2000, NCEA added Multiracial as a category, separated Asian and Pacific Islander into two categories, and changed Native American to American Indian-Native Alaskan (McDonald, 2000b).

Minority teachers are underrepresented when compared to minority students, who make up one quarter of the Catholic school population (24.7%) (McDonald, 2000b). In Catholic schools where the student enrollment is at least 50% minority, the faculty is more diverse. In their study of 311 ethnically diverse schools, O'Keefe and Murphy (2000) found that 45% of elementary teachers and 33% of secondary teachers are minorities. There is equal likelihood of Hispanic teachers being employed at the elementary or secondary level (13% versus 12%), but Blacks are three times more likely to be enrolled in elementary schools (18%) than in secondary schools (6%).

Where school leadership in ethnically diverse schools is concerned, few principals are minorities (elementary = 16%; secondary = 10%). Hispanic principals are equally represented on the elementary and secondary level at 7%. Blacks account for 6% of the principals in ethnically diverse elementary schools and 2% of those for secondary schools.

Religious Background

At one time, one could assume that the overwhelming majority of Catholic school teachers was Catholic. This is no longer the case. The NCEA began to publish the religious background of faculty in 1998. That year non-Catholics made up 12.1% of teachers in Catholic schools (McDonald, 1998c). By 2000, the percentage of non-Catholic faculty jumped to 14.5%. A higher percentage of non-Catholic teachers is employed on the secondary level (19.1%) than on the elementary level (12.7%) (McDonald, 2000b).

Professional Preparation and Experience

The standard measures for the preparation of teachers in public and private schools are formal degrees, state certification, and teaching experience. Where Catholic school teachers are concerned, researchers consider Catholic school attendance an additional measure of preparation worth studying.

Academic Preparation

By the mid-1980s, almost all Catholic school teachers possessed a minimum of a bachelor's degree and nearly a third had earned a graduate degree (Convey, 1992). Data from the United States Department of Education's *School and Staffing Survey* (SASS), most recently collected in 1993-1994, reveal that Catholic elementary teachers (96%) were slightly less likely to hold a bachelor's degree than public elementary teachers (99%) but more likely to hold one than teachers in other private schools (91%). In contrast, Catholic secondary teachers (99%) were more likely to possess a bachelor's degree than either public (98%) or other private (91%) secondary teachers (Schaub, 2000).

An examination of advanced degrees indicates that public elementary teachers (44%) were nearly twice as likely to have earned a master's degree than their counterparts in Catholic (24%) or other private (27%) schools. Catholic secondary teachers (51%) exceeded both public (50%) and other private (37%) school teachers in master's degrees. Catholic (3%) and other private (3%) secondary teachers were the most likely to hold doctorates compared to any other group of teachers of any level or type of school.

On a related note, data collected during the 1999-2000 school year from a representative sample of American Catholic high school religion teachers revealed that the percentage of full-time religion teachers who hold an advanced degree in theology, religious studies, or religious education fell from 57% in 1985 to 41% in 2000 (Cook, 2000, 2001b).

Certification

State teacher certification is considered the initial stamp of approval for the teaching profession. Using SASS data, Schaub (2000) reports that in 1993-1994, almost all (94%) public elementary teachers were state certified in any field whereas roughly 7 out of 10 (71%) Catholic elementary teachers and 6 out of 10 (60%) teachers in other private schools held state teacher certification. Also, very few public elementary school teachers (8%) were not certified in their main field whereas fully one-third (33%) of Catholic elementary teachers and one-half (49%) of other private school teachers were teaching outside their main teaching field.

At the secondary level, a comparison of teachers certified in any field between public (95%), Catholic (67%), and other private (54%) schools yields similar results to the elementary comparison. This is also true of the comparison between public (8%), Catholic (36%), and other private (55%) school teachers who teach outside their main field. It is worth noting that far fewer high school religion teachers are state certified in any subject than their colleagues who teach secular subjects (47% versus 67%). This comparison is problematic insofar as only two states—Nebraska and Wisconsin—certify religion teachers. Nonetheless, the statistic draws attention to the uniqueness of religion teaching within the education profession, especially with regard to pedagogical training (Cook, 2001b).

Teaching Experience

On average, public school elementary teachers have slightly more teaching experience than do Catholic and other private school elementary teachers (14.8 years compared to 12.4 and 11.1 years, respectively).

At the secondary level, the difference in average teaching experience between public (15.9 years) and Catholic school teachers (14.4) is merely 1.5 years. As is the case for elementary teachers, secondary teachers at other private schools have the fewest years of teaching experience (11.7) (Schaub, 2000). Statistics about Catholic high school religion teachers merit special attention. Cook (2001b) discovered that almost half (41.5%) of the teachers in a national sample of Catholic high school religion teachers had five years or less experience teaching religion.

Looking to the future, the problem of inexperienced teachers could worsen for Catholic schools if present trends continue. O'Keefe (1999) reports that young teachers (<25) are leaving private schools (including Catholic) at an alarming rate (17.1%), which is more than seven times higher than the rate for public schools (2.4%). Having a balanced faculty in terms of teaching experience blends the wisdom of veteran teachers with the enthusiasm of novice teachers. A school whose faculty is heavily weighted at one end of the experience spectrum risks either extreme instability or extreme stagnation. If present trends continue, private schools will suffer these negative effects.

Catholic School Background

Research suggests that a teacher's own educational background is the most critical factor in the formation of that teacher. In essence, teachers teach as they were taught (Bryk, Lee, & Holland, 1993). Teachers who attended Catholic schools can draw upon personal experiences to inform their philosophy and practice and to help them serve as carriers of Catholic school culture and builders of faith community.

In a study involving 1,076 elementary teachers nationwide, Kushner and Helbling (1995) reported that 57.1% of the respondents attended Catholic elementary school for at least seven years. Nearly half (48.4%) attended four years of Catholic high school, and 37.5% earned their undergraduate degree from a Catholic college. With regard to secondary teachers, the only available national data collected during the 1990s involved religion teachers. Data provided by Cook (2001b) noted that two-thirds (65.6%) of American Catholic high school religion teachers attended a Catholic high school and two-thirds (62.6%) attended a Catholic college or university.

Distinctive Qualities and Roles

Church documents pertaining to Catholic education have uniformly stressed the special vocation of teachers. Furthermore, the documents have stressed that teachers of all subjects play a major role in carrying forward the religious mission of the Catholic educational project (National Conference of Catholic Bishops, 1976). As the transition from vowed religious to lay teachers with diverse backgrounds proceeded during the 1990s, the desired qualities, extended role expectations, and specialized formation of Catholic school teachers continued to be paramount.

Desired Qualities

Some researchers have sought to pinpoint the attributes teachers must possess to make them effective in the mission-related aspects of Catholic school teaching. In an effort to answer the question, "what is the profile of the ideal Catholic school teacher," Shimabukuro (1993) analyzed nine Roman and American Church documents to identify the characteristics of the ideal Catholic educator. Based on the frequency of citations in Church documents, she delineated five characteristics. In the order of frequency, Shimabukuro determined that the ideal Catholic school teacher: 1) fosters spiritual growth in students, 2) is vocationally prepared, 3) builds community, 4) forms humanity, and 5) is professionally prepared. In her book, *A Call to Reflection: A Teacher's Guide to Catholic Identity for the 21st Century*, Shimabukuro (1998), reconfigured her research in the form of five teacher commitments and provides concrete behaviors that describe each of these commitments.

Religious knowledge is an attribute that some believe teachers must possess in order to share faith and otherwise participate in the faith-based mission of Catholic schools. Cook (1990) investigated the religious literacy of Catholic secondary educators in the Diocese of Erie, Pennsylvania by administering the knowledge section of the Assessment of Catholic Religious Education (ACRE III) onsite at all the high schools. Cook found the overall religious literacy to be "good," according to ACRE measures for high school juniors and seniors. However, Cook also discovered that one-third to one-half of all the educators could not define basic terms such as Immaculate Conception, Paschal Mystery, and Infallibility. The data revealed that the best predictor for a person's score on the ACRE III instrument was the number of years of Catholic school attendance.

Results from these studies strongly suggest that formal Catholic faith formation and prolonged experiences with Catholic schools increase the likelihood that a Catholic educator will possess the desired qualities to contribute to the religious mission of Catholic schools. In teacher recruitment and selection, these findings suggest that Catholic educational leaders should seek candidates who have this background and these attributes. Furthermore, Catholic school leaders should emphasize these attributes in the professional development and evaluation of faculty and staff.

Role Expectations

Teachers live out their specialized vocation by integrating faith with learning and life and culture, actively participating in the faith life of the school, and bearing witness to Christ and his gospels through words and actions (Sacred Congregation for Catholic Education, 1982). In *The Vocation of the Catholic Educator*, Jacobs (1996) contended that to achieve excellence, Catholic educators must become "mindful" of their ministerial role. The goal is for teachers to become more deliberate about integrating their school's faith-based mission with teaching and learning.

Many studies indicate that Catholic teachers are "mindful" of their vocation and their role as moral educators. Dorsey (1992) verified that the elementary teachers (grades 5-8) in her sample perceived themselves as modeling gospel values in the classroom. Principals and students agreed with this perception. Using a national sample, Kushner and Helbling (1995) confirmed in *The People Who Work There* that 94.5% of Catholic elementary teachers understand their role in student religious development and that 96% feel an obligation to foster the faith of their students.

Catholic high school teachers also recognize their vocation and the role they play in the spiritual and faith formation of students, although to varying degrees. In *Catholic Schools and the Common Good*, the authors noted that teachers who were interviewed often discussed the ministerial aspects of their job (Bryk et al., 1993). In a study of first and second year teachers at certain Jesuit schools, Donovan (1995) found that one-half of those interviewed viewed themselves as moral educators. However, most participants did not think their administrators placed much emphasis on this aspect of their career nor did they know anything about Ignatian pedagogy. Cioppi (2000) concluded in a study of teachers in selected Philadelphia Catholic high schools that many teachers were unclear about their role in the evangelizing mission of their schools.

Regarding the ministerial role of Catholic educators generally, one or more study reached each of the following conclusions: 1) Teachers who attended Catholic schools are more likely to view themselves as moral educators; 2) Teachers who have taught longer in Catholic schools are more likely to understand and commit to their role as moral educator; 3) Teachers with more hours of religious inservice or other forms of continuing education are more likely to perceive themselves as moral role models.

Religion teachers play a pivotal role in Catholic schools. The Congregation for Catholic Education (1988) declares, "The religion teacher is the key, the vital component, if the education goals of the school are to be achieved" (#96). Religion teachers undoubtedly recognize the importance of their work. However, research suggests that they lack consensus regarding the nature of their role: religious instruction or catechesis. Cook (2001b) reported that high school religion teachers were almost evenly split as to whether their primary role was religious instruction or catechesis (45% versus 55%). To be effective in either catechesis or religious instruction, a teacher should know and believe Church teaching. Galetto (1996, 2000) investigated what elementary religion teachers know and believe about the teachings of the Church. One of Galetto's key findings demonstrated that Catholic school attendance and formal coursework preparation to teach religion were major predictors for both knowledge and personal belief among elementary religion teachers. In short, the amount and manner of exposure to religious education determine knowledge and belief. The Congregation for Catholic Education (1988) underscores the need for formal preparation: "an unprepared teacher can do a great deal of harm (#96). Everything possible must be done to ensure that Catholic schools have adequately trained religion teachers" (#97).

Specialized Formation

Understanding that the religious mission of Catholic schools will only be realized to the extent that all teachers participate, the call for specialized formation for Catholic educators resounds in Church documents and research studies alike. In *Lay Catholics in Schools*, the Sacred Congregation for Catholic Education (1982) stridently declared:

> The concrete living out of a vocation as rich and profound as that of the lay Catholic in a school requires an appropriate formation, both on the professional plane and on the religious plane....All too frequently, lay Catholics have not had a religious formation that is equal to their general, cultural, and, most especially, professional formation. (#60) Formation is indispensable; without it, the school will wander further and further away from its objectives. (#79)

For their part, many researchers have uniformly confirmed the need for specialized and systematic pre-service and continuing formation for Catholic educators; the intent is to develop the identified qualities and skills that teachers need to be effective in their vocation (Cioppi, 2000; Donovan, 1995; Jacobs, 1996; Kushner & Helbling, 1995).

Where should Catholic educators receive this specialized pre-service and continuing formation? Most Church officials, scholars, and practitioners agree that schools, dioceses, religious congregations, and colleges and universities must share this responsibility. For its part, Catholic higher education played a large role in the professional education of Sister-teachers earlier this century during the Sister Formation movement (Jacobs, 2000; Traviss, 2000). As the number of lay teachers increased, Catholic officials looked again to Catholic higher education for assistance. In a pastoral letter concerning Catholic higher education, the National Conference of Catholic Bishops (1980) was unequivocal about the need for specialized training, and Catholic higher education's role in addressing the need:

> Teacher preparation programs adequate for public schools are inadequate for teachers in Catholic schools. This need is urgent and can best be met by the Catholic colleges and universities who alone possess the unique resources and desire to be a service to the Catholic community. Catholic institutions of higher education which have teacher preparation programs are urged to provide Christian formation programs for educators who are evangelizers by call and covenant and mission. (p. 6)

Although Church officials and scholars alike have urged Catholic higher education to provide specialized preparation for Catholic educators, recent research findings call into question the extent to which Catholic postsecondary institutions have responded. For instance, Jones (2000) found that although teacher educators in California Catholic colleges and universities perceived that they should be preparing teachers to be moral educators, they addressed only on a limited basis student moral development and the teaching strategies that foster it.

Furthermore, many teacher educators in Catholic higher education are unsure or unaware of their role in providing specialized preparation for beginning Catholic educators. White (1995) discovered that Catholic school principals and Catholic university teacher educators differed in their views of what competencies beginning Catholic elementary school teachers should possess. The differences between teacher educators and principals were statistically significant in four of five areas. Most notably, principals rated ministerial competencies and spiritual qualities more important than did teacher educators. White concludes, "It is apparent that many Catholic colleges and universities in California are concerned with the state credential requirements and have very little concern for the distinctive needs of Catholic schools" (p. 112). The assumption held by teacher educators is that specialized formation can be done at the school level.

Some research studies have investigated models of specialized formation for current teachers. DiPaola's (1990) research involving elementary religion teachers and Mulligan's (1993) research involving teachers of all subjects reached similar conclusions. Either or both researchers concluded that ministerial and spiritual formation of teachers should be: 1) based on personal experiences; 2) offered in a collaborative environment; 3) centered on the practical; and 4) grounded in principles of adult learning.

To conclude, professionalism as it relates to teaching in Catholic schools requires two types of preparation: teaching-related and vocation-related (Bryk et al., 1993; Jacobs, 2000). Vocation-related preparation is specialized formation that encompasses the spiritual and ministerial dimensions (National Conference of Catholic Bishops, 1980). Whereas Sister-teachers of the Sister Formation movement in earlier decades lacked professional training, lay teachers today lack vocational preparation. Perhaps the need of this age is a Lay Teacher Formation movement. Just as Catholic colleges and universities participated then, they need to participate now (Jacobs, 2000; Traviss, 2000).

Goal Consensus

Research on effective schools suggests that having a shared set of values regarding school purpose and goals is a leading indicator of school effectiveness (Convey, 1992). Bryk et al. (1993) argued in *Catholic Schools and the Common Good* that the high level of values cohesion in Catholic schools is one core feature that characterizes them as communal organizations and distinguishes them from public schools.

Additional data collected during the 1990s centered on consensus about school mission and reinforced the notion that Catholic educators share common views regarding school mission. Kushner and Helbling (1995) drew this conclusion in their study that involved a national sample of Catholic elementary teachers. Data from the *School and Staffing Survey* for 1993-1994 established that there was more consensus among elementary teachers in Catholic (95%) and other private schools (95%) regarding their school's central mission than among teachers in public schools (87%). Within the Catholic elementary school universe, teachers in parish or diocesan schools agreed more about the school mission than teachers in religious order schools (96% versus 85%). On the secondary level, a wider gap existed between teachers in private (Catholic = 90%; other private = 92%) and public (79%) schools regarding consensus about school mission. In the realm of Catholic schools, consensus levels were relatively the same among teachers in parish, diocesan, and religious order schools—approximately 90% (Schaub, 2000).

Among the doctoral dissertation studies during the 1990s that addressed mission-related congruence and consensus, two dealt primarily with teachers. Paulino (1990) found a lack of congruence between teachers and school leaders on Guam relative to religious beliefs and values. Leaders scored higher than teachers on most subscales.

Mueller (1994) studied the goal congruence and consensus of principals, brother teachers, and lay teachers in American Lasallian schools with regard to school goals. In terms of goal congruence, Mueller noted that all three groups agreed that their schools attached less importance to each goal in reality than in the ideal. Vowed brothers were the most dissatisfied with how the common vision was lived out in the schools. In terms of goal consensus, Mueller observed more agreement about Lasallian goals as they were idealized than as they were operationalized. Lack of agreement occurred most often between religious brothers and lay teachers.

Paulino's (1990) and Mueller's (1994) dissertation studies made similar observations regarding teachers' views about mission-related school values and goals. Each or both noted that administrators and vowed religious held views more congruent with mission than lay teachers. Not surprisingly, among their recommendations were the following: 1) Emphasize the mission-related values and goals of the school in teacher recruitment and selection; and 2) Design systematic staff development to deepen faculty and staff commitment to school mission.

Work Conditions

Studies show that conditions of the work environment greatly influence job satisfaction. Environmental factors such as rapport with administrators, colleagues, students, and parents, teacher empowerment, and perceptions about school problems have enormous impact on how much teachers enjoy their profession. In addition to the environmental factors that Convey (1992) discussed in *Catholic Schools Make A Difference*, this update considers two more—parental support and teacher perceptions of school problems.

Rapport with Administrators

Administrative support and open communication are important to teachers. Schaub (2000) compares the responses of private, Catholic, and public teachers to the *School and Staffing Survey* item: "The principal knows what kind of school he/she wants and has communicated it to the staff." On the elementary level, the affirmative responses were nearly identical among Catholic (88%), other private (89%), and only slightly lower for public (83%) teachers. On the secondary level, the highest percentage of affirmative responses came from teachers in other private schools (90%), followed by Catholic teachers (86%), with less agreement among public teachers (77%).

Participation in Decision Making

As professionals, teachers appreciate a large measure of autonomy in the classroom and participation in school-wide decision making. Classroom control and school influence contribute to a teacher's sense of job satisfaction. Data from the *School and Staffing Survey* revealed that on two measures of classroom control, course content and textbooks, many more Catholic teachers believe they have control than do public teachers. Yet, teachers in other private schools believe they have even more control over what transpires in their classrooms (McLaughlin, 1997).

Teacher Perceptions of Self-Determination
Class content (Catholic = 71.4%; total private = 74.9%; total public = 60.5%)
Class textbooks (Catholic = 65.0%; total private = 68.8%; total public = 55.2%)

Where school policy is concerned, teachers in all three sectors believe they have less influence than they do in their classroom. Catholic teacher perceptions of influence are somewhat lower than those of teachers in other private schools, but much higher than those of teachers in public schools (McLaughlin, 1997).

Teacher Perceptions of Their Influence on Selected School Policies
School Discipline (Catholic = 56.1%; total private = 59.2%; total public = 34.9%)
School Curriculum (Catholic = 48.4%; total private = 55.7%; total public = 34.3%)

Collegiality

Even though teachers like autonomy, friendly and cooperative relationships among faculty and staff contribute to job satisfaction. The degree to which teachers get along is also a strong determinant of a school's climate, which in turn affects student learning. Collegiality is essential for a Catholic school faculty if they are to model faith community. On the *School and Staffing Survey*, teachers were asked to respond to the item: "There is a great deal of cooperative effort among staff." Catholic teachers (88.6%) answered affirmatively more than public teachers (77.5%) but less than private school teachers overall (90.5%) (McLaughlin, 1997).

Relationship with Students

Because of the relational nature of Catholic education, the student-teacher relationship is one of paramount importance. Because students and teachers in Catholic schools relate on several levels, including the spiritual level, their relationship is characterized by Christian personalism—a personal relationship that is guided by Christian principles (Bryk et al., 1993; Jacobs, 1996). At the spiritual level, Jacobs (1996) calls the encounter between student and teacher "an intimate communication between souls" (p. 37).

Due to the emphasis on education of the whole person, teachers in Catholic schools take on additional roles in their relationships with students in and out of the classroom. Each teacher acts as counselor, coach, mentor, guide, and role model. Bryk et al. (1993) observed significant endorsement for these extended roles among teachers, parents, and students. For their part, parents often referred to teachers as "dedicated" and "committed." Students spoke of their appreciation of the personal care and attention they received from teachers. Overall, the authors note, "such teacher personalism, which seemed to pervade the myriad social encounters within the schools, was infectious, pulling students strongly toward engagement in school life" (p. 99).

Parental Support

When teachers feel supported by parents, their sense of efficacy increases and their stress level brought on by the demands of teaching decreases. Furthermore, when the home and school are partners in a child's education, this web of adult support that Coleman et al. (Coleman & Hoffer, 1987; Coleman, Hoffer, & Kilgore, 1982) refer to as "social capital" positively influences a child's learning. Schaub (2000) reports that among elementary teachers, Catholic (85%) and other private school (84%) teachers experience much more parental support than do public teachers (58%). The difference is even more dramatic on the secondary level (Catholic = 83%; other private = 84%; public = 43%).

Teacher Perceptions of School Problems

According to the *School and Staffing Survey*, teachers in public, Catholic, and other private schools selected identical problems as the top three problems in their schools and ranked them in the same order of seriousness. Even though teachers in the three sectors had identical rankings, the percentage of public school teachers who chose each option to be a moderate or serious problem in their schools was often two or three times higher than that of Catholic and other private school teachers. Teachers perceived the most serious problem to be apathetic or unprepared students (public = 71%; total private = 28%; Catholic = 26%). Teachers identified the second most serious problem as student attendance (public = 53%; Catholic = 23%; total private = 21%). For the third most serious problem, teachers selected poverty or racial tension (public = 38%; total private = 16%; Catholic = 13%). Catholic educators ranked the remaining problems in the following order: physical conflict or weapons (10%), robbery or vandalism (9%), alcohol or drugs (8%), and dropouts (2%) (McLaughlin, 1997).

To conclude, the overwhelming majority of Catholic educators enjoy their work environments. They feel a strong sense of community that is characterized by affirming social interactions among teachers, administrators, students, and parents. These interactions are rooted in an ethic of caring that governs school relationships and positively impacts a teacher's work life (Bryk et al., 1993).

Commitment and Satisfaction

The degree to which teachers are committed and satisfied greatly impacts student learning and overall school effectiveness. Furthermore, teacher commitment and satisfaction are very much linked to teacher motivation and, ultimately, to teacher attrition, which has tremendous implications for teacher recruitment and retention. Research confirms that there is a direct relationship between commitment and satisfaction (Convey, 1992). In other words, committed teachers are more likely to be satisfied, and vice versa. When listing future research priorities at the end of *Catholic Schools Make a Difference*, Convey (1992) specified the need for more research about teacher commitment and satisfaction.

Commitment

Commitment is characterized by loyalty, identity, and involvement. Catholic school teacher commitment can be classified three ways—organizational (mission), professional (teaching), and job. Tarr (1992) classified commitment of teachers in Catholic schools in terms of organization (mission), teaching (profession), and job. Teachers who fall into the first category are attracted to the faith-based nature of Catholic schools. Those in the second category are attracted to the academic environment of Catholic schools. And those in the third category do not view teaching as either a vocation or a profession.

What builds teacher commitment to the faith-based mission of their schools? Research suggests that working conditions and school environment influence a teacher's commitment to mission (Bryk et al, 1993; Squillini, 1999, 2001). Teachers who experience collegiality, administrative support and recognition, values consensus, and efficacy develop a deep sense of community and form strong cultural bonds with the community's mission. Based on quantitative analysis of 23 measures of communal organization, Bryk et al. (1993) drew this conclusion in *Catholic Schools and the Common Good*: "the greater prevalence of communal school organization in the Catholic sector accounts for much of the observed difference between Catholic and public schools in the commitment of their teachers and the engagement of their students" (p. 287). In short, community builds commitment.

Are there any personal or professional characteristics of teachers that predict commitment to mission? In her study of 940 full-time elementary and secondary Catholic educators in Boston, Tarr (1992) found that the best predictors for commitment to mission are Catholic school teaching experience and the importance of religion in one's life. An important, albeit less critical, factor is Catholic school attendance. In sum, personal valuing of religion and prior socialization in Catholic schools increases the likelihood that a teacher will be committed to mission.

How might Catholic educational leaders increase their chances of hiring someone who will be committed to the mission of the school? 1) Consider these criteria in the hiring process—personal religiosity, prior attendance, and teaching experience in Catholic schools (Tarr, 1992), and willingness to build community (Bryk et al, 1993); 2) Be clear about school mission and related teacher expectations in the interview and hiring process (Tarr, 1992).

Satisfaction

There are intrinsic and extrinsic factors associated with job satisfaction. Intrinsic factors, those relating to the work itself, include student achievement, self-learning, sense of accomplishment, and enjoyment. Extrinsic factors, those relating to work conditions and environment, include collegiality, student-teacher rapport, parent and administrative support, control over classroom and influence on school policy, recognition and appreciation, opportunities for advancement, and salary and benefits (Convey, 1992).

Catholic educators tend to enjoy high levels of job satisfaction (Bryk et al, 1993). On the *School and Staffing Survey*, teachers were asked to respond to the following question, "if you could go back to college days and start over again, would you become a teacher or not?" Agreement with this statement among Catholic teachers (77.6%) fell slightly below that of total private teachers (78.4%) but considerably above public teachers (64.0%) (McLaughlin, 1997). Within the Catholic school realm, Schaub (2000) reports almost no difference in agreement between elementary (78%) and secondary teachers (77%).

What intrinsic and extrinsic measures motivate Catholic educators and lead to job satisfaction? In terms of intrinsic factors, Lee's (1991) study of secondary teachers in Guam and Squillini's (1999, 2001) study of elementary teachers in the Archdiocese of New York point to the teacher perception of doing important and meaningful work as a determinant of job satisfaction. Other intrinsic factors include professional growth and sense of service (Lee, 1991). In terms of extrinsic factors, both studies reinforced the importance of overall working conditions. Participants in Squillini's (1999, 2001) study specified the following extrinsic factors as important: autonomy, administrative support and recognition, student motivation, rapport with students, and collegiality among teachers.

With respect to satisfaction measures that are specifically related to Catholic schools, Squillini (1999, 2001) found that nearly two-thirds (63%) of the respondents in her study said that the opportunity to work in a faith community is very important to job satisfaction. Furthermore, Tarr's (1992) data revealed a relationship between commitment and satisfaction. Teachers who were committed to mission were significantly more satisfied with their jobs. Lastly, Chikri (2000) discovered a direct correlation between perception of mission and job satisfaction. The more positive the perception about mission, the more satisfied the teacher. Chikri noted that teachers who were active in parishes and attended worship services, as well as teachers who have worked longer in Catholic schools were more likely to have positive perceptions of school mission.

Dissatisfaction

Although Catholic educators like their jobs, salaries are a major source of dissatisfaction. When asked to respond to this statement on the *School and Staffing Survey*—"I am satisfied with my teaching salary," Catholic elementary teachers were half as likely to agree with this statement than were teachers in other sectors (Catholic = 26%; public = 44%; other private = 46%). Among Catholic teachers, those in religious schools (35%) were more satisfied than those in parish (27%) or diocesan (23%) schools. Catholic high school teachers were more satisfied than elementary teachers (42% versus 26%) but slightly less satisfied than public (47%) or other private (51%) teachers. Among Catholic teachers, again those in religious order schools (45%) were more satisfied than those in parish (39%) or diocesan (39%) schools (Schaub, 2000).

Comparative analysis elucidates dissatisfaction with salaries. Catholic educators are underpaid compared to teachers in other sectors. On average, Catholic elementary teachers make 54% of a public school salary ($17,926 versus $33,116). Catholic high school teachers fare better but still only make 73% of the average public school salary ($25,089 versus $34,387). The salary gap between Catholic and public teachers widens with teaching experience. Although the gap is less severe on the secondary level, the most experienced Catholic elementary teacher makes approximately $16,000 less than a similar teacher in a public school. Within the Catholic school network, the average elementary teacher makes about $7,200 less than his or her high school colleagues. In public schools, the difference is about $1,300 (Schaub, 2000).

In conclusion, Catholic educators make a huge financial sacrifice. Philosophically, having grossly underpaid teachers is a social justice issue (National Conference of Catholic Bishops, 1990). Pragmatically, large salary disparities have tremendous implications for recruitment and retention, especially during a time of teacher shortages.

Teacher Shortage Issues

In 1983 Catholic school principals reported few serious problems finding qualified teacher candidates. In fact, the oversupply of teachers that existed in the United States enabled Catholic schools to make the transformation from predominantly vowed religious teachers to predominantly lay teachers (Bryk et al, 1993).

Concern about teacher shortages began to resurface nationwide in the mid-1980s. During the 1987-1988 school year, The National Center for Education Statistics began collecting data with the *School and Staffing Survey* to chart supply and demand to analyze its influences and sources. Causes of the recent teacher shortages include fewer new college graduates entering teaching, expanding enrollments, demands for smaller class sizes, and an aging teaching force nearing retirement. Experts estimate that U.S. schools will hire 2.2 million teachers over the next 10 years (Broughman & Rollefson, 2000; O'Keefe, 1999).

Catholic schools now exist in an increasingly competitive teacher market. For many schools, teacher shortages—brought on in large part by fierce competition—have reached crisis proportions. In a recent survey, approximately 9 out of 10 Catholic superintendents reported that a teacher shortage exists in their diocese (O'Keefe, 1999). In another study, 86% of a nationally representative sample of Catholic high school administrators reported a shortage of qualified religion teacher candidates (Cook, 2001b).

Recruitment and Retention

Teacher shortages must be examined in terms of attracting teachers and keeping them. The annual attrition rate in private schools is almost double that of public schools. More alarming is the fact that younger teachers are leaving private schools at a high rate (O'Keefe, 1999). Almost half of the Catholic school superintendents responded in a survey that 50% of the teachers hired in 1994 have left their jobs (Curtin, 2001). Moreover, in a national study of high school religion teachers conducted during 1999-2000, 4 out of 10 said they plan to cease teaching religion within five years (Cook, 2001b).

In *Catholic Schools Make a Difference*, Convey (1992) stressed the need for more research on what attracts teachers to Catholic schools and what motivates them to stay. What attracts new teachers? Prehn (2000) surfaced nine reasons why recently hired teachers sought employment at Jesuit high schools: the desire to work in a specifically Jesuit institution; the conviction that teaching was one's vocation and supported in Jesuit schools; the desire to contribute back to an alma mater that had provided a quality education; the recognition that among Catholic high schools, the Jesuit high schools paid the best; a recognition that students were capable and faculty peers were respected; and lastly, the benefit of a free Jesuit high school education for one's children.

What retains teachers and what influences them to leave? Research by Barrett-Jones (1993) and Squillini (1999, 2001) confirms that religious mission, Catholic character, and faith community motivate teachers to remain in Catholic education and that salary is a factor that influences their decision to leave.

Among current and past elementary teachers in Fort Wayne-South Bend, Indiana, Barrett-Jones (1993) determined that responses to survey questions that centered on four topics—safe school environment, emphasis on instruction, sharing faith with students, and salary offered—predicted 83% of stayers and 42.5% of leavers. Stayers stated that belief in Catholic education and factors related to Catholic identity such as sharing faith with students, opportunity to teach values and morals, and caring community strongly influenced their decision to remain in Catholic education. Conversely, leavers cited salary and benefits among the factors that impacted their decision to leave.

In Squillini's (1999, 2001) study of job satisfaction factors that influence commitment and longevity among experienced full-time Catholic elementary teachers in the Archdiocese of New York, survey participants were asked to rate 14 possible steps Catholic schools could take to encourage teachers to stay. The highest percentage (77.9%) of respondents rated improvement of salary and benefits as most important. Benefits increased in importance with longevity. The second highest percentage (66.1%) of teachers rated "foster a stronger commitment to creating a Catholic-Christian environment" as a very important step to encourage longevity.

Researchers have frequently recommended the following recruitment and retention strategies to address the teacher shortage: Improve salaries and benefits and make them portable; partner with Catholic higher education in the recruitment and formation of Catholic educators; involve religious congregations in the formation of Catholic educators; emphasize school faith community in recruiting and selecting teachers and strengthen school faith community to retain them; intensify national recruitment efforts and showcase local models; and expand a Catholic teacher service corps.

Catholic Teacher Service Corps Initiatives

Just as volunteer programs such as Teach for America have been created to ease the teacher shortage in under resourced public schools, similar initiatives have been started to serve Catholic schools. Although many are in their infancy, 87 volunteer programs across the nation currently provide teachers for Catholic elementary schools and 67 provide volunteer teachers to secondary schools. These programs are sponsored by a variety of Catholic organizations such as Catholic colleges and universities, religious congregations, and individual parishes and schools. Many participants in these programs are recent college graduates who are motivated by the desire to serve. Most are attracted to these Catholic teaching corps because of the mix of elements that characterize these programs: community living, spirituality, and teaching (O'Keefe, 1999).

Founded in 1994, Notre Dame's Alliance for Catholic Education (ACE)—the nation's largest university-based program—sends out approximately 160 recent college graduates annually to serve Catholic schools, primarily in the south. Almost two-thirds (61%) of ACE graduates have remained in teaching. Most continue to serve in Catholic schools (Pressley, in press). As these Catholic teacher service programs grow and mature, more quantitative and qualitative research is needed to assess the impact they make on Catholic education relative to the teacher shortage.

SUMMARY

1. The two Church documents issued during the 1990s that pertained to Catholic education—*The Catholic School on the Threshold of the Third Millennium* (Congregation, 1997) and *In Support of Catholic Elementary and Secondary Schools* (National Conference, 1990)—collectively addressed three themes related to teachers. In essence, Church officials underscored the extended student-teacher relationship, teaching as a vocation, and salary and benefits as a social justice issue.

2. Some demographic characteristics of Catholic educators changed during the 1990s. Faculty growth exceeded student growth, which resulted in improved student-teacher ratios. Elementary schools accounted for three-fourths of faculty growth. Vowed religious decreased by one-half, to 7%. Minority and non-Catholic representation grew slightly. Public school teachers hold more advanced degrees than Catholic elementary teachers but fewer than Catholic secondary teachers. The number of high school religion teachers who possess a master's degree in their field has dropped since 1985. Catholic educators are less likely to be state certified than public educators, and have slightly less teaching experience. Almost half of high school religion teachers have taught religion five years or less. A majority of Catholic elementary teachers attended a Catholic elementary or high school but only one-third attended a Catholic college. In light of its positive impact that research suggests, Catholic school attendance warrants more monitoring and intensified study.

3. During the 1990s, some research focused on the distinctive qualities and roles of Catholic educators. Findings demonstrate that most Catholic educators recognize the ministerial aspects of their role. High school religion teachers lack agreement on whether their primary role is religious instruction or catechesis. Most people connected with Catholic education recognize the need for specialized formation, yet research indicates that teacher educators may not understand their role. A systematic Lay Teacher Formation movement might very well meet the needs of today's Catholic educators the way the Sister Formation movement met their needs in earlier decades.

4. The overwhelming majority of Catholic educators enjoy their work environments, especially the affirming social interaction with administrators, colleagues, students, and parents. Teachers feel a strong sense of community that positively impacts their work life, which ultimately leads to higher levels of job satisfaction and commitment. Overall, Catholic educators are very committed to mission, although data reveal differences among administrators, vowed religious, and lay teachers. Research has also shown that personal valuing of religion and prior socialization in Catholic schools as a student and teacher build commitment and positively influence job satisfaction. Overall, Catholic educators, especially those who are committed to mission, exhibit high levels of job

satisfaction. The major source of dissatisfaction is salaries. There is a wide gap between the salaries of public and Catholic school teachers, which becomes wider for more experienced teachers. The disparity is worst at the elementary level.

5. Although an oversupply of teachers during the 1970s and 1980s helped Catholic schools ease the transition from religious to lay, the 1990s brought teacher shortages that have become severe. As a result, Catholic educational leaders have stepped up recruitment and retention efforts. Catholic teacher service corps such as Notre Dame's Alliance for Catholic Education (ACE) show promise for providing a new source of recruits. In terms of retention, research indicates that faith community and compensation greatly influence decisions by teachers to stay or leave Catholic schools. The entire Catholic community must work together to strengthen faith community in Catholic schools and simultaneously improve salaries and benefits.

CHAPTER 6

PARENTS: THE PRIMARY AND PRINCIPAL EDUCATORS

JAMES M. FRABUTT

INTRODUCTION

Parents are the primary and principal educators of their children. The church has upheld this fundamental parental right and duty as primordial and inalienable (Congregation for Catholic Education, 1988; John Paul II, 1982; National Conference of Catholic Bishops, 1994). The daily lives of parents and children contain countless instances that allow for the development of the person and therein the vitality of the whole church. In the words of Pope John Paul II, "The future of humanity passes by way of the family" (# 86). Parents embrace their role as educators when they immerse themselves in their children's education and the broader life of the school community. For this reason, it is critical to examine the research interface of parenting and family with Catholic education. In addition, changes in family structures, systems, and demographics over the last quarter century make it imperative that Catholic educators and catechists stay informed of the most current research and practice for dealing effectively with children and families. This chapter reviews research focusing on the intersection of parenting and family life with educational issues and concerns. Major topics covered include parent involvement, parenting and children's development, family dynamics and children's functioning, parental choice of schools, and parent education and parenting programs.

PARENT INVOLVEMENT

Bauch (1991) examined the reasons for parent choice and involvement for minority (59% African American, 27% Hispanic) families in a study involving 1,070 parents of ninth through twelfth graders in five inner city Catholic schools. Three dimensions of parent involvement believed to influence learning were included: participation, decision making, and communication. Analyses of variance demonstrated that parents' reasons for school choice were associated with their participation in school-related activities. Specifically, parents that chose discipline as their primary reason were more likely to report involvement in school-related activities than parents that reported that their child's choice was the primary reason for choosing the school. Further multiple regression analyses indicated that the strongest predictors of participation were parents' choice for a discipline or safety reason, parents' church participation, and parents' expectations for their child's educational attainment. For the communication domain, ethnicity emerged as the strongest predictor. Significant effects were also detected for educational attainment, church participation, and income. Churchgoing African American parents and high socioeconomic status parents were likely to communicate more frequently with teachers than their counterparts.

Bauch and Goldring (1996) further pursued the linkage between school choice and involvement through an examination of the context of school responsiveness to parents under different choice arrangements. The study sample included parents (N = 575) from three types of school choice arrangements: Catholic, single-focus specialty public magnet schools, and multifocus public magnet schools. After controlling for income and ethnicity, parents in the different choice arrangements differed in their reasons for school choice, perceptions of school responsiveness, and parent involvement. Parents chose Catholic and single-focus magnet schools more frequently for discipline and safety reasons. Of the three arrangements, parents only chose Catholic schools for moral reasons. The authors also investigated the extent to which parent-school interactions differed as a function of school-choice arrangements. Based upon discriminant analysis, findings indicated that in Catholic and single-focus magnet schools, parents were more likely to report (a) having current information about school policies, (b) helping at school and serving on committees, and (c) checking over or helping with homework. Catholic schools and single-focus magnet schools were more likely to (a) provide information about course selection and how to help students, (b) be effective in communicating with parents and helping them to feel at ease in approaching the school, (c) seek advice from parents regarding school decisions, and (d) require parent volunteering. A second discriminant function distinguished along a private-public school dimension. After controlling for income, Catholic parents were more likely to contact the school and to enforce rules at home. Furthermore, "parents in Catholic schools were more likely to perceive their schools as providing effective communication with parents and making parents feel at ease in approaching the school, and were less likely to require parent volunteering" (Bauch & Goldring, 1996, p. 15).

Bauch and Goldring (1996) also examined the nature of the relationship between parent involvement and teacher decision making in three different school settings: Catholic schools, multifocus magnet schools, and single-focus public schools. Survey data were collected from teachers and parents of seniors in a total of 13 schools located in three urban areas of the United States. Canonical correlation was employed to explore the interrelationships of levels of parent involvement and teacher decision making. Different patterns emerged between parent involvement and teacher decision making across the three types of school choice settings. Results for Catholic schools suggested that a combination of "more involvement in school activities and opportunity for involvement, but less participation in decision making and less involvement around a child's educational issues, correspond with more teacher influence in decision making" (1996, p. 418). In single-focus schools, low levels of parent involvement were associated with low levels of teacher decision making. In multifocus magnet schools, "lower levels of teacher decision making are associated with higher levels of parental participation in school activities, but lower levels of parent involvement in their child's education" (p. 420). These findings suggested that Catholic schools might be developing a partnership mode of parent-teacher relations, beyond that measured in the single-focus or multifocus public schools. However, the results also indicated that parents are treated somewhat as clients in the Catholic school, as they appeared not to have a significant role in the school organization. Bauch and Goldring noted that, from a practical perspective, their study

> cautions us to consider how the improvement of parent involvement
> could be threatening to teachers who may not wish to include parents'
> opinions and ideas in their decisions and how increased teacher decision
> making could mitigate the influence of parents in school matters. (p. 425)

More research is needed on the dynamics of shared power in the collaborative efforts of parents and teachers in education matters.

During the last decade, several dissertations have explored elements of parent involvement. For example, Benevento (1997) examined the relationship between teachers' perceptions' of parental involvement in Catholic schools. Parents (N = 122) and teachers (N = 86) from eight schools in the Archdiocese of Newark completed measures of parent involvement, parent participation, and perceptions of quality of school. Effects of socioeconomic status were detected in this study, such that as educational and occupational background of parents increased, perceptions of the opportunities the school provided for parents to learn about education and their children decreased, as did their perceptions of their involvement in personnel decisions. As the number of children in the school increased, parents exhibited lower perceptions of parent involvement in shaping the school's budget and policies. Results indicated that parents who were members of the parent association perceived parents as less involved in educational choices and were not as satisfied overall with the school as parents not in the parent association. Parents reporting high achievement of their children had higher perceptions of parental involvement and satisfaction with the school. Significant differences were not reported between parents' and teachers' perceptions of parental involvement, with one exception: parents felt they were able to participate in more learning activities about education and their children than did teachers. Finally, in examining the relationship between overall satisfaction with the school and parents' perceptions of involvement, Benevento (1991) reported that higher parent satisfaction was associated with increased perceptions of parents' involvement as shapers of school policy and decreased involvement as learners and as supporters of school.

Research on social capital by Coleman and Hoffer (1987) provided the conceptual basis for Chilampikunnel's (1995) dissertation examining the relationship of parental involvement in school-related activities at home, school-home communication, and parental attitude toward school to outcome indicators such as students' academic performance, attendance, and self-esteem. Families of elementary school children (N = 317) from six Catholic schools completed a demographic questionnaire, the Hopkins Survey of School and Family Connections (HSSFC) (Epstein & Salinas, 1993), and a Parent Involvement Questionnaire designed by the investigator. Findings demonstrated significant correlation between involvement in school-related activities at home, school-home communication, and parental attitude toward school with children's attendance, performance, and self-esteem. The most important predictor of these outcomes was parental involvement in school-related activities.

An issue of the *Private School Monitor* devoted to parent involvement featured two articles that specifically addressed parental involvement practices in Catholic schools (Mastaby, 1993; Muller, 1993). Mastaby conducted a descriptive analysis of a diverse, inner city parochial school. Results indicated the presence of a strong, supportive parent community that believes in the traditional value of education. Attendance at school functions was greatest for activities that directly involved children in terms of grades, entertainment, and awards. Specific barriers that prevented attendance at school functions were examined including factors such as safety, finance, work schedules, childcare, and daily life routines.

Muller (1993) analyzed data from the National Education Longitudinal Study (NELS) of 1988 to determine whether parents who send their children to Catholic schools are also more involved with their child than parents with children in public schools and whether this involvement makes a difference in the performance of the student. Survey findings indicated that Catholic school parents are 40% more likely to volunteer, participate in the parent teacher organization, and know more parents of their child's friends when compared to parents with similar characteristics who send their child to public school. Both sets of parents engage in home-based involvement (e.g., talking with child, providing supervision after school) at similar rates. Muller also determined whether association between involvement and performance are the same for public and Catholic school students. Talking with parents about current school experiences is a strong predictor of math test performance for both Catholic and public school students. Regression analyses also demonstrated that three parental monitoring activities (restricting television on weekdays, supervision by an adult after school, and number of friends parents know) were associated with math test scores for public school students, but showed no relationship for Catholic school students. It was hypothesized that Catholic schools may impose more regulation on the lives of students than public schools. As a consequence, any association between parental activity and academic performance for any individual child-parent relationship is removed.

Building on research on the influence of class and culture on parent-school interactions, Smrekar (1994, 1996) examined family-school interactions across social class in three organizationally different school settings: a Catholic elementary school, a magnet elementary school, and a public elementary school. The investigation employed a qualitative, multiple-case study methodology including semi-structured interviews (with parents, teachers, principals, parents' outreach coordinators, school secretaries, and PTA officers), observations of parent interactions with school officials, and examination of school documents. Smrekar found that overarching differences in family organization in response to parents' employment status greatly outweighed any differences due to income and material resources among parents. The patterns of stress and coping in regard to the work-family intersection provide direction to families' relationships with schools. As a result, school processes and structures that promote social cohesion, commitment, and communication (highlighted in-depth in the magnet school case study) are effective mediators of the influence of social class on family-school relations.

Quantitative research on parental involvement is complemented by a qualitative inquiry conducted by Donovan (1999). The unit of analysis for the investigation was a K-8 Catholic elementary school in the Diocese of Scranton, Pennsylvania. Data were collected through several methods including personal interviews (principal, 6 full-time teachers, 18 parents), review of documents and records of the school's parental involvement program, and administration of a two-part Likert questionnaire. Donovan reported a strong parental presence in the areas of monitoring extracurricular school events and fundraising. In contrast, parents reported little participation in areas such as curriculum revision, textbook selection, budgeting, and policymaking. Interview and questionnaire data indicated that parental participation was encouraged for co-curricular and extracurricular activities but not for activities considered professional in nature. In sum, the parental involvement philosophy at this school most approximated the teacher's helper paradigm (Bauch, 1990; Uderos-Blackburn, 1996) and stands in contrast to a parents-as-partners model (Riley, 1994) or a full empowerment of parents' concept (Sarason, 1995).

Parental involvement in school governance and decision making was addressed in Convey's (2000) 10-year follow-up of O'Brien's (1987) nationwide survey of bishops' and priests' perceptions of the value, effectiveness, funding practices, and future structure of Catholic schools. Conducted in 1996, survey results were based on completed questionnaires from 184 bishops and 1,036 priests. Across the entire survey, the greatest increase in agreement from 1986 to 1996 occurred for the item, "Parents must be given a substantial role in the development of policy for Catholic schools" (Convey, 2000, p. 81). From 1986 to 1996, bishops' agreement was recorded at 63% and 85%, respectively. Although priests' agreement with the item was lower than bishops' agreement (40% in 1986 versus 68% in 1996), there was a significant change of 28 percentage points. Additional items not included in the 1986 survey indicated more support from bishops than priests for parents' voice in governance and the needs for boards for all schools. Convey also provided percent agreement findings for subgroups of priests (pastor – school, pastor – no school, associate, etc.) revealing that pastors of parishes with schools were not quite as supportive as other pastors.

Parenting and Children's Development

McCormack initiated a program of research (1995, 1998, 1999) focused on formative parenting (defined as the process of communicating parenting practices that are foundational to healthy development) and its relationship to the holistic psychosocial development of children. McCormack's (1995) dissertation examined how well the Catholic elementary school functions as an agent of formative parenting. Responses from 332 parents identified specific formation needs such as: (a) communicating the components of socialization, self-esteem, prosocial behavior, democratic family atmosphere and identity formation; (b) suggesting strategies or practices for developing these components; (c) encouraging consistency in parenting practices, and (d) providing guidelines for discipline, sibling rivalry, peer relations, and angry behavior. McCormack (1999) reported that according to questionnaire data, parents felt that the school functions at least fairly well as an agent of formative parenting. Interview data, however, elicited a different pattern. A majority of parents (83%) felt that the Catholic school in terms of parenting had not helped them. As to why they evaluated high on the questionnaires, parents reported that they were pleased with the academic program, approved of the school atmosphere, or perceived that they had been helped vicariously by teachers' interactions with their children.

McCormack (1999) reported follow-up research that explicitly sought to uncover the parenting practices that contribute to the foundation of identity formation within children. Principals of 16 schools submitted the names of 93 children (from grades K-12) that met specified criteria, such as "appears secure and comfortable," "has a sense of personal boundaries," "demonstrates positive social behavior," "follows through with tasks," and "is accountable for consequences of actions." Parents of these children were then invited to participate in the research project. Among this sample, McCormack noted a great amount of "attentive parent presence," described as consistent availability to and interaction with the child. For the first three years of life, each of these children had experienced attentive presence of a parent throughout the day or a stable, consistent caregiver within a private home-type daycare. As part of the research protocol, parents reported (independent of each other) the practices they had used during the past year that might explain why their child displayed security, autonomy, prosocial behavior, and accountability on a consistent basis. Across families, parents mentioned similar parenting practices that likewise mirrored discussions of effective parenting practices in the developmental psychology research literature. For example, their parenting styles featured limit-setting, positive affect, expectations of responsibility, provision of encouragement, and freedom with concomitant accountability.

Similar to McCormack (1995), Gorman's (1996) dissertation investigated the relationship of parenting practices to the holistic development of the child. Specifically, the study explored the particular parenting that parents, administrators, and teachers in Catholic elementary schools of a California archdiocese perceived as the most likely to both empower and encourage parents in promoting healthy child development. A survey instrument provided to parents, teachers, and administrators assessed three domains: (a) parenting practices most important to the process of fostering the holistic development of children, (b) the degree to which the Catholic school assists parents in the formative areas of parenting, and (c) areas of parenting in which parents desired assistance and the areas perceived by administrators and teachers as practices in which parents need assistance. All three groups identified parenting practices that are conducive to a democratic family atmosphere, self-esteem, identity formation, and prosocial behavior as important. Significant differences emerged between parents on one hand, and parents and teachers on the other, such that teachers and administrators identified more than twice as many practices in which parents needed assistance than did parents. The study concluded that families clearly have formative parenting needs that Catholic schools must attempt to meet through the development and implementation of comprehensive parent education programs.

Family Dynamics and Children's Functioning

Written for educators, parents, and anyone that works with children, Garanzini (1995) author of *Child Centered, Family Sensitive Schools: An Educators Guide To Family Dynamics* (NCEA) dedicated to the overarching goal of understanding the impact of family dynamics and structures on the school setting. The book is divided into three parts. The first provides a theoretical framework (family systems theory) within which the developmental and environmental needs of children can be understood. Part one also explores, through case study vignettes, varieties of healthy families (dual-career homes, single-parent homes, blended families, and adoptive families) and how the relational and developmental needs of children are met in differing family configurations. The second section of the text is devoted to examining the counterpoint to healthy family structures and explores in-depth dysfunctional family styles. Family pathologies such as substance abuse, family violence, and the "fragile family" are discussed. Linkages are presented between various dysfunctional family styles and the resultant psychological and behavioral difficulties manifested by children at home and school. Finally, part three provides suggestions and guiding principles for intervening with families, as well as recommendations for increased consultation and cooperation among child-serving professionals.

As a lesson in educational leadership for parent and child guidance, Garanzini (2000) has also written about dealing with narcissistic families. Narcissistic families are those that exhibit an unhealthy level of enmeshment, are excessively demanding, poorly differentiated, and unrealistic in their expectations of the child and the school. Families such as these are especially prone to unnecessary advocacy for their child as a result of their anxiety over the demands of the school combined with the parents' feelings of inadequacy. Since narcissistic parents view the child's poor performance as a reflection on themselves, the parents in turn project their anger and disappointment onto those who are the source of the poor evaluation (often the child's teacher or principal). Garanzini (2000) detailed strategies for handling narcissistic families and their children: (a) reinterpret negative behavior of the child and parents as a call for help, (b) model appropriate behaviors and boundaries, (c) stress the child's need to take responsibility, and (d) help the child learn to defer gratification and internalize rewards. In terms of implications for Catholic educational leadership, Garanzini delineated several elements that could assist educators and administrators in dealing with narcissistic families. For example, acquiring knowledge and skills, especially in regard to the psychological literature on family dysfunction, is recommended. Other strategies suggested are working with teams (as opposed to compartmentalized strategies and uncoordinated interventions), appraising and developing the resources of the school community, and lastly, espousing a commitment to continuous spiritual and psychological growth.

Parent Education and Parenting Programs

Scheinfeld (1993) authored a text designed to assist in creating parent education courses for refugee and immigrant parents, with a special emphasis on those who are having difficulty in parent-child relations. The guide is based upon three parent education projects sponsored and coordinated by the North American office of the International Catholic Child Bureau. Each of the projects was conducted at a separate site and featured an eight-week course for Cambodian refugees who were having difficulties in their parenting roles. Scheinfeld described the common theme of the program as parental empowerment, wherein "each program asks parents to take a hard look at themselves, their children, and their situation, and to take action to prevent and improve conflictual parent-child relationships that are harmful to parent, child, and the family as a whole" (p. 2). The guide contains a detailed chapter on the implementation of the parent education program in each of the three sites including topics such as (a) staff perception of parents' needs, (b) goals for the course, (c) principles underlying course design, (d) weekly description of course components, and (e) staff assessment and evaluation of the course. These case studies provide an array of experiences, common obstacles, and shared aims that are meant to assist in the design of a locally tailored program. Although Cambodian refugee families were the participants in the parent education program described in the guide, Scheinfeld noted that the results have broad application to other refugee and immigrant groups. The guide also contains several chapters that provide program-planning advice based on the content of the program descriptions as well as outcome evaluations of the three parent education programs.

Research indicates that the most effective sexuality education occurs when both the parent and the school cooperate to educate the child about sexuality. Accordingly, Martens (1996) conducted a program evaluation targeted at whether a religious based sexuality education program (the "In God's Image Program") would positively impact parent-child comfort and communication about sexuality. The program is meant to complement informal education in the home and to provide a developmentally sound approach that encourages parental involvement. Furthermore, the program is meant to counter negative attitudes toward sexuality and to alleviate the generational cycle of discomfort with addressing sexuality that is experienced in many families. The research was a qualitative, multisite investigation in which 115 eighth-grade students from five socio-economically and racially diverse schools voluntarily participated in the 10-week sexuality curriculum. One of the program components at the end of each lesson included a worksheet to be taken home and discussed with parents. At the completion of the curriculum, focus groups were conducted with students and 46 parents. The focus group findings revealed more frequent and more comfortable communications about sexuality for both parent and child. Moreover, students reported an increase in their knowledge of Church teachings in regard to sexuality, with 79% of eighth-graders indicating that the program had influenced them to postpone sexual involvement.

Parental Choice of Schools

Several dissertations in the 1990s examined the role of various demographic variables and motivational constructs in order to better understand parental choice of schools. Gibson (1993) examined demographic and educational variables to explain the motivation of suburban Milwaukee parents in choosing private elementary schools (Catholic, Jewish, Independent, or Lutheran) for their children. Data for the investigation were gathered through surveys and telephone interviews. Gibson found that of parents who chose Catholic schools, 98% of the mothers were Catholic and 80% of them had attended private schools themselves. Relevant educational variables that emerged from parents choosing Catholic schools included religion, moral values, and committed teachers. When compared to parents initially choosing Catholic schools, Gibson reported only a slightly different pattern of relevant educational variables for those parents who transferred their children following dissatisfaction with public schools, noting the importance of religion, moral values, and warmth of school climate.

A dissertation by Esposito (1993) focused on parental choice among Roman Catholic schools, public schools, and parish-catechetical programs for 306 parents of fifth- and sixth-grade students. Survey methodology was used to explore the relationships among demographic variables, selected constructs (superior goal attainment, strong mutual commitment, organizational jeopardy, and school environment), and subsequent parental choices. Significant differences were found between Catholic school parents and their public school counterparts for the importance of superior goal attainment as a determinant of parental choice. All three groups, and especially the Catholic school parents, reported strong concerns in regard to organizational jeopardy, as parents perceived a serious financial threat to the future viability of their school environments. For the school environment construct, all three school types evidenced stronger social cohesion than alienation in relation to their communities. Results also revealed that Catholic school parents participated in their schools at higher rates than did the other two groups and that they embraced the uniqueness of their school more than their counterparts. Esposito concluded that to the extent that they patronize such schools and report satisfaction with the educational programs, parents of children in Catholic schools and parish-catechetical programs attained optimally effective instructional environments.

Noting parents' increasing involvement in school choice, Gallanter (1994) explored parent selection factors at three private elementary schools (two private independent, one Catholic). A descriptive, cross-sectional, survey research methodology allowed for data collection from faculty, staff, and parents through a questionnaire format. Analysis of the parent selection factors revealed that the most important reason parents selected private schooling was to avoid public schooling, which they perceived as offering less than a quality education. Teachers were also an important influence on parents' choice and selection. Overall, parents sought small schools with small class sizes because of their desire for greater individual attention for their child.

The purpose of Taylor's (1996) dissertation was to examine the reasons associated with parents' choices of specific types of private schools (Roman Catholic, Episcopal, Independent, Jewish, and Fundamentalist Christian). Survey data were gathered from 401 randomly selected families from 30 private high schools in a 50-mile radius of Miami, Florida. The survey employed a Likert type rating scale that emphasized general variable domains such as academics, religions and values and morals, nurturing educational environment, and proximity and convenience of the school. Differences across types of schools emerged across several variables: (a) quality of instruction, (b), commitment of teachers, (c) emphasis on religion, (d) small class size, (e) well-defined academic goals, (f) proximity of the school's location, (g) preparation for desired secondary schools and colleges, and (h) convenience of school's operation schedule. Taylor found that parents appeared to look for a school that would satisfy the special needs of their child and would be compatible with their own values, morals, and personal philosophy.

Biddle (1997) conducted a longitudinal inquiry of a specific urban elementary school to explore the reasons that predominantly non-Catholic parents choose to send their children to a Catholic elementary school.

Data collected over a 10-month period included a parent survey, formal and informal interviews, participant observation, and review of school documents. With an enrollment of 250 students, the elementary school, located in an economically distressed area, was 100% African American and 90% non-Catholic. The parent survey, which provided the data in regard to reasons for school choice, consisted of three open-ended questions. Returned surveys were supportive of the school overall and mirrored reasons and explanations found in the literature. Parents noted "the school's sense of community, differences from the public schools, reputation for academic excellence, emphasis on values, the development of a faith community, and emphasis on discipline and order" (p. 72). Tuition aid was not a motivating factor for parents. Interviews revealed that tuition aid provides an opportunity, but it is not a determining factor for parents. Parents saw the distinguishing features of the school to be its smaller class size, emphasis on academic standards, teacher interest in students, discipline and order, and attention to values and sense of community.

VARIOUS TOPICS

Social Capital

Coleman identified the religious dimension as the foundation of the Catholic school as functional community. A dissertation by Saunders (1992) explored this contention more specifically by investigating the impact of the family's social capital on the religious outcomes of eighth-grade students in Catholic elementary schools. Students and parents (N = 248) completed questionnaires assessing religious, academic, and social values and parent-child interactions. When operationalized as predictors of religious outcomes, particularly those involving practice, religious predictors enhanced overall prediction beyond the effect of the academic and social predictors. The student's perception of the school was a strong predictor of several religious outcomes, particularly those of a cognitive nature. By partitioning the sample into three groups (students with two Catholic parents, students with parents of mixed religious backgrounds, and students of single parent families) Saunders detected limited evidence that a strong set of religious predictors does compensate for structural (single parent family) and functional (parents of different religious backgrounds) deficiencies in the family.

Teachers' Perceptions of Parental Support

Schaub (2000) provided a profile of American Catholic school teachers based on data from the U.S. Department of Education's *Schools and Staffing Survey*. In 1993-1994, the nationally representative sample of teachers responded to items assessing teacher attitudes, one of which targeted parental support ("I receive a great deal of support from parents for the work I do"). Survey results indicated a dramatic difference between Catholic and public school teachers' perceptions of the amount of perceived parental support for teaching activities. For the item above, 85% and 83% respectively, of Catholic elementary and secondary school teachers expressed agreement. In contrast, 58% and 43% respectively, of public elementary and secondary school teachers agreed. These findings are noteworthy in that higher levels of perceived parental support contribute to teachers' overall views of the working conditions in their schools, which in turn are commonly associated with teacher quality and retention.

Parents' Perceptions of School Staff

A dissertation by Sullivan (1995) explored the perceptions of parents regarding the important aspects of a program of quality education and the effectiveness of laypersons and religious in delivering the program in the Diocese of Fall River, Massachusetts. Two key themes from the research literature provided the foundation for this investigation: (a) a shift from religious instruction and formation to academic quality in parents' primary reasons for choosing Catholic schools, and (b) parents' concern regarding the effects on the schools of the decline in the number of religious, and the increase in the number of laypersons. Questionnaires were completed by 465 parents with children in the Catholic schools in the diocese. Structured interviews also supplemented these data. Sullivan reported that parents showed interest in strong academic programs and demonstrated equally strong interest in moral and value development. Data indicated that while parents' perceptions were not affected by demographic variables such as age and education, perceptions were affected by grade level of their children and by administrator of the school. Lastly, although a majority of parents reported that it made no difference who fostered characteristics associated with academics and values, a majority of parents perceived that religious would do better at fostering characteristics associated with religion.

CHAPTER 7

STUDENTS IN CATHOLIC SCHOOLS

RICHARD J. MCGRATH, OSA

MINORITY AND AT-RISK STUDENTS AND CATHOLIC SCHOOLS

Research from 1965 through the 1990s indicates that Catholic schools have a beneficial effect on the educational outcomes of minority and at-risk students both in inner city and disadvantaged areas of the nation. Findings consistently point to a "Catholic school effect" (Coleman, Hoffer, & Kilgore, 1982) through improved test scores, increased likelihood of graduation from high school and college, supportive climate, and improved educational aspirations as a result of experience in Catholic education.

Catholic School Minority Enrollment Growth

Catholic schools experienced a renaissance beginning in the mid 1980s. Through the decade of the 1990s and beyond, Catholic school growth has continued in several areas of the nation. From 1993 to 2000, overall Catholic school student enrollment increased by 86,000 students, with half of the Catholic schools reporting that they maintained a waiting list for admission (Augenstein & Meitler, 2000). More than 50% of Catholic elementary schools now provide preschool programs with 94% having kindergartens. Minority enrollment has increased to 656,393 students, or 24.7% of total enrollment. Non-Catholic students enrolled are 353,628 or 13% of total enrollment; many of these students are minority students.

Of the 1,221 Catholic high schools nationwide, 62.2% are coeducational, 14.5% are all male schools, and 21.3% are all female schools. Over 32% of the schools are classified as urban, 12.9% as inner city schools, 21.4% as suburban, and 21.4% as rural (McDonald, 2000b). Two hundred and fifty new Catholic elementary schools and 38 Catholic high schools have opened since 1985 (Meitler, 2001). These new schools added a total of 88,323 elementary seats and 20,296 secondary seats for a total of 108,619 new seats available for Catholic school children nationwide. In the year 2000 alone, 41 new elementary schools and 10 new secondary schools opened, the largest number of openings since 1985. The National Catholic Educational Association (NCEA) reports that nearly 100 schools are currently in the planning or building stages. Although a period of consolidation, closure, and bleakness appeared in the 1960s and 1970s, and sometimes continues in urban and inner city schools, there is clearly a boom of new Catholic school openings in many areas (McDonald, 2000b). Since 1992 Catholic schools have opened at the rate of 21 per year.

While nationwide Catholic school enrollment has increased by 3.8% in the last decade, the market share of Catholic education dropped from 6.3% to 5.6% during the same period. Enrollment has increased in the Plains, the Southwest, the West, and the far West. Declines have taken place in New England, the Midwest and the Great Lakes regions (Augenstein & Meitler, 2000; Guerra, 1998).

Most recent data on Catholic high school enrollment show that student bodies are composed of 76% Caucasian students, 8% African American, 10% Hispanic or Latino, 4% Asian or Pacific Islander, 1% native

American, and 1% other (Guerra, 1998). Private, religious, and parish high schools report a larger percentage of minority students than diocesan run high schools. Catholic high schools on the average are 81% Catholic, 15% non-Catholic, and 4% non-Christian. Two hundred and thirty Catholic high schools serve student populations that are more than one-third minority. There are 94 Catholic high schools of this group whose student populations are more than one third Hispanic,[1] and 60 schools whose student populations are more than one third African American. Eleven Catholic high schools report student populations that are both one third or more Hispanic and one third or more African American and these schools are included in both categories. Sixteen Catholic high schools have student populations that are more than 90% students of color. Five of these schools report that all students are either Hispanic or African American (Guerra, 1998).

The percentage of minorities in all Catholic schools has more than doubled in the past 30 years. In 1970 minority enrollment amounted to 10.8% of the Catholic school population. In 1980 that increased to 19.4% and by 2000 was 24%. In the same period of time, the percentage of African American enrollment increased from 6.5% to 7.8%. The percentage of Asian Americans increased from .5% to 3.5%. The Hispanic enrollment rose from 2.5% to 10.7% (McDonald, 2000b). Non-Catholic student enrollment rose from 2.7% in 1970, to 11.2% in 1980 and 13.4% in 2000 (McDonald, 2000b). Reasons often cited for growth in minority enrollment include population increases, economic prosperity extending into minority communities, a greater emphasis being placed on the needs for basic Christian values and religious instruction, the emergence of school choice, and aggressiveness in Catholic school marketing (Augenstein & Meitler, 2000).

Catholic School Climate and Minority Students

Catholic schools have a distinct climate: an atmosphere that encourages and supports the learning process among students of all types. This distinctive climate aids Catholic schools in providing a quality education for inner city and minority and at-risk students, encouraging them to excel in academic pursuits and personal development. Consistent features of Catholic school climate include generally smaller enrollment, highly structured academic programs, devoted and loyal faculty who receive substandard salaries, and the practice of regular religious experiences. Catholic schools attempt to promote complete intellectual, spiritual, athletic, and social development of their students (Daly, 1996).

Catholic schools provide a setting where each child is valued. The schools are pleasant, supportive, respectful, and expect success from minority students. Environments are safe and teachers enforce the need for students to be well prepared for the future (Bean, Eichelberger, Lazar, Morris, & Reed, 2000).

Catholic schools influence their students' choices, which result in the more equitable social distribution of course taking among all social classes. Research drawn from the NELS of 1988 focused on mathematics, an area of the curriculum in which learning is particularly responsive to school experiences. Correcting for demographics and academic characteristics, it was found that Catholic school students take more advanced math courses. Catholic schools influence their students to take more academically challenging and risky courses than do independent schools. Catholic schools provide more equality and equitability in determining who completes advanced coursework in a normative leveling or common school effect for all students, than are found in public schools. Evidence suggests that Catholic schools are not especially selective in admitting students, particularly with regard to academic ability. This finding works against the commonly held belief that Catholic schools are selective and therefore pick only the best students. Evidence shows that taking the most appropriate courses makes a substantial difference in learning, particularly in mathematics. Results indicate that Catholic schools employ this nonselective model while providing a common school effect without being selective with regard to clientele (Lee, Chow-Hoy, Burkam, Geverdt, & Smerdon, 1998).

Catholic schools provide faith formation and values. Teachers view the formation of Christian character in the Catholic school as a non-negotiable, which is gospel centered, environmental, cross-curricular, and essential in this society where values are lacking (Groome, 1998; Thibeau, 1999).

Catholic schools work hard at racial harmony, appreciate diversity, and enforce strong discipline. The commitment of parents and teachers helps build a supporting community with close friendships between students and teachers (Gerson, 1997; Jones, 1997).

Catholic schools have a distinctive social environment that is highly regarded by both students and adults. Catholic schools, regardless of location, share major characteristics and an unwavering commitment to an academic program for all students regardless of background, race, or life experiences. Catholic schools provide an academic organization designed to promote an atmosphere with a caring environment and a social organization deliberately structured to advance it. They have an inspired ideology that directs institutional action toward social justice and an ecumenical and multi-cultural world (Bryk, Lee, & Holland, 1993).

Typically Catholic high schools feature well-organized classes where students are kept on track, teachers are prepared, and there is an expectation that all students can learn. High standards of homework, attention, discipline, and production are required of all students. Catholic schools have adequate technology and basic instructional materials. External interruptions are rare, and there is a heavy emphasis on teacher directed activities. Data suggest a high level of student engagement in classroom instruction and a very small portion of students who are not engaged. There are six times fewer incidents of cutting class, and refusing to obey the teacher; students are twice as likely not to talk back and half as likely to instigate attacks on teachers compared to public schools. Positive attitudes toward school and teachers are evident. A vast majority of students believe that the academic quality of the school they are in is either good or excellent, and agree that their school has a good reputation in the community (Bryk et al., 1993).

Catholic secondary schools are not highly selective in admissions, accepting 88% of all students who apply. In making the selection of a Catholic school, parents cited reasons such as perception of the school having smaller class size, stronger teacher interest in students, emphasis on academic standards, discipline and order, attention to values, and a sense of community. Minority parents, 90% non-Catholic, cited the reinforcement of values emphasizing pride and respect instilled in students by the school and its teachers as very influential in selection (Biddle, 1997). Tuition aid in determining attendance was not a motivating factor (Archer, 1997b). Parents and students voluntarily select the school exhibiting a willingness to join the community and accept its values. Virtually every Catholic high school has a written code of conduct including a dress code, standards for social behavior, and a list of prohibited behaviors. Consequences are clear and provide for violations up to and including expulsion. Standards in Catholic high schools are widely understood by parents, students, and school personnel. Catholic high schools have shared organizational beliefs and articulate an explicit moral understanding of the purposes of education. They work at developing a sense of personal responsibility and commitment to hard work. They conscientiously seek to shape and engage students in character building (Bryk et al., 1993).

Catholic secondary schools utilize a set of shared activities having a direct bearing on climate. First among these activities is a core academic curriculum uniting students for the same purpose, providing equitable academic opportunities among social classes, and resulting in a strong common school effect. They promote extensive extracurricular involvement and require students and faculty to engage in religious activities which strengthen a sense of community and relationship, including service programs in which students respond to the larger community (Bryk et al., 1993).

It is clear that the academic success of poor minority students in Catholic schools is attained with significantly smaller financial resources than those spent by public schools (Delpit, 1996; Groome, 1998). Data gathered from 5th and 6th grade African American, Latino, Indochinese, and Caucasian students demonstrated that parents intervene in children's private (including Catholic) school education when the child's academic performance is low regardless of ethnicity. High achievement among minorities in schools is associated with beliefs about ability and not about effort (Bempechat, Drago-Severson, & Dindorff, 1994).

Relative to their public school peers, Latino students in Catholic schools believe more strongly that success is due to ability. Both Latino and African American students in Catholic schools are much less likely than their public school counterparts to believe that success should be attributed to external factors such as luck. For African American students, the type of school they attend appears to be more important in supporting their beliefs about success or failure. African American students attending Catholic schools are less likely than their public school peers to blame failure on external factors (Bempechat, Graham, & Jimeniz, 1997; Delpit, 1996; Groome, 1998).

Latino and African American students in Catholic schools are encouraged to assume more personal responsibility for their intellectual development. The overall philosophy of Catholic schools is one that leads children to believe in their intellectual abilities and to strive for academic excellence. The cause of serving and advancing the poor and marginalized in society is shown in schools by clearly communicated structure, classroom discipline, demanding curriculum, and consistently high expectations in standards for both social behavior and academic performance (Bempechat et al., 1994). In Catholic schools students are more likely to attribute achievement to higher ability indicating the environment of Catholic schools may foster positive beliefs about achievement (Delpit, 1996). Catholic schools have built a reputation for academic distinction by adhering to a relatively straightforward doctrine of excellence, rooted in profound faith and a covenant to both educate and elevate the disadvantaged (Groome, 1998).

Organizational Effects

Data from *High School and Beyond* (HSB) yields a body of evidence converging to show that success in Catholic secondary schools can be attributed to three important influences. First, Catholic schools have a teaching philosophy that believes in the ability of all students to succeed. This philosophy is supported by school principals who show a clear vision, and teachers who establish appropriately high expectations for students. Second, Catholic school structure leads to success. Catholic schools are a school based management system. In schools with large minority populations, faculty and staff are unfettered by layers of bureaucracy that characterize public schools. They solve problems at the building level themselves and are accountable to themselves, parents, and students (Bryk et al., 1993). Third, Catholic schools adhere to a strictly academic core curriculum. Generally, every parent, child, and teacher works toward the same goal, which is college preparation and admission (Groome, 1998).

Catholic school tracking and placement are unrelated to race and ethnicity. The educational experiences of lower track students are much more demanding when compared to public schools. Teachers in Catholic schools have implicit faith in the child and the child's ability to learn, which encourages children to have faith in their own abilities. Children come to believe that academic success is due to ability and that failure is not the result of lack of ability. Teachers in Catholic schools may provide the kind of feedback that encourages positive attitudes about learning (Bempechat, Graham, & Jimenez, 1996).

Catholic schools encourage the participation of parents who report that teachers and principals make them feel at home in their children's school and that the school is a welcoming non-threatening place. Parents have a sense that children's teachers care not only about the student but also about the entire family, which fosters a sense of shared goals focused on academic excellence (Bempechat et al., 1997).

The organizational structure of the Catholic high school compensates for the differences students bring to the school in academic preparation (Bryk et al., 1993). Catholic school students on average scored higher than their public school peers, but differences disappeared when specific school and classroom level variables were taken into account such as time on homework, number of math classes taken, and disciplinary climate. Differences in the average achievement between public and Catholic schools are more directly linked to key organizational conditions that vary across the two sectors. The typical Catholic high school has more internal diversity with regard to race and income than the typical public school. Catholic high schools provide more advanced academic courses and fewer vocational courses. Seventy-two percent of Catholic school students study an academic program while only 10% concentrate in vocational studies. Public schools typically feature an even distribution between academic programs, advanced academic programs, and vocational tracks. Data indicated that a focused curriculum and high standards exist in Catholic schools (Bryk et al., 1993; Ravitch, 1996).

While the character of instruction in many Catholic high school classrooms is rather ordinary, Catholic school students described teachers as patient, respectful, and happy with their work. Catholic school students were similar in their interest in school but much more likely to praise the quality of instruction and the school's reputation than public school students. Catholic school minority students were more likely to report that their teachers enjoyed their work and were more respectful and patient than public school teachers. Catholic school students seem to put more emphasis on testing and homework than appears in public schools (Bryk et al., 1993).

Academic Climate and Minority Students

Data support the generalization that Catholic school students take considerably more academic courses than public school students. Typically, students in all Catholic high schools take an average of over a year and a half more of mathematics and a half-year more of foreign language. Analysis shows that Catholic school graduates averaged 16 credits in core academic subjects compared to 13 credits for public school graduates (Bryk et al., 1993).

In comparing vocational track students, Catholic school vocational track students take an extra year of mathematics, while science and social studies enrollment is about the same as public school students. Catholic school vocational students generally take a slightly greater number of English courses. In the academic track Catholic school students take 12% more academic courses than public school students. The larger enrollment in academic courses in Catholic schools compared to public schools results from two factors: the substantially greater percentage of students enrolled in the academic track in Catholic schools, and a greater emphasis on academic coursework for students not in academic programs in Catholic schools (Bryk et al., 1993).

Catholic schools take a direct and active role in deciding what their students should learn and create an academic structure to advance their agenda. This approach contrasts strongly with characterizations of public high schools as shopping malls where market forces and free choice dominate. In public schools less academically gifted and at-risk young people are more likely to enroll in non-academic courses. The Catholic school, with its emphasis on a common core of academic experience and a structure that limits levels of student choice, compensates for some of the powerful differentiating influences in society where minority children are viewed as inferior learners. This academic organization works as a strong integrating influence on both students and adults, bonding them together in a common school that encourages the best efforts of each person (Bryk et al., 1993).

At the elementary level urban Catholic elementary school students are more likely to study core academic subjects such as English, math, science, history, and social studies than their public school counterparts. They are twice as likely as urban public school elementary students to take remedial English and math; however, lab sciences are served better in public schools. Catholic school elementary students are less likely to take foreign language but more likely to receive computer education, religion class, and experiences in music and art. The non-academic subjects are generally not offered in Catholic elementary schools (Sebring & Camburn, 1992).

Catholic elementary school students are more likely to participate in sports, science fairs, newspaper and other extracurricular activities than public school students. Catholic school students indicate that their teachers express strong feelings about student competence and concern for their students. Minority students in Catholic schools in less affluent rural areas may take fewer courses, participate less in extracurricular activities, and not appreciate their teachers as much as students in urban Catholic schools. Generally, Catholic school students regardless of geography are satisfied with school climate. Students from lower socioeconomic status (SES) families in Catholic schools have higher praise for teachers than those of medium and high SES families. Catholic school parents are more likely to speak often with their children about plans for high school than are public school elementary parents (Sebring & Camburn, 1992). Non-Catholic students help drive the Catholic school effect if they attend Catholic grade schools (Sander, 1999).

Minority Academic Achievement

When adjusting for religious preference, the rate of African American students enrolled in Catholic schools exceeds the enrollment of Whites and Hispanics (Bryk et al., 1993). In public schools the academic talents of African American students are largely untapped, underutilized, and unrecognized (Irvine & Foster, 1996). Catholic schools challenge the idea that African American and Hispanic students are not able to rise above the adversity of their disadvantaged backgrounds and poor educational systems (Bryk et al., 1993).

The academic effects of the Catholic school education on minority and at-risk students remained an interesting question through the 1990s. Some have found either no Catholic school effect or a very modest positive effect on test scores (Akerhielm, 1993). Others find no Catholic school effect on White student test scores but significant positive effects on Black and Hispanic test scores (Sander, 1996). Yet, there is no shortage of positive results; data indicate that eight years of education in Catholic elementary schools has a positive effect on the academic achievement of minority students in mathematics, reading, and vocabulary test scores, but perhaps not as much on science (Sander, 1996).

Data collected from the third follow-up survey of *High School and Beyond* 1980 sophomore cohort, indicate that positive Catholic school achievement effects among minority students depend on greater emphasis on core curriculum, organizational aspects such as school discipline, and the decentralized nature of Catholic education. Catholic schools spend on the average 50% or less than public school elementary per pupil expenses and have fewer bureaucrats in their system (Akerhielm, 1993; Bryk et al., 1993).

Math Scores

Heritage Foundation researchers analyzed math scores from the 1996 National Assessment of Educational Progress test (NAEP) taken by African American fourth and eighth-grade students in the District of Columbia's public and Catholic schools. Controlling for family background factors such as number of parents, family income, reading materials in the home, and education of parents, findings indicated that the average African American eighth grader in a District of Columbia Catholic school performs better in math than 72% of their public school counterparts. Nationwide, on the average, Catholic school students in the fourth grade scored 6.5% higher in math than public school students; the difference is widened to 8.2% higher for Catholic school children by the time they reach eighth grade compared to public school students. The self-selection criticism was addressed by integrating more SES and family background characteristics into the research model (Johnson, 1999).

Findings suggest that over time students in private and parochial schools may continue to outperform their public school counterparts. Results indicate an expanding difference in outcomes depending on the length of time in Catholic education (Butler, 2000). Catholic schooling for these students had a more significant academic effect than decreasing class size.

More striking than the improvement in test scores is the relative impact of Catholic schools compared to other variables. Taken separately, the statistical effects of Catholic schooling are more important than a family's income or belonging to a two-parent family. For fourth graders, attending a Catholic school had almost four times the effect on standard math scores as living in a two-parent home, and 10 times the effect of attending a slightly more affluent public school. For eighth grade students, attending a Catholic school had nearly twice the beneficial academic effect of having a mother who attended at least some college (Greene & Peterson, 1996; Johnson, 1999).

Other data found smaller but still significant differences between the scores of Catholic school eighth graders who were White or African American compared to public school students. Minority students in Catholic schools exhibit higher levels of math proficiency than their public school counterparts. In Catholic schools 26% of Hispanic students and 29% of African American students have intermediate levels of math skills compared to 16% of public school students in both racial minority groups. The achievement gap between racial minorities and Whites is smaller in Catholic schools than public. A significantly lower percentage of students have test scores in the lowest quartile in Catholic schools (Sebring & Camburn, 1992).

High School and Beyond (HSB) yielded data on mathematics achievement for high school students. Differences in achievement between White and minority students in Catholic high schools are smaller than in public schools with regard to mathematics. If Catholic schooling continues, the differences become even less. The achievement advantage in mathematics of White students compared to minority students increases in public high schools during the last two years of schooling, whereas the gap actually decreases between White and minority students in Catholic high schools (Bryk et al., 1993).

By senior year lower middle class minority students attending Catholic high schools are achieving 4.5 years ahead of their counterparts in the public sector in mathematics. For minority students the difference between public and Catholic schools is larger than the gains in learning between White students in public and Catholic schools. Minorities in Catholic high schools learn at a rate of approximately 65% faster than that of the average public school sector student, and more than 100% faster than their minority counterparts in public education (Bryk et al., 1993).

The basic pattern established in previous research is confirmed; mathematics achievement is less dependent on a student's social and racial background in Catholic schools than in public schools. Reasons for these results have to do with increased likelihood of minority students in Catholic high schools being placed in mathematics courses more often than they would be in public schools. Minority students in Catholic high schools are much more likely to take advanced courses in mathematics than public school students. Minority students taking math courses in an academic track are more likely to take more math courses and therefore to produce better academic math results than students who do not take them. Public school students' personal and academic background plays a substantial role in determining their subsequent academic experiences. These findings support previous research that the organizational structure of Catholic high schools modifies the effects on achievement of the differences that students bring to the school. A comparison of Catholic school minority achievement to public school minority achievement in mathematics shows that on the average, senior year achievement is 3.2 years higher in Catholic than public schools. The size of the achievement gap between White and minority students in Catholic and public schools is 2.0 years less in Catholic schools than in public schools, a substantial difference (Bryk et al., 1993).

The advantage in attending Catholic high schools for students from lower SES with regard to mathematics achievement decreases as the social class of the student increases and becomes less important as the social class of both Catholic and public school students rises. The Catholic school advantage remains for minority students when comparing students in the average Catholic school to students in the average public school. It grows even larger for minority students in Catholic schools compared to disadvantaged students in public schools. As the perceived quality of the public school decreases, the advantage to minority students in attending Catholic schools increases. The biggest advantage is accrued to the most disadvantaged students on the average (Bryk et al., 1993).

Reading and Science

Hispanic and African American students are more likely to be reading at an advanced level in Catholic schools than public schools. Catholic school Hispanic students perform better in reading than public school students. In Catholic elementary schools, 29% of African American students are reading at an advanced level compared to 17.5% in public schools. Data indicate that gaps in reading proficiency are considerably smaller in Catholic schools between minority and White students than in public schools. Achievement in reading is more equitably distributed across the student body in Catholic schools than in public schools (Sebring & Camburn, 1992).

National Assessment of Educational Progress (NAEP) data examining reading proficiency found that significantly more Catholic school students are enrolled in advanced placement English than public school students (Bryk et al., 1993).

Adjusting for socioeconomic status, students in Catholic schools in science are less likely than in public schools to score in the lowest quartile and more likely to perform in the upper range. The gap between science test scores of students who are traditionally disadvantaged and advantaged students is smaller in Catholic schools. In science, both Hispanic and African American students, as well as Asian students, scored better than their counterparts in public schools. Males and Asians in Catholic schools are significantly more likely to perform better than public school males and Asians. White students and Asian students generally have higher test scores than African Americans and Hispanics in Catholic schools (Sebring & Camburn, 1992).

Other Achievement Areas

Hispanic and African American students are more likely to score better in history and social studies in Catholic schools. Similarly 47% of Asian students scored in the highest quartile in Catholic schools in social studies compared to 30% in public schools (Sebring & Camburn, 1992).

National Educational Longitudinal Study (NELS) data controlling for race, religious affiliation, and parent level of schooling found large positive differences in test scores for Black and Hispanic students who attend religious schools, and effect even more pronounced in urban areas. Differences in positive test score achievement were even larger than other research (Neal, 1997b) for Black and Hispanic students in urban areas, particularly in large central cities (Figlio & Stone, 1997).

College Board scores for college bound seniors who take the SAT point to an advantage for students from religiously affiliated schools on the verbal test of between 23 and 27 points, and on the math test of between 4 and 13 points including all types of students. Students who attend independent private schools obtained an advantage over their public school counterparts of between 45 and 50 points both on verbal and math test scores. Catholic schools are included in these private school statistics (College Board, 1999). While private schools do not have a direct effect on public school achievement, study data indicate that more competition with the public sector increases the quality of public education (Sander, 1999).

Recent outreach efforts to aid minority communities are being attempted around the country by the Catholic community. A mission school model in new schools has been applied in New York, Chicago, and other major urban areas. At some of these schools, students are allowed to attend class as well as to hold down jobs to enable them to pay tuition and succeed economically (Archer, 1997b). Latino students are taught in both English and in Spanish. Families make a contribution toward tuition. It is reported that there are almost 2,000 such schools around the country, which generally have a very limited enrollment (Anderson, 1999).

The phenomenon of better performance in Catholic education by minority students when Catholic school outcomes are compared to public school outcomes when controlling for background variables is known as the Catholic school effect. Research suggests that Catholic schools educate low income minority students differently than public schools, particularly in their treatment of African American students, and are producing better academic outcomes (Bryk et al., 1993).

Minority Aspirations

NELS data indicate that the most important predictors of aspirations for African American eighth-grade students were grades. High academic achievers had higher aspirations in spite of poverty status. Students from poor neighborhoods often had low aspirations and low vocational predictions. High parent expectations produce students more likely to seek higher education and attend Catholic schools. Students attending a Catholic school were more likely to have higher career expectations (Smith-Maddox, 1994).

Attending a Catholic high school raises the probability of finishing high school and entering college for inner city students by 17%. This is twice as large as the beneficial effect of moving from a one to a two-parent family, and two and a half times as large as the effect of raising parents' educational level from a high school dropout to a college graduate (Evans & Schwab, 1995). Catholic schools have a particularly strong effect on the aspirations of students with the lowest probability of graduation: inner city Black students, students in urban areas, and those with the lowest test scores. Neal (1997b) analyzed the effects of Catholic secondary schools on high school and college graduation rates and future wages. Controlling for selection bias by using data from the National Catholic Educational Association (NCEA), a survey of churches and church membership, and merging the information with NELS data, he found that African American and Hispanic students attending urban Catholic schools were more than twice as likely to graduate from college as their counterparts in public schools. Of African American and Hispanic Catholic high school graduates who started college, 27% graduated compared to 11% from urban public schools. In addition, the probability of inner city students graduating from high school increased from 62% to 88% when they were placed in Catholic secondary schools. When compared to their public school counterparts, minority students in urban Catholic high schools can expect roughly 8% higher wages in the future (Neal, 1997b).

Catholic high school minority students are more likely to plan to attend college and indeed attend it. Evidence indicates a steady downward drift in post secondary plans from grade 8 through grade 12 among public school students. However, data suggest a slight increase among Catholic high school students in educational aspirations over the last two years of high school. In grade 8, 70.9% of Catholic elementary school students planned to attend college compared to 52.5% of public school students. By grade 12, Catholic school student college expectations remained at 65.5%, while public school student college plans shrunk to 41.4%. Since the percentage of those in Catholic secondary school academic tracks in grade 10 is 71.5% compared to 38% from public schools, evidence supports the contention that Catholic high schools exert institutional influence on their students toward academic achievement and plans which include college after high school. Students with comparable academic and family backgrounds are much more likely to be enrolled in academic tracks if they attend a Catholic high school (Bryk et al., 1993).

Transferring

Transferring from one school to another has effects on post high school aspirations. Students who transfer from Catholic elementary schools to public high schools are moving into a less academically competitive environment, and are much less likely to have college plans at the point of high school entry than their Catholic elementary school counterparts who remain in the Catholic school sector. Their educational ambitions are similar to those of the public school elementary group who attend public high schools. Students who remain in public education for high school and Catholic elementary school students who transfer to public high schools are more likely to attend larger non-selective public schools where the average achievement is considerably below that found in the Catholic sector. These students are more likely to enroll in a general or vocational program and to take considerably more vocational and business courses than students who attend a Catholic high school (Bryk et al., 1993).

In general, students who transfer from a public elementary into a Catholic high school either at the end of eighth grade or during their high school career are more affluent, better prepared academically, and have higher educational aspirations than students who attend a public high school. Students who transfer from public elementary schools to Catholic high schools attend schools whose average sophomore year achievement level is over one half standard deviation higher than the school selected by the Catholic to public transfer group. It is also slightly higher than the average achievement level of high schools chosen by those students continuing in the Catholic sector (Bryk et al., 1993).

The substantially higher tuition charges of Catholic secondary schools as compared to Catholic elementary schools may constitute a barrier to access for students from poor and minority families. Low family discretionary income is a strong deterrent against choosing a Catholic high school for many families. Other factors that predict a transfer to public high school from Catholic elementary school include larger family size and non-Catholic religious status. Factors that influence the decision to attend a Catholic high school include higher parental education and greater educational ambition (Bryk et al., 1993).

Evidence suggests that students who transfer from public elementary schools chose a Catholic high school primarily for academic reasons. These students are more likely to enroll in an academically oriented single sex Catholic school. In this regard the choice of a Catholic secondary school may be viewed as a way of pursuing an option generally unavailable in the public sector; that of a single sex secondary education. There is evidence that lower achieving students in Catholic elementary schools choose to move to a public high school where the academic orientation is less demanding and where there is greater opportunity for enrolling in business and vocational courses (Bryk et al., 1993).

High School Graduation Rates

Data gathered from the NELS on urban minorities, urban Whites, non-urban minorities, and non-urban Whites indicate that Catholic high schools have better graduation rates in communities where public high schools have low graduation rates. Public school graduation rates for urban minorities are low, but the Catholic school graduation rate for urban minorities is actually higher than the rate for public school White students. Ninety-one percent of Black and Hispanic students who attend Catholic secondary schools in urban areas graduate from high school. By contrast 62% of Blacks and Hispanics who attend urban public schools graduate. For urban Whites the Catholic school graduation rate is 87% while the public school graduation rate is 75% (Neal, 1997b). By adjusting for the effects of selection, the probability of high school graduation remains at 62% for Black and Hispanic students in public schools. In urban Catholic schools with the same demographic characteristics as public schools including parents' education, occupation, family structure, and reading materials, the graduation rate is 88% when adjusting for selection. While this percentage is below the non-adjusted rate of 91%, it is far above the public school rate of 62%. Catholic schools increase the probability of graduation from high school by 26%. The effects of Catholic school on urban White graduation rates are positive but smaller than those experienced by minority students. The public school graduation rate among Whites was found to be 75%. When the same type of students attended a Catholic school, the rate rose to 85% (Neal, 1997b).

The fact that Catholic school students remain in school longer than public school counterparts indicates a brighter future for them. Because they are more likely to finish high school, Catholic school students are more likely to attend and to complete college. This remains the case even when the effects of family background and home environment are removed (Neal, 1997b).

Dropping Out

Those who drop out of high school suffer severe social consequences. In the past two decades individuals with less than a high school diploma have suffered an absolute decline in real income and dropped further behind individuals of more education. Data from the National Educational Longitudinal Study of 1988 (NELS), followed up in 1990 and 1992, revealed that students who dropped out of school before the tenth grade were highly unlikely to obtain subsequent education, including a high school equivalency degree (Teachman, Paasch, & Carver, 1996). Variables including family arrangement, divorce-separation, and stepparent or additional partner, attendance at Catholic school, and changing schools were examined. Results indicated that children who attend Catholic schools have greater access to social capital than those who do not. Children in Catholic schools are more likely to have parents who know the parents of their closest friends, are more concerned with their schools, experience more parent-child interaction, and are less likely to have changed schools. This pattern of effects demonstrates a considerable stability of relationships experienced by these students. Evidence suggests that attendance at a Catholic school and living with both biological parents is associated with additional social capital possessed by the child. For a child who attends a Catholic school, the odds of dropping out of school are reduced by 45% (Teachman, Paasch, & Carver, 1996). The number of times a child changes schools is related to dropping out of school; each additional change of schools is associated with a 34% increase in the likelihood of dropping out of school. Children who come from families with greater parental financial resources are less likely to drop out of school. There is a strong positive relationship between attending a Catholic school and a parent's and a school's connectivity and thus, a reduced likelihood of dropping out. Families that send their children to Catholic schools connect quite closely with the school (Teachman, Paasch, & Carver, 1996).

Adolescents from families with incomes in the bottom 20% of the income distribution are six times more likely to drop out than adolescents from families in the top 20% of the income distribution. Latino students are more likely than White students to leave school before graduating and the rate for Black students falls between the two (Ekert & Drago-Severson, 1999).

Catholic high schools have a significant negative effect on the high school dropout rate. This effect is particularly large for Blacks and Hispanics in urban areas. The effect is not so great for White students but still significant (Sander & Krautmann, 1995). While it is reported that 14.4% of students in public schools and 11.9% of students in private schools leave high school between sophomore mid-year and senior mid-year, the rate is 3.4% in Catholic schools (Peterson, Meyers, Howell, & Mayer, 1993). Catholic high school dropout rates are one-fourth of those in public school. Minority students in both Catholic and public high schools are more likely to drop out than White students; however, the dropout rates for minorities in Catholic schools are considerably less. It is reported that 18% of Blacks and 16% of Hispanics who attend public schools drop out compared to 7% and 11% in Catholic schools. The Hispanic dropout rate is 2.5 times the rate for Blacks and 3.5 times the rate for non-Hispanic Whites (Tamara, 1998). Less advantaged students are considerably more likely to leave school early (Bryk et al., 1993). Social class is not as strongly related to dropping out in Catholic schools as in public schools. Not only is the average dropout rate lower in Catholic schools, but the social background of students is also less strongly associated with the likelihood of dropping out before graduating in Catholic schools than in public schools (Bryk et al., 1993; Groome, 1998).

In Summary

Evidence indicates that academic achievement, particularly for minorities, is higher in schools with orderly environments. The academic structure and environment within Catholic schools exerts an influence toward academic pursuits and excellence for all students, and in particular, has a positive effect on minority students. A more equitable social distribution of achievement is associated both with high levels of minority achievement and low differentiation by social class. Research from 1965 to the present day indicates that family background variables such as income, parental educational levels, and parental educational aspirations are less important in the academic achievement of minority students in Catholic schools than they are in public schools. Minority students in Catholic schools are more apt to experience the common school effect where students are more likely to be treated the same rather than treated differently because of their race or background. Such characteristics as intelligence, achievement, motivation, gender, religious affiliation, and race are less related to African American academic achievement in Catholic schools than in public schools. Several school related variables, perhaps acting in concert, seem to contribute significantly to the academic achievement of African American and minority students in Catholic schools. Researchers have continually discounted the selection effect in their work by controlling for variables and comparing students, schools, and families in similar situations. Viewed as a whole, the work of Coleman and his colleagues (Coleman et al., 1982) and the subsequent research by other scholars indicates that on the average minority students in Catholic high schools learn more than public school students with similar backgrounds and ability levels especially in urban areas (Evans & Schwab, 1995; Neal, 1997a). Because Catholic high schools have a much larger proportion of students pursuing academic programs, results showing academic improvement and superior performance should not be surprising. Catholic high schools more equitably distribute achievement among social classes by providing a similar academic program and expectations for all students (Bryk et al., 1993; Irvine & Foster, 1996).

Minority students attending Catholic schools are more likely to have higher career expectations and have a higher probability of finishing high school than those attending public schools. Attending Catholic schools increases the likelihood of minority students planning to attend, attending, and graduating from college. Transferring out of Catholic school to public school reduces career aspirations while transferring into Catholic school raises expectations and likely post high school achievement.

SINGLE SEX CATHOLIC EDUCATION

When secondary education began in the United States, students were ordinarily segregated by sex. The shift to public coeducation from single sex schools in modern times occurred with relatively little or no controversy. Local school boards examined the efficiency of the school system and determined that one school for both boys and girls would save money. Single sex education in Catholic schools is limited almost exclusively to secondary schools since 99.3% of Catholic elementary schools are coeducational (Guerra, 1998). Catholic high schools in the United States were almost entirely single sex schools until after World War II; the movement toward Catholic coeducation began to spread in the 1960s and 1970s as single sex education in high schools and colleges declined. The primary reasons for change were legal, social, and economic. Catholic high schools built during that time were often coeducational or co-institutional, and many single sex schools began accepting students of the opposite sex (Bryk et al., 1993). Title IX Legislation made public single sex schooling virtually extinct (Lee & Marks, 1992). Title IX has probably contributed to the decline of single sex private schools as well.

Single Sex School Advantages

Supporters of single sex education believe that the male-female differences in the timing of physical and cognitive maturation, as well as the differences in the social and moral development of boys and girls indicate that schooling is best tailored to each sex while meeting their unique needs. Researchers have found benefits for both boys and girls in single sex education (Hawley, 1993). Single sex advocates argue that coeducation does not allow for the optimal discipline instruction needed by young males, given their greater tendency to restlessness and aggression. Adolescent boys may be easily distracted by female classmates and are less focused on schoolwork. Males from disadvantaged backgrounds need special attention and focus (Reese & Corrin, 1995; Whitehead, 1994). Single sex schools may facilitate male bonding and optimized character development for both high school and college males (Mael, 1998). However, neither coeducational nor single sex schools are immune from sexism or sexual harassment (Lee, Marks, & Byrd, 1994).

For some families single sex Catholic high schools have a particular attraction. Families from a higher social class with greater financial ability often enroll students in single sex Catholic schools where there is a reputation for a strong academic climate, relatively high levels of fiscal and faculty resources, a perception of teachers of high quality, and a reputation for academic achievement. These schools are more likely to be sponsored by religious orders. Data indicate that families may apply different criteria in selecting a secondary school for boys than they do for girls (Bryk et al., 1993). Families with female students are more likely to be more attracted to a single sex school with a strong religious climate if they have had previous Catholic elementary experience, a sense of personal religiousness, are Catholic, and come from a large family. Boys are somewhat more likely to attend high achieving single sex schools with more affluent classmates and greater faculty resources. The choice of single sex education for girls is made because such a school offers elite socialization and a protective environment for girls where they are allowed to flourish undistracted by boys. The choice of single sex education for boys is made by families who believe that a stronger academic education is their primary concern and that it will be received at a single sex school compared to a coeducational private school (Lee & Marks, 1992).

All boys' Catholic schools tend to enroll the most advantaged students while all girls' Catholic schools the least. Tuition is higher in single sex schools than in coed schools; per pupil expenditures are highest in all boys' schools but lowest in all girls' schools. Generally speaking all boys' Catholic high schools are larger than girls' schools and operate larger classes. Boys' schools tend to pay teachers higher salaries than do girls' schools. All girls' schools are generally smaller, have more favorable student-teacher ratios, and a more intimate personal environment. The emphasis is on academic achievement for boys and a safe social environment for girls. Boys' schools strive for academic and economic efficiency. They focus on delivering an academic program to students in relatively large groups (Bryk et al., 1993).

Single Sex School Climate

Studies find that in coeducational classrooms both men and women teachers pay more attention and give more encouragement to boys than girls. To counterbalance these effects, single sex Catholic schools concentrate their attention in classrooms that are filled with all boys or all girls (The Case, 1997).

It is argued that by separating the sexes in education, certain distracting traits of our culture, such as materialism, drug use and abuse, violence and personal irresponsibility, and a tendency toward abusing other people, play a less central role in the academic life of the school (Riordan, 1994). Regardless of gender, single sex school students are more likely to experience a positive school climate than coeducational students (Min, 1991).

All girls' schools have a strong impact on levels of career commitment and sex role attitude of girls. Both boys and girls at single sex schools are influenced directly in choosing their major areas of study in college and beyond. All girls' schools encourage students to choose more traditionally male oriented majors while all boys' schools may encourage students to enter less male oriented fields. Girls' single sex schools' influence on occupational aspirations for girls may not be as great as for boys. The differences between types of schools in terms of gender composition have more significance for the development of girls than boys (Min, 1991).

Data gathered on all girls' schools indicate that these schools produce more positive outcomes with regard to individual freedom, respect for individuality, caring for a community, and students focused on learning and empowerment. The all girls' school experience gives students invaluable opportunities to develop the competency and connectedness that define their identities and prepare them for the real world (Carstensen, 1999).

The climate in single sex schools has distinctive effects on the girls and boys who attend them. High School and Beyond (HSB) data reveal that girls from single sex schools report more positive schooling experiences, more teacher attention, perceive that teachers pay ample attention to them, and are interested in them. They tend to express more liberal attitudes regarding sex role models and to choose more male oriented fields of study than coeducational girl students. They are more likely to commit to a future career choice while in high school and to display liberal attitudes toward the roles of men and women. They have a higher positive level of self-concept and are inclined to display a stronger internal locus of control. They are more likely to respond that they have control over their actions and their consequences (Min, 1991; Reese & Corrin, 1995).

Girls attending a single sex Catholic school have a significantly higher positive math self-concept compared to those attending a coeducational public school (Fuller, 1997). They tend to assume more leadership responsibilities and functions than girls in coeducational high schools (Fox, 1993; Steinbrecher, 1991).

Single sex school climate plays an important part in the attitude toward science of female students. Females from single sex Catholic settings revealed a greater confidence in science classes and less anxiety. They were less likely to perceive science as male oriented and were more likely to see same sex science teachers as positive role models than were public coeducational students (Cipriani-Sklar, 1996). Higher grade point averages correlate with a positive attitude toward science. Single sex girl students who pursue science come from a school environment that nourishes an internal locus of control, emphasizes individuality over gender, and challenges female students who challenge themselves, to take responsibility for learning, and to be open minded (Sexton, 1991).

Single sex girls' schools encourage students to have more positive relationships with teachers, and to be more visibly active in school affairs than coeducational high schools. They have substantial positive direct influence on the school life of the girls, especially regarding the amount of teacher attention received. Single sex girls' schools tend to reinforce a positive self-concept, good school grades, racial pride, and support for the type of school (Min, 1991).

Indirect academic benefits for girls include a greater likelihood of single sex peers pursuing serious academic and leadership roles with more opportunity to receive instruction from accomplished female teachers and role models. Single sex schools may reduce some of the distractions of sexual attention for adolescent boys and girls, concerns over sexual harassment, and the limitations imposed on leadership roles for females in coeducational schools (Mael, 1998).

Boys at all boys' Catholic schools experience a more positive and active social life, receive positive attention from teachers, and are more likely to be actively involved in school programs. They are more likely to be devoted to the importance of family, display liberal attitudes toward sex roles, express a positive self-concept, and have an internal locus of control compared to coeducational counterparts in public schools. They are more likely to choose occupations with higher prestige than are boys from coeducational schools (Min, 1991).

Single Sex Schools and Minority Students

Data from HSB indicate that Catholic all boys' schools have the highest minority enrollments and their students are more advantaged than coeducational Catholic school counterparts in terms of social class. Girls in all girls' Catholic schools are generally less advantaged than boys in all boys' schools and are more similar to girls in coeducational Catholic schools. Adjusting for variables such as student background, academic curriculum track, and school social class, research found that girls in all girls' Catholic high schools are more likely to associate with academically oriented peers and to express positive interest in mathematics and English (Bryk et al., 1993).

High-risk minority students may be aided by single sex instruction to help overcome negative environmental forces. Single sex instruction combined with close attention to the individual student had a positive effect on ethnic and racial identity, commitment, and academic development for students. Minority students in single sex schools may receive significantly higher academic grades and test scores (Gordon, 2000; Scott, 1999; Staponska, 1999). Single sex schooling for minority boys has achieved demonstrable benefits that have been replicated (Mael, 1998; Sander & Krautmann, 1995).

Public school advocates have promoted single sex education for minority students, both male and female, as a way of overcoming problems inherent in inner city education. These proposals are often subject to strong objections because they seem to give up the goal of racial desegregation and because they violate Title IX. Commentators acknowledge the value of single sex public education and would like to see programs that allow single sex education to proceed (Fox-Genovesse & Podles, 1995). They are aware of the objections raised by those who might use single sex education as a regression, a loss of civil rights, and de facto discrimination. Public sector efforts to provide single sex schooling and gain its benefits have been conducted on the west coast, the east coast, and in some states in between. Because of disagreement and objections the public sector may not make a significant contribution to single sex education (Fox-Genovese & Podles, 1995). The issue of whether coeducation reduces gender stereotypes or fosters gender confusion is a central point of contention between coeducation and single sex advocates (Fox-Genovese, 1994; Lee, Marks, & Byrd, 1994).

Academic Achievements

Using HSB data, it was found that attending single sex schools positively affects academic achievement. Every one of the statistically significant effects on academic achievement favored single sex schools. Positive boys' single sex school effects are largest in sophomore year and are somewhat diminished by senior year. Girls in all girls' schools receive an academic benefit that increases in size from sophomore to senior year. Gains in reading and science achievement are statistically significant for girls in single sex schools. The all girls' effects on academic achievement stand out, since these students are not taking more academic courses than girls in coed Catholic schools (Bryk et al., 1993; Min, 1991).

Girls in single sex schools do more homework and enroll in more academic courses than in coed schools. Boys enroll in more math and science courses than in coed schools (Min, 1991). Academically, students in single sex Catholic schools spend significantly more time on homework than in coed Catholic schools, and this is especially true for girls. Boys in all boys' Catholic schools are less likely than boys in coed Catholic schools to enroll in vocational classes. Girls take slightly more vocational offerings and social science courses than their coed counterparts (Bryk et al., 1993).

The effects produced by single sex schools do not depend on school resources but on the atmosphere at a single sex school and student enrollment in academic courses. Students in both Catholic all boys' and all girls' schools rate the schools and the quality of teaching more positively than students in Catholic coeducational high schools. Single sex schools may produce positive environments for learning as well as positive environments for teaching—two factors that are closely intertwined (Bryk et al., 1993).

Attendance at an all girls' Catholic high school doubles the learning in science for Catholic school girls over the course of their junior and senior years. While girls in coed Catholic schools are making two years of progress, their single sex counterparts are making four. Evidence gathered coupled with field observations provides strong support for a conclusion that there are significant academic outcome differences favoring attendance in single sex schools. These effects are especially pervasive for girls. While there are positive effects for all boys' schools, the evidence does not show as strong an effect as it does for girls (Bryk et al., 1993).

Mathematics comparisons are often used as a more easily evaluated discipline with regard to male and female differences and single sex and coeducational school differences. Data revealed that there are imbalances in classrooms in which traditionally male disciplines such as math, science, and mechanics are taught. High school age females may not hold intrinsically negative attitudes toward math; rather male students and teachers may convey to their female classmates and students their stereotypic view that math is unfeminine. At the same time, some single sex schools for females are not immune to promoting stereotypic female limitations in some subject areas (Lee et al., 1994).

HSB data for Catholic single sex high schools which are predominantly White show that female students do better academically than in coeducational schools. In Catholic schools that have a large minority population, both sexes do better with single sex education (Riordan, 1993). The greatest gains in single sex schooling occurred with Hispanic and African American males and females. In coeducational classrooms the differences between male and female performance appear first during high school. Females participate less than males in coeducational science, math, and calculus classrooms (Meece & Eccles, 1993). Differentiation by gender becomes a fact of the coeducational classroom.

Contrary to previously discussed research, LePore and Warren (1997), using NELS Data, found that boys who attend single sex Catholic high schools had slightly higher achievement test scores than boys in coed Catholic high schools, although the differences were not always statistically significant. However, girls in single sex and coed Catholic schools had roughly equivalent scores in achievement tests. Data showed no significant differences in gain scores between single sex and coeducational high school students over a high school career. They also found no significant differences in locus of control and self-esteem between single sex and coeducational schools. They observed no such academic achievement superiority in all girls' schools found in other research and found no positive statistically significant effects of attending single sex schools. Although single sex school boys had higher achievement test scores in grades 8, 10, and 12 than boys in coeducational Catholic schools, they found no positive achievement test score improvement for girls in single sex schools (LePore & Warren, 1997). Further research in this area may explain the differences in results found by LePore and Warren.

Aspirations and Affective Outcomes

In the areas of educational aspirations, locus of control, self-concept, and sex role attitudes, research found that these effects generally favored single sex schools with a more significant level of effects occurring for students in all girls' schools. The effect of an all girls' school on the educational aspirations of its students is significant at sophomore year and grows until senior year. Female school students also display a more positive outcome with regard to locus of control and self-concept, outcomes not found to the same degree in boys' schools. When measuring students' views about women's roles in society, girls' school students were considerably less likely to show stereotypical sex role attitudes than girls in coed schools. From sophomore to senior year, girls show a decline in stereotyping about women's roles. Boys in all boys' schools hold a slightly more sex stereotypical view than coed school boys, but the difference disappears by senior year. Sexual stereotyping attitudes are not necessarily an outcome of an all male environment in a Catholic school (Bryk et al., 1993).

Affectively, boys in single sex schools who aspire to higher-level occupations are inclined to be less devoted to family. Those who hold the importance of family in high regard are more likely to express traditional attitudes toward sex roles. Those with higher socioeconomic status and higher grades are more inclined to be positive toward themselves. Boys with higher grades were more likely to have a strong internal locus of control. Those who have taken more advanced math and science courses and received positive attention from teachers, are more likely to express strong career aspirations, family commitment, a positive self-concept, and an internal locus of control (Min, 1991).

Attendance at a single sex high school has long-term positive effects, which are stronger for graduates of girls' schools. Graduates from single sex boys' and girls' schools continue to have higher educational aspirations and attend more selective colleges. Graduates from all girls' Catholic high schools have more integrated attitudes toward sexual stereotyping, are more likely to be involved in college activities, and are satisfied with their college experiences (Bryk et al., 1993). Both boy and girl graduates from single sex high schools were very likely to have plans for attending graduate school. Generally, the results of single sex education appear more positive for girls than boys. The young women in a single sex high school may be more aware of their full human potential in an atmosphere free of the social pressure they would experience in a coed high school. Academic attitudes and behaviors, as well as high achievement in Catholic single sex schools, is accompanied by very positive reports from students about their schools (Bryk et al., 1993).

IN SUMMARY

In summary, most research indicates important positive effects for single sex Catholic schools according to a variety of criteria. Academic achievement in specific areas, continued gains in academic achievement over a high school career, future educational plans and aspirations, affective measures such as locus of control and self-concept, and sex role stereotyping all seem to receive specific positive advantages in single sex schools. The effect of the single sex organization is the most plausible explanation for the observed success of single sex education (Bryk et al., 1993). The effects appear to be more pronounced for females than for males (Moore, Piper, & Schaefer, 1993).

The majority of research studies on single sex education are concerned with the academic and socio-emotional benefits of single sex schools for women. Discussion about the values of single sex schools benefiting males have either received less attention and support or have been insufficient to override resistance to what critics perceive as preserves of male dominance (Mael, 1998).

---

[1] The editors are aware of the ongoing debate surrounding the use of the terms Latino and Hispanic and have chosen to use the term adopted by the author of the original source.

TEACHING
AND LEARNING

CHAPTER 8

GIFTED EDUCATION IN CATHOLIC SCHOOLS

LESLIE S. REBHORN

Few programs for gifted and talented students in Catholic schools are described in the professional literature. However, those programs for which descriptions have been published represent a wide variety of effective and creative approaches to serving the academic needs of gifted and talented students. Unfortunately, research results have been published on only a small fraction of the programs that exist. Research on best practices in gifted education provides guidance for schools seeking to develop or modify programs for these learners, and much of that research is applicable to Catholic schools. This chapter will summarize published research on gifted education in Catholic schools, and will highlight additional research findings that can inform educators seeking to establish programs for gifted learners.

THE CURRENT STATUS OF GIFTED EDUCATION IN CATHOLIC SCHOOLS

The National Research Center on the Gifted and Talented (NRC/GT) conducted a national survey (Archambault, Westberg, & Brown, 1992) of over 7,000 third- and fourth-grade teachers, of whom almost 1,000 were teachers in private, predominantly church-related, schools. The study was replicated in Australia (Whitton, 1997) with another 400 teachers, of whom 138 taught in Catholic schools. The survey "was designed to determine the extent to which gifted and talented students are receiving differential education in the regular classroom setting" (Archambault et al., 1992, p. 2). The findings were the same for all types of schools across both countries and in all types of communities: "Third and fourth grade teachers make only minor modifications in the regular curriculum to meet the needs of gifted students" (Archambault et al., 1992, p. 2; Whitton, 1997, p. 38). The results of this comprehensive survey challenge educators in all schools to better address the academic needs of these learners.

Kelzenberg (1993) surveyed the 103 Catholic elementary schools in the Archdiocese of Saint Paul-Minneapolis to determine the range and scope of programs for the gifted, and to obtain information about the characteristics of those programs. Findings from the survey indicated that only one-third of the schools that responded to the survey provided specific programs for gifted and talented learners, and that only one-third of the schools that provided programs also effectively planned and evaluated the provisions. The programs incorporated a variety of provisions: several schools offered gifted students opportunities to work in homogeneous groups on projects for science fairs, creative writing, spelling and geography bees, and special art courses; other schools supported forms of acceleration, such as grade-skipping or telescoping in reading and mathematics. Other provisions included independent study opportunities, and "pull-out" programs in thinking skills or in specific content areas.

For schools with gifted programs, Kelzenberg (1993) found that administrative leadership was perceived as important to program maintenance, and that teacher nomination was the identification procedure most commonly utilized. The survey further revealed that enrichment opportunities provided for all students were considered by many schools to be sufficient for gifted learners, and that budget constraints were perceived as the major obstacle to providing programs for gifted and talented students.

Wojcikewych (1996) described a full-time program, a Catholic day school for 130 academically gifted fourth through eighth-graders. The Father Sweeney School for the Academically Gifted Child, in Peoria, Illinois, challenges its students to "think creatively, critically and independently at an accelerated rate" (p. 68). Provisions of the school include departmentalized subject areas, foreign language instruction, and cross-disciplinary teaching.

Leroux (1990, 1992) documented a program pairing gifted high school students with community mentors. Students from St. Paul's Catholic High School in Ottawa, Ontario, were released from regular classes to attend a special class in which they developed plans for independent projects, received skills training, and investigated methodologies related to their projects. Several teachers at the school helped identify community mentors in the areas of the students' interests. The students and mentors worked together during after-school hours, often for periods of several months. At the end of the school year, the students presented their products to a panel composed of several administrators, school consultants, community mentors, and a university professor. The program was deemed so successful that it was expanded to other nearby Catholic high schools, and attracted additional community and university mentors and sponsoring agencies.

Sherman (1984) described a biochemistry course she developed for high ability secondary students. The author taught the senior-level honors course at Ursuline Academy, a private Catholic college-preparatory high school for young women in St. Louis, Missouri. The course encompassed demanding topics and experiments, featured frequent field trips, and utilized high-level reading materials and resources, including college laboratory manuals.

Beyond the classroom, media specialists writing in *Catholic Library World* have expressed interest in meeting the learning needs of gifted and talented students (Margrabe, 1978; Stockton & DuChateau, 1984). Margrabe (1978) identified six goals for involving the Library Media Center (LMC) in the school's total curriculum; third on her list was "to identify and stimulate gifted and talented students not otherwise recognized outside the LMC, or to enrich those already identified" (p. 283). Margrabe (1978) suggested several ways for media specialists to work with gifted students. Stockton and DuChateau (1984) addressed various aspects of working with gifted students, including guidelines for recognizing them if they are not formally identified for a special program, recommendations for appropriate literature and materials, and suggestions for teaching research techniques.

Research on Gifted Programs in Catholic Schools

McClelland (1989) compared motivational and strategy variables in achieving and underachieving gifted students in sixth through ninth grades in the Edmonton (Alberta, Canada) Catholic School System. The research was not conducted on the school programs, but rather focused on attributes of the students themselves, and revealed qualitative differences in the motives and strategies employed by the two groups of gifted learners.

Hughes (1984) similarly studied attributes of gifted students, investigating the relationship between gifted girls' attitudes toward traditionally defined feminine roles and aspirations toward math-related careers. The sample consisted of gifted children in grades four through seven, in five Catholic elementary schools in the diocese of Brooklyn, New York. Hughes noted a decline in the number of girls, but not boys, identified as gifted after the fifth grade; she recommended further investigation of the phenomena, and also suggested that math curricula be enriched in order to encourage gifted girls' career awareness in that area.

Leroux has investigated academic and social development (Leroux, 1997) and self-concept (Wright & Leroux, 1997) in gifted adolescents grouped together for instruction at a French Catholic secondary school in Ottawa, Ontario, Canada. Leroux's results provide insight into the perceptions of the students regarding grouping and labeling, and useful observations regarding the effectiveness of various teaching styles and strategies.

Casey, Casiello, Gruca-Peal, and Johnson (1995) employed several interventions designed to raise student achievement in heterogeneous classrooms in a secondary parochial school for girls. The interventions included "integrated use of cooperative grouping techniques, the implementation and monitoring of student goals, and the development of student awareness of the intelligent behaviors concept" (Casey et al., 1995, p. i). Student achievement increased across all classes for students of lower ability, and increased in three of four classes for students of average or high ability.

Rizza (1997) also studied academically talented female adolescents; she conducted a qualitative analysis of girls' experiences in classrooms and girls' perceptions of the factors associated with learning. Of the sample of 20 gifted eleventh graders, half were students at a single-sex Catholic high school, and half attended a public coeducational high school. Through interviews and observations, Rizza (1997) discovered that "the participants from both sites had many common characteristics and behavior patterns associated with learning and perceptions leading to success" (p. 168). She also found "several subtle differences . . . related to the school environments" (p. 168), including aspects of academics, such as required courses, selection of courses, grades, and test scores; students' access to services such as guidance; and the perception of community at the two schools, "evident in the extracurricular activities and amount of interaction between students and teachers" (p. 168).

Cooper (1993) evaluated aspects of a summer enrichment program for gifted students in grades three through six from Catholic schools across the Diocese of Dallas, Texas. The program, the DeBusk Enrichment Center for Academically Talented Students (DECATS), debuted in the summer of 1990, and Cooper made it the focus of her doctoral dissertation several years later. Via survey, she collected evaluation data from students, parents, and teachers on the academic environment, development of thinking and learning skills, leadership development, environment and community, spiritual development, parent and student services, and overall program. While some opportunities for improvement—such as strengthening the guidance component—were revealed by the survey, the majority of the data indicated that the program did an excellent job of attaining its goals and meeting a variety of needs of the students and parents.

Research-Based Recommendations for Gifted Education Programs

Research on effective methods of responding to gifted students has pointed to a variety of strategies available to schools, including ability grouping, acceleration, curriculum compacting, Talent Searches, and various programming arrangements.

Shore, Cornell, Robinson, and Ward (1991) analyzed recommended practices in the field of gifted education, and grouped the 101 practices they located into categories, including "advocacy and administration," "identification and assessment," and "curricular and program policies." The authors further stratified the practices into seven levels according to the strength of research evidence supporting them. The levels ranged widely—the top two levels were described as having either "good" or "some" research support for the practices, as well as indication that appropriate differentiation for gifted learners was also associated with each practice assigned to those levels; the bottom three levels were described as "recommended practices applicable to all children," "recommended practices for which there is some evidence that they are inappropriate," and "a recommended practice strongly refuted." The research results pertaining to each recommended practice were reviewed and critically discussed, with subsections for each practice describing current knowledge, implications for action, and needed research. The book provided thorough and comprehensive analysis of research on, and implications for, aspects of gifted programming.

Recommended practices (Shore et al., 1991) in the category of "curricular and program policies" that enjoyed either strong or some research support were:

- Acceleration should be used.
- Include career education, especially for girls.
- Intervention should be adapted to levels of giftedness.
- Ability grouping is appropriate.
- Stress affective as well as cognitive growth.
- Materials should be high in quality and reading level, require complex verbal responses, and avoid repetition.
- Provide a qualitatively different curriculum, at least part-time.
- Take learning styles into account.
- Employ professional end-products as standards. (pp. 280-281)

Delcourt, Loyd, Cornell, and Goldberg (1994) investigated the effects of a variety of programming arrangements on learning outcomes for elementary students. Over 1,000 students in 14 school districts in 10 states participated in the study over a two-year period. Four popular types of programming arrangements—within-class, pull-out, separate class, and special school—were compared for effects on academic and affective development. Regarding achievement, the researchers concluded that gifted students who attended special programs performed better than gifted students who were not placed in special programs: "Specifically, children in Special Schools, Separate Class programs, and Pull-Out programs for the gifted showed substantially higher levels of achievement than both their gifted peers not in programs and those attending Within-Class programs" (p. vii). The researchers hypothesized that this outcome might be due to the relationship between the programs' content and the focus of the assessment instrument: "With Special School and Separate Class programs traditionally emphasizing academics, it is important to note that the Pull-Out programs in this study also had a strong academic orientation" (p. xiii).

In terms of affective development, students who spent more time with gifted peers (students in separate classes or special schools) had lower perceptions of their own academic abilities than did students who spent more time in heterogeneous classes (gifted students in the comparison group and gifted students in pull-out or within-class programs). Delcourt et al. (1994) noted, "this is an appropriate outcome based on social comparison theory" (p. xiv).

Acceleration

Acceleration is frequently mentioned in the professional literature (Assouline, Colangelo, Lupkowski-Shoplik, & Lipscomb, 1998; Feldhusen, Proctor, & Black, 1986; Proctor, Black, & Feldhusen, 1986; Rogers, 1991a; Southern & Jones, 1991) as an effective response to gifted learners. Acceleration takes a plethora of forms, including early admission to school, accelerating in a content area, grade skipping, radical acceleration of two or more years, and early admission to college. It is one of the "strongly supported practices" critically reviewed by Shore, Cornell, Robinson, and Ward (1991). Southern and Jones (1991) edited a comprehensive review of the research, practices, and issues related to acceleration.

Proctor, Black, and Feldhusen (1986) reviewed 21 studies on early admission of selected children to elementary school. Studies comparing the accelerants with their older classmates "consistently report data favorable to early admission" (p. 71). Studies that matched early entrants with similarly able peers that did not start school until the following year "suggest that the early entrants gained a year without apparent harm. Further, delaying school entrance of a child who is able and ready may result in negative consequences" (p. 72). The authors also generated guidelines for grade advancement of able children (Feldhusen, Proctor, & Black, 1986), based on their review of the research.

A few years later, Rogers (1991a) conducted a "best-evidence synthesis," examining the results of 314 studies on acceleration; Rogers grouped the studies into 12 categories that included early entrance, grade skipping, subject acceleration, concurrent enrollment (in high school and college), and early admission to college. Rogers noted that the outcomes of acceleration vary among the options, indicating that schools and families should continue to make decisions on an individual basis, considering the nature of the child and matching individual characteristics and needs with specific options. Rogers also concluded that none of the various types of acceleration had negative academic, social, or emotional impact, and that most forms of acceleration led to positive academic outcomes (Rogers, 1991a).

Guidelines for acceleration, specifically whole-grade skipping in the years between kindergarten and eighth grade, have been proposed and formalized in a research-based instrument entitled the *Iowa Acceleration Scale* (IAS) (Assouline et al., 1998). The IAS form and manual were designed for use by educators and parents working together, with student input. The IAS guides the group through collection of data, and analysis and weighting of important variables. Use of the *Scale* yields documentation of the student's strengths and areas of concerns, and a numerical end-product to inform the decision about acceleration.

ABILITY GROUPING

Ability grouping is another type of response to the different needs of learners in a heterogeneous setting. In recent years, issues surrounding ability grouping have been raised amid much controversy. Like acceleration, ability grouping is one of the recommended practices for gifted education that enjoys good research support (Shore et al., 1991), but ability grouping can also encompass other practices that ranked high on that list, such as "intervention should be adapted to levels of giftedness" and "provide a qualitatively different curriculum, at least part-time" (p. 280). Grouping practices have been the focus of two extensive reviews and analyses of research (Kulik, 1992; Rogers, 1991b) commissioned by the National Research Center on the Gifted and Talented (NRC/GT).[1] Findings from these meticulous analyses are reproduced here at some length, due both to the strong research base that supports the findings, and to the wide applicability of the findings to schools desiring to meet the needs of highly able learners.

Kulik (1992) analyzed 127 studies on five types of ability grouping—XYZ grouping, within-class grouping, cross-grade grouping, accelerated classes for gifted students, and enrichment classes for gifted learners. Descriptions of the five types of grouping arrangements vary, as do their effects on student achievement. Kulik (1992) noted that the effects of the various grouping arrangements depend on program features, especially the extent to which curriculum is adjusted to fit the needs of the learners. As part of Kulik's systematic approach, the effect sizes for each study were coded, as were selected features of each study, such as methodological characteristics, and program characteristics.

XYZ grouping refers to the practice of assigning students to instructional groups—high, middle, and low—by test scores and other school records. All three groups cover the same curriculum. Kulik (1992) concluded that:

> Pupils in middle and lower classes in XYZ programs learn the same amount as equivalent pupils do in mixed classes. Students in the top classes in XYZ programs outperform equivalent pupils from mixed classes by about one month on a grade-equivalent scale. Self-esteem of lower aptitude students rises slightly and self-esteem of higher aptitude students drops slightly in XYZ classes. (p. vii)

In contrast to XYZ programs, cross-grade and within-class grouping arrangements provide students of different ability with different curricula. Cross-grade grouping refers to the practice of separating children in several grade levels into a larger number of instructional groups, crossing grade levels to mix students of similar ability for instruction in a particular subject. As an example, Kulik (1992) described the Joplin plan, which originated in Joplin, Missouri, during the 1950s: "During the hour reserved for reading in the Joplin schools, children in Grades 4, 5, and 6 broke into nine different groups that were reading at anything from the Grade 2 to Grade 9 level" (p. xii). Within-class grouping refers to creating ability-level groups within a single class:

> A teacher…would use test scores and school records to divide her class into three groups for their arithmetic lessons, and she would use textbook material from several grade levels to instruct the groups….The teacher would present material to one group for approximately 15 minutes before moving on to another group. (Kulik, 1992, p. xii-xiii)

Both of these grouping arrangements can be effective:

> The average gain attributable to cross-grade or within-class grouping was between 2 and 3 months on a grade-equivalent scale. The typical pupil in a mixed-ability class might gain 1.0 year on a grade-equivalent scale in a year, whereas the typical pupil in a cross-grade or within-class program would gain 1.2 to 1.3 years. Effects were similar for high, middle, and low aptitude pupils. (Kulik, 1992, p. xiii)

Accelerated classes typically offer bright students the opportunity to cover material at a faster pace than they would in a mixed-ability class. Kulik (1992) analyzed the results of 23 studies on acceleration:

> All of the studies examined moderate acceleration of a whole class of students rather than acceleration of individual children. In each of the comparisons involving students who were initially equivalent in age and intelligence, the accelerates outperformed the nonaccelerates. In the typical study, the average superiority for the accelerates was nearly one year on a grade-equivalent scale of a standardized achievement test. (p. xiv)

Kulik's meta-analysis on grouping arrangements also included 25 studies of enrichment classes for gifted students. Kulik (1992) found that

> In the average study, students in the enriched classes outperformed equivalent students in mixed classes by about 4 to 5 months. Children receiving enriched instruction gained 1.4 to 1.5 years on a grade-equivalent scale in the same period during which equivalent control children gained only 1.0 year. (p. xiv)

Guidelines from Meta-Analytic Studies of Ability Grouping

Following the analysis of the results of the research on ability grouping, Kulik (1992) offered guidelines, and related research support, gleaned from the meta-analysis.

Guideline 1: Although some school programs that group children by ability have only small effects, other grouping programs help children a great deal. Schools should therefore resist calls for the wholesale elimination of ability grouping.

Research support: The effect of a grouping program depends on its features. It is important to distinguish among programs that (a) make curricular and other adjustments for the special needs of highly talented learners, (b) make curricular adjustments for several ability groups at a grade level, and (c) provide the same curriculum for all ability groups in a grade.

Guideline 2: Highly talented youngsters profit greatly from work in accelerated classes. Schools should therefore try to maintain programs of accelerated work.

Research support: Talented students from accelerated classes outperform nonaccelerates of the same age and IQ by almost one full year on the grade-equivalent scales of standardized achievement tests.

Guideline 3: Highly talented youngsters also profit greatly from an enriched curriculum designed to broaden and deepen their learning. Schools should therefore try to maintain programs of enrichment.

Research support: Talented students from enriched classes outperform control students from conventional classes by 4 to 5 months on grade-equivalent scales.

Guideline 4: Bright, average, and slow youngsters profit from grouping programs that adjust the curriculum to the aptitude levels of the groups. Schools should try to use ability grouping in this way.

Research support: Cross-grade and within-class programs are examples of programs that provide both grouping and curricular adjustment. Children from such grouping programs outperform control children from mixed classes by 2 to 3 months on grade-equivalent scales.

Guideline 5: Benefits are slight from programs that group children by ability but prescribe common curricular experiences for all ability groups. Schools should not expect student achievement to change dramatically with either establishment or elimination of such programs.

Research support: In XYZ grouping, all ability groups follow the same course of study. Middle and lower ability students learn the same amount in schools with and without XYZ classes. Higher ability students in schools with XYZ classes outperform equivalent students from mixed classes by about one month on a grade-equivalent scale.

Ability Grouping for Enrichment

Rogers (1991b) also addressed the issue of ability grouping in her analysis of 13 previous syntheses of research covering ability grouping for enrichment, cooperative learning for regular instruction, and grouping for acceleration. Her analysis produced conclusions specific to each area, as well as recommendations for ability grouping involving gifted students.

Across the five meta-analyses, the two best-evidence syntheses, and one ethnographic research synthesis, the following conclusions can be drawn:

1. While full-time ability grouping (tracking) for regular instruction makes no discernible difference in the academic achievement of average and low ability students, it does produce substantial academic gains for gifted students enrolled full-time in special programs for the gifted and talented.

2. High ability student groups have more extensive plans to attend college and are more likely to enroll in college, but the research has not been able to substantiate that grouping directly influences this. Likewise, research has not been able to substantiate that there are marked differences in the quality of teachers who work with high ability students or in the instructional strategies and learning time apportioned in such classes. It is probable that the substantial gains in achievement reported for gifted and talented students in six of the eight research syntheses is produced by the interaction of greater degrees of learning potential, teachers who are interested in their students and in their subject, and the willingness of gifted students to learn while in a classroom with other interested, high ability learners.

3. Ability grouping for enrichment, especially when enrichment is part of a within-class ability grouping practice or as a pullout program, produces substantial academic gains in general achievement, critical thinking, and creativity for the gifted and talented learner.

4. Ability grouping, whether for regular instruction or enrichment purposes, has little impact on gifted students' self-esteem. When full-time grouping is initiated, there is a slight decrease in self-esteem, but in special programs for gifted students, there are no changes in self-esteem. Enrichment pullout programs show only a small but positive increase in self-esteem.

5. Ability grouping for the gifted produces a moderate improvement in attitude toward the subjects in which students are grouped. A moderate improvement in attitude toward subject has been found for all ability levels when homogeneously grouped on a full-time basis.

6. Ability grouping is not synonymous with "tracking." It may take many forms beneficial to gifted learners, including full-time enrollment in special programs or classrooms for the gifted, regrouping for special subject instruction, cross-grade grouping for specific subjects or for the entire school curriculum, pullout groups for enrichment, and within-class ability grouping, as well as cluster grouping. The major benefit of each grouping strategy for students who are gifted and talented is its provision of the format for enriching or accelerating the curriculum they are offered. It is unlikely that grouping itself causes academic gains; rather, what goes on in the group does.

Cooperative Learning for Regular Instruction

Across the two major meta-analyses and one best-evidence synthesis on the academic and nonacademic effects of mixed ability cooperative grouping, the following conclusions may be drawn:

1. Cooperative learning in mixed-ability groups for regular instruction cannot be shown to be academically beneficial for gifted and talented learners. Likewise, there is no research below the college level to support cooperative learning in like-ability groups for gifted students.

2. Although there is some evidence to support sizable academic effects for those forms of cooperative learning that incorporate individual task accountability, little research has been reported which would allow this to be extrapolated to the gifted population.

3. Although there is some evidence to support sizable affective outcomes for mixed ability cooperative learning, particularly for the acceptance of culturally diverse and academically handicapped students, no research has been reported which would allow this to be extrapolated to the gifted population.

Grouping for Acceleration

Across the one meta-analysis and one best-evidence synthesis on accelerative practices for gifted students, the following conclusions about grouping for acceleration can be drawn:

1. Grouping for the acceleration of curriculum for gifted students produced substantial academic gains for the forms of Nongraded Classrooms, Curriculum Compression (Compacting), Grade Telescoping (Rapid Progression at Junior or Senior High), Subject Acceleration, and Early Admission to College. Advanced Placement programs were found to produce moderate, nearly significant academic gains as well.

2. Those forms of acceleration for which groups of gifted learners may be involved do not appear to have a direct impact on self-esteem, either positively or negatively. It is apparent that a host of other environmental, personological, and academic variables are more directly involved with changes in self-esteem.

Recommendations for Practices Involving Ability Grouping

Based on conclusions drawn from the research syntheses, the following guidelines are offered for educators who are considering various grouping options for gifted students.

Guideline One: Students who are academically or intellectually gifted and talented should spend the majority of their school day with others of similar abilities and interests.

Discussion: What forms this option may take are open—both general intellectual ability grouping programs (such as School Within a School, Gifted Magnet Schools, Full-time Gifted Programs, or Gifted Classrooms) and full-time grouping for special academic ability (such as Magnet Schools) have produced marked academic achievement gains as well as moderate increases in attitude toward the subjects in which these students are grouped.

Guideline Two: The Cluster Grouping of a small number of students, either intellectually gifted or gifted in a similar academic domain, within an otherwise heterogeneously grouped classroom can be considered when schools cannot support a full-time gifted program (either demographically, economically, or philosophically).

Discussion: The "Cluster Teacher" must, however, be sufficiently trained to work with gifted students, must be given adequate preparation time, and must be willing to devote a proportionate amount of classroom time to the direct provision of learning experiences for the cluster group.

Guideline Three: In the absence of full-time gifted program enrollment, gifted and talented students might be offered specific group instruction across grade levels, according to their individual knowledge acquisition in school subjects, either in conjunction with cluster grouping or in its stead.

Discussion: This "cross-grade grouping" option has been found effective for the gifted and talented in both single subject and full-time programming (i.e., Nongraded Classrooms).

Guideline Four: Students who are gifted and talented should be given experiences involving a variety of appropriate acceleration-based options, which may be offered to gifted students as a group or on an individual basis.

Discussion: It is, of course, important to consider the social and psychological adjustment of each student for whom such options are being considered as well as cognitive capabilities in making the optimal match to the student's needs.

Guideline Five: Students who are gifted and talented should be given experiences which involve various forms of enrichment that extend the regular school curriculum, leading to the more complete development of concepts, principles, and generalizations.

Discussion: This enrichment could be provided within the classroom through numerous curriculum delivery models currently used in the field, or in the form of enrichment pullout programs.

Guideline Six: Mixed-ability Cooperative Learning should be used sparingly for students who are gifted and talented, perhaps only for social skills development programs.

Discussion: Until evidence is accumulated that this form of Cooperative Learning provides academic outcomes similar or superior to the various forms of ability grouping, it is important to continue with the grouping practices that are supported by research.

Curriculum Compacting

Curriculum compacting refers to the practice of assessing how much of the curriculum to be taught in a given year has already been mastered by students, and replacing it with more appropriate or more challenging material (Reis, Burns, & Renzulli, 1992). This technique is useful for classroom teachers who use it to better meet the academic needs of gifted learners. The NRC/GT conducted research (Reis, 1992) to "examine the effects of staff development on elementary teachers' ability and willingness to implement" (p. 4) this strategy. Some of the findings from this study (Reis, 1992) are as follows:

- Ninety-five percent of the teachers were able to identify high ability students in their classes and document students' strengths.
- Approximately 40-50% of traditional classroom material was compacted for selected students in one or more content areas in mathematics, language arts, science and social studies.
- When teachers eliminated as much as 50% of the regular curriculum for gifted students, no differences in the out-of-level post achievement test results between treatment and control groups were found in Reading, Math Computation, Social Studies and Spelling.
- In Math Concepts and Science, all 3 treatment groups scored significantly higher on the out-of-level post test than did the control group whose curriculum was not compacted. (p. 4)

The results of the study have encouraging implications for educators seeking to respond to the learning needs of gifted students.

Talent Search

In the context of gifted education, the term "Talent Search" refers to a multi-step approach to determining a gifted student's level of functioning and then providing appropriate educational opportunities based on that assessment (Assouline & Lupkowski-Shoplik, 1997; Olszewski-Kubilius, 1998b). Typically, all students in a given grade within a school or school district are assessed using the same standardized achievement instrument. For highly able students, the grade-level tests are often inadequate for assessing the students' actual level of achievement—students who score near the top on such batteries might score even higher if the assessment instruments included more items at the upper levels. An analogous situation would be if the reader were to respond to the item, "What is 2 + 2?" The reader would no doubt respond correctly, but the "test" certainly did not tap the extent of the reader's knowledge of mathematics, and would not be useful in prescribing an appropriate placement or level of challenge for mathematics work. Gifted students encounter the same phenomenon when they are assessed using standardized, grade-level achievement tests. The response to this situation, as implemented by the Talent Search approach, is to employ out-of-level tests to more accurately ascertain students' levels of achievement.

Talent Search centers across the United States serve all 50 states, and offer individual students access to out-of-level testing as part of the process of determining the student's level and prescribing appropriate educational opportunities. The tests used are designed for students at least two years older than Talent Search participants, and the scores are accompanied by recommendations for interventions within schools and via summer programs offered at colleges and universities across the country.

The Talent Search approach has been used within the field of gifted education for almost 30 years, and has generated much research. Olszewski-Kubilius (1998a) reviewed studies conducted on the validity and effects of Talent Search scores and programs, and concluded that Talent Search scores have been found to "provide a valid indication of level of developed reasoning ability and learning rate within several domains that can be matched to educational programs adjusted for pacing and content" (Olszewski-Kubilius, 1998a, p. 135). She also found that Talent Search scores have high predictive validity for future high school and college achievement, and that students who "partake of special summer or accelerated school programs are more likely to take a more rigorous course of study in high school and attend more selective colleges" (Olszewski-Kubilius, 1998a, p. 134).

OPEN ISSUES

Single-Sex Schools

There is some indication in the literature that single-sex schools (a descriptor that applies to many Catholic secondary schools) may confer academic advantages upon gifted girls (Kerr, 1997; Rimm, 1999). After surveying over 1,000 eminent women on the factors that contributed to their success, Rimm (1999) noted that approximately twice as many of the women studied had attended parochial or private schools, compared with children in the general population. The women surveyed viewed their attendance at single-sex schools as positive. In addition, "approximately 20 percent of the successful women admitted that boys and social life adversely affected their seriousness about school and learning during their middle- and high-school years" (Rimm, 1999, p. 9).

On the other hand, other research has suggested that positive outcomes attributed to single-sex learning environments may in fact be due to other factors. The American Association of University Women (AAUW, 1998) recently released a report that reviewed research pertaining to single-sex education, and concluded that the benefits of such separation are not clear:

> Although research finds that girls tend to view the single-sex classroom as more conducive to learning, and express greater confidence in this environment, research has also demonstrated consistently that girls' math and science achievement, measured by a variety of means, has not shown statistically significant gains in the single-sex classroom. Those studies that investigate girls' achievement in single-sex schools and conclude that school type does not affect outcomes typically ascribe the raw differences in scores to factors such as the selectivity of the school or the socioeconomic advantages of those parents opting for single-sex education. (AAUW, 1998, p. 34)

Still other variables may include class size and school size, quality of teaching, lack of gender bias in teaching, and the nature of the curriculum.

The Development of Gifted Education Programs in Catholic Schools

Some authors have noted a disinclination on the part of Catholic schools to develop programs for gifted and talented students (Campbell & Carney, 1987; Cooper, 1993; Kelzenberg, 1993). Others have urged the promotion of appropriate services for gifted students within Catholic schools (Fiedler, 1985; Hall, 1985; O'Laughlin, 1982). O'Laughlin (1982), describing the future of Catholic schools, envisioned that "programs...for gifted students will become a more prominent part of the curriculum" (p. 324). Fiedler (1985) reported that a needs assessment conducted in the Springfield, Illinois, diocese had indicated that "teachers felt they needed more information and support for the slow learner and the gifted in the classroom" (p. 44).

A strong call for Catholic schools to develop programs for gifted students was issued by Sr. Suzanne Hall (1985), then the Executive Director of the Special Education Department of the National Catholic Educational Association. She served as editor of a brief but comprehensive overview of the practical issues surrounding implementation of appropriate programming for gifted students in Catholic schools. In the booklet, entitled *Challenging Gifted Students in the Catholic School,* Hall (1985) and the other authors addressed program development from a goals-oriented perspective, focusing in turn on the school, the classroom, the student as a person, and the student as a member of a community. A wide array of programming options was presented within a continuum of Catholic educational configurations. Although currently out of print, the publication is worth obtaining for its thorough, practical approach and the wealth of information it contains. The preface likened the need to appropriately educate gifted students to the need for the greater society to "deal creatively and effectively with the pluralism which exists in all facets of our life together," (p. iii) and called this challenge a "truly 'catholic' educational adventure" (p. iii). Educators were urged to accept this challenge on behalf of all students:

> As Catholic educators, we are called to respond to all students. In doing this, we not only affirm the reality of pluralism, but more importantly, we demonstrate that pluralism can, in fact, be dealt with in our Catholic schools. This is in keeping with the teachings of our church which exhort us, as educators, to appreciate and enhance the uniqueness of each person, and thus to challenge each person to the fullest realization of his/her potential. (Hall, 1985, p. iii)

Two years after the publication of Hall's (1985) booklet, Campbell and Carney (1987) described "the failure of Catholic educators to...identify their most gifted and talented students and to provide programs for them" as "the Achilles heel of Catholic education" (p. 24). Campbell and Carney noted that the situation did not result from a lack of gifted students: "Surely Catholic schools have always had more than their share of intelligent, motivated students" (p. 24). The authors attributed the lack of programs to the problems of identification of students and allocation of resources. Kelzenberg (1993) echoed the concern about budget constraints, and further noted that many educators believe that enrichment regularly provided to all students is sufficient to meet the educational needs of gifted learners. Cooper (1993) theorized that concerns about elitism among Catholic educators is another important factor, and reported that gifted education in Catholic schools lacks a national forum:

> The Catholic school system...must address these needs [of gifted students] in the same fashion as must the public sector. Yet, there is no national focus on gifted education within the Catholic system, as evidenced by the fact that no information on Catholic school gifted programs is available in the national data base. (p. 11)

CONCLUSION

This review of research on gifted education programs in Catholic schools reveals that there is ample opportunity for educators to move toward providing challenges for gifted and talented learners. The research on successful gifted education programs in Catholic schools, coupled with research on effective gifted education programs in other settings, provides guidance for educators seeking to establish or enhance such programs. The reader is holding a volume that updates research on Catholic schools presented in the preceding volume, published a decade ago (Convey, 1992). That volume had no chapter on gifted education in Catholic schools; this chapter represents a strong editorial statement regarding the need for such programs. Ten years in the future, in the volume succeeding this one, what will the research tell us about Catholic schools' efforts to challenge gifted learners?

[1]Research for these reports (Kulik, 1991; Rogers, 1991) was supported under the Javits Act Program (Grant No. R206R00001) as administered by the Office of Educational Research and Improvement, U.S. Department of Education. Grantees undertaking such projects are encouraged to express freely their professional judgement. These reports, therefore, do not necessarily represent positions or policies of the Government, and no official endorsement should be inferred.

Portions of these documents have been reproduced within this chapter with the permission of the National Research Center on the Gifted and Talented.

CHAPTER 9
SERVING STUDENTS WITH SPECIAL NEEDS IN CATHOLIC SCHOOLS

H. ROBERTA WEAVER
MARY F. LANDERS

INTRODUCTION

In John Convey's (1992) book, *Catholic Schools Make a Difference,* there was no chapter addressing the education of students with special needs in Catholic schools. That omission may have been because research on the subject is woefully lacking. The review of Catholic special education research literature uncovered only a few dissertations (Burgoon, 1997; Curran, 1984; Depp-Blackett, 1997; Faerber, 1949; Frey, 2000; Meyer, 1998). There were, however, a number of non-research sources that when reviewed, as noted in the reference listing, painted a picture of social-justice oriented Catholic educators who have promoted and provided education for students with disabilities. Two particularly rich resources were Behrmann (1971) and Buetow (1985, 1988).

The purpose of this chapter is to provide an abbreviated historical account with emphasis on the 1980s and 1990s of Catholic education in the United States for students with special needs. Addressed, in particular, are those students with cognitive impairments identified as learning disabilities (LD), including attention deficit disorders (ADD), attention deficit hyperactivity disorders (ADHD), and mild mental retardation (MMR). These populations are referred to as "high incidence," meaning they make up the majority of the individuals identified as disabled in the Individuals with Disabilities Education Act (IDEA 1997), formerly the Education of the Handicapped Act (PL 94-142). These are the students who would most frequently present themselves within Catholic school-aged populations. Many students with learning disabilities, attention deficit disorders, and mild mental retardation appear as any other child of their age group. Their differences are not discovered until they are in an educational setting where they are expected to perform in the same manner as their peers and are unsuccessful. Their disabilities are referred to as "hidden handicaps." These children need specialized instruction and individualized learning strategies if they are to succeed in the general education curriculum.

Catholic school education has been a part of the history of the Church in the United States beginning with missionaries who attempted to establish a school with every parish. Archbishop John Carroll charged parents in 1789 with the responsibility for the religious education of their children. The Third Plenary Council of Baltimore echoed his charge in 1884, as did the National Conference of Catholic Bishops in 1972. The scope of Catholic schooling was broadened by religious communities of women, from schools as avenues to religious life or religious leadership among the affluent laity, to the education of the children of the poor and disadvantaged (Buetow, 1985; Curran, 1984). The Catholic Education Association, now known as the National Catholic Educational Association (NCEA), was formed in 1904 (Buetow, 1985; Curtin, 1999). Evidence of coursework on the education of the mentally retarded was found as early as 1917 at Fordham University (McKillop, 1971). Until the early 1950s, however, Catholic schooling was directed toward individuals without disabilities. Attention to the individual with disabilities was limited to custodial or residential care, not education. As McKillop (1971) states, "Educational efforts of parochial schools, on the one hand, and the residential schools for the handicapped, on the other, developed separately and independently" (p. 34). St. Coletta School, a residential school, opened in 1904, was one of the first educational programs for students with disabilities (Theodore, 1959). As various programs for the education of students with special needs were developed they operated independently of one another. There was no system for coordinating services or sharing resources. The Archdiocese of New York and the Archdiocese of St. Louis were among the few that had "a relatively complex network of such classes as a regular part of the elementary program" (McKillop, 1971, p. 34). The establishment of the NCEA Department of Special Education in 1954 provided the structure and forum for nationally coordinating educational efforts and for addressing the challenge of allowing students with disabilities "to share in the blessings of a Catholic education like their normal (nondisabled) brothers and sisters" (Behrmann, 1971, p. 6). Behrmann's review of the data collected on Catholic special education services indicated that there were progressive special education programs that had been introduced by Catholic special educators. Three of these programs are described as: self-contained classes in parish schools; part-time special education class for basic subjects and part-time regular class for social studies, homeroom, and so forth; and full-time special schools, residential and day, for individuals with disabilities. Hall (1981) pointed out that the challenge of serving students with special needs in Catholic schools evolved slowly. It was not until PL 94-142 in 1975 that the public schools were mandated to serve all students with disabilities. The public schools responded to the federal law. The Catholic sector, on the other hand, had no single official Church body charged with administrative authority to govern (Youniss & Convey, 2000). Catholic schools configured as parish schools, interparish schools, diocesan schools, private religious order affiliated schools, and charter schools, reported to many different masters. However, in 1972, 1978, and 1988, the Bishops did address the education of students with disabilities as Catholics. In 1972 in their pastoral message, *To Teach As Jesus Did,* the Bishops addressed the right of the handicapped (persons with disabilities) to receive religious education as a challenge of the Catholic community (Sacred Congregation, 1972). In 1978 (United States Catholic Conference) in their *Pastoral Statement on Handicapped People*, the bishops reiterated that persons with disabilities should be integrated within the normal Catechetical activities (Bishop, 1995) and 10 years later, on the anniversary of that pastoral statement, again "encouraged conversion of mind and heart so that all persons with disabilities may be invited to worship and to every level of service as full members of the body of Christ" (Perry, 1989, p. 23). The bishops' statements did not go unheeded (Hall, 1979, 1981). Catholic educators during the 1970s began serving students with disabilities in less segregated settings (Hall, 1981).

NCEA LEADERSHIP

The National Catholic Educational Association is the largest private professional association in the world (McDonald, 2000a), but has no formal authority because it is a voluntary association (Horrigan, 1978). The departments within NCEA, therefore, can facilitate the education of students with disabilities in Catholic schools through information dissemination, advocacy, leadership and services.

Department of Special Education

In 1954, 50 years after the founding of NCEA, the Department of Special Education was formally recognized (Behrmann, 1971). The department existed to support the work of dioceses and schools involved in special education—namely, the day schools and residential centers. Children, youth, and young adults with mental retardation and varying levels of Down syndrome made up the largest populations in both day schools and residential settings (A. Dudek, personal communication, June 25, 2001). It offered "professional services to those interested in special education in the form of conventions and institutes, publication of a national

Directory of Catholic facilities in this area, a periodic Newsletter, and consulting services" (Behrmann, 1971, p. 5). Msgr. Behrmann, the executive director of the special education department also authored the first book written on Catholic special education. Father C. Albert Koob, then president of NCEA, in the foreword of the book, commended Behrmann for "professional leadership in a field of human concern, too long overlooked" (Behrmann, 1971, p. vi). Leadership of the department moved to Suzanne Hall, S.N.D.de N. who continued to advocate for Catholic education of students with special needs in the least restrictive environment (Hall, 1979, 1981). By the end of the 1980s, the Special Education Department's newsletter was predicting that the role of special education would change in the next decade and would become more integrated with regular education than it had been in the past (Hall & Dudek, 1987b). In 1986, NCEA surveyed all of its members to determine the effectiveness of the departments and offices. Survey results indicated that the Department of Special Education and two additional offices were significantly underused. As a consequence, the Department of Special Education was closed in 1991 (A. Dudek, personal communication, June 25, 2001).

Department of Elementary Schools

Under Dr. Kealey's leadership as executive director, the department published a statement on appropriate inclusion (NCEA, 1999) suggesting that, "to teach as Jesus did," requires not only acceptance, but also understanding and respect for all students, their parents, and their teachers. Antoinette Dudek, formerly in the Department of Special Education, assumed an advocacy role for students with special needs (DeFiore, 1999) and in 1998 authored the book, *Is There Room for Me?*, giving practical ideas and providing encouragement for Catholic educators striving to serve all Catholic students. As a direct result of Jubilee justice, the *Making Room for Me* seminar series was launched. The first two meetings, in 2000 and 2001, brought together Catholic educators nationwide to share and learn from one another about educating students with disabilities (Dudek, 2000; Kealey, 2001a). A third seminar is being planned for 2002. Additionally, the Department of Elementary Schools offers workshops focused on children with special needs at the annual NCEA Convention.

Department of Secondary Schools

A perusal of the NCEA Convention and Exposition programs for 1995 through 2000 revealed that there has been an increased focus by the Department of Secondary Schools with sessions and strands offered each year that addressed issues related to students with special needs. In 2001 there were five sessions. The 2000-2005 strategic plan for the Secondary Department shows commitment to the special needs learner in the strategies identified for achieving a diversity or inclusivity goal (NCEA, 2000). The goal and strategies are:

Diversity or Inclusivity Goal: To assist Catholic secondary schools in establishing environments of openness, trust, and respect for and appreciation of differences, reflecting a commitment to inclusiveness as a hallmark for their Catholic identity.

Strategies:

- To promote in Catholic secondary schools an understanding of diversity that incorporates issues of gender, special needs, socio-economic status, sexual orientation, ethnicity, race, and culture.
- To assist Catholic secondary schools in assessing the extent to which diversity issues are being acknowledged and addressed in policy, practice, and programs.
- To produce resources for Catholic secondary schools that will assist them in establishing programs and curricula that promote an understanding of and appreciation for issues of gender, sexual orientation, and special needs.

Achievement of this goal has the potential to change Catholic education at the secondary level for students with special needs.

CURRENT DEMOGRAPHY

Although Faerber (1949) reported that Catholic high schools enrolled students with IQs as low as 70 in the 1940s, educating children with exceptionalities was not given national attention until the 1950s (Behrmann, 1971; Buetow, 1985). Sheehan (1999) cited that in private schools, including Catholic, two percent of the students are identified as students with special needs. Recent NCEA survey data, summarized in Tables 1, 2, and 3 compiled by the Elementary and Secondary Departments (Guerra, 1988; Kealey, 1996, 1998a, 2000) provide a snapshot of the incidence of various disability groups being served in today's Catholic schools. Table 1 shows that across the five-year period, 1995-1999, there were students with disabilities attending the elementary and middle schools sampled in the survey. There was no information on the average size of the schools sampled so the percent of the school population with disabilities could not be discerned. However, the average number of students per school remained fairly constant across the years, indicating that students with disabilities have been a continual presence.

Table 1: Percent of US Catholic Elementary and Middle Schools Represented in Survey and Average Number of Students with Disabilities per School

Report Year	Percent of all US Catholic schools represented	Average number of students per school classified as disabled
1995	8%	15 students
1997	9.8%	17 students
1999	5.6%	14 students

Source: *NCEA Balance Sheet for Catholic Elementary Schools* (Kealey 1996, 1998a, 2000)

Table 2 identifies the disabilities of the students reported in Table 1 and the percent of the schools reporting that they serve students with disabilities. The categories of learning disabilities (LD) and ADD/ADHD, two of those categories associated with mild cognitive impairments, are present in the schools. The category of mild mental retardation (MMR), the other high incidence handicapping condition, was not a response choice on the survey. The schools reporting that they had students with LD and ADD/ADHD among their populations were not asked the grade levels of the students, nor the average number of years a student with disabilities attended the school. The value of such information would be to contrast it with Curran's (1984) finding that there was a significant difference between the number of students enrolled in second grade (101) and in the sixth grade (62), indicating that perhaps the students were not supported to remain in the upper grades.

Table 2: Percent of US Catholic Elementary and Middle Schools with Students with Selected Disabilities

*Category	**1995	1997	1999
Learning Disabilities	NR	66.5%	79.4%
ADD/ADHD	NR	74.9%	74.2%
Speech Impairments	NR	62.4%	73.7%
Physical Disabilities	NR	19.7%	19.6%
Hearing Impairments	NR	24.8%	24.8%
Visual Impairments	NR	16.2%	15.3%
Autism/Nonlanguage Learning Disorders	NR	5.2%	10.8%
Emotional/Behavioral	NR	5.5%	20.8%

Source: *NCEA Balance Sheet for Catholic Elementary Schools* (Kealey 1996, 1998a, 2000)
*Mild Mental Retardation or Mental Retardation were not categories listed for selection on the survey

The Secondary Department's report (Guerra, 1998) reflected data received from approximately 84% (1,015) of the Catholic high schools in the United States. Information on students with disabilities was addressed in the chapter on school programs. Table 3 shows the program offerings with specific reference to accommodations made for students with disabilities.

Table 3: Percentage of U.S. Catholic High Schools Serving Students with Disabilities and without Accommodations

Program Services	Percentage of Schools
Students with disabilities are served within the school's programs, but with no special accommodations	37% (Approximately 375 schools)
Accommodations are provided for students with disabilities	32% (Approximately 325 schools)

Source: Table 5, p. 22, (Guerra 1998)

There were no data about the characteristics of the students with disabilities who received accommodations and those who did not. Although there were general questions addressing the dropout rate and the reason for leaving the school prior to graduation, there was no indication of the graduation rate of students with disabilities. The data about students reported in chapter six, *Patterns of Diversity*, addressed ethnic, religious, and socioeconomic diversity, but not disabilities. This pattern of reporting was consistent with Riordan's (2000) summary of the demographics of students in Catholic high schools from 1972-1992. He also did not mention students with disabilities. He did, however, offer that due to declining enrollments, Catholic schools are becoming highly academic and costly. He predicted that "in the end, Catholic schools would have to relinquish the short-lived but much-loved definition of 'common school' that was bestowed on them in the 1980s" (Riordan, 2000, p. 50). This prediction would not bode well for students with disabilities. Hallinan (2000), on the other hand, suggested the future of Catholic schools might be to better serve certain populations (i.e., slow learners, described as being students with learning disabilities) that are underserved in the public schools. From her perspective, serving these students who have few educational alternatives, would be congruent with the Vatican II directives to serve the needy.

PROGRAMS AND SERVICES

The vision and desire generated in the early 1950s to educate every Catholic, including those with disabilities (Behrmann, 1971), was given new impetus by the passage of PL. 94-142 in 1975 and the Bishops' pastoral statements of 1972 and 1978 (Hall, 1981). Advocacy by parents of students with disabilities, Catholic leadership, and general social-justice thinking nationwide converged in the early 1980s to inspire a vision of Catholic educational programs and services for students with disabilities and their teachers. O'Laughlin's (1982) report of the results of an NCEA Delphi probe concerning the future of Catholic schools substantiated this vision. One prediction made for the 1985-2000 period was that, "programs for handicapped (students with disabilities) and for gifted students will become a more prominent part of the curriculum" (p. 324). Programs were established in the 1980s and the 1990s at both the elementary and the high school levels for children described as having learning disabilities, low-severity learning problems, mild retardation, and dyslexia as well as programs making accommodations for students with hearing and visual deficits enabling those populations to move out of segregated settings and into the mainstream of Catholic education. Hall (1979, 1981) provided a representation of a continuum of services and the meaning of "least restrictive environment" for Catholic schools.

Figure 1. Least Restrictive Environment-A Continuum of Services

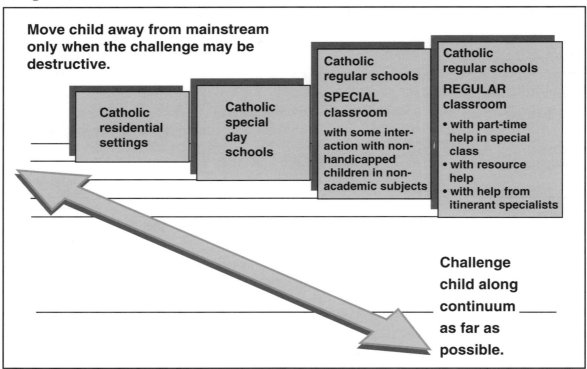

Source: Hall (1979). Special education becomes special. *Momentum, 10,* p. 22.

Serving students with special needs required making the most appropriate placement, (e.g., residential facilities, day schools, special classrooms within regular Catholic schools, and regular classrooms within the Catholic school), and then challenging the child to move as far along the continuum as possible. Hall (1979) saw regular Catholic schools as an option for students with disabilities. She challenged Catholic educators to embrace the least restrictive environment concept for students with disabilities.

Following is a discussion of a limited number of examples of Catholic programs that have committed to educating individuals with disabilities and have been documented in the literature. Some of these programs stand alone as independent schools while others are diocesan efforts, and still others have university connections.

Segregation to Integration

Schools such as the Archbishop Ryan Memorial School for Children with Hearing Impairments founded in 1912 and the St. Lucy Day School for Children with Visual Impairments founded in 1955, both in the Archdiocese of Philadelphia, provide examples of transitions from segregated to integrated services (Fleming & Moeller, 1996; Hall & Dudek, 1987a). Initially the Archbishop Ryan Memorial School served only a deaf population. Since that time, the institute has expanded its services to students with hearing impairments and has a mainstreaming component in addition to the regular elementary curriculum. St. Lucy's, affiliated with St. Alice School, provided a continuum. Students needing a segregated program are afforded one at St. Lucy. Students who are capable of being mainstreamed are provided the opportunity to attend St. Alice School where a vision consultant is available to teachers, parents, and students. Students who find success at St. Alice are then afforded the opportunity to attend their own parish school.

Individual School Efforts

Elementary level program examples range from intensive remediation to full inclusion (Alexander, 1988; Frey, Hecker, Hardy, Herzog, Paulette, & Robinson, 2000; Hall & Dudek, 1986; Helfrich, 1988; Potyrala, 1993; Ryan, 1988; Walker, 1999). The BRIDGE program (Hall & Dudek, 1986) began in 1982 and sought to identify, assess, and serve students with learning disabilities using individualized methods and materials in a resource room setting. The purpose was to enable the students to bridge their learning disabilities and resume full time placement in their homerooms. Eighty percent of the students were able to fully achieve this goal. Five percent had to be subsequently placed in a special education setting.

Resource rooms in Maryland (Helfrich, 1988) and Texas (Alexander, 1988) also provided separate class instruction for students with learning disabilities with the goal of returning the students to the mainstream classroom. The resource room in Texas served as a laboratory school for Our Lady of the Lake University. Inclusive efforts, serving the student with disabilities in the general educational program, given whatever supports are needed, have been documented in the 1990s.

Holy Family School in New York included a boy with Down syndrome for six years (Ryan, 1988). The primary goal was acceptance of the young man for the gifts he brought to offer, not academic achievement commensurate with his peers. Academics, however, were not overlooked. Expectations were commensurate with the student's cognitive gifts.

St. Jude's program (Potyrala, 1993) came into being through the efforts of an educational consultant, who was also a parent of a student with Down syndrome and a member of the Diocese of Wichita, Kansas Inclusive Education Task Force. The purpose of St. Jude's program was to include all learners for both social and academic reasons. Remediation of academic deficits is not the primary goal. The same can be said of Walker's (1999) program. He stated, "this author is in the process of establishing an inclusive atmosphere based on community need…when a child comes to us with a physical challenge or learning need, we accommodate that individual student" (p. 7).

Dayton Catholic Elementary (Frey et al., 2000), an urban school, makes accommodations for learners with different needs using a team problem-solving approach to identify learning and teaching strategies appropriate for individual students.

At the secondary level schools have designed programs to accommodate students with mild to moderate disabilities (Carter, 1997; Chilinskas, 1989; Joller, 1995; Laengle, Redder, Somers, & Sullivan, 2000; Manese, 1999; Matuszek, 1999). Some programs have an academic focus, others a social integration purpose, and some choose to address both the academic and social dimensions. Chilinskas (1989) reported a program in New Jersey designed to meet the academic, social, and emotional needs of high school students with IQs ranging from approximately 65 to 90. Students were served in a self-contained room for certain subjects and were mainstreamed for others (e.g., Essentials of Math and Consumer Mathematics). During the first year in lieu of mainstreaming, all the students took an organization-study skills class. For students who could not succeed in the general academic program, integration with peers was accomplished through peer tutoring done in the special education classroom. Additional socialization was achieved using the established extra-curricular teams and clubs.

The program established at Cincinnati Purcell Marian High School (Carter, 1997; Matuszek, 1999) also addresses the inclusion of students with mild mental retardation. A special educator facilitates the program, but it is built, as the principal states, "on a strong conviction of the entire Purcell Marian family that we are all invited to the same table" (p. 3).

Springfield Catholic Central High School in Ohio runs a school-within-a-school model, entitled Success Central, for first year students who have experienced academic difficulties in the past and may or may not have an IEP (Laengle et al., 2000). Students attend a summer program designed to bolster math and reading skills prior to entering the first year. They attend the same general classes as their peers. These classes are often team-taught by the Success Central coordinator and the general educator. Additional tutoring is also provided. Support in subsequent years is less structured, but provided based on individual student need.

The program at Santa Margarita Catholic High School for students with learning difficulties and attention problems is being evaluated for implementation throughout the Orange County California Diocese (Manese, 1999). The program supports students enrolled in a rigorous college preparatory program. It features ongoing educational support, promotes student-self advocacy, teacher and counselor training, parent education, and comprehensive assessment and diagnostic procedures.

At Vandebilt Catholic High School in Louisiana a multi-sensory teaching methods program for students with dyslexia and average to above-average IQ was established (Joller, 1995). In addition to the multi-sensory approach, students are offered "skills" English in grades 8 through 12. Students may also take a non-credit resource class on organization, study skills, time management, and social skills.

Diocesan Supported Efforts

Hall (1981) reported that the Catholic dioceses of Brooklyn, St. Louis, Philadelphia and Camden were among the pioneers in educating students with disabilities in the least restrictive environment. The Archdiocese of St. Louis, Department of Special Education developed and published in 1958 a revised *Curriculum Guide for Use in the Special Ungraded Classes for the Educable Mentally Retarded* Child (Hegemann, 1971). In addition, Hall (1981) described a number of Catholic schools with programs for students with special learning needs that operated during the 1970s in the dioceses of Minneapolis-St. Paul, Houston, Chicago, Jackson, New Orleans, Biloxi, and Baton Rouge.

Curran (1984) cited Cathedral Grammar School in the Boston Archdiocese as a model for educational programming. The school employed two special educators and had an individual education plan for all students integrating these students into the regular classrooms as appropriate. The program, funded by the Archdiocese, student tuitions, and additional grants, served students with IQs ranging from borderline intelligence to gifted.

The Diocese of Kansas City-St. Joseph's (1998) inclusive education program derived its philosophy of inclusion from an interpretation of the document issued by the National Congress of Catholic Schools for the 21st Century (NCEA, 1991). This document encouraged all Catholic school educators to open their minds, hearts, and doors to an increasingly diverse world, suggesting to the Diocese that part of this diversity includes children with disabilities. The Diocese produced a handbook (1998) on inclusive Catholic education, defining inclusion as, a philosophy of teaching that relies on the ability of educators to promote an environment that respects and reverences the rights of all students to learn in regular classrooms in Catholic schools. Parents of students with special needs established the Foundation for Inclusive Religious Education (F.I.R.E.) that supports the inclusion of students with special needs (Denzer, 2000).

In the Diocese of Venice, Florida, a resource program, Dreams Are Free, was initiated in 1994 (Cottrill, 1996). It was created to support teachers at all grade levels in their efforts to provide for the diverse learning needs of students with low-severity learning problems. The program is built on a triad concept of collaboration between and among the student, the teacher, and the parent. Students benefit from the program by employing the learning strategies that are identified and build upon the student's individual learning strengths and needs.

Ramirez (1996) produced a handbook to guide Catholic elementary schools in designing and implementing diocesan-supported programs for students with special needs. The handbook reflects lessons learned from establishing programs for students with special needs in the Diocese of Oakland, California. Included in the handbook are guidelines for establishing a Diocesan wide organizational structure, staff development training information, and local school site based program components.

Support Service Efforts

The Business Leadership Organized for Catholic Schools (BLOCS) was established in 1980 in the Archdiocese of Philadelphia to provide scholarships to inner city schools and students (Prendergast, 1998). BLOCS aided 34 elementary schools and five learning centers in 1996-1997. One center funded was for students with learning disabilities. BLOCS provided tuition aid, a family assistance grant, and training for teachers at the center. Working with the Archbishop of Philadelphia, the administrators of BLOCS continue to focus on providing an affordable, solid, value-centered education for students and their families.

The Kennedy Institute continues to provide leadership for the inclusion of students with special needs in the Archdiocese of Washington, DC (Sileo & Allen, 1999; Walker, 1999). The Catholic Schools Inclusion Project goal was designed to establish replicable models for inclusion that could be gradually introduced into all the elementary and secondary schools in the Archdiocese. The project has an assessment component, site analysis, a phase-in process, and a phase-out process. Professional development provided over the course of the project in each school creates the foundation for the professionals to implement inclusive practices efficiently and effectively once the project has ended.

Universities Support Efforts

Cardinal Stritch University in Wisconsin working closely with St. Coletta School provided training for teachers and supervisors in the area of mental retardation (Theodore, 1959). St. Coletta served as a laboratory school, for the observation and study of individuals with mental retardation. Collaboration between the university and St. Coletta's led to the development and publication of a series of curriculum monographs beginning in 1959 (Hegemann, 1971). These publications, along with the curriculum guide of the Archdiocese of St. Louis were the first educational guides for teachers of students with mental retardation.

Two universities in Ohio have worked closely with parents and educators interested in integrating and including students with special needs into religious and Catholic educational settings. The University of Dayton in 1989 through the Office of Ministry and Religious Education Services, renamed the Institute for Pastoral Initiatives, launched a conference on Inclusive Catholic Education (ICE). Its mission was to provide attendees with practical ways to bring children with disabilities into the regular classroom (M. Bishop, personal communication, May 2001). The ICE conference has become an annual event, featuring nationally recognized speakers and conference attendees from across the country (P. Carter, personal communication, June 2001). An outgrowth of ICE has been the Network of Inclusive Catholic Educators (NICE). NICE supports inclusive Catholic education through quarterly newsletters, an interactive website, consultation, and limited resources (e.g., videotapes of ICE sessions). Xavier University in Cincinnati in collaboration with the Archdiocese of Cincinnati in 1994 agreed to provide coursework on special education and consultation for teams of teachers, principals, and directors of religious education (Merrill, Tessarolo, & Blessing, 1999). The yearlong training and supported consultation of the teams was further enhanced by the SPARC (Seton Professional/Parent Archdiocesan Resource Center). SPARC, a depository of teaching materials and books for parents and professionals, supported the on-going efforts of the Xavier trained teams at their work in their home schools and programs.

In Iowa, St. Ambrose University in collaboration with the Davenport Diocese embarked upon a three-year project to provide teacher in-service through graduate coursework and by placing special education trained individuals in schools to support and facilitate in classroom accommodations (Ristow & Wieser, 2000). Additional grant money from the St. Vincent's Foundation, supplied needed student materials. The project has been designed for the Diocese to gradually assume and support it with limited assistance from St. Ambrose University.

RELATED RESEARCH

Five research studies in the form of doctoral dissertations (Burgoon, 1997; Curran, 1984; Depp-Blackett, 1997; Frey, 2000; Meyer, 1998) were found to address the education of students with disabilities in Catholic schools. Curran (1984) addressed the incidence of students with disabilities in Catholic schools; Burgoon (1997) and Meyer (1998) investigated service delivery options for students with disabilities in Catholic schools; Frey (2000) reported on the critical elements of in-service training for teachers serving students at risk; and Depp-Blackett (1977) examined and analyzed federal law and case law related to serving students with special needs in Catholic and private schools.

Curran's (1984) study was conducted within the context of the conversations following the 1978 pastoral statement on handicapped people (people with disabilities) of the United States bishops (United States Catholic Conference). The superintendent of the Archdiocese of Boston's department of education had established a special education committee to identify the incidence of students with disabilities in the Catholic schools and the services provided. Initial investigations found that some of the local parochial schools were identifying and serving students with special needs. This finding led to a desire to expand the opportunities for students with special needs. Curran's study (1984) was limited to the Catholic schools in the Boston Archdiocese and investigated three elements: the identification of students with disabilities; the retention of students with disabilities; and the percent of students with disabilities in the Catholic schools as compared to the public schools. Data collected showed that the classroom teachers were as good at identifying the students with learning disabilities, defined as students who fell below the 20th percentile, as were the standardized instruments administered. Another finding was that there were fewer children with disabilities in the sixth grades than there were in the second grades. Administrators indicated that it was more difficult to meet the older students' needs than the younger. The final finding of Curran's study was that the public schools had twice as many students with special needs (an 11.6% incidence rate) as did the Catholic schools (a 5.8% incidence rate). Curran suggested that more incidence studies be done to reveal a broader picture of the opportunities afforded students with disabilities in Catholic schools. He also recommended the development of training programs to insure the integration of all children into the parochial school system and identified Cathedral Grammar as a model for serving students with disabilities in the general education program.

Burgoon (1997) studied three different models, School A, School B, and School C, for serving the educational needs of students with disabilities in the St. Louis Archdiocese. School A's program began in 1950 with two special education classrooms housed in rooms standing empty in an elementary school. The special education program ran independent of the other classes in the building. These parallel programs ran until 1994 when the school personnel chose to meet the needs of students within the general education classrooms. School B's program began in 1992 as a pilot inclusion program for students identified as having learning disabilities, being at-risk, or manifesting other health impairments. A learning consultant and a counselor were hired. An enrichment center was also established. School C was established on the philosophy that providing in house training to make all teachers experts was preferable to adding special education staff. Grants provided teachers with training opportunities at a local college, support for a learning consultant, and in-service training. Although the models differed, the primary goal of each model was to provide children with disabilities the opportunity to be educated in general education with their nondisabled peers. In addition, each school had a process for staff and parents to work together to develop working plans to assist students and keep track of their progress. Burgoon (1997) found across the models common elements needed for success. Needed elements were: on-going staff development; collaboration; teaming; identification of student strengths and needs and progress monitoring; modifications and adaptations; alternative assignments; cooperative learning strategies; developing multiage classrooms; and flexibility to work with individuals or small groups in classrooms. The importance of each element varied by staff, program, and student needs. Burgoon (1997) outlines a recommended staff development plan for educators implementing an inclusion program.

Meyer (1998) examined the evolution of the St. Anthony School for Exceptional Children to the establishment of a St. Anthony School network in the Diocese of Pittsburgh. After 37 years as a segregated program for students with mild or moderate developmental delays (mental retardation), St. Anthony School branched out to nine sites employing a resource room model with inclusion as an option. Meyer used observations, interviews, conversations, archived documents, and a survey to examine the process and the effect of the change on staff, parents, and programs. Meyer compared survey responses gathered in 1990 to those gathered in 1996 and found greater support for inclusion in 1996 than in 1990 especially among the non-teaching staff and the parents. The teacher responses were similar on both surveys. Teachers indicated that the major weakness in the whole move was lack of sufficient in-service. Meyer found this to be a major concern of teachers and administrators. Another finding was the importance of good staff relationships and collaborative skills among the special educators, the general educators, the non-teaching staff, and the administrators. A major weakness of the programs was time to plan. Principals tried to arrange schedules, but there did not seem to be enough time during the school day. Having students with disabilities in the building had both positive and negative effects. On the one hand, some administrators felt they had an increased load, especially with behavioral issues. On the other hand, having the students with disabilities in the building elicited such comments as, "it makes us more sensitive and aware of diversity" and "it made religion much more alive for everybody in the building" (p. 85). Information provided by parents ranged from accounts stating they were very involved in the change process, to having no information about proposed changes, to being forced to move their child to another building because of a top-down decision. Meyer's (1998) recommendations for educators making similar changes included the following: engaging the teachers and parents in the change process; defining the roles and responsibilities of the special educators for most effective service delivery; providing on-going staff development; and making provision for collaborative planning time.

127

Frey (2000) investigated the development of teachers learning to use a collaborative problem-solving model to identify strategies for supporting at-risk students in an urban Catholic elementary school. She looked at the support systems and practices needed to help the teachers develop the skills implicit in the problem-solving model. She found that before she could train the teachers, she had to develop trust and become a member of the community. Once she was accepted, then the teachers were open to learning a new approach to addressing student challenges. Notes kept of the collaborative problem-solving sessions revealed that teachers were able to identify their own in-service needs; they developed greater openness for sharing issues; they gained a greater understanding of both student and curriculum development; and they developed better interpersonal communication skills to deal with conflict. Frey attributed all of these gains to the following: "building rapport, understanding the learners *(teachers)* [italics added], staying long enough (over-time learning)" (p. 204), and active participation (hands-on) on relevant (day-to-day) issues.

Depp-Blackett (1997) did an exhaustive review of federal regulations and case law relevant to special education to discern the responsibilities of Catholic and private schools and those of public schools. She found that students with disabilities can be served in Catholic and private schools, but knowledge of the law by Catholic educators is necessary to assure that the student is afforded all the services to which he or she is entitled. There is a need to do more pre-service and in-service education of teachers, administrators, and school boards regarding special education law as it relates to Catholic and private schools. Staying abreast of the special education law requires, in Depp-Blackett's opinion, addition of a knowledgeable person if one is not already employed. She further recommends Catholic schools take the initiative for greater collaboration with public school personnel because the research shows that public schools will not seek out private schools or their students with special needs.

CONCLUSIONS, FUTURE RESEARCH, AND RECOMMENDATIONS

This review evidences that students with special needs are being educated in Catholic schools. What is not known is the percent of the 2,647,301 current enrollees (McDonald, 2001b) that represent students with disabilities. It is not known how many Catholic children of school age with disabilities are denied access to a Catholic school (Owen, 1997). However, it is known that there are advocates for Catholic education of students with disabilities (e.g., clergy, parents, educators, and funding groups); that some of the advocates implement programs and that these programs are not without controversy; and that a variety of models for educating students in Catholic schools with their same aged peers exist. From the limited research, it can be concluded that more than one model can be effective. It is known that staff development is a major element of successful programs; that parent involvement is a necessary ingredient to creating programs for the education of students with disabilities; that a supportive local administrator makes a difference in the quality of a program; that the presence of students with disabilities in a building can be value added for understanding human dignity; that Catholic schools must design their own model of service delivery because they do not have the same resources as the public schools (McDonald, 2000a; Sheehan, 1999); and that Catholic schools operate as independent entities rather than as related members of a system. There is no collective vision for the education of Catholic students with special needs. The choice to serve students with diverse academic needs in Catholic schools is ultimately a school-by-school decision (Weaver & Landers, 2000).

The field of Catholic special education is ripe for research. There are so many questions and issues to be addressed.

1. **How are programs for students with special needs in Catholic schools funded?** A study of the source of resources of existing programs needs to be done. Knowing how to sustain these programs beyond the startup or pilot phase is critical.

2. **What expertise is really needed to educate students with special needs?** So often, it is assumed that the presence of a fulltime special educator is a necessary ingredient. Studies looking at the knowledge, skills and attitudes (Wagganer & Standhardt, 1987) needed by all persons involved could better inform staffing pattern decisions.

3. **What factors have the most positive effect on the academic achievement of students with and without disabilities?** Knowing what makes a difference for students is needed to inform program decisions.

4. **Can the presence of students with disabilities affect the teaching and learning of Catholic values?** Perhaps this needs to be a study of adults who attended Catholic schools that did and did not have students with disabilities present. As Sumarah (1993) states, "theories and techniques will come and go, but a deep respect for one another is the most fundamental component of exceptionality and service delivery" (p. 25).

5. **Do strategies like cooperative learning and peer tutoring facilitate the learning of students with disabilities and without disabilities?** A study of this sort would get at the question of students with disabilities taking time away from the instruction of students without disabilities.

6. **What types of technology are effective in meeting the needs of students with disabilities?** Technology is a kind of support for instruction and learning, not the only answer to meeting the needs of a diverse population in our classrooms. A study demonstrating the effectiveness of various technology supports can guide instructional decision making.

7. **What are the characteristics of administrators who move beyond what can't happen because of limited resources to providing programs for students with disabilities?** We need to identify the motivation, the strategies of support given faculty and staff, and the ability to sustain.

Research is needed to inform decision making. There is no question that Catholic schools should be about educating all Catholics who have been given the gift of life. Modern medicine has increased the diversity of the population and social justice has raised expectations for the range of students to be served in Catholic schools (Hall & Dudek, 1987b). Research and proven practice need to guide the future of Catholic special education.

In addition to research, there are some general recommendations to be gleaned from this review of Catholic special education.

1. Current data collection instruments need to be redesigned to provide a better understanding of the incidence of students with disabilities in Catholic schools and how they are succeeding.

2. Including students with disabilities in the conversation and data collection when talking about diversity (Dudek, 1994) would be another step toward acknowledging this population. All Catholic educators need to continue to advocate for all learners. Without conversation, the issue of educating students with special needs can be quietly dismissed.

3. There is a need for special education resources to be coordinated and shared more systematically. Diocesan schools, through the Catholic schools office, could share resources to support consultants, volunteers, and instructional and learning materials.

4. Ongoing staff development needs to be focused and skill based. Meaningful, relevant in-service is based on an analysis of teacher skills related to the population of students being served and must be delivered over time. Skill building is a process.

5. Parents need to be seen as a valuable resource that can support integrated programs. Teams of parents of students with and without disabilities make dynamic spokespersons. They can also serve as a resource for schools when other parents question integrated programs or to support parents of students with disabilities.

6. Students are another valuable resource often overlooked that should be utilized. At the high school level, groups of students working in conjunction with special education majors at local universities and colleges can provide support services to students with disabilities through programs such as Project Support, a Council for Exceptional Children (CEC) initiative.

7. More diverse instructional strategies are needed to meet the needs of a more diverse student body. Technology, differentiated instruction, and cooperative learning are a few of the options for moving from the *sage on the stage* instructional approach to the *guide on the side* instructional approach. Students need to be the focus of learning rather than the objects of instruction.

Catholic education is at the crossroads (Youniss & Convey, 2000) and the presence of students with disabilities must be a part of the future conversation. The *taking care of* mentality must shift to *empowerment* if both the student with disabilities and the student without disabilities are expected to come to accept and appreciate the *likeness of God* that each individual exemplifies.

CHAPTER 10
LEARNING STYLES

DOROTHY D. MILES

LINDA J. BUFKIN

ANN M. RULE

Institutions change so slowly that we are often not aware of the changes until we look back at the past. This is especially true of the Catholic Church with its strong emphasis on tradition. Karl Rahner, one of the greatest theologians of the modern era, maintained that the church's rootedness in tradition was both a strength and a weakness. The heavy reliance on past practice provides a solid foundation for current undertakings, but the uncritical acceptance of all parts of traditions can paralyze ongoing growth and development (Rahner, 1981). Understanding the need to embrace what is good in the past, but to look to the future with hope, we turn our attention to schools and to pedagogical practices. In this chapter we will take a brief look at educational theories and practices in the near past, since the 1950s and before 2001, focus on our present educational theories and practices, and then make some projections about the future of education. It is important to remember, as with any theories and practices, acceptance and implementation vary widely.

In the past, both students and teachers were relatively homogeneous groups. Schools were designed to meet the needs of White, middle class families who valued education and supported the efforts of the teacher to impart knowledge to their children. When students progressed far enough through the system to begin to cultivate their differences, those who did not value education left the system, while many who stayed were placed in separate vocational, college preparatory, or special educational settings. Homogeneity (in as far as was possible) in the classroom was thus preserved. In this type of teacher-centered classroom, the content was inert, and students were passive (Vatterott, 1995). Students were expected to learn individually and to compete with their classmates to achieve good grades and academic honors. Students were assessed chiefly by means of paper and pencil tests to ascertain how much knowledge they had retained and could give back on the tests. Successful students received good grades and those who were headed for college were accepted into various institutions of higher learning. There was a heavy emphasis on linguistic and logical-mathematical learning and assessment. Even measures of intelligence measured "g" or general intelligence, or at the most, linguistic and logical-mathematical intelligence. Teaching methods, primarily the lecture method, were those that had been used for many years and were often accepted as worthwhile based on anecdotal evidence.

The change from homogeneous to more heterogeneous classes reflects a national trend, as the population of the United States is becoming more diverse. The percentage of Whites in our culture is decreasing, with the percentage of African Americans and Asians showing slight growth and the Hispanic population showing the largest increase (Morganthau, 1997). Because the cultural diversity of students within our schools is increasing, the role of the teacher in fostering students' pride and respect for their own cultures has increased. According to Au and Kawakami (1991), when children can take pride and ownership in their cultural heritage, achievement in school increases. Classrooms include children who are not only racially, ethnically, and linguistically diverse, but the movement referred to as inclusion is aimed at including all children with special needs, who are diverse in terms of cognitive and physical skills, in regular classrooms. Many studies have indicated that separate education for students with special needs has not been effective. The principle of inclusion has been encouraged by legislators and adopted by many educators with the result that students identified with special needs are more and more frequently being included in the regular classrooms.

Presently, education is in the midst of sweeping changes which are rooted in research based theories and methods. One of the greatest problems in educational research is that the funds for research and development are pitifully inadequate (Gage, 1990). There is encouraging work being done, however, with resulting theories that are transforming educational practices.

BRAIN-BASED LEARNING

One relatively new area of research is brain-based research. According to Caine and Caine (1991), "brain-based learning involves acknowledging the brain's rules for meaningful learning and organizing/teaching with those rules in mind" (p. 4). The guiding principle for brain-based learning is that "brain research establishes and confirms that multiple complex and concrete experiences are essential for meaningful learning and teaching" (Caine & Caine, 1991, p. 5). In brain-based learning, teachers are seen as facilitators and guides rather than as "deliverers of knowledge." Brain-based learning is guided by a set of 12 principles:

1. The brain is a complex adaptive system.
2. The brain is a social brain.
3. The search for meaning is innate.
4. The search for meaning occurs through "patterning."
5. Emotions are critical to patterning.
6. Every brain simultaneously perceives and creates parts and wholes.
7. Learning involves both focused attention and peripheral perception.
8. Learning always involves conscious and unconscious processes.
9. We have at least two ways of organizing memory.
10. Learning is developmental.
11. Complex learning is enhanced by challenge and inhibited by threat.
12. Every brain is uniquely organized. (Caine & Caine, 1997, p. 19)

These guiding principles have several implications for how we educate children of today and in the future. Some of these implications are that the beginning of a child's life is critical to learning; learning and maturation cannot really be separated; the environment affects the brain physiologically; and the time scale of change varies enormously (each brain appears to have its own pace) (Caine & Caine, 1991).

Larsen (2000) acknowledged that emerging brain research would become a critical consideration in the development of future religious education programs and texts. The patterns that are involved in religious rituals, celebrations, and rites of passage are often packed with emotional energy and present themselves as an area ripe for study in brain research. Some researchers are turning their attention to parents and to parenting behavior in an effort to assist in the prosocial development of children (Bennett, Finn, & Cribb, 1999; Frabutt, 2001). Thus, it appears that brain research is poised to influence early developmental practices, even those associated with religious rituals in the home, parenting styles, and broader institutional religious practices.

In the past, brain research was extremely difficult to conduct. Some of the older research including brain growth and spurts (Epstein, 1978); the Triune Brain (MacLean, 1978); and Hemisphericity (Sperry, 1968) have led educators to examine and explore more closely how children learn. Researchers today can use new tools, such as Magnetic Resonance Imaging (MRI); Positron Emission Tomography (PET); and Computerized Axial Tomography (CAT) that were unavailable in the past. These tools have added tremendously to our knowledge about how the brain works (Jensen, 1998). According to Gardner (1999), imaging techniques have allowed us to look at brain activity as it is happening. He lists seven brain and mind findings that "ought to be kept in mind by anyone concerned with education" (Gardner, 1999, p. 81):

1. The tremendous importance of early experience;
2. The imperative of "Use it or lose it;"
3. The flexibility (plasticity) of the early nervous system;
4. The importance of action and activity;
5. The specificity of human abilities and talents;
6. The possible organizing role played in early childhood by music;
7. The crucial role played by emotional coding. (Gardner, 1999, pp. 81-82)

Gardner also states that a "surprisingly large role is played by heredity in the performances achieved by human beings…It seems that half of the variation is due to genetic factors. That is, roughly half of the variability found with a general population proves to be a function of individual genetic history, while the remaining half, roughly, is due to (typically differing) individual experiences in the world" (Gardner, 1999, p. 83). This statement implies that educators need to provide rich environments conducive to learning; to help students create their own environment and be active in it; to provide gentle care; to provide appropriate social environments; and to stimulate the brains of children by providing challenges and reducing stress (Sprenger, 1999).

COGNITIVE LEARNING THEORIES

Cognitive psychologists have also formulated important theories of learning that are influencing the way we teach. Two important theories of cognitive learning are the information processing model and the levels of processing theory. The information processing model most frequently cited is that of Atkinson and Shiffrin (1968). As explained and elaborated upon by Morris (1993) and Slavin (2000), the model consists of three components of the memory system. The first component is the sensory register. We are continuously bombarded by stimuli which must enter our memory system through the sensory register (seeing, hearing, touching, smelling, etc.). The sensory register can only attend to these stimuli for a second or two. That which is attended to is passed on to the next compartment, the short term or working memory, and the rest of the stimuli is forgotten. It is important for teachers to remember that in order for information to enter the system to begin with, students must pay attention to it. Teachers can encourage attention to information by making it vivid, interesting, and relevant to the students.

The second compartment, short term or working memory, is what is in our immediate consciousness. We can hold information in this compartment for about 20 to 30 seconds. The amount of information is also limited to about five to nine bits of information for adults. Although this short-term memory is often regarded as an informational bottleneck, there are various techniques such as using multiple stimulus dimensions (e.g., visual and auditory), recoding, and mnemonic devices, which a teacher can use to aid students to receive, process, and remember the information (Miller, 1994). We can maintain information longer than 20 to 30 seconds through simple rehearsal, which is repeating the information (Baddeley, 1990), or by chunking information together. Chunking involves categorizing information into meaningful units rather than as discrete information. We can think of chunking by using an analogy to money. Seven pennies (or bits of information) are limited in value. However, if we chunk our money together into categories and turn it into seven quarters, we have increased our amount of money (or information). This limited capacity of working memory has significant implications for teachers in designing and delivering lessons (Sweller, vanMerrienboer, & Paas, 1998). Teachers can remember to avoid bombarding students with too much information at a time, to give them time for rehearsal, to categorize discrete bits of information, and to use visual aids for permanent reference, thus freeing up working memory to be used on the current task. Teachers should also be aware that children have much less capacity in their short term memories (the average number of items for children 6 years of age is two to three items) and adjust their instruction accordingly.

The third compartment is the long-term memory. Theoretically, long-term memory is our permanent storage of all of our experiences and information we have accumulated. It is often called our knowledge base. Information in long-term memory is unconscious until it is retrieved by the short-term memory. Although we may think that a memory has been lost, it may simply be inaccessible, perhaps because it is stored in a place in long-term memory that the short-term memory cannot access at the moment (Slavin, 2000). Researchers believe that long-term memory consists of three types of memories (Squire, Knowlton, & Musen, 1993). One is personal experience, called episodic memories that seem to be organized in storage by when and where they happened (Tulving, 1993). Teachers can furnish personal experiences, such as field trips, vivid visual pictures and videos, and hands-on experiences to encourage students to store some information as episodic memories. A second type of information stored in long-term memory is semantic memories. These are discrete facts. Teachers can encourage organization of discrete facts into hierarchies and meaningful units. Relating new information to information already in long term memory also increases its meaning for students. Procedural memories, or the "how to" procedures (how to write a paragraph, how to factor an equation), depend on meaningfulness also, and the degree to which the material is learned, as well as the active involvement of the student. Teachers can provide practice in order for students to retain procedural memories.

Another information processing theory that has been widely accepted by cognitive psychologists is the levels-of-processing theory (Craik, 1979, Craik & Lockhart, 1972). In this theory, memory depends on the amount of mental processing that is involved in learning this material. For instance, if students see the word antiaircraft (shallow processing), they are much less likely to remember it than if they also say the word or spell it (deep processing). If students also learn the meaning of the word and how antiaircraft were used as a defensive method in World War II (elaborative processing), then they are most likely to remember the word in the future. Teachers who remember this theory will make information relevant and meaningful to their students.

CONSTRUCTIVISM

Another theory that is gaining acceptance and changing our educational practices is constructivism. Constructivism is a theory about learning and knowledge (Brooks & Brooks, 1993) rather than a specific method of teaching. Constructivists believe that the learner constructs knowledge internally and gives meaning to new knowledge by relating it to this internal construction. Constructivism is a view of knowledge acquisition, which emphasizes knowledge construction in contrast to traditional approaches that emphasize knowledge transmission from the teacher to the student (Applefield, Huber, & Moallem, 2001).

Jean Piaget was one of the most influential proponents of constructivism. His work focused on cognitive development and the formation of knowledge and then used constructivism as a way of describing how children learn about their world. Piaget supported the idea that the mind meets the environment in an extremely active, self-directed way (Flavell, 1985). Piaget describes a learning environment where teachers provide the opportunities for students to think and explore. Both teachers and students engage in the process of learning (Brooks & Brooks, 1993).

Vygotsky (1962) also provided a foundation for constructivism. While Piaget studied individual processes, Vygotsky emphasized the importance of social interaction in cognitive development. His concept of the zone of proximal development is exemplified by having students work on tasks that can be completed with the assistance of a person competent in completing the task (Applefield, Huber & Moallem, 2001). The task may be mediated by a more skilled peer or a teacher who provides the support (scaffolding) that allows learners to construct their own knowledge. Vygotsky's framework emphasized a more communal element and took into consideration the power of the community to shape the learning, skills, and mores of children. This construct is highly compatible with Catholic education in general, for it acknowledges the transformative power present in the example and leadership of an assembled community, such as a parish.

Vygotsky (1962) believed that one of the first tasks of the child is learning the sign systems of the culture such as language, writing systems, and numerical systems. When the individual has learned these signs, she or he can learn from others. When these signs become internalized they are used in independent thinking and problem solving. Vygotsky theorized that children first use the speech of others or "private speech" to solve problems (self-talk is an example). Later, private speech becomes internalized, silent, and what we call "thought" (Vygotsky, 1962).

Gauvin (2001) continues the discussion of the importance of social processes on cognitive development. She states, "several social processes exert influence and direction on cognitive development. These include interpersonally direct processes like interaction in the child's zone of proximal development and guided participation" (p. 30). The teacher can keep in mind the importance of language and other sign systems that lead to better problem-solving and thinking skills. Class discussions can stimulate the thinking and learning process.

The adoption of the theory of constructivism leads to classroom practices that are student-centered rather than teacher-centered. This involves significant changes for both teachers and students. In the past, classrooms tended to be teacher-centered and content-centered. The content was inert, and the student functioned in a passive role. The student focused on the answers desired and tried to shape responses until they resembled a prototype. With the constructivist, student-centered classroom, the primary activity is not inert content, but the involvement of individual students upon the curriculum (Vatterott, 1995). Students try out new ideas for themselves as they develop and test hypotheses. What goes on inside their heads, or the models that an individual constructs in his or her mind are crucial to understanding (Scherer, 1999). Students organize, construct, and transform the content to have personal meaning, and as a culminating event, create a unique product (Gage, 1990). The role of the teacher changes to one of a mediator between the curriculum and the students, and an assessor of the quality of the final product.

When learners build on previous knowledge, they grasp concepts enabling them to move from simply knowing material to understanding it. Constructed knowledge promotes critical thinking, which allows students to integrate concepts within and between disciplines; to represent concepts in multiple forms; and to justify, defend, and reflect on the concepts (Ward, 2001). When students are actively engaged in the construction of knowledge, their learning is reflected in the restructure of their cognitive maps. The teacher facilitates this by providing an environment in which students undergo a certain amount of cognitive dissonance and by devising tasks that challenge their current thinking. These tasks are represented by instructional practices such as hands-on activities and questioning techniques that delve into students' beliefs and turn them into hypotheses to be tested. An atmosphere which is non-threatening allows students to examine their beliefs (Richardson, 1997).

While the focus in constructivism is on the learner, the teacher has a critical role as facilitator. The teacher facilitates the construction of knowledge. When a student develops an idea that may not be accurate, the teacher provides examples and opportunities to see other ideas that challenge the student's thinking. This allows students to rethink their ideas and integrate the new information. This process of assimilation and accommodation is ongoing as the student constructs knowledge. Constructivist teaching practices enable learners to internalize and reshape, or transform new information (Brooks & Brooks, 1993).

The current emphasis on constructivism is evident at all levels of schooling from preschool through higher education. Focus is on the learner's construction of knowledge through meaningful learning experiences with the teacher serving as mediator and facilitator. Through a variety of activities, learners may construct what they are learning. There is emphasis on choicemaking by students, implementation of a student driven curriculum, development of critical thinking skills, incorporation of active learning, efforts to meet individual needs and alternative forms of evaluation (Bufkin & Bryde, 1996).

Both the National Council of Teachers of Mathematics and the American Association for the Advancement of Science have proposed conceptual changes in teaching that reflect a constructivist philosophy (Applefield, Huber, & Moallem, 2001). Literature based approaches to reading and emergent literacy as well as process approaches to writing are drawn from constructivism (McCarthey, 1994). The National Association for the Education of Young Children also provides guidelines for appropriate practice with young children, which originate in constructivist theory about how knowledge develops (Bredekamp & Copple, 1997).

COOPERATIVE-COLLABORATIVE LEARNING

Consistent with the theories of constructivism are classroom methods called cooperative learning. Over time, cooperative learning is slowly replacing "competitive" learning. Sylwester (1995) attributes this to the idea that

> historically, humans have developed into a cooperative species, assigning community tasks so that the group could benefit from the strengths of each individual....Our race became a dominant form of life because we tended to help, not kill, one another. (p. 177).

Johnson, Johnson, Holubec, and Roy (1984) stated that the push for cooperative learning resulted because of two crises: crises in achievement and crises in socialization. They continued by stating that lower SAT scores, the lack of quality in the work force, the low scores of students in science and math, functional illiteracy, feelings of isolation, feelings of being disconnected, feeling unattached and without purpose or direction all served as catalysts in promoting cooperative learning.

The terms cooperative and collaborative are often used interchangeably. Gerlach (1994) states, "collaborative [cooperative] learning is based on the idea that learning is a naturally social act in which the participants talk among themselves. It is through talk that learning occurs" (p. 8). Cowie, Smith, Boulton, and Laver (1994) state, "Cooperative learning is the opportunity to learn through the exploration and expression of diverse ideas and experiences in cooperative company" (p. 48). Cooperative-collaborative learning techniques have common characteristics: group goals, individual accountability, equal opportunities for success, team competition, task specialization, and adaptation to individual needs (Slavin, 1995). Johnson, Johnson, Holubec, and Roy (1984) state that cooperative learning methods also emphasize four elements: face-to-face interaction, positive interdependence, individual accountability, and interpersonal and small group skills.

Research shows that "cooperative learning is an effective strategy in inclusive classrooms" (Halvorsen & Nealy, 2001, p. 19) and that "cooperative structures prepare students for the world outside of school while ensuring the students acquire and master both academic and interpersonal skills" (Halvorsen & Nealy, 2001, p. 20). In fact, some scholars have argued that cooperative learning is an inherently Catholic pedagogical model in that it explicitly teaches students to be concerned for others (Nuzzi & Rogus, 1993: Nuzzi, 1998). Jensen (1998) states that " cooperative groups...do two important things: 1) when we feel valued and cared for, our brain releases neurotransmitters of pleasure—this helps us enjoy our work more; and 2) groups provide a superb vehicle for social and academic feedback" (p. 33). When examining the impact of cooperative groups on early adolescents, Stevenson (1998, p. 31) states, "intellectual development is enhanced when youngsters actively explore their world by having firsthand interactions with people and objects in their environment." As educators, we realize that early adolescence can be a difficult time for students, and that actively engaging them with their peers seems to help them in developing a sense of self as well as assisting them in achieving academically.

Zemelman, Daniels, and Hyde (1998) state, "cooperative learning activities tap the social power of learning better than competitive and individualistic approaches" (p. 8). Although cooperative learning is more difficult to implement and requires a higher level of expertise on the part of the teacher, supporters claim that these methods are consistent with democratic values of fairness, respect for diversity, and personal responsibility (Sandhu, 1996). A Department of Labor survey reported in *Education* (Sparapani, Abel, Easton, Edwards, & Herbster, (1997) suggests that employment needs for 2000 are for workers who can work cooperatively, make decisions, and think critically. In this same article, the authors claim, "over the past several years cooperative learning has been presented as a means for classroom teachers to enable students to be more interactive and cooperative and, perhaps, prepare them more adequately for the society of the twenty-first century" (p. 252).

MULTIPLE INTELLIGENCES

Concurrent with and consistent with the theory of constructivism is Howard Gardner's theory of Multiple Intelligences (MI). In the early 1980s, Gardner's model forced educators to reevaluate their thinking on how children, adolescents, and adults learn. His theory on MI is powerful, mainly because "he backs it up with research from a wide variety of fields including anthropology, cognitive psychology, developmental psychology, psychometrics, biographical studies, animal physiology and neuroanatomy" (Armstrong, 1993, p. 13). Each intelligence that Gardner established had to meet a specific set of criteria: each intelligence had to be capable of being symbolized; each intelligence had its own developmental history; each intelligence had to be vulnerable to impairment through insult or injury to specific areas of the brain; and each intelligence had its own culturally valued end-states (Armstrong, 1993).

In his early work, Gardner (1984), described 7 intelligences:

- Linguistic intelligence: the capacity to use language.
- Logical-mathematical intelligence: understanding the underlying principles of some kind of a causal system.
- Spatial intelligence: the ability to represent the spatial world internally in your mind.
- Bodily kinesthetic intelligence: the capacity to use your whole body or parts of your body to solve a problem, make something, or put on some kind of production.
- Musical intelligence: the capacity to think in music, to be able to hear patterns, recognize them, remember them, and perhaps manipulate them.
- Interpersonal intelligence: understanding other people.
- Intrapersonal intelligence: having an understanding of yourself, of knowing who you are, what you can do, what you want to do, how you react to things, which things to avoid, and which things to gravitate toward (Checkley, 1997).

In the 1990s, Gardner updated his thinking to include an eighth intelligence—Naturalist. Naturalist intelligence is the human ability to discriminate among living things as well as sensitivity to other features of the natural world (Checkley, 1997).

Research in the area of MI has continued since the 1980s. Lazear (1991) summarized the major research findings from "psychology, medicine, education, business, cognitive patterning, sociology, anthropology, brain research, linguistics, biofeedback, and the human potential movement" (p. 187) with respect to MI. Major research findings for MI include:

- Intelligence is not a static reality that is fixed at birth. It is a dynamic, ever-growing, changing reality throughout one's life. Intelligence can be improved, expanded, and amplified.

- At almost any age and ability level one's mental functioning or mental processes can be improved. In fact, intelligence can be taught to others. One can learn how to be more intelligent by activating more levels of perception and knowing within daily living.
- Intelligence is a multiple phenomenon that occurs in many different parts of the brain/mind/body system. There are many forms of intelligence, many ways through which people know and understand themselves and the world.
- A stronger, more dominant intelligence can be used to train a weaker intelligence. Much of one's full intelligence potential is in a state of latency due to disuse, but it can be awakened, strengthened, and trained. (Lazear, 1991, p. 189)

Gardner's theory of MI has important implications for education because he challenges the view of the past that intelligence is narrow and is solely inborn. He feels that the amount of each of the (eight) intelligences varies with the individual, leading him to conclude that we have different kinds of minds, therefore the role of teachers is to help students use their particular combination of intelligences to learn (Checkley, 1997). Campbell (1995) suggested that we examine six areas including: pedagogy (multiple entry points into content areas); curriculum (thematic and interdisciplinary, arts based, project based, apprenticeships); assessment (multiple forms of documentation); role of the teacher (becomes a resource person); role of parents and community members (more involvement); and the school mission (education for understanding). Other educators such as Bruce Campbell (1994) and Thomas Armstrong (1993) have also suggested that teachers and school administrators should rethink how children and adolescents are taught in school settings. Their books are filled with suggestions and ideas on how to integrate the ideas of MI into classroom settings.

MI thinking is especially relevant for Catholic educators in as much as MI pedagogy has an explicitly theological dimension. Though not articulated by Gardner in the original study, the multiple intelligences provide people of religious faith with a psychological framework for understanding and appreciating what Catholic educators have for decades called the "image of God" in each student. Nuzzi (1999) argues for this deeper, theological understanding of the intelligences, even going so far as to suggest that MI approaches, in their embrace of diverse learning styles, are more congruent with the catholicity of Catholic education than more narrow or focused classroom strategies. Nuzzi recognizes the challenge of the Catholic educator to teach gospel values in persuasive and engaging ways, and feels that religious educators need a methods course in teaching religion and that Gardner's MI theories are particularly relevant to religious education.

A provocative and creative application to MI theory can be seen in Eucharistic celebrations—the Mass. The Mass is "a veritable festival of the multiple intelligences" (Nuzzi, 1996, p. 4.). With but a casual understanding of the research supporting MI theory, most Catholic educators would easily be able to identity the various ways in which the Mass touches on all the intelligences. As such, the Mass can be understood not only as central liturgical prayer, but also as psychologically expansive, intelligence-rich, and respectful of the full range of human giftedness.

EMOTIONAL INTELLIGENCE

Denham (1998) states "differences in emotional competence have a very real impact on how children work and play together and on their feelings of mastery" (p. 13). She goes on to say that "emotional competence is fundamental for the ability to interact and form relationships" (p. 14). In her developmental model of the socialization of emotional competence leading to social competence, Denham indicates that socialization of emotion: modeling, reactions, and coaching, lead to the understanding and expression of emotions by children. This understanding and expression of emotions then lead to social competence and emotion regulation. She says that social competence is an "accurate interpretation of others' emotions (which) provides important information about social situations" (p. 178).

Peter Salovey of Yale University divided emotional intelligence into five areas: (1) self-awareness, or being aware of and understanding your own emotions (2) managing your moods, or keeping your moods in check and avoiding impulsivity (3) empathy, or putting yourself into another's shoes and "feeling with" that person, (4) motivation, or setting attainable goals and developing enthusiasm and persistence toward those goals, and (5) social skills, or learning cooperation, how to build relationships and fit in with a group (Reissman, 1999).

Daniel Goleman describes emotional intelligence as a different way of being smart. He notes that the five areas described by Salovey can help you to use your feelings to make good decisions in life. He contends that IQ contributes only about 20% to the factors that determine life success, leaving 80% for everything else (O'Neil, 1996). In his book, *Emotional Intelligence*, Goleman (1995) describes many examples of research that indicates that youngsters who are able to control their impulses at a young age are much more likely to be successful academically and more stable emotionally and were better liked by teachers and peers than those who chose immediate gratification when they were preschool age. Goleman also makes the point that the emotional centers of the brain are closely connected to the prefrontal areas where working memory is located. Since working memory is limited in size, and is the center where all learning takes place, one can see that emotional states such as anger or anxiety can interfere with learning. Some school systems such as the New Haven schools have developed emotional literacy lessons that are part of the daily school curriculum (O'Neil, 1996). Goleman feels that this curriculum is working because the district is finding that students are better able to control their impulses, their behavior has improved, and they have better skills in handling conflict and interpersonal problems (O'Neil, 1996). The Child Development Project in Oakland, CA has a literature-based emotional literacy curriculum that is used by teachers (Murray, 1996). For more information on emotional literacy programs, contact The Collaborative for the Advancement of Social and Emotional Learning (CASEL), Yale Child Study Center, P.O. Box 207900, New Haven, CT 06520-7900; (203-785-6107).

CHARACTER EDUCATION

The issue of character education is one that has waxed and waned in U.S. schools. The recent spate of violence by and among our school children has sparked new interest in what most are calling character education. In a national poll (Rose, Gallup, & Elam, 1997), over 90% of respondents agreed on traits such as honesty, democracy, and acceptance of others as values that should be "taught" in the schools. While presently, most states provide no substantive funding for character education in public schools, most encourage schools to offer character education. Suggestions from educators regarding character education are: include the community and the family (Vessels, 1998; Zarra, 2000), use direct instruction of shared, core ethical values (Ryan & Bohlin, 1999; Zarra, 2000); teachers and other adults need to model good character (Lasley, 1997); use heroic stories to illustrate good character (Six ways, 2001); encourage service to others (Six ways, 2001); hold students accountable for actions and words (Six ways, 2001); teach responsibility and care for others (Loughran, 1999).

As Thibeau (1999) points out, "Catholic educators have a proven and lasting program to guide the character-building effort" (p. 14). Cronin (1999) points out that Catholic schools have a commitment to share with families the development of character in their children. Cronin adds that character education involves more than teaching rules but it includes the total school experience. It must be meaningful to students. Loughran (1999) adds that being a catechist is more than imparting knowledge, it is also being a character builder. She calls the role of the religious educator important because "we are the examples and motivators" (p. 65). Thibeau (1999) stresses that the entire school community must make the effort to build character in every student, all the time. Character building should be cross-curricular. "Given the relative autonomy of Catholic schools, the integration of Gospel-centered character development across all curriculum areas is expected and achievable" (p. 16). Catholic educators have been highly successful in this effort, especially because of the high degree of articulation between home and school (Cronin, 1999), the emphasis on the connection between spirituality and religious education in moral development (Nuzzi, 2001), and the recognition of the role of parents in the moral and cognitive development of their children (Frabutt, 2001).

TECHNOLOGY

With the fast growth of technology, the nation's schools are faced with challenges around the basic availability of technology, the quality of equipment, the appropriate integration of technology into the curriculum, and preparation of teachers to provide meaningful technology experiences for their students. In public school settings, 99% of teachers report having a computer available somewhere in their school with 84% having at least one computer available in their classroom. Teachers also report that it is more likely they will use computers and the Internet when available in their own classroom. Currently schools provide one computer for every six students on the average (NCES, 2000).

There are clear differences in availability of computers relevant to schools with minority enrollments. Schools with lower minority enrollments (less than 20%) were more likely to have Internet available than those with minority enrollment over 50% (NCES, 2000). Even when there are enough computers, the use of technology is less in the poorer public schools. Lack of access to computers at home is also an issue, with children from lower socioeconomic groups having fewer opportunities to use computers in their home setting (Johnston, 2001). This issue has been described as the "digital divide" and an issue that must be addressed if there are to be equitable educational opportunities for all children.

Teachers report three major barriers to the use of computers including the lack of computers, lack of release time for teachers to learn how to use computers, and lack of time in the schedule for students to use computers (NCES, 2000). Only one-third of teachers reported feeling well-prepared or very well prepared to use computers and the Internet for classroom instruction (NCES, 2000). Currently teachers who do feel competent with computers use them in a variety of ways with students in the classroom such as: word processing, creating spreadsheets, doing research on the Internet, drill and practice, analyzing data, and solving problems. Teachers reported that they used computers to create instructional material, gather information for planning lessons, and communication, as well as for other administrative tasks (NCES, 2000).

Even with these varied uses, there has been a broad range of quality in interactions and technology activities in which children engage. In an effort to address standards related to technology, the International Society for Technology in Education (ISTE) called for the establishment of guidelines for students as well as teacher preparation. ISTE called for programs

> that provide effective educational settings to enable students to become capable information technology users; information seekers, analyzers, and evaluators; problem solvers and decision makers; creative and effective users of productivity tools; communicators, collaborators, publishers, and producers; and informed responsible and contributing citizens. (2000 p. 2)

The new learning environments to support these goals use student-centered instruction, multisensory stimulation, collaborative work, activity and inquiry-based learning, promote critical thinking and informed decision making and represent authentic, real-world contexts (ISTE, 2000).

Based on these ideas, the National Educational Technology Standards (NETS) project developed standards in six categories for students:

- basic operations and concepts
- social, ethical, and human issues
- technology productivity tools
- technology communications tools
- technology research tools
- technology problem-solving and decision-making tools (ISTE, 2000).

In addition to the six categories of standards, NETS provides profiles for Technology Literate Students (PK-12), which guide the development of effective programs.

An important aspect of the effective use of technology in the classroom is the integration of the computer into the curriculum. Teachers' planning should be centered on student needs and the curriculum and the next consideration should be how to integrate technology. Technology should contribute to and enhance the curriculum rather than shaping the curriculum. Lockard and Abrams (2001) describe the process of integration as seeking to identify those places where the computer can increase learning effectiveness, enable learners to do what they otherwise could not, or teach significant life skills.

Even with the increasing numbers of computers, the full impact of technology is yet to be seen. Classrooms with fully integrated technology have tremendous potential for changing the way students engage in learning.

DEVELOPMENTALLY APPROPRIATE EDUCATION

All of these trends in education are having an effect throughout our school systems, both public and private, and from preschools to high schools. For a brief look at the various levels of schooling, let us first examine the concept of developmentally appropriate practice, which took root in early childhood education. Developmentally appropriate practice (DAP) is not a specific curriculum or "rigid set of standards that dictate practice. Rather, it is a framework, a philosophy, or an approach to working with young children" (Bredekamp & Rosegrant, 1992, p. 4). DAP is based on constructivist theory and has become the practice which exemplifies constructivism in the classroom.

Developmentally appropriate practice is based on the idea that professionals will make decisions about children based on three considerations:

- Age-appropriateness. Professionals should consider what is known about predictability of development within a given age range and provide activities and materials appropriate to support development.
- Individual appropriateness or the individual interests and ability of each child. This calls for adaptation of curriculum to meet the needs of individual children.
- The importance of social and cultural context in developing meaningful learning for children (Bredekamp & Copple, 1997).

In her review of research, Charlesworth (1998), indicates that children who participate in developmentally inappropriate preschool and kindergarten academic activities do less well in academic achievement, rate lower on behavior evaluations, and tend to be perceived as less motivated when compared with children attending more child-initiated or DAP programs. In addition, studies that followed these children into the elementary grades are consistent with preprimary results indicating that attendance in DAP programs appears to be related to overall positive benefits related to achievement and behavior outcomes in students from varying backgrounds.

Developmentally appropriate practice also emphasizes the whole child perspective including physical, social, emotional, and cognitive development. Learning in a DAP classroom often occurs through play which engages children in activities relevant to their lives yet organized to promote inquiry and critical thinking.

The guidelines for DAP are organized around five interrelated areas of practice: "creating a caring community of learners, teaching to enhance development and learning, constructing appropriate curriculum, assessing children's development and learning, and establishing reciprocal relationships with families" (Bredekamp & Copple, 1997, p. 16).

The classroom implications for developmentally appropriate practice include the use of integrated curriculum with curriculum content emerging from children's interests and needs. Careful observation of and conversation with children provide direction for curriculum. Materials and activities are concrete, real and relevant to the children as well as non-sexist and multicultural. Children are encouraged to explore these materials in a variety of ways. Opportunities for making choices about materials and activities are available with adults serving as facilitators of learning. Extensive interactions with peers and teachers allow for the development of social skills. Behavior issues are addressed in a positive manner such as use of redirection. Developmentally appropriate practices include establishing partnerships with parents by involving them with all aspects of the classroom. Parents participate in decision-making and are respected for their expertise and beliefs (Bredekamp & Copple, 1997).

Diversity is central to all components of developmentally appropriate practice. In a developmentally appropriate classroom children learn to recognize diversity's value and its presence in our lives (Perry & Duru, 2000). Diversity can relate to cultural or linguistic differences as well as differences in abilities. Children and their families form distinct cultural and linguistic groups that must be recognized with sensitivity and respect (Gestwicki, 1999).

Although the guidelines for DAP are designed for children from infancy through age eight, the implementation of these practices has been the most widespread with young children through the kindergarten level. Increasingly, primary classrooms are adopting the guidelines and addressing the issues of age appropriateness, individual appropriateness, and becoming more responsive to social and cultural contexts.

The idea of developmentally appropriate practice may be extended to the middle school level. In 1989, the Carnegie Council on Adolescent Development (CCAD), described five desirable characteristics of effective 15-year-olds: an intellectually reflective person; a person enroute to a lifetime of meaningful work; a good citizen; a caring and ethical individual; and a healthy person. From these characteristics, the CCAD continued with a set of recommendations, which today form the core of middle school education. When considering the five desirable characteristics of effective 15-year-olds, the emotional, physical, social, and intellectual development of emerging adolescents must be closely examined.

With respect to physical development, Wiles and Bondi (2001), said that accelerated physical development begins in transecence (typically 10-14 years of age); in pubescent girls, secondary sex characteristics continue to develop; a wide range of individual differences among students begins to appear; glandular imbalances occur; boys and girls tend to tire easily, but won't admit it; fluctuations in basal metabolism may cause students to be extremely restless at times and listless at others; and boys and girls show ravenous appetites and peculiar tastes.

In social development, Wiles and Bondi (2001) state that the affiliation base broadens from family to peer group; peers become sources for standards and models of behavior; society's mobility has broken ties to peer groups and created anxieties in emerging adolescents; students are confused and frightened by new school settings; students show unusual or drastic behavior at times; "puppy love" emerges with a show of extreme devotion to a particular boy or girl; youth feel that the will of the group must prevail and sometimes can be almost cruel to those not in their group; boys and girls show strong concern for what is right and for social justice; they are influenced by other regulation but reserve the right to question or reject suggestions of adults.

In examining emotional development, Wiles and Bondi (2001) say that erratic and inconsistent behavior is prevalent—anxiety and fear contrast with reassuring bravado. Feelings of transescents "tend to shift between superiority and inferiority" (p. 35). They continue by saying that "at no other time in development is he or she likely to encounter such a diverse number of problems simultaneously" (p. 35).

The intellectual development of transescents was addressed by Wiles and Bondi (2001) when they wrote:

> middle school learners prefer active over passive learning and prefer interaction with peers during learning activities; students are usually very curious and exhibit a strong willingness to learn things they consider useful; students often display heightened egocentrism and will argue to convince others or to clarify their own thinking; independent and critical thinking emerges; studies show that brain growth in transescents slows between the ages of 12 and 14. (p. 36)

Keeping in mind all of the important changes occurring in the life of a transescent, middle schools must become more responsive to the needs of this group of students. According to Jackson and Davis (2000) "over time, much has been learned about what affects student outcomes in learning positively" (p. 5). Researchers describe the process of effectively educating transecesents as Developmentally Responsive Education. Important characteristics of Developmentally Responsive Middle Schools, as characterized by the National Middle School Association are:

1. Educators committed to young adolescents
2. A shared vision
3. High expectations for all
4. An adult advocate for every student
5. Family and community partnerships
6. A positive school climate (Knowles & Brown, 2001, p. 51).

Therefore, developmentally responsive middle schools provide:

- Curriculum that is challenging, integrative and exploratory
- Varied teaching and learning approaches
- Assessment and evaluation that promote learning
- Flexible organizational structures
- Programs and policies that foster health, wellness, and safety
- Comprehensive guidance and support services (Knowles & Brown, 2001, p. 51).

Developmentally responsive middle schools have become an important aspect in the education of transcesents. The important and often confusing changes in their social, emotional, intellectual and physical development have a tremendous effect on the student's ability to learn. However, we must not forget that "within the trials and tribulations of early adolescence are the opportunities to forge one's own identity, to learn new social roles and to develop a personal code of ethics to guide one's own behavior" (Jackson & Davis, 2000, p. 7).

Developmentally appropriate practice at the high school would include the understanding of adolescents at high school age and being responsive to their needs and levels of cognitive and emotional maturity. The adolescent, by high school, has moved from a strong reliance on family and teachers for models to a greater reliance on peers. One of the important tasks of adolescents, according to Erikson (1959) is the development of a strong identity. This task is difficult because of the many possibilities, the variety of models, and the conflicting messages and values received by the adolescent. Erikson felt that during this stage, the adolescent is in a state of "moratorium" or a time when they may try on many different identities before forming a strong self identity. David Elkind (1978) addressed a characteristic called adolescent egocentrism. He described this egocentrism in terms of two aspects: one is personal fable or the feeling that one is unique and no one else can possibly understand how they feel; the other is the concept of the imaginary audience which is the feeling that everyone else is watching the personal appearance and behavior of the adolescent. Originally, Piaget felt that cognitive development was complete by high school age and so these individuals should be able to use logical, hypothetical deduction and to systematically test hypotheses. In 1974, however, even Piaget admitted that most adults use formal operational thinking in just a few areas in which they have the most experience. The educator should keep in mind that adolescents are in varying stages of social, emotional, and cognitive development, therefore a variety of approaches and strategies must be used to reach each student.

Theodore Sizer has challenged the idea of the comprehensive high school in several books: *Horace's Compromise* (1984), *Horace's School* (1992), and *Horace's Hope* (1996). He argues that the high schools are too big and too disjointed to offer students deep and coherent learning. Teachers do not get to know their students well enough to mentor them. Further, he feels that the present system of evaluating students with tests is narrow and does not measure whether students can use the information they have learned at school in the real world. Sizer's (1992) specific suggestions for the high school are:

- all students would follow the same curriculum;
- students should take fewer subjects in greater depth;
- students would mount exhibitions and portfolios to demonstrate their progress;
- high schools would be subdivided into houses of between 200 to 220 students;
- the school year would be extended from 36 to 42 weeks.

What will be the look of the schools in the future? The National Commission on Teaching and America's Future (NCTAF) has given us a blueprint for improving our schools by reforming five areas:

- Professional standards for teachers linked to standards for student learning;
- Redesigned teacher education including a year-long internship, mentoring for all first year teachers and ongoing professional learning opportunities;
- Teacher recruitment strategies that are more aggressive;
- Rewards for teachers who demonstrate knowledge and skill;
- Schools that are organized for student and teacher learning (Darling-Hammond, 1997b).

If we imagine our ideal schools of the future, they would certainly include all of the areas mentioned by the Commission. We can imagine some other changes. Pre-K though elementary schools would be student-centered while students learn the basics of our mathematics and verbal language. They would hone these skills and use them for learning to read and compute and to communicate and work with others. They would use technology, chiefly computers, as learning tools. They would meet in smaller classes and have the same teacher(s) for more than one year.

Middle schools are already a step ahead in terms of organizing time for teachers to plan curriculum and learn from each other. They also might put student and teacher teams together for more than one year, and continue the learning skills and technological processes students will need to become lifelong learners. They would begin to develop hypothetical-deductive skills and use a variety of information sources (library, internet, etc.) to analyze and solve problems.

High schools could be the areas where most radical changes take place. As Wilkinson (1996), points out, secondary schools need to "become that place which produces, rather than imports, curricular excellence" (p. 37). He recommends that secondary schools stop building new facilities and put their limited funds into technology that allows students to learn outside the school walls. More students could be served by one building unit because all students would not be attending at the same time. Students could access information from a distance and from multiple sources. Interactive videos and electronic classrooms could provide both verbal and written communication between teachers and among students. Assignments could be submitted electronically. Students would also be able to participate in athletics, extracurricular activities, and attend assemblies of interest. For academics, students could meet frequently and directly with teacher-mentors and other students focusing on a topic of study. Students would maintain a relationship with a teacher-mentor who could remain with the student for their time in high school. Students would employ or learn research skills and display their findings in some format such as exhibits or portfolios that could be viewed by family and faculty. Assessment would go beyond the paper and pencil tests to include authentic assessment of the products of the students' efforts. The political pressure to produce good scores based only on limited paper and pencil tests would broaden to include these more authentic, real-world techniques of assessment.

Any and all of these changes are possible because good ideas almost always begin with a dream. Perhaps our greatest dream is analogous to the "audacious goal" set by the National Commission on Teaching and America's Future, "by the year 2006, America will provide all students with what should be their educational birthright: access to competent, caring, and qualified teachers" (Darling-Hammond, 1996, p. 193). In working to achieve such dreams, Catholic educators, by a renewed commitment to the vocation of teaching, help the church change for the better.

CHAPTER 11
TECHNOLOGY

JEANNE HAGELSKAMP, SP

INTRODUCTION

For the past quarter century, Church documents have acknowledged the important role of technology in life today. In *To Teach as Jesus Did,* the National Conference of Catholic Bishops (Sacred Congregation, 1972) noted that:

> Technology is one of the most marvelous expressions of the human spirit in history, but it is not an unmixed blessing. It can enrich life immeasurably or make a tragedy of life. The choice is [ours] and education has a powerful role in shaping that choice. (#33)

In addition, the Church has recognized the necessity of preparing students for the scientific and technological world in which they live without neglecting their spiritual formation (Congregation for Catholic Education, 1988, 1997) or academic areas such as the humanities (Congregation for Catholic Education, 1988). In their 1997 document *Catholic Schools on the Threshold of the Third Millennium*, the Congregation for Catholic Education (CCE) submitted that

> the Catholic school should be able to offer young people the means to acquire the knowledge they need in order to find a place in a society which is strongly characterized by technical and scientific skill. But at the same time, it should be able, above all, to impart a solid Christian formation. (#8)

Furthermore, educators have been admonished to update themselves continually (Sacred Congregation for Catholic Education, 1982) and to equip their facilities with the tools needed to adequately provide such preparation for life in the third millennium (Congregation for Catholic Education, 1988). According to the CCE, the ultimate task of educators is to assist young people to discover the harmony between faith and science so that, in their professional lives, they will "be better able to put science and technology to the service of men and women, and to the service of God" (1988, #54).

At the National Congress on Catholic Schools for the 21st Century, Convey (1991) identified 10 challenges that Catholic educational leaders faced if Catholic schools were to remain viable. Among those challenges, Convey called Catholic schools to "adequately prepare their students to assume their responsibilities as citizens in a world in which technological and scientific advances rapidly are changing into one global community" (p. 39). According to Convey, not only must Catholic schools "commit themselves to a full program of computer education and…integrate computers wherever possible into their curricula," but more importantly, they have a responsibility to "educate their students as citizens of this global community" (p. 40) by helping their students to:

> (1) become more aware of the global community in which they live; (2) appreciate the cultures and values of different peoples in this global community; and (3) when possible, act to alleviate some of the problems of the global community which modern technology has helped to identify. (p. 40)

Catholic schools have embraced this challenge and have wrestled with questions about the ways in which technology can assist in effecting their mission (Braun, 1992; Broekman, 1997; Corrado, 1997; Doyle, 1998; Hutchison, 1998). In addition to grappling with such philosophical questions, educators in the Catholic school system have considered practical issues as well. As might be expected, a substantial amount of thought has been given to technology planning (Brennan, 1997; DeZarn, 1997; Dudek, 1996; Haney, 1997b; Stuckey, 1995, 1997a, 1997b; Waggenspack, 1997); staffing (Erhart, 1997); staff development (Brigham, 1992a; Clifford, 1998; Krupka, 1997; Manning, 1994; Power & Brosnan, 1992; Sine, 1994); technology and special needs (Dudek, 1999); technology and problem solving (Marion & Monroe, 1992); integration of technology into the curriculum (Bashian, 1991; Bouton, 1997; Brooks, 1997a; Dudek, 1997; Fleming & Moeller, 1996; Holian & Chismar, 1991; Lester, 1996; Lewis & Boudreaux, 1992; MacKenthun, 1992; National Catholic Educational Association, 1995; Oberlander, 2000; Shaner, 1992; Stegall, 1998; Zajac, 1995; Zukowski, 1992); funding (Bergan, 1997; Connelly, 1997; McDonald, 1997a, 1997b, 1998a, 1998b; National Catholic Educational Association, 1993; Schwartz, 1992); the future of technology (Czarnota, 1994; Sherman, 1994; Thornburg, 1997, 2000; Zukowski, 1997c); media literacy (Trampiets, 1997, 2000); and collaborative partnerships with parents and other schools (Anderson, 1993; Butler, 1992; Chin, 1997; Collura, 1995; Froman, 1992; Kinney, 1997; Morse, 1997; Tracy, 1996; Wirth, 1996). Moreover, numerous articles have considered the theological, moral or ethical implications of technology and Internet use (Heltsley, 1996, 1998; Mann, 1992; Smith, 1995; Traviss, 1997; Zukowski, 1997d, 1999); gender equity issues (Brooks, 1999a, 1999b; Heltsley, 1996, 1998; Traviss, 1997); and the use of technology in religious education (Abel, 1992; Albertson, 1992; Beecroft, 1992; Campbell, 1996; Cerveny, 1995; Kimball, 1992; Ritzel, 1995; Trampiets, 1995; Zukowski, 1995, 1997a).

Still others (Cimino, 2000a, 2000b; Coburn, 1994, 1995; Garlitz, 1992) have highlighted best practices in schools across the United States. The 1994-1995 volume of *Today's Catholic Teacher* featured monthly articles by Coburn in which she cited "Profiles in Success." The following year, Coburn highlighted schools that had been participants in the *New Frontiers* program. From 1998 through 2000, *Today's Catholic Teacher* recognized exemplary technology programs in schools through their annual "Catholic Schools for Tomorrow: Innovations in Technology" competition. In 1999, the Selected Programs for Improving Catholic Education (SPICE), a joint venture of the National Catholic Educational Association (NCEA) and the Jesuit Institute at Boston College, focused on "Forming Innovating Learning Environments Through Technology" (Cimino, 2000a). They sought to identify the best programs in the country that "seamlessly weave the use of technology into every aspect of the learning experience for students," (Cimino, 2000b, p. 2) either through teacher training or through the education and training of students. Eleven such programs were identified in Catholic elementary and secondary schools and (arch)diocesan offices and have been resources for other schools in the country.

For the past decade, every issue of *Today's Catholic Teacher* has featured an article on technology. In an early series, entitled "Technology for Technophobes" and "Moving Ahead with Technology," Coburn (1992a, 1992b, 1993) provided teachers with information on the use of technology for instructional and managerial purposes in the classroom. Coburn's articles during the 1994-1995 and 1995-1996 academic years were dedicated to best practices in schools. Brooks (1996, 1997b, 1998, 1999b, 2000) authored articles in subsequent years, running series such as "Technology Tools for Teaching" and "Technology in the Classroom." Though some of these articles focused on acquisition or location of equipment, most emphasized some aspect of technology integration.

Among the plethora of articles, dissertations, and journals that have focused on technology in Catholic schools, few have been research-based. Rather, most have provided concrete advice, based on experience, for other educators to consider as they scrambled to meet the challenges posed by the Church documents and the National Congress on Catholic Schools in the 21st Century. As such, those pieces, though instructional and informative, will not be reviewed in this chapter.

AVAILABILITY OF TECHNOLOGY

The National Center for Education Statistics (NCES), the National Catholic Educational Association (NCEA), and Quality Education Data (QED) have examined trends in the acquisition and use of technology in Catholic schools and in staff development. The first of the NCES studies (Heaviside & Farris, 1997) was done in 1995, as part of a larger project which examined advanced telecommunications in a variety of private schools. A follow-up survey (Parsad, Skinner, & Farris, 2001) was undertaken in 1998-1999. In both NCES surveys, the data were generally reported in four categories: all private schools, Catholic schools, other religious schools, and non-sectarian private schools. Statistics gathered by NCEA were reported biannually as part of a larger balance sheet of income and expenses for Catholic elementary schools, from 1995 through 1999, as well as from annual staffing surveys. The QED data (Tyre, 1998, 2000) were attained in cooperation with NCEA through two surveys, one in 1997-1998 and one in 1999-2000. O'Keefe (2000) reported the information from several of these surveys. For purposes of this chapter, however, data contained herein are derived from the original reports.

In the first NCES survey (Heaviside & Farris, 1997), of the 873 respondents, 323 (43%) were Catholic schools. The 1998-1999 survey (Parsad, Skinner, & Farris, 2001) included 844 respondents, of which 361 (43%) were Catholic schools. Each of the NCEA studies was based on the financial information garnered from all the U.S. Catholic elementary schools that reported to NCEA. The QED statistics (Tyre, 1998, 2000) included both Catholic elementary and secondary schools. The 1998 survey was based on a reponse of over 6,550 schools (78%), while the response rate of the 2000 survey was 50%, or nearly 4,200 schools.

Number of Computers

In the 1995 NCES survey (Heaviside & Farris, 1997), the Catholic schools fared better than most other religious schools in availability of advanced telecommunications. Of the schools represented in the survey, there were approximately 31 computers per Catholic school, nearly twice that of other religious schools. However, the student to computer ratio in Catholic schools was slightly higher than that of other religious schools: Catholic schools averaged about 10 students per computer, while other religious schools averaged 9.

According to NCES (Parsad, Skinner, & Farris, 2001), by 1998-1999, the mean number of computers per Catholic school had increased to 49, slightly more than twice the mean number in other religious schools. On average, 41 of the 49 computers were designated for instructional purposes. Furthermore, the ratio of Catholic school students to instructional computers was 8:1, better than the 9:1 ratio of other religious schools. This ratio was approximately double that which the president's committee of advisers on science and technology had recommended in 1997.

The QED study (Tyre, 2000) also found an 8:1 ratio of students to computers. Furthermore, it ascertained that during the 1999-2000 school year, administrators planned to purchase an average of 9.4 additional computers, and intended to add still another 9 computers in 2001-2002. The study also noted that, for instructional purposes, the Windows platform outnumbered the Apple-Mac platform by a ratio of 3:2, slightly greater than the 7:5 ratio in the 1997-1998 academic year (Tyre, 1998). Approximately six laptops (platform not indicated), often used on a student-checkout basis so that schools could begin to address equity issues, were present on the typical Catholic school campus in 1999-2000, whereas in 1997-1998 they were virtually non-existent.

Computer Labs

According to the data gathered by NCEA (Kealey, 1996), in 1994-1995, 83% of the U.S. elementary schools represented had computer labs. Whereas 89% of the schools in the mideastern section of the United

States reported having at least one lab, only 79% of those in the Southeast had them. Across the U.S., the average Catholic elementary lab had 18 computers and students typically spent an average of 51 minutes per week there. Approximately 68% of the elementary classrooms had computers, and the typical classroom had two computers.

Two years later, in 1996-1997, the percentage of Catholic elementary schools reporting computer labs had risen to 87% (Kealey, 1998a). Again, the percentage was largest in the Mideast, where 93% reported having labs; moreover, schools in the Plains states were least apt to have a lab, with only 80% reporting a lab. The typical lab had 20 computers, and students averaged 52 minutes per week in the lab. There was a more significant increase in classroom accessibility to computers, with 75% (up seven percentage points over two years) of the classrooms having at least one computer, and the typical classroom had two.

By the 1998-1999 school year, 90% of the Catholic elementary schools had computer labs (Kealey, 2000). The largest percentage of labs was reported in the New England states, with 96% indicating presence of a lab. The Plains states remained lowest, still at 80%. While the average number of computers in the typical lab remained at 20, the average time students spent in the lab each week increased by 11 minutes (21%) to 63 minutes. Progress was made in individual classrooms, with 81% of the classrooms reporting at least one computer (up six percentage points in two years). Furthermore, the typical classroom reported having three computers, up one from the previous report two years prior. For the first time, principals were queried about teacher proficiency with computers. Respondents suggested that approximately 45% of the teachers were proficient at using computers.

Use of Peripherals

The 1999 QED study (Tyre, 2000) found a larger number of peripherals in place than ever before. In schools that had Web TV, two such units could be found. The typical school also had 11 TV monitors and 3 DVD players. Moreover, each Catholic school had, on the average, at least one digital camera, 1.6 scanners, 2.4 LCD projectors, 3.9 laser printers, and 2.5 videodiscs. Perhaps most impressive was the 561% jump in ownership in assistive and adaptive devices available for special needs students, from less than one such unit in 1997 to 4.5 units in 1999.

Internet Access

According to the 1995 NCES study (Heaviside & Farris, 1997), 35% of Catholic schools had at least some Internet access, compared with 16% of other religious schools. However, only 6% of all computers in Catholic schools had Internet access, while 5% of all computers in other religious schools had such access. Nonsectarian schools had nearly four times as many Internet-accessible computers as did the Catholic schools. Among Catholic schools with Internet access, 48% had only one computer connected to the Internet, 37% had 2-5 computers connected, 3% had 6-9 computers Internet-accessible, and 12% had 10 or more computers connected; the mean number of Internet-connected computers was five. For the Catholic schools, these statistics translated to a dismal 174 students per computer with Internet access, comparable to other religious schools (171:1) but sorely different from the 25:1 ratio for non-sectarian schools. Moreover, 35% of Catholic schools that did have Internet access did not provide it in any instructional room (classroom, lab, media center, art room, etc.); 39% had one instructional room with Internet access; 18% had 2-3 instructional rooms so-equipped; and only 7% had five or more instructional rooms with Internet access.

The 1995 NCES survey (Heaviside & Farris, 1997) also gathered information about extent of use of any types of wide area networks (WANs), including Internet. In schools with such networks, Catholic administrators (35%) were twice as likely to use them to a moderate or large extent than those in other religious schools

(17%). Approximately 27% of the Catholic school teachers used WANs moderately or extensively, slightly more than those in other religious schools (23%), but less than nonsectarian school teachers (43%). Moderate to extensive use of WANs by students in Catholic schools was about 24%, slightly more than those in other religious schools (21%), but only slightly more than half of non-sectarian school students (45%). It would appear, then, that there was a strong correlation between ease of accessibility and actual use of such networks.

From 1995 to 1998, the NCES reported substantial gains in numbers of Catholic schools with Internet access. According to data gathered in the 1998-1999 survey (Parsad, Skinner, & Farris, 2001), 83% of the Catholic schools had Internet access, up significantly from the 35% indicating such access three years earlier. Additionally, this percentage was significantly greater than that of other religious schools (54%) or nonsectarian schools (66%).

However, the Catholic schools lagged behind nonsectarian schools in the total number of instructional computers with Internet access: the number of Internet-connected computers in nonsectarian schools (40) was more than double the number of such computers in Catholic schools (18). In addition, nonsectarian schools boasted a lower ratio of students to instructional computers with Internet access (7:1) than did Catholic schools (19:1) or other religious schools (18:1). Moreover, while Catholic schools reported approximately 27% of their instructional rooms with Internet access, the nonsectarian schools indicated that 41% of their instructional rooms had Internet access, whereas other religious schools had only 18% of their instructional rooms so equipped. In the Catholic sector, of schools with Internet access, 12% had no instructional rooms equipped with Internet, 41% had only one such instructional room, 16% indicated that 2-4 instructional rooms had Internet access, while 31% reported five or more instructional rooms as being Internet accessible. According to the U.S. Department of Education, National Center for Education Statistics (2000), impressive gains were made in Internet access within a three-year period, for between 1995 and 1998, the ratio of students per Internet-accessible computers had improved from 174:1 to 16:1 in the Catholic schools.

The QED results (Tyre, 1998, 2000) were similar, finding that 84% of all Catholic school classrooms had at least one computer with Internet access (up 285% from two years before), as did 89% of administrative offices. In 1997-1998, there were, on the average, about 12 classroom computers with Internet access, and by 1999-2000, that number had grown to nearly 17. However, QED provided a more optimistic view of connectivity from labs and media centers, reporting that by 1999, "virtually all" Catholic schools provided Internet access both from their computer lab(s) and from their library or media center.

The annual survey of Catholic schools for the same time period provided information about geographic differences in accessibility to the Internet. According to the 1998-1999 annual statistical report on schools, enrollment and staffing (McDonald, 1999b), there were 8,217 elementary, middle, and secondary schools in the U.S. Of these, 4,932 (60%) reported having student access to the Internet. The Plains states showed the largest percentage (72.4%) of their schools with access. Furthermore, the Southeast reported 68% access. The West-Far West reported least accessibility, with only slightly more than half (51.3%) indicating Internet availability for students.

The 1998-1999 NCES study (Parsad, Skinner, & Farris, 2001) also reported greater availability to the World Wide Web (WWW), with 81% of Catholic schools reporting accessibility, according to their data. Nearly two-thirds of students (63%) had access to the World Wide Web, while almost three-fourths of teachers (73%) and administrative staff (77%) had the World Wide Web available to them. As before, availability of the technology did not necessarily suggest use. About 30% of students, 34% of teachers, and 40% of administrative staff who had World Wide Web accessibility rarely or never used it. Furthermore, the survey found that, by 1998-1999, e-mail was available to at least some constituents in 79% of Catholic schools. Nearly two-thirds (66%) of faculty had e-mail access, while less than one-third of students (31%) were connected. Over three-fourths (78%) of administrative staff had e-mail accessibility. Again, its actual use varied significantly. Nearly half (48%) of teachers who had e-mail accessibility rarely, if ever, used it; similarly, 60% of students and 30% of administrative staff for whom it was available reported little or no usage of e-mail.

The 1999-2000 annual statistical report on schools, enrollment, and staffing (McDonald, 2000b) showed a nearly 14% increase in numbers of Catholic schools with student access to the Internet, with 6,017 (73.9%) of the 8,144 schools reporting student access to the Internet. In four geographic regions, over three fourths of the schools offered student Internet access: the Southeast, 80%; Plains, 79%; New England, 78%; and Mideast, 77.4%. In the Great Lakes region, 72.5% reported student Internet access. Again, the West-Far West trailed significantly, with only 61.0% reporting availability of the Internet to students.

Plans for Future Accessibility to Internet

From 1995 to 1998, the number of Catholic schools without Internet access declined significantly. Furthermore, by 1998, those without such access were much more likely than previously to indicate that they anticipated gaining access in the future. In 1995, of the 65% of schools without Internet access, only half of them were planning for those services in the future (Heaviside & Farris, 1997). This percentage, while surprisingly small, exceeded those in the other private schools. Of the 84% of other religious schools without access, only 34% reported planning for it in the future; similarly, of the 68% of nonsectarian schools without Internet capabilities, only 38% were planning for future access.

By the 1998-1999 survey (Parsad, Skinner, & Farris, 2001), of the 17% of Catholic schools without Internet access, nearly three-fourths (74%) indicated that they hoped to acquire Internet access in the future. Comparatively, of the 46% of other religious schools without Internet connections, only 41% intended to gain access; of the 34% of nonsectarian schools without connections, 38% hoped to gain access in the future. These statistics suggest that there may be philosophical differences across types of private schools about the value of Internet access, with Catholic school educators more convinced of the benefits of Internet availability for their students.

Legal Implications

As the Internet has become commonplace in schools around the country, one of the concerns of educators has been its potential to expose students to sexually inappropriate materials. This issue may explain, at least in part, the reluctance of some schools to prepare for Internet availability. In an effort to mitigate opportunities for access to such sites, schools have invoked the use of filters. In the public sector, such filters have been the target of litigation (Kosse, 2001). While some plaintiffs have argued for their required use in public schools, libraries, and other public forums where children and adolescents may have Internet access, others have decried their use, claiming that civil liberties have been violated. To date, courts have not rendered a final disposition on such cases. In an effort to avoid legal action, many schools have utilized acceptable use agreements (AUPs), signed by both students and their parents. However, according to Kosse, the alleged violation of First Amendment Rights and the vagueness of many AUPs have made them vulnerable to court action as well. Although Catholic schools are governed by a different set of rules, the court ruling on filters may be deemed applicable to Catholic schools, particularly if schools have purchased computers with government funds. Thus, use of AUPs may provide Catholic schools with more latitude.

In addition to concerns about appropriateness of materials available to minors (Kosse, 2001; Shaughnessy, 1997), copyright and software licensing issues have raised legal and ethical tensions for Catholic educators (Shaughnessy, 1995, 1997). According to Shaughnessy (1997), for some educators, "the motive of helping students learn is a sufficient excuse for failing to comply with the law" (p. 70). She noted that such behavior fails the moral, ethical, and legal standards that Catholic educators espouse and admonished teachers to comply with "fair use" guidelines outlined in Section 107 of the Copyright Law of 1976.

Barriers to Acquisition of Advanced Telecommunications

In the 1995 survey (Heaviside & Farris, 1997), 72% of Catholic schools without Internet access cited lack of designated funds as a barrier to their acquisition. Other reasons given by these schools were poor equipment (47%), too few telecommunications access points in the building (44%), difficulty in accessing telecommunications equipment (32%), inadequate hardware upkeep and repair (29%), and concern about student access to inappropriate materials (19%). The 1998-1999 survey (Parsad, Skinner, & Farris, 2001) did not break down the information about barriers to acquisition of advanced telecommunications by type of school; thus, comparable data for 1998-1999 cannot be reported here. However, information was gathered about the types of support that private schools got for advanced telecommunications. Of the Catholic schools, 73% received funding of some sort; 62% obtained support for hardware; 51% garnered support for software; 46% obtained technical assistance; 41% accessed assistance for training; and 25% received support in gaining network access.

The E-Rate Program

One major funding support was the E-rate discount program. According to the NCES survey (Parsad, Skinner, & Farris, 2001), in 1998-1999, over half (51%) of the Catholic schools applied for the E-rate discount program, whereas only 15% of nonsectarian schools and a mere 9% of other religious schools sought the discount. According to NCES, of the Catholic schools that applied for the 1998 E-rate program, nearly one-fourth (23%) were eligible for a 60% discount; 14% were eligible for a 50% discount; 45% were entitled to a 40% discount; and 18% earned the minimum 20% discount. The 1998-1999 annual statistical report on schools, enrollment, and staffing (McDonald, 1999b) did not receive data from all (arch)dioceses about E-rate application, but the responses suggested that at least 40% of the Catholic schools had applied. Of those that made application, 84% of them were funded (McDonald, 2000b). The QED study (Tyre, 2000) reported an application rate of 48% during the 1998-1999 year. According to QED, 42% of schools that were represented in the 1998-1999 study reported that they had received a discount during that year, averaging over $14,000 per school.

Of Catholic schools that did not apply in 1998, nearly half cited the complicated application process as their major deterrent. Another 20% failed to apply because the discount was too low; 15% had never heard of the program; and 1% were opposed to the program in principle. While the percentage of schools that had never heard of the program may, at first glance, be surprisingly high, it is quite small in comparison with the percentage of other religious schools (59%) or nonsectarian schools (60%) for whom the program was unknown (Parsad, Skinner, & Farris, 2001).

The QED study (Tyre, 2000) noted that slightly fewer Catholic schools (44%) applied for E-rate discounts for the 1999-2000 academic year, but nearly two-thirds of those expected to receive a discount.

Web Pages, Remote Accessibility, and Distance Learning

While in the 1998-1999 NCES report (Parsad, Skinner, & Farris, 2001), the Catholic schools outpaced either other religious schools or nonsectarian schools in both e-mail and WWW access, only about half (52%) of Catholic schools had their own web page (slightly more than the 45% of other religious schools), while over two-thirds (68%) of nonsectarian schools could boast their own page. Few private schools (only about 10%) had a computer system that could be accessed by students from home; for Catholic schools the percentage was smallest (8%). Furthermore, the study found that while nearly half (48%) of Catholic school teachers invoked some type of advanced telecommunications for teaching, less than one-tenth of them (8%) used advanced telecommunications for distance learning for their students. However, QED (Tyre, 2000) reported that 16% of Catholic school teachers have used the distance learning format themselves to participate in professional development or technology training.

Types of Connections to Wide Area Networks

The 1995 NCES survey (Heaviside & Farris, 1997) noted that the majority (95%) of Catholic schools using wide area networks accessed the Internet via modem connections. However 14% reported some use of SLIP/PPP network connections, 2% used 56kb connections, 1% used T1 lines, and 2% reported at least some use of ISDN lines. (Note: Because some schools reported multiple types of connections, the percentages do not sum to 100%.)

These modes of accessibility changed significantly within three years, for according to the 1998-1999 NCES study (Parsad, Skinner, & Farris, 2001), 65% reported using a dial up connection, 27% used dedicated lines, 17% had an ISDN connection, 13% used cable modem, and 1% used wireless connections. Of those with dedicated lines, the majority (63%) were still using modems, though much faster (56kb); however, 41% were benefiting from T1 or DS1 lines; and about 18% had fractionalized T1 lines. (Again, because several schools indicated multiple types of connections, the percentage sum exceeds 100%).

Use of Local Area Networks

The QED study (Tyre, 2000) found that in 1998, less than one-fourth of Catholic schools were linked by local area networks (LANs). However, within one year, that percentage jumped significantly, for in 1999, over 60% reported the use of LANs, with an average of 16 rooms and over 40 machines being connected in the typical school. The server of choice, by a ratio of more than 2:1, was Windows NT.

STAFF SUPPORT FOR ADVANCED TELECOMMUNICATIONS

In 1995, of Catholic schools with Internet access, 15% had a full-time network administrator, while 50% had a part-time person and 35% had no single individual (Heaviside & Farris, 1997). Rather than inquire about a "network administrator," the 1998-1999 survey (Parsad, Skinner, & Farris, 2001) asked about persons primarily responsible for supporting advanced telecommunications. By 1998-1999, 19% of Catholic schools with Internet access had a full-time paid technology director, and 21% had such a part-time person. Another 29% indicated that there was a teacher for whom technology coordination was part of his or her full-time job. Interestingly, for 16% of the schools, volunteers were used as technology coordinators, either from among the teaching staff (9%) or from the parents or other resources (7%). Outside contractors or consultants were used by 7% of the schools. No person was designated as responsible for technology in 8% of schools with Internet access. According to QED data (Tyre, 2000), in 1999 the average Catholic school had 1.2 full-time technical support staff members.

The 1998-1999 NCES study (Parsad, Skinner, & Farris, 2001) found that assisting teachers with the integration of technology into the curriculum was often assigned as one of the duties of the technology coordinator or others. Over half (56%) of those persons to whom such responsibility was assigned indicated that their services were generally invoked to a moderate or large extent. Only 33% suggested that their services were infrequently used for such purposes. For 11% of the technology coordinators, assisting teachers with such integration was not part of their job.

By 1998-1999, Catholic schools were more apt than other religious schools but slightly less apt than nonsectarian schools to recognize the services their students could provide in the maintenance of telecommunications systems. About half (51%) of Catholic schools used their students to some degree in telecommunications maintenance, whereas only 38% of other religious schools did so. The nonsectarian numbers were similar to those in the Catholic sector, with nonsectarian schools utilizing students to a moderate or large extent slightly more often than the Catholic schools.

STAFF DEVELOPMENT FOR ADVANCED TELECOMMUNICATIONS

One might wonder whether the lack of use of available networks noted throughout this report was based on inconvenience, inadequate staff development, or philosophical objections. While staff development information was not available in the 1995 NCES report (Heaviside & Farris, 1997), at least some staff development in advanced telecommunications occurred in 88% of Catholic schools in 1998-1999 (Parsad, Skinner, & Farris, 2001). According to the latter report, the training varied, with 85% offering some staff development in use of computers; 74% in integration of technology into the curriculum; 66% in use of Internet; and 30% in some other type of telecommunications training. Of the schools that provided training of some type, 26% mandated participation; 31% encouraged it with incentives, but did not mandate it; and 37% left it up to the teachers to initiate their participation in training. The QED findings (Tyre, 2000) were less promising. While 13.4% of all professional development activities in Catholic schools in 1999 covered technology or integration skills as more than half of the particular professional development activity, and another 23% of professional development meetings incorporated technology or its integration as one-fourth to one-half of the total content covered, nearly 64% of all professional development activities were devoid of technology-training content.

TECHNOLOGY INTEGRATION INTO THE CURRICULUM

One of the most prominent programs for fostering technology integration has been the *New Frontiers for Catholic Schools* program. Founded in 1992 and co-sponsored by the University of Dayton and the National Catholic Educational Association, the annual summer event draws 10 to 12 teams of three people who desire to investigate possibilities, draft a vision, and form a network of peers who will provide mutual support in the process of technology integration (Haney, 1997a). The team philosophy is founded in research that top-down mandates for technology integration are ineffective and lack momentum and inventiveness (Zukowski, 1997b). During the four-day seminar, each team drafts a working document for the design of an integrated interdisciplinary plan for their school. According to Zukowski, the program, which provides leadership, direction, and support to the teams, advocates

> a new paradigm which understands that the purpose of Catholic education is not to transfer knowledge but to create environments and experiences that bring students to discover and construct knowledge for themselves, to make students members of communities of learners that make discoveries and solve problems. (p. 53)

Furthermore, Zukowski (1997b) contended that in monitoring *New Frontiers* teams subsequent to their participation in the program, the technologies that they have created can be considered effective educational tools if they have met the following criteria:

- Conversation within the learning environment has been enhanced
- Collaboration and teamwork have offered greater opportunities than individualism
- Radical conversion or transformation in ways of thinking or being in relation to one another and the world has been experienced by students or teachers within the educational setting
- New opportunities for community have been created
- New paradigms of creativity for problem solving and reasoning with regard to academic and religious insights have been found
- A greater awareness for the need and value of contemplation in a world deluged with information and interaction has been achieved.

Bouton (1997) conducted a survey of *New Frontiers* graduates to determine the effectiveness of the program during its first four years (1992 through 1995) and to identify initiatives designed by graduates so that they could be shared with others. Because most teams who had been in attendance at one of the four workshops had been represented by their principal, technology coordinator, librarian, and a faculty member, those were the personnel included in the sample. The sample consisted of 23 of the 44 schools that had participated in *New Frontiers*, and included 15 principals or librarians and 28 teachers. The 43 total responses comprised 32% of the 134 participants in *New Frontiers* from 1992 to 1995.

While nearly one-third of the schools had a technology plan in place before attending *New Frontiers*, 93% of the respondents reported having such a document at survey time. Furthermore, the number of schools with technology coordinators increased from 31% prior to attendance in *New Frontiers*, to 69% at the time of the survey. Prior to *New Frontiers*, only 46% of attendees considered themselves technologically competent, whereas afterwards, 78% did so. In addition, 87% of respondents reported that *New Frontiers* had had *some effect* (47%) or *great effect* (40%) on staff development in technology: 60% of the faculty in over two-thirds of the reporting schools had received training in technology. Approximately one-third of the teachers trained in technology use it to support classroom learning at least 75% of the time. For those who did not do so, funding was the significant limitation. Still, funding increased after participation in *New Frontiers*. While prior to the workshop, all but one school spent less than $20,000 annually; afterwards the same schools spent over $50,000 per year.

Participant respondents noted that the *New Frontiers* program had a strong impact on their understanding that technology should be used as a means to an end, and to a large extent as a communications tool, rather than as an end in itself. That focus has prompted better writing among students in writing classes in which technology was used. Teachers reported that they, too, enjoyed benefits such as a healthy sense of curiosity and a renewed enthusiasm for their work. They view themselves as facilitators of learning rather than imparters of knowledge.

Communications with parents and alumni were more fully automated. More schools reported using computer software to do scheduling, record report cards, keep attendance records, and post grade books. Libraries became media centers. Publications were done using authoring software. Half had networked their computers since participating in the program.

Respondents noted that if they could do it all over again, they would move more slowly, make sure the principal's enthusiasm was reflected in budgeting and in philosophical support, and would do more teacher training at the outset.

THE ROLE OF THE PRINCIPAL IN TECHNOLOGY IMPLEMENTATION

While infrastructure and hardware concerns may be major factors in technology planning, it appears that one of the most significant factors in successful technology implementation is the disposition of the principal toward technology. Stegall (1998) sought to discover indicators of successful technology programs in Catholic schools. Although literature existed in the public sector, there was none for the Catholic schools. Subsequently, in fall, 1997, Stegall surveyed 79 elementary schools in four dioceses in south Texas. Of these schools, she received responses from 54 schools. The survey included indicators of successful technology programs, based on the literature from the public sector and validated by experts in educational technology, and examined factors such as staff development, the principal's attitude toward technology, outside support, the existence of a technology plan, a computer curriculum, a computer teacher, a technology committee, Internet access, and student-to-computer ratio.

Stegall (1998) found that 85% of the schools that responded had a computer curriculum; 81% had a computer teacher; 59% included technology in their budgets; 56% had a technology plan; 44% employed technology committees; 33% received funding from external sources; and 31% had Internet access. When questioned about their attitudes toward technology, 100% of the principals either *strongly agreed* (74%) or *agreed* (26%) that technology was an important component of a Catholic school. Moreover, 96% of the principals had a strong interest in technology, and 87% of them strongly agreed that they were quite knowledgeable about computers.

Subsequently, Stegall (1998) isolated the seven schools with the highest scores in technology integration to look for common factors among them. In these seven schools, the student-to-computer ratio was 6:1, rather than the 9:1 ratio for the entire sample. All seven schools had a computer teacher, computer curriculum, and six of the seven had a technology plan and a technology committee. Despite these commonalities, the schools varied widely in demographic statistics: size (146 – 620 students), location (urban, suburban, rural), and per pupil expenditures ($1671 - $3042).

Stegall (1998) visited each of the seven schools and interviewed their principals and two teachers. Among the principals, four were female and three were male; two were religious, while five were lay. SES of the schools also varied, with one from a low SES area, one in a high SES region, and five in middle SES areas. Principals were creative in their financing of technology. While for one school, technology was a completely budgeted item, another designated money from an annual fundraiser for several years. Others used money from cash reserves, tuition, fundraising, technology fees, grants, and other donations. One school received a $50,000 check for technology from a parishioner, after an announcement appeared in the parish bulletin describing technology as a major weakness in an assessment done prior to an accreditation visit.

Universally, however, when asked what was the driving force behind the technology program, the item most consistently mentioned by either principals or teachers was the principal's strong interest in technology, his or her beliefs in the benefits it could provide to the students, and his or her subsequent willingness to support those convictions by appropriate actions: allocation of resources, hiring of technology personnel, staff development, and so on.

SOFTWARE EVALUATION

While infrastructure, hardware, funding, and staff development were elements cited by principals and teachers as important in technology implementation, the purchase of software for student use cannot be overlooked. In an effort to familiarize teachers with available software, since 1994, each issue of *Today's Catholic Teacher* has featured reviews of educational software. However, in the past 10 years in the Catholic sector, very little research has been undertaken to examine either the appropriateness or effectiveness of the software that is being used in Catholic schools. Two doctoral dissertations, both from the University of San Francisco, have attempted to fill the gap.

Popular Software, Transmission of Values, and the Digital Divide

Heltsley (1996, 1998) sought to discover which computer software programs were most popular and most frequently employed by students in Catholic elementary schools. Once identified, the study examined whether differences existed in the quality, quantity, and kinds of programs present in Catholic elementary schools in economically disadvantaged areas as compared with those in more economically advantaged areas. Finally, the study sought to identify the extent to which computer software programs, implicitly or explicitly, contained values antithetical to or supportive of the educational philosophy of a Catholic school. According to Heltsley, such examination was crucial, for the values that are implicitly taught through software are a part of the "hidden curriculum" which, according to Jackson, Boostrom, and Hansen (1993), is more effective than the explicit curriculum of the school in the development of students' moral maturity.

Heltsley (1996) used a mixed methodology of survey and content analysis. Surveys were received from four fifth-grade students and their principals in a sample of 120 Catholic elementary schools spanning all 12 (arch)dioceses in California. Each of the 120 schools was categorized into one of three economic status categories: high, middle, or low.

Analysis of Most Popular Software Programs

Students were allowed to list three of their favorite software programs for use in school. Although 355 software titles were generated, the five most frequently named programs, cited by 73% of all the student respondents, were *Oregon Trail* (35%), *Where in the World is Carmen Sandiego?* (10%), *Where in the USA is Carmen Sandiego?* (10%), *Math Blaster* (10%), and *KidPix* (10%). *Oregon Trail* was the program of choice across the three SES subgroups as well. Reasons for preferring the given programs, based on the total number of responses given by the students, were that they were fun (34%), educational (26%), in game format (14%), a simulation of real life (13%), allowed for choice or control (12%), language arts related (11%), involved drawing and graphics (11%), math-related (8%), geography-related (5%), or were versatile (5%).

Teachers' picks for students were somewhat different. *Oregon Trail* was also the favorite choice of teachers (19%) and *Math Blaster* was also on their favorite list (8%) as well. Thereafter, however, their choices differed from those of the students and included more integrated utility software packages: *ClarisWorks* (8%), *Microsoft Works* (7%), and *The Writing Center* (7%). The two Carmen Sandiego programs ranked at the bottom of the teachers' top 10 list.

Heltsley (1996) applied content analysis to students' five most frequently used pieces of software. Frequencies and percentages were computed for positive and negative values with regard to violence or aggression and cooperation and competition, as well as to fairness of representation for males and females, people of color, and individual differences. For each piece of software, Heltsley performed five hours of coding.

Oregon Trail II, favored by 35% ($f = 125$) of the students and 19% ($f = 64$) of the teachers, seemed to provide a mixed set of values to its users. Although the content analysis revealed little violence or aggression in the software, there was no cooperative behavior required to successfully complete a journey and there were few representations of persons working together. Furthermore, there was significant under-representation of females and people of color. At the same time, there were some counter-stereotypical representations as well. Both males and females provided solid and poor advice, desired rest, noticed beauty, complained about hardships, and so on. Some individual differences and religious differences were also noted. Program design allowed for individual differences of students to be accommodated, for a pause mode allowed for intermittent breaks by students who were "on the journey." Additionally, most text was presented in both visual and auditory format.

The second most popular educational software package was *Where in the World is Carmen Sandiego?* This program had two play modes: explore mode and game mode. While the explore mode contained actual photographs, video clips, and names and information of actual persons and events, the game mode used caricatures. In the explore mode, females were severely under-represented; however, the ratio of persons of color to White persons exceeded four to one.

In play mode, *Where in the World is Carmen Sandiego?* had nearly equal pictorial representations of males and females; however, there were 210 male referents but only 81 female referents. On the other hand, there were 462 sentences (4153 words) spoken by females and only 286 sentences (2589 words) spoken by males. The play mode incorporated randomized hair color, skin color, glasses, and canes, and characters varied in gender, race, height, weight, and other physical attributes. Software design virtually excluded a visually impaired student from using explore mode; in game mode, more accommodations were possible. Furthermore, though structured for a single player, it could be used as a cooperative venture on the part of students. Violence and aggression were not prominent, and good manners were portrayed.

The third-ranked program was *Where in the USA is Carmen Sandiego?* According to Heltsley (1996), while the program demonstrated some sensitivity to appropriate representation of Native Americans by use of real photos and state scripts, the same was not true for Asians or African Americans. A wide range of heights and weights was used for both males and females, whether good or bad, and there was respect for different religions. Multiple learning styles were also supported. Among characters, there was some evidence of provision for physical limitations and there was little gender stereotyping. However, inclusive language was not always used. Moreover, violence and aggression were present. Although no accommodations were made for multiple players, students could cooperate in decision-making and solving clues.

Math Blaster was fourth choice among students. In five hours of play, Heltsley (1996) noted that females were significantly underrepresented. Despite the dominance of the male gender, women were portrayed in a positive light as they demonstrated ability to solve given problems or assumed leadership positions. Unfortunately, the majority of strategies used to solve problems in *Math Blaster* were violent, aggressive, or destructive. Furthermore, there were several subtle messages that would be antithetical to the philosophy of Catholic schools: anything alien is bad; bad people are ugly; a person's skin color or other physical differences is reason to single that person out; attack persons can be used to solve problems; and force is an appropriate way to eliminate a problem. There were negative messages about doing math: solving math problems was punishment for not shooting enough trash. Competition was also prevalent, for students competed against their own best score. In its behalf, *Math Blaster* projected some positive messages as well. Recycling and other care of the earth were evident; proper use of safety glasses was advocated; occupants of a spaceship were allowed to depart before it was blown up.

Kid Pix was students' fifth most favorite program. In this drawing program, persons were infrequently represented. When they were, their representations were often indistinguishably male or female. In addition, a variety of individual differences were represented. Furthermore, the program provided ability to switch between English and Spanish. This was the only program in which there were no winners or losers. It was untimed and could be used cooperatively. There was no violence or aggression, except that players were allowed to destroy their own creations with a stick of dynamite accompanied by an explosion.

In summary, then, through her content analysis of the five most popular software programs, Heltsley (1996) found that each of the software programs contained messages supportive of and antithetical to the espoused values in Catholic schools. Some programs perpetuated stereotyping while others were designed to avoid them; some were violent or aggressive, while others were not; most promoted competition, while others allowed for cooperation.

The survey also queried principals about the importance of evaluating educational software. There was nearly universal agreement (61% *strongly agreed* and 35% *agreed*) that the software should be evaluated. However, when asked about the presence or absence of eight given values in the software in their schools, most were *uncertain*. Apparently, then, although principals believed that software evaluation was a necessity, few had scrutinized the software in their schools and could not attest to the values contained therein.

The Digital Divide

The Heltsley (1996) study also examined differences in numbers and types of computers in schools according to SES. Using ANOVA, she found significantly different numbers of computers by SES ($F = 5.86$, $p = .0039$). High SES schools had, on the average, nearly 42 computers available to students, while middle

SES schools had 28.8 and low SES schools had 27 computers for students. Additionally, there were significantly more Macintosh computers in high SES schools than in either middle or low SES schools ($F = 10.70$, $p = .0001$). On the average, high SES schools had 16.6 Macintosh computers available to students, while middle SES schools had only 6 and low SES schools had only 3.9.

Furthermore, there were differences in the types of programs that were used in the various SES groups. The high SES schools were significantly more likely than middle or low SES schools to have paint and draw programs available ($F = 4.30$, $p = .0162$) and to have Internet access ($F = 5.38$, $p = .0061$). Low SES schools were significantly less likely than the others to have computer languages and utility programs available to them ($F = 5.11$, $p = .0078$). Across all groups, 73% of all students used word processing programs; 51% used drill software; 50% used games, and 41% used math games. However, for the low-income group, the most frequently used software was games (82%), whereas word-processing dominated in middle (87%) and high (80%) income groups. In the low-income group, the second most frequently used software was drills, used by 75%, while word-processing ranked third, with 50% of students using it. Math calculation software ranked fourth among low-income schools, with 36% of students using it. In the middle SES schools, drills also ranked second, used by 53% of those students, followed by games (43%), and math calculation software (43%). In the high SES schools, the pattern was notably different. Second most frequently used was math calculation software (43%), followed by sound and drawing programs (34%), followed by drills (29%) and games (29%).

The different SES groups also expressed different impediments to their school's ability to use computers effectively. All three groups suggested that weakness in teachers' knowledge about computers was a serious problem, although not all groups named it as the most serious. Among low SES schools, finances was cited first (62%), followed by too few computers (52%), outdated equipment (52%), teachers' knowledge (41%), and teacher training (31%). Middle SES principals cited the same five problems, though in different order: teachers' knowledge (66%), outdated equipment (59%), teacher training (50%), finances (47%), and too few computers (41%). High SES schools did not list too few computers among their five top problems, but included developing appropriate lessons. Their ranked list included teachers' knowledge (51%), teacher training (47%), developing lessons (38%), finances (32%), and outdated equipment (29%). Apparently, then, the digital divide had already manifested itself in Catholic schools by 1996, as evidenced in differences in hardware, software, and problems related to implementation of technology.

Effectiveness of The Geometer's Sketchpad

While Heltsley (1996) analyzed specific software for its implicit conveyance of values supportive of or antithetical to the philosophy of Catholic schools, Lester (1996) examined one piece of software, *The Geometer's Sketchpad*, to determine whether there was a difference in achievement of geometric knowledge between students who used a technology tool versus those who used a textbook and classic geometry tools: compass, protractor, ruler, and straightedge for instruction of high school geometry. She hypothesized that those using *The Geometer's Sketchpad* would achieve a higher mean score on a test of geometric knowledge and construction than subjects who received instruction using a textbook and traditional tools. She also speculated that students using *The Geometer's Sketchpad* would formulate generalizations in the form of conjectures indicating higher geometric concept development than those subjects who received instruction using a textbook and conventional geometry tools.

Lester (1996) used a posttest-only control group quasi-experimental design, with two levels of instruction. Subjects were members of two intact geometry sections in a northern California all-girls Catholic high school. One intact group was deemed the treatment group and received technology-based instruction using *The Geometer's Sketchpad*, while the other intact group was designated the control group and used a geometry textbook and classic geometric tools. Third quarter geometry grades of subjects participating in the study were used as a covariate to account for individual differences existing up until the time of treatment. The study extended over 16 class periods, three of which were devoted to post-testing and one devoted to taping interviews with subjects in the treatment groups. On the posttest, Lester measured three dependent variables: geometric knowledge, geometric constructions, and geometric conjectures. Subsequently, Lester interviewed students from the treatment group to attain qualitative information about their learning experience.

Lester (1996) found a moderate correlation between the third quarter geometry grade and each of the dependent variables: geometric knowledge ($r = .66$); geometric constructions ($r = .42$); geometric conjectures ($r = .60$). Using analysis of covariance to control for prior geometric achievement, based on third quarter geometry grade, she found no significant difference ($F = .26$, $p = .61$) in mean score for geometric knowledge between the treatment group ($M = 33.35$, $SD = 11.88$, $n = 20$) and the control group ($M = 31.20$, $SD = 14.73$, $n = 27$). Again, controlling for prior geometric achievement, there was no significant difference ($F = .49$, $p = .49$) in mean scores for geometric constructions between the treatment group ($M = 22.00$, $SD = 3.24$) and the control group ($M = 20.15$, $SD = 6.14$). However, for geometric conjectures, there was a significant difference ($F = 5.23$, $p = .03$) in achievement scores between the treatment group ($M = 14.45$, $SD = 5.29$) and the control group ($M = 9.74$, $SD = 6.17$). Effect size was found to be .81, suggesting a large difference between the two means. Whereas approximately 30% of the control group attained a score of 50% or better on the conjectures section of the posttest, 70% of those in the treatment group scored 50% or better. Furthermore, for the conjectures test, each student solved eight problems. In the treatment group, then, the 20 subjects solved a total of 160 problems. Of these, 80 of the solutions (50%) were scored at level 3 thinking (based on a scale with maximum 3 the highest level). In the control group, however, there were 216 total solutions, of which 61 (or 28%) were considered level 3 thinking.

Students in the treatment group were subsequently interviewed. According to Lester (1996), "their comments corroborated findings on the experience of sharing an intellectual partnership with *Sketchpad* to extend cognitive capacities to optimize learning" (p. 137). Students noted that constructing and transforming geometric figures was made easier through use of *Sketchpad*. They also found that measuring and recording information was made visible through charts and labeling and that they could more easily verify accuracy of data through observation of multiple cases. They acknowledged that being able to visualize dynamic transformations of figures deepened their understanding of circles. It also gave some students the confidence they needed to be able to make conjectures and reason to conclusions. However, transferring those skills in the absence of the computer was confusing and difficult for other students.

The dissertations of Heltsley (1996) and Lester (1996) have provided valuable information to educators, both in the Catholic and public sectors, about the value and impact of given software on our students. While Lester's analysis was decidedly focused on the content and curricular import of the software, Heltsley's scarcely addressed the academic value; rather, it considered the moral and ethical messages embedded in popular software packages.

TECHNOLOGY AS A MOTIVATOR

Heltsley (1996) noted that the most common reason cited by students for choosing given programs as their favorites was that they "were fun." This motivational reason was mentioned by 34% of the students. The educational incentive was second, named by only 26% of students. Thus, it appears that use of technology can be a motivator in student learning. A study by Samaras and Wilson (1998) provided further evidence of this proposition.

Samaras and Wilson (1998) investigated African American families' perceptions of an after-school family involvement program that had been implemented in two inner city schools, one public and one Catholic. Among the research objectives, the study sought to determine families' perceptions of the value of technology in the children's learning. The program invited families to tell, write, and then key-in family stories on computers, with university faculty and students serving as computer assistants. The program was implemented in the Catholic school during the first four months of 1997. An interview protocol was administered to families. Additionally, secondary data were gathered using computer-documented family stories, children's drawings, computer-generated quick-take pictures, and researcher observations and field notes. Families consistently indicated that they were attracted to the program because of the computer component and saw it as a way of becoming prepared for the future.

TECHNOLOGY AND ADMINISTRATION

Over the past 10 years, more and more schools have moved from manual record keeping to the use of technology. In many instances, schools have invested in integrated software packages that provide economy of time, for data shared among offices need to be input only once, and revisions are updated simultaneously across offices. Cresci (2000) sought to determine whether schools' administration operations were significantly more efficient with the use of computers and the applications they supported. Additionally, Cresci presented an action proposal that addressed the need for continuous availability, data integrity, ease of use, high performance, and system and application accountability. It included an outline of 10 application systems within a school setting that could be accessed by one another: a management control system, discipline reporting system, guidance tracking system, electronic mail system, attendance reporting, school billing, tuition billing, grade reporting, schedule generation, and budget reporting.

Cresci (2000) used survey methodology to measure efficiency both with and without the use of technology, and to draw a correlation between the two to determine relevance of technology for administrative operations and efficiency. The survey consisted of two parts, one which was designed to measure the school's efficiency based on its utilization of technology and its creation and implementation of a technology plan. Part B measured the self-reported overall efficiency of the principal.

The survey was sent to the 453 elementary or secondary schools in the Archdiocese of New York and the Diocese of Brooklyn. Of the 453 surveys mailed, 139 (30.7%) were returned. These were scored, using a rubric designed by Cresci (2000). The scores for technology use and overall efficiency were paired for each principal and plotted. For the graph, the best fit line, its equation, and the Pearson r were determined.

For the elementary schools, the slope of the regression line was .389, and r = .28. For the high schools, however, the results were much different, with the slope of the regression line equal to -0.1506 and $r = -0.12$. Cresci (2000) conjectured that the insignificant secondary school results were due to the technological proficiency of the principals and staff, resulting in a feeling of no greater efficiency based on the technology. The personnel in general were comfortable using phone answering machines, VCRs, automated bookkeeping systems, and computerized media center card catalog systems. CD-ROM usage was related to availability of computer laboratories in the schools. Few schools reported availability or use of video disc players, Interactive Distance Learning (IDL), or fiber optic lines. Secondary principals made greater administrative use of e-mail, the World Wide Web, and databases than did elementary principals. Nonetheless, they did not perceive themselves as more efficient. For the 139 schools combined, the correlation between use of technology and overall efficiency was $r = 0.25$.

SUMMARY

In the last 10 years of the twentieth century, Catholic schools made significant progress in their acquisition and use of technology for instructional purposes. However, while there has been a fair amount of research relative to numbers of pieces of equipment, connections to local or wide area networks, frequency of staff development, and similar statistics, there has been little research about the effectiveness of the use of technology in the Catholic schools. It would seem that the research agenda in Catholic schools for the next decade must include studies about student gains when technology is used in the educational process. Additionally, studies will need to examine the size of the digital divide so that strategies can be devised for reducing it so that Catholic schools can be true to their mission of providing quality education to all of their students.

SOCIAL, FISCAL, AND POLITICAL CAPITAL

CHAPTER 12

CATHOLIC SCHOOL DEMOGRAPHY: CHANGES FROM 1990-2000

FRANK X. SAVAGE

INTRODUCTION

This chapter describes the demographic changes that have taken place in Catholic schools from about 1990 to 2000. After sketching a portrait of Catholic schools in 1990 including the major points and trends highlighted by John Convey in *Catholic Schools Make a Difference* (1992), the chapter will explore changes in the number, types, distribution, location, and new construction of schools. Changes in school enrollment including market share, Catholic versus non-Catholic enrollment, ethnic and cultural background percentages of total enrollment, and changes in staffing will also be presented. Information regarding increases in tuition, per-pupil cost, and salaries of school administrators and teachers will also be explored.

Most of the data presented in this chapter were gleaned from reports based on data collected by the National Catholic Educational Association (NCEA) and from reports issued by the National Center for Education Statistics (NCES) of the United States Department of Education. Information on new school construction was based on data collected by Meitler Consultants, Inc. that was reported in *Catholic School Growth 1995 to 1999* (Augenstein & Meitler, 2000).

SUMMARY OF CATHOLIC SCHOOL DEMOGRAPHICS 1990

Schools

In the fall of 1990, there were a total of 8,587 Catholic schools in the United States (Brigham, 1992b). Of that number, 7,291 were elementary and 1,296 were secondary schools (Brigham, 1992b). This represented almost a 9% decline since 1982-1983 in total Catholic schools and an 8.3% and 12.6% decline in elementary and secondary schools respectively. Consolidation was attributed as the major reason for school realignment (Brigham, 1992b). Table 1 presents the number and percentage of total schools by the six geographical regions identified by NCEA (NCEA). [1]

Table 1: Elementary and Secondary Schools by Region 1990-1991		
	Number	**%**
Elementary		
New England	477	6.5
Mideast	2,050	28.1
Great Lakes	1,933	26.5
Plains	848	11.6
Southeast	791	10.9
West-Far West	1,192	16.4
United States	**7,291**	**100.0**
Secondary		
New England	107	8.3
Mideast	364	28.1
Great Lakes	271	20.9
Plains	147	11.3
Southeast	180	13.9
West-Far West	227	17.5
United States	**1,296**	**100.0**
All Schools		
New England	584	6.8
Mideast	2,414	28.1
Great Lakes	2,204	25.7
Plains	995	11.6
Southeast	971	11.3
West-Far West	1,419	16.5
United States	**8,587**	**100.0**

Source: (Brigham, 1992b)

NCEA identifies four types of schools according to the authority of school administration (Brigham, 1990). The four types are parish, inter-parish, diocesan, and private. Figure 1 represents the percentage of each type of Catholic elementary school during the spring of 1990.

Figure 1: **Types of Catholic Elementary Schools, Spring 1990. Source: (Brigham, 1992b).**

Figure 2 provides the same representation for Catholic schools. In the spring of 1990, both elementary and secondary schools were predominately located in urban areas.

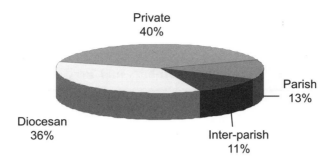

Figure 2: **Types of Catholic Secondary Schools, Spring 1990. Source: (Brigham, 1992b).**

Approximately 34% of Catholic schools were located in urban areas, 31% in suburbs, 23% in rural areas, and 12% in inner city (Brigham, 1990). Brigham (1990) noted that the number of elementary schools declined by 601 since the base line year of 1981-1982. However, during the same period inter-parish and diocesan elementary schools had increased by 197 or 3.2% (1990). Catholic secondary schools had declined by 174 during the same years and showed a slight increase in the percentage of inter-parish and diocesan schools. The majority (75.7%) of Catholic secondary schools were either private or diocesan. In 1989-1990, parish secondary schools accounted for 13% of all Catholic secondary schools—down from 21.6% in 1981 (1990). Brigham also observed that the increase in elementary and secondary inter-parish and diocesan schools in the last decade (1981-1989) underlines the reorganization of Catholic education through consolidation. We will see this trend continue into the 1990s as the Catholic population migrates and enrollment numbers increase.

Enrollment and Staffing

The total number of students enrolled in Catholic schools grades pre-kindergarten through grade 12 in the fall of 1990 was 2,575,815 (Brigham, 1992b). Of this number, 100,376 children were enrolled in preschool programs, 1,883,906 students in grades K-8 and 591,533 in grades 9-12 (Brigham, 1992b). Table 2 illustrates enrollment numbers and percentages by regions.

Table 2: Fall 1990 Enrollment Numbers and Percentages by Regions

Elementary	Numbers	Percentage
New England	109,633	5.8
Mideast	556,176	29.5
Great Lakes	493,462	26.2
Plains	186,234	9.9
Southeast	229,280	12.2
West-Far West	309,121	16.4
All Regions	**1,883,906**	**100.00**
Secondary		
New England	44,481	7.5
Mideast	188,635	31.9
Great Lakes	136,383	23.1
Plains	47,660	8.1
Southeast	70,613	11.9
West-Far West	103,761	17.5
All Regions	**591,533**	**100.00**
All Schools		
New England	154,114	6.2
Mideast	744,811	30.1
Great Lakes	629,845	25.4
Plains	233,894	9.5
Southeast	299,893	12.1
West-Far West	412,882	16.7
All Regions	**2,475,439 ***	**100.00**

* Represents K-12 total. Regional Pre-K enrollment figures were not compiled before 1991-92
Source: (Brigham, 1992b)

In 1990, slightly over 23% of the Catholic school student population came from four ethnic groups: Black, Hispanic, Asian, and Native American. Catholic elementary and secondary schools had approximately the same percentage of ethnic enrollment with 23.4% of enrollment for elementary schools and 22.7% for secondary schools (Brigham, 1992b).

NCEA data have shown a gradual increase in non-Catholic students between 1982 and the early 1990s (Brigham, 1992b). In 1990, the non-Catholic student enrollment was 11% for all elementary schools, 14.5% for secondary schools, and 11.9% for all Catholic schools (Brigham, 1992b). There were significant regional differences in non-Catholic enrollment. The Plains region had the lowest percentage of non-Catholic enrollment with only 5.5% of students. The Southeast and the West-Far West had the highest percentage with 16% and 14.6% respectively (Brigham, 1992b).

In 1990-1991, there were 131,198 full-time teachers in Catholic schools. Lay women (89,718) represented the largest group with slightly more than 68%. Lay men were the second largest group with approximately 18% followed by sisters with slightly less than 11% and brothers and priests with slightly more than 2%. In 1990, lay men and women comprised almost 87% of Catholic school teachers (Brigham, 1992b).

Trends 1990

The number of Catholic schools continued to decline into 1990 due to consolidations and the movement of Catholic families away from neighborhoods with Catholic schools (Convey, 1992). The declining enrollment of Catholic elementary and secondary schools that began after the 1964-1965 school year continued through 1990. Convey in *Catholic Schools Make a Difference* (1992) states that "by 1990, over three million fewer students attended Catholic school, compared with 1965" (p. 51). Convey lists several factors that contributed to the decline; namely, diminished birth rate, migration of Catholic families to areas without Catholic schools, higher cost of Catholic schooling, greater acceptance of public schools on the part of Catholic parents, and changing social attitudes (p. 51). While the overall number of Catholic school students was decreasing, the relative proportion of students from the four major ethnic and cultural groups was increasing (1992). Similarly, the proportion of non-Catholic enrollment was also increasing (1992).

CHANGING CATHOLIC SCHOOL DEMOGRAPHY 1990-2000

The 1990s saw the continuation of some trends and the reversal of others. The school age population in the United States increased each year of the decade for an overall increase of 13.9% (NCES, 2001). Catholic school enrollment began to increase reversing the trend of declining enrollment that started in 1965. The number of schools continued to decline but this was offset by the construction of new schools. A significant number of Catholic schools reported waiting lists. Regional demographic trends observed in the total population were reflected in Catholic school enrollments, staffing, and the distribution of Catholic schools. These trends and related information will be explored in the following sections that highlight the changes in Catholic schools between 1990 and 2000.

Number, Type, and Distribution of Schools

In the fall of 2000 there were 8,146 Catholic schools. Of that number 6,920 were elementary/middle schools and 1,226 secondary (McDonald, 2001b). The number of schools declined by 441 or 5% from the 1990 fall total of 8,587. Elementary schools declined by 371 from the 1990 total of 7,291. Secondary schools declined by 70 from 1,296. Both elementary and secondary schools declined approximately 5% over the 10-year period. The rate of decline was offset by the amount of new school construction that took place during the same period. A discussion of new school construction follows later in this chapter.

Table 3 shows the distribution of schools by region. Regional numbers and percentage of totals are presented for elementary and middle schools, secondary schools, and totals for all schools. Statistics for the 1990-1991, 1995-1996 and 2000-2001 school years are provided for comparison. Southeast and West-Far West regions showed increased percentages of schools with respective increases of 1% and 1.3% over their 1990 percentages. The New England and Plains regions showed slight declines. The Mideast and Great Lakes regions showed the greatest declines over their 1990 percentages with decreases of 1.3% and 0.8% respectively. These slight to moderate changes in percentages reflect the changing population trends in the last decade (McDonald, 2001b).

Table 3: Regional Distribution of Elementary, Middle, and Secondary Schools

	1990-1991		1995-1996		2000-2001	
	No.	%	No.	%	No.	%
Elementary/Middle						
New England	477	6.5	458	6.5	452	6.5
Mideast	2,050	28.1	1921	27.4	1853	26.8
Great Lakes	1,933	26.5	1819	25.9	1773	25.6
Plains	848	11.6	800	11.4	794	11.5
Southeast	791	10.9	805	11.5	827	12.0
West-Far West	1,192	16.4	1212	17.3	1221	17.6
United States	**7,291**	**100.0**	**7,015**	**100.0**	**6,920**	**100.0**
Secondary						
New England	107	8.3	96	7.8	94	7.7
Mideast	364	28.1	340	27.7	332	27.1
Great Lakes	271	20.9	260	21.2	257	20.9
Plains	147	11.3	140	11.4	137	11.2
Southeast	180	13.9	171	13.9	178	14.5
West-Far West	227	17.5	221	17.9	228	18.6
United States	**1,296**	**100.0**	**1,228**	**100.0**	**1,226**	**100.0**
Totals All Schools						
New England	584	6.8	554	6.7	546	6.7
Mideast	2414	28.1	2261	27.4	2185	26.8
Great Lakes	2204	25.7	2079	25.2	2030	24.9
Plains	995	11.6	940	11.4	931	11.4
Southeast	971	11.3	976	11.8	1005	12.3
West-Far West	1419	16.5	1433	17.7	1449	17.8
United States	**8,587**	**100.0**	**8,243**	**100.0**	**8,146**	**100.0**

Source: (McDonald, 2001b, p.7)

Slight changes occurred in the percentages for types of schools. The percentage of parish elementary and middle schools declined over 5% while the inter-parish, diocesan, and private elementary school types have a combined increase of 5.3%. The largest increase in elementary and middle schools was 3.1% for inter-parish schools. Secondary schools showed a decrease of slightly less than 2% in parish schools with a very small increase in inter-parish schools. The percentage of diocesan secondary schools decreased almost 1% for the same period. Private schools, the largest category of Catholic secondary school types, increased over 2%. Figures 3 and 4 illustrate these changes.

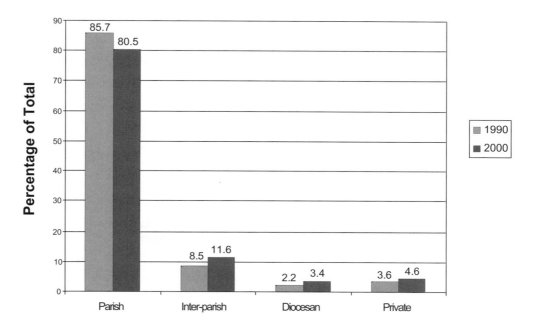

Figure 3: Types of Catholic Elementary/Middle Schools Comparison Between Spring 1990 and Spring 2000. Source: (Brigham, 1992b; McDonald, 2001b)

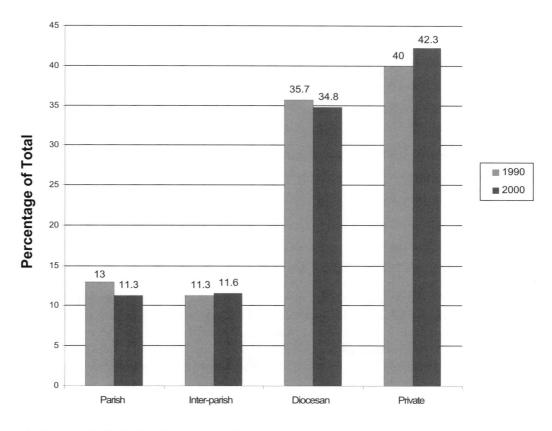

Figure 4: Types of Catholic Secondary Schools Comparison Between Spring 1990 and Spring 2000. Source: (Brigham, 1992b; McDonald, 2001b)

In the spring of 1990, 34% of Catholic schools were located within urban areas, 12% in the inner city, 31% in suburbs, and 23% in rural areas (Brigham, 1990). In the spring of 2000, 33% were located in urban areas, 13% in inner city, 33% in suburbs, and 21% in rural areas. In 1990, 46% of Catholic schools were located in urban and inner city areas. The percentage remained unchanged for 10 years despite population changes and financial difficulties (McDonald, 2001b). Figures 5 and 6 compare the distribution of schools in 1990 and 2000.

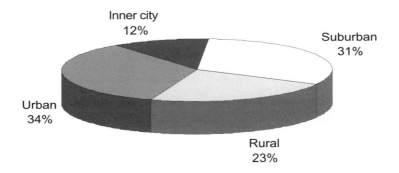

Figure 5: **Percentage of Catholic Schools by Location Spring 1990. Source: (Brigham, 1992b; McDonald, 2001b).**

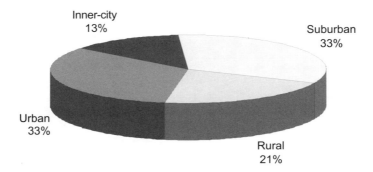

Figure 6: **Percentage of Catholic Schools by Location, Spring 2000. Source: (Brigham, 1992b; McDonald, 2001b).**

New Schools

The decline in the number of schools from 1990-2000 was offset by the construction of new schools. In 1994, Meitler Consultants, Inc. in collaboration with the NCEA Department of Chief Administrators of Catholic Education (CACE), began a systematic process of collecting data regarding the construction of new Catholic schools. Until this time, many Catholic educational leaders felt that a trend toward new school construction was underway but were unable to confirm it empirically. The initial research focused on new school construction over an 11-year period from 1985-1995. The first report was published by NCEA in a 1997 publication titled *New Catholic Schools 1985-1995.* The report documented that 134 new Catholic schools opened with 51,370 new seats between 1985 and 1995 (Augenstein & Meitler, 2000).

Meitler Consultants continues to annually update the data on new school construction. In 1999, NCEA commissioned a revised report authored by John Augenstein and Neal Meitler (2000). The revised report showed that for the 15-year period 1985-1999, 230 new Catholic schools opened with 87,807 seats. Of that number, 204 were elementary schools and 26 were secondary schools. The Southeast, West-Far West and Plains regions constructed the greatest number of new schools. Reflecting the population migration, the majority of new schools were constructed in the suburbs. Fifty-five percent of new elementary schools and 42% of new secondary schools were located in the suburbs. However, new schools were also constructed in urban, inner city and rural areas (Augenstein & Meitler, 2000). Figures 7, 8, 9, and Table 4 detail the growth and location of new school construction from 1988-1999.

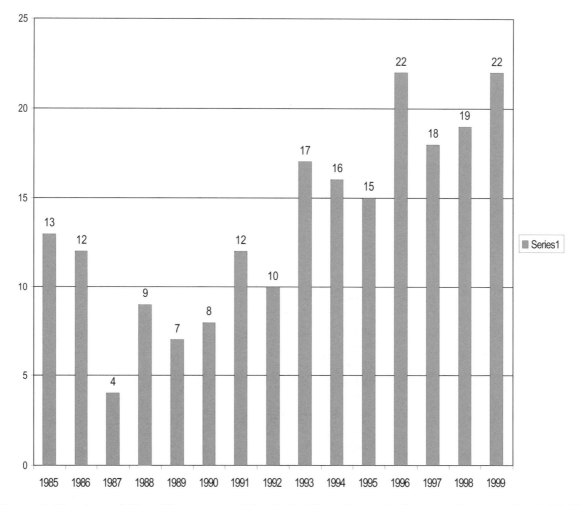

Figure 7: **Number of New Elementary Schools by Year Opened. Source: (Augenstein & Meitler, 2000, p. 13).**

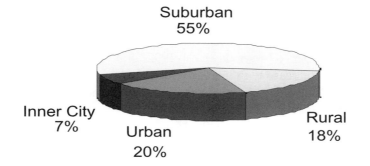

Figure 8: **Location of New Catholic Elementary Schools Built Between 1985 and 1999. Source: (Augenstein & Meitler, 2000, p. 13).**

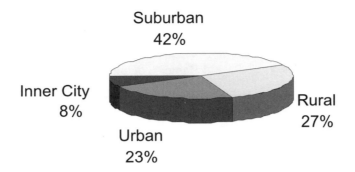

Figure 9: **Location of New Catholic Secondary Schools Built Between 1985 and 1999. Source: (Augenstein & Meitler, 2000, p. 13).**

Table 4: Number of New Secondary Schools Opened by Year 1985-1999	
Year	**Number**
1985	1
1986	1
1987	3
1988	2
1989	1
1990	0
1991	1
1992	1
1993	2
1994	0
1995	2
1996	4
1997	1
1998	6
1999	1

Source: (Augenstein & Meitler, 2000, p. 27)

Enrollment

In the 1992-1993 school year, the trend of declining Catholic school enrollment that started in 1965 halted with an increase of 0.66% or 16,767 over the 1991-1992 total (Brigham, 1993). The remainder of the decade saw enrollments continue to increase with increases in all but two years.[2] The overall increase in PreK-12 enrollment was 71,486 or 2.8% from 1990 to 2000. Catholic elementary school enrollment (Pre-K-8) increased 1.8%. Secondary school enrollment (9-12) increased 6.1%. The percentage of total enrollment for the Mideast and Great Lakes regions declined in the 1990s. However, these two regions still enrolled more than half (52.6%) of the Catholic school age population. During the same period, the percentage of total enrollment in the Southeast and West-Far West regions grew by 2.4% from 28.6% of total enrollment in 1990 to 31% in 2000 (McDonald, 2001b). Figures 10, 11, and 12 chart changes in PK-12, PK-8, and 9-12 from 1990 through 2000.

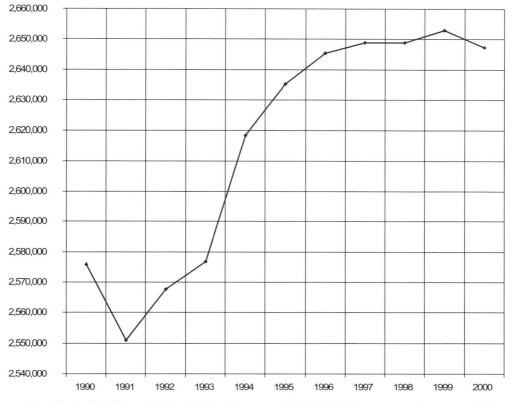

Figure 10: Catholic School PK-12 Enrollment 1990-2000. Source: (Brigham, 1992b, 1993, 1994, 1995; McDonald, 1999b, 2000b, 2001b; Metzler, 1998; Milks, 1997; Savage & Milks, 1996).

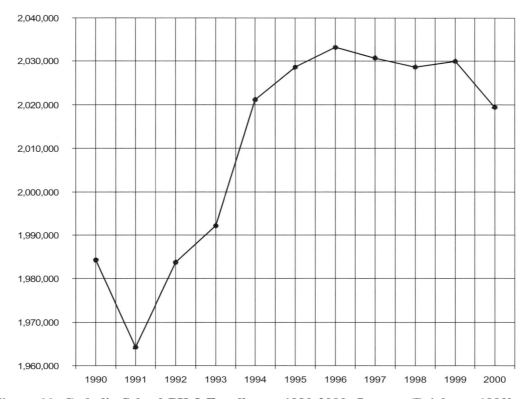

Figure 11: Catholic School PK-8 Enrollment 1990-2000. Source: (Brigham, 1992b, 1993, 1994, 1995; McDonald, 1999b, 2000b, 2001b; Metzler, 1998; Milks, 1997; Savage & Milks, 1996).

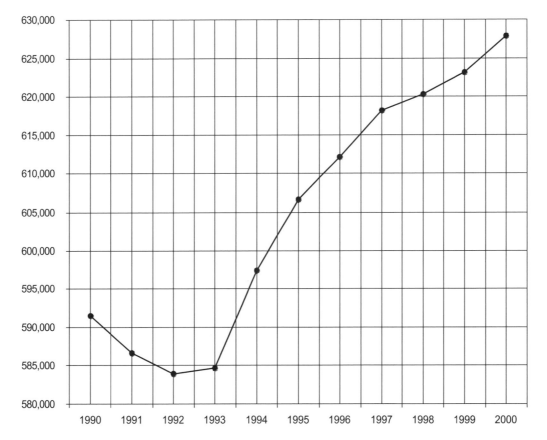

Figure 12: **Catholic School Enrollment Grades 9-12 1990-2000. Source: (Brigham, 1992b, 1993, 1994, 1995; McDonald, 1999b, 2000b, 2001b; Metzler, 1998, Milks, 1997; Savage & Milks, 1996).**

In 1990, NCEA reported student ethnic background in five categories: Black, Hispanic, Asian, Native American and other. In 2000 there were 7 categories.[3] The changes in reporting ethnic background underscore the increasing cultural and ethnic diversity in the United States population that are reflected within Catholic schools. However, between 1990 and 2000 enrollment of students from ethnic and cultural groups, exclusive of "White" and "Other" has remained fairly constant at approximately 23% to 24% of the total Catholic school student population nationally. Regional enrollment differences vary widely with the West-Far West having the highest percentage of minority enrollment with 48% and the Plains the lowest with 8.8%. Table 5 shows a breakdown of minority enrollment by region.

Table 5: Catholic School Ethnic Minority Enrollment Percentages by Region: 2000-2001

Region	%
New England	14
Mideast	27
Great Lakes	17
Plains	9
Southeast	21
West-Far West	48
National	25

Source: (McDonald, 2001b, pp. 16-17)

The percentage of non-Catholic enrollment of total Catholic school enrollment has increased 1.6% from 1990 to 2000. In 1990, non-Catholic children represented 11.9% of Catholic school students (Brigham, 1992b). In 2000, the percent had grown to 13.6% (McDonald, 2001b).

The decade of 1990 was a period of growth for Catholic schools. The enrollment decline ceased and enrollment began to gradually increase. New schools were built. Catholic schools enjoyed a level of respect that caused many to look at them as models for educational reform. Augenstein and Meitler in their report *Catholic School Growth 1985-1999* (2000) list seven reasons for this recent growth in Catholic schools:

1. The growth of the U.S. population and the increased number of school-age children
2. The intentional and more assertive marketing of Catholic schools to the public
3. The unprecedented economic growth that began in 1991 and continued to the end of the decade
4. The avoidance of unpopular and failing public schools
5. The belief that Catholic schools are safe places for children to learn and that parents have more opportunities to be involved in their children's education
6. The heightened need for instruction in Christian values and doctrine
7. The increased desire for parental choice in education. (pp. 6-7)

The data that document the growth of schools and enrollment in the 1990s also present some challenges for the future. While the growth in enrollments in the 1990s is cause for celebration among Catholic educators, the difficulty in retaining students through eight grades of elementary school continues to be a problem (Kealey, 2001b). Using NCEA enrollment figures, Figure 13 tracks the first grade class in fall of 1990 through eight years to the fall of 1997. The difference between the 1990 first grade enrollment and the enrollment of that class in the eighth grade of 1997 is 50,353 students, which is erosion of 21.7% of the 1990 class enrollment. Figure 14 illustrates the percentage of decline between grades. Loss of enrollments is especially acute between grades 1 and 2 (4.9%) and 6 and 7 (4.9%). Catholic schools are addressing the challenge of student recruitment. The challenge of student retention still needs attention.

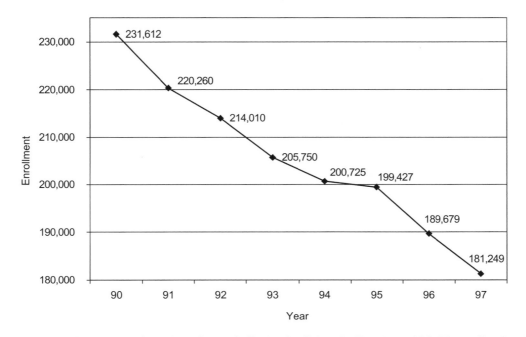

Figure 13: **Student Migration Out of Catholic Schools Tracks 1990 First Grade through 1997 Eighth Grade. Source: (Brigham, 1992b, 1993, 1994, 1995; McDonald, 1999b, 2000b, 2001b; Metzler, 1998; Milks, 1997; Savage & Milks, 1996).**

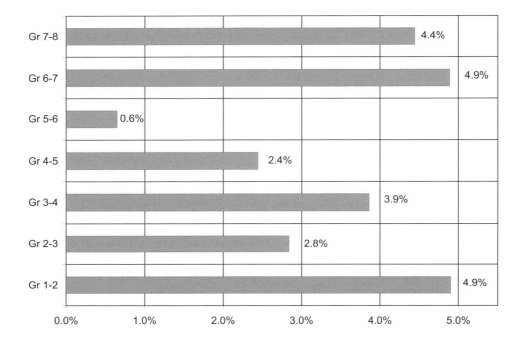

Figure 14: **Percent of Enrollment Decline Between Catholic Elementary School Grades Tracks 1990 Grade 1 through 1997 Grade 8. Source: (Brigham, 1992b, 1993, 1994, 1995; McDonald, 1999b, 2000b, 2001b; Metzler, 1998; Milks, 1997; Savage & Milks, 1996).**

While Catholic school enrollment increased in the 1990s, so too did the total student age population in the country. A comparison between total U.S. elementary and secondary school enrollment, which includes public and private schools, and Catholic school enrollment indicates that Catholic schools continued to lose market share. From 1990 to 2000 total elementary and secondary school enrollment in the United States increased from 46.4 million to almost 53 million—a cumulative increase of 13.9% (NCES, 2001). The cumulative increase for Catholic school enrollment was 2.8% for the same period. A review of the enrollment statistics shows that Catholic schools' market share of the school age population decreased from 5.55% in 1990 to 5.0% in 2000. The Catholic school enrollment increase from 1990 to 2000 was 71,487 students. If the same market share of 5.55% had been maintained, the enrollment increase would have been 341,279 or an increase of 13.25%. The fall 1999 *Cara Report* (Froehle, 1999) in a special section on Catholic schools indicated a decline in market share of the Catholic school age children from 40% in 1950 to 21% in 1998. Clearly there are still more marketing and promotion challenges ahead. Figure 15 gives a graphic comparison of changes in the Catholic school enrollment to total school age enrollment and an indication of a declining share of the Catholic enrollment of the total school age enrollment.

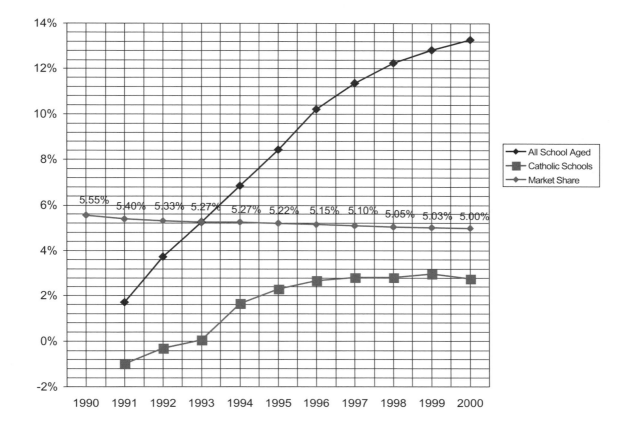

Figure 15: **Comparison of Total Elementary and Secondary Enrollment Change to Catholic School Enrollment Change with Catholic School Market Share 1990-2000. Source: (Brigham, 1992b, 1993, 1994, 1995; McDonald, 1999b, 2000b, 2001b; Metzler, 1998; Milks, 1997; NCES, 2001; Savage & Milks, 1996).**

The construction of new schools and increasing the capacity of existing schools is another challenge related to Catholic school enrollment. Augenstein and Meitler (2000) claim, "There is a substantial unmet demand for Catholic schools in some areas of the country. If new Catholic schools were constructed in all areas with waiting lists, total Catholic school enrollment would be considerably higher than it is today" (p. 5). The Meitler research pointed out that in the period between 1985 and 1999 newly constructed Catholic schools created 87,807 new seats (Augenstein & Meitler, 2000). Had the capacity of Catholic schools not been increased, it is doubtful if Catholic schools would have experienced the enrollment increases of the 1990s and probably would have experienced an even greater loss of market share (Augenstein & Meitler, 2000).

Since 1997-1998, NCEA has reported the number of schools with waiting lists. On average, 44% of all schools have waiting lists (McDonald, 1999b, 2000b, 2001b; Metzler, 1998). Table 6 shows the percentage of schools with waiting lists by region and by year. Waiting lists may seem like a blessing to veteran Catholic educators who have endured the anguish of schools with empty desks. However, from another perspective it is discouraging that over 40% of Catholic schools in the country do not have the capacity to serve the needs of parents wanting Catholic schooling for their children.

Table 6: **Percentage of Schools with Waiting Lists by Region and Year**

Region	1997-1998	1998-1999	1999-2000	2000-2001
New England	66.7%	68.5%	69.5%	60.8%
Mideast	37.4	36.4	49.0	37.3
Great Lakes	25.9	28.7	29.5	30.9
Plains	32.5	31.2	33.0	35.1
Southeast	56.4	58.2	57.2	57.1
West/Far West	51.9	52.0	54.8	62.8
United States	**40.8**	**41.4**	**45.7**	**44.0**

Source: (McDonald, 1999b, 2001b; Metzler, 1998).

Staffing

Full time equivalent teaching staff grew from 131,198 in 1990 (Brigham, 1992b) to 161,496 in 2000 (McDonald, 2001b)—a 23% increase. The percentage of lay faculty increased from 87% (Brigham, 1992b) to 93% (McDonald, 2001b). In 1990, religious and clergy accounted for 13.3% of teaching staff in Catholic schools (Brigham, 1992b). In 2000, religious and clergy represented 6.5% of Catholic schools' professional staff (McDonald, 2001b). Table 7 compares the religious clergy and lay composition of Catholic schools' faculties from 1991-1992[4] and 2000-2001.

Table 7: **Full Time Equivalent Professional Staff 1991-2000 Comparison**

	1991-92		2000-01	
	No.	%	No.	%
Elementary				
Sisters	11932	10.9%	6008	5.4%
Brothers	242	0.2%	161	0.1%
Priests	726	0.7%	221	0.2%
Lay women	87408	80.1%	95305	85.1%
Lay men	8776	8.0%	10243	9.2%
Total	**109,084**	**100.0%**	**112,402**	**100.0%**
Secondary				
Sisters	4,083	9.2%	2,121	4.4%
Brothers	1,624	3.7%	1,053	2.2%
Priests	1,728	3.9%	931	2.0%
Lay women	20,660	46.7%	24,593	50.1%
Lay men	16,155	36.5%	20,096	41.3%
Total	**44,250**	**100.0%**	**49,093**	**100.0%**
All Schools				
Sisters	16,015	10.4%	8,129	5.0%
Brothers	1,866	1.2%	1,214	0.8%
Priests	2,454	1.6%	1,152	0.7%
Lay women	108,058	70.5%	119,898	74.6%
Lay men	24,951	16.3%	30,339	18.9%
Total	**153,344**	**100.0%**	**161,496**	**100.0%**

Source: (Brigham, 1992b; McDonald, 2001b)

In 1997-1998, NCEA began reporting ethnic background and non-Catholic numbers and percentages of Catholic school faculties. The data include all full and part-time staff. The vast majority of Catholic school staff members are White. That percentage varied from a low of 85.9% in 1999-2000 (McDonald, 2000b) and a high of 90.4% in 1998-1999 (McDonald, 1999b). Staff members from other ethnic backgrounds comprise 10% to 15% of Catholic school faculties. In the years reported, the percentage of non-Catholic faculty varied from a low of 12.1% in 1997-1998 to a high of 14.5% in 1999-2000. On average for the four reported years non-Catholics comprised 14% of Catholic school faculties. For elementary schools the percentage was 12.2%. For secondary schools it was 17.6% (McDonald, 1999b, 2000b, 2001b; Metzler, 1998).

Cost, Tuition, and Salaries

NCEA collects data on Catholic school finances on a two-year cycle with the report on secondary schools issued on even numbered years and the elementary school report on the odd numbered. The observations made here are based on those reports.

United States Catholic Elementary Schools & Their Finances 1991 (Kealey, 1992) reported data collected for the 1990-1991 school year. The publication reported that $969 was the average tuition charged for one child of a parishioner to attend a Catholic school. Regional differences in average tuition ranged from a low of $824 for the Great Lakes region to $1,171 for the West-Far West region (1992). The average materials fees were $98 (1992). Tuition and materials fees covered 58.66% of the average per-pupil cost of $1,819 (1992). Other sources of income made up the difference with parish subsidy covering about one-third the cost (Kealey, 1992).

In *Balance Sheet for Catholic Elementary Schools: 1999 Income and Expenses*, Robert Kealey (2000) reported financial information for the 1998-1999 school year. In 1998-1999, the average tuition for one child from the parish was $1,787 (2000)—an 84.4% increase over eight years. Tuition covered 62% of the per-pupil cost (2000). As in 1990, the regional differences varied but the Great Lakes still had the lowest average tuition with $1,373 and the West-Far West the highest with $2,309 (2000). The average cost of materials paid by parents was $290 (2000). The average per-pupil cost in 1998-99 was $2,823 (2000), an increase of 55.2% from 1990. The amount of parish subsidy as a percent of total revenue declined to less than 24% (2000). Figure 16 illustrates the average tuition and per pupil cost in Catholic elementary schools for the five numbered years of the 1990s. Figure 17 shows that tuition as a percentage of per pupil cost has increased 10% over the same period.

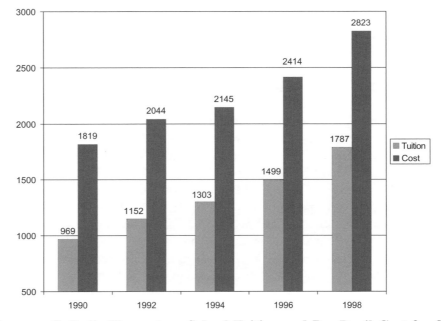

Figure 16: **Average Catholic Elementary School Tuition and Per Pupil Cost for Selected Years. Source (Kealey, 1992, 1994, 1996, 1998a, 2000).**

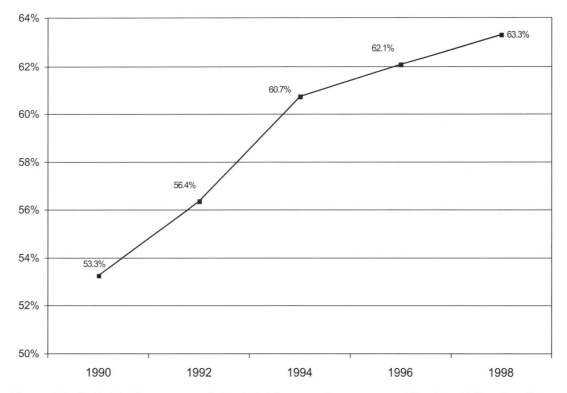

Figure 17: **Catholic Elementary School Tuition as a Percentage of Per Pupil Cost for Selected Years (Fees Excluded). Source: (Kealey, 1992, 1994, 1996, 1998a, 2000).**

Regarding administrator and teacher salaries, in 1990-1991 the average lay elementary principal's salary was $30,153 and the average salary for a beginning lay elementary teacher with a bachelor's degree was $14,514. The average salary for all other teachers was $17,597 (Kealey, 1992). By 1998-1999 the average lay elementary principal's salary had risen 44.6% to $43,599. The average salary for a new teacher with an undergraduate degree rose 31.2% to $19,047, and the average salary for all teachers rose 49.8% to $26,361 (Kealey, 2000). While these salary increases seem significant, they must be viewed in light of salaries paid to a Catholic school principal or teacher's public school counterpart. The average salary paid a public school elementary principal in 1998-1999 was $67,348. The average for middle school principals was $71,499. This translates to a salary gap of 35% to 39% between the average salary paid a Catholic school elementary principal and public elementary or middle school principal in 1998. The average salary gap for teachers for the same period is over 36% (Kealey, 2000).

For Catholic secondary schools, the median tuition cost in the 1989-1990 school year was $2,299. This represented 65% of the per-pupil cost of $3,517 (Guerra, 1990). Tuition, per-pupil cost, and tuition as a percent of per-pupil cost varied by region and type of secondary school. The West-Far West and New England regions had the highest tuition ($2,800 and $2,632), per-pupil cost ($3,566 and $3,456) and the largest percent of per-pupil cost (79% and 76%) (Guerra, 1990). The Plains region had the lowest tuition ($1,470), per-pupil cost, ($2,739), and tuition as a percent of per-pupil cost (53%) (Guerra, 1990). In 1998-1999, the median tuition for Catholic secondary schools was $4,000, an increase of 74%. The per-pupil cost for the average Catholic secondary school in 1998-1999 was $5,571. New England and the West-Far West had the highest tuition rates in 1998-1999 with median tuition rates of $4,785 and $4,720 respectively (Tracy, 2001). This represents increases since 1989-1990 of 45% and 41%. Data collected in 1998 indicate that, on average, Catholic secondary tuition covers between 70% and 80% of school operating costs (Guerra, 1998). Figure 18 compares the average ninth grade tuition and the median per pupil cost for selected years. Figure 19 shows the percentage of per pupil cost that tuition covers for the same years.

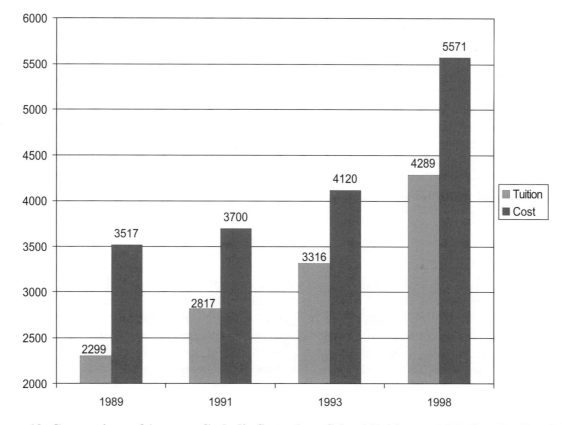

Figure 18: **Comparison of Average Catholic Secondary School Tuition and Median Per Pupil Cost for Selected Years. Source: (Guerra, 1990, 1993, 1995; Tracy, 2001).**

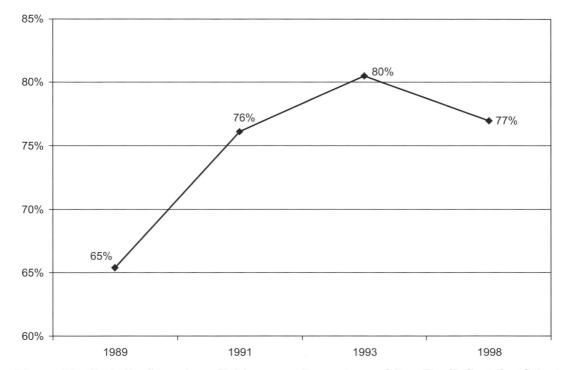

Figure 19: **Catholic Secondary Tuition as a Percentage of Per Pupil Cost for Selected Years. Source: (Guerra, 1990, 1993, 1995; Tracy, 2001).**

In 1990, the average salary for a lay secondary principal was $41,300 (Guerra, 1990). In 1999, the average lay salary for the chief administrator of a Catholic secondary school had increased 47.5% to $60,900. For schools that had a head administrator (e.g., president) the average principal's salary was $51,600 (Tracy, 2001). The median salary for a Catholic secondary school teacher in 1990 was $22,081 (Guerra, 1990). By 1999, the median salary had increased 35% to $29,800 (Tracy, 2001). As with Catholic elementary school principals and teachers there is a salary gap between Catholic secondary school principals and teachers and their public school counterparts. There is an even greater gap between their salaries and those of their colleagues in other private schools. Sister Mary Tracy (2001) in *Mission and Money: A CHS 2000 Report on Finance, Advancement, and Governance*, reports, "The Catholic secondary school's salary for the head of school is about 79% of the National Association of Secondary School Principals (NASSP) reported average salary, and 50% of the National Association of Independent Schools (NAIS) figure" (p. 17).

SUMMARY

The decade of 1990 was significant for Catholic schools. The 27-year enrollment decline stopped and enrollment numbers gradually began to increase. The number of schools continued to decline, but a significant number of new schools were constructed. Changes in regional distribution of schools reflected the general population shifts in the country as a whole. The number and percentage of schools and Catholic school enrollment increased slightly but significantly in the West-Far West and Southeast regions. Ethnic and multicultural enrollment remained steady at approximately 24% of total enrollment. However, in some regions, most notably the West-Far West, ethnic and multicultural enrollment increased to the point that soon the ethnic category "White" may become a minority. Despite the growth of the 1990s, Catholic educational leaders cannot afford to be complacent. Aggressive marketing and promotion of Catholic schools are still needed to not just increase enrollment but to increase market share and retain students once they enroll in Catholic schools. School waiting lists need to be reduced by increasing capacity through the construction of new and expanded schools. This must be done while keeping a careful eye on the total school age population which is projected to peak overall in 2005, for elementary grades in 2001, and for high school grades in 2006 (NCES, 2001). The cost of Catholic schools will always increase. Catholic educational leaders will always be challenged by the dilemma of setting tuition at an affordable level and paying appropriate wages to teachers and administrators. School development efforts are needed to ensure that reliable sources of income are generated that will keep tuition affordable and provide wages and benefits that will attract and retain the best teachers and administrators. These are big challenges, but if addressed, Catholic schools will continue the growth of the 1990s into the 2000s.

[1] NCEA divides the nation into the following six geographical regions: **New England** (Connecticut, Maine, Massachusetts, New Hampshire, Rhode Island, Vermont); **Mideast** (Delaware, District of Columbia, Maryland, New Jersey, New York, Pennsylvania); **Great Lakes** (Illinois, Indiana, Michigan, Ohio, Wisconsin); **Plains** (Kansas, Minnesota, Missouri, Nebraska, North Dakota, South Dakota); **Southeast** (Alabama, Arkansas, Florida, Georgia, Kentucky, Louisiana, Mississippi, North Carolina, South Carolina, Tennessee, Virginia, West Virginia); **West/Far West** (Alaska, Arizona, California, Colorado, Hawaii, Idaho, Montana, Nevada, New Mexico, Oklahoma, Oregon, Texas, Utah, Washington, Wyoming).

[2] Enrollment for the 1998-99 school year was essentially unchanged from the previous year with a decline of 24 students reported. The 2000-01 school showed a decline of 5,737 students or -0.2%.

[3] In 1995, Caucasian or "White" was reported as a specific category. Until that year "White" was included in the "other" category. In 1996 the Asian category changed to Asian/Pacific Islander. The 1998-99 report added "Multiracial" to the categories. In 1999-2000, "Native Hawaiian/Pacific Islander" became a distinct category apart from "Asian," "Native American" changed to "American Indian/Native Alaskan" and the designation "unknown" was added.

[4] In 1991-92, NCEA began to introduce the statistical breakdown of the brothers/priests category into two distinct categories (Brigham, 1992).

CHAPTER 13
GOVERNANCE AND ADMINISTRATION

PATRICIA M. KELLEHER

Until the mid-1960's, Catholic school governance, including finances, was based on the ownership model. Parishes, dioceses, and religious congregations were owners and operators and therefore the recognized authority figures; the pastor, bishop, and elected congregational leaders, were the decision makers. (Sheehan, 1991, p. 22)

A review of the past methods of school governance and administration, the reasons for necessitating change or adaptation of these methods, and discussion of the emerging new models that will shape the vision of Catholic schools in the 21st century are included in this chapter. The information will be reviewed in light of strengthening the Catholic identity of Catholic schools and the role that the spiritual formation of Catholic school leaders plays in this process

This review will show the influence Vatican II has had on the role of the laity in the future governance and administration of Catholic schools. As Sheehan (1991) noted, "the question is not who owns the school but rather what is the Church's understanding of decision making in the operation of schools" (p. 22).

Research on governance and administration in Catholic schools by Hocevar and Sheehan was presented at the National Congress for Catholic Schools for the 21st Century in 1991. Data garnered through the studies of Convey (1992) and Bryk, Lee, and Holland (1993) laid the foundation for this review of research, which is inclusive of the years 1990-2000.

Hocevar (1991), in her theme paper "Catholic School Governance," cites challenges to the governance of Catholic schools as: "(1) a future creative governance model which can support the mission of the Catholic schools; (2) the future relationships which can be developed for the Catholic school community and the governing authority; and (3) future possibilities for the resources and financing of Catholic schools" (p. 6). Convey (1992) indicated that a "long-range, strategic planning" study by dioceses should "result in the development of policies concerning finances, governance, curriculum, marketing and public relations, and development programs for the schools, as well as a coordinated plan for the future placement of the schools in the diocese" (p. 190). Reflection on these studies may initiate ways to insure the future of Catholic schools and the value they contribute to education in the United States.

Bryk, Lee, and Holland (1993) looked at the issue of governance in Catholic schools and identified four significant ideas to be addressed when discussing this issue:

the nature of their fiscal and legal authority varies depending upon the particular type of Catholic school; the interpretation and implementation of governance systems vary substantially across dioceses depending on the orientation and interests of the individual bishop; variations in the organizational control of religious orders who provide staff for schools add another dimension; and Vatican II opened to laypersons new opportunities to exercise responsibility for Catholic institutions. (pp. 148-149)

Bryk et al. (1993) indicate that new governance and administrative policies may vary with the type of Catholic school, but that the underlying issues of excellent fiscal management and the new role of the laity are similar. The most important factor, however, is how the Catholicity or spirituality of the school will be implemented and integrated into the environment.

REASONS FOR CHANGE

The decline in the numbers of priests and religious brothers and sisters is one of the main reasons for the necessity for the change and adaptation of the governance and administration in Catholic schools. Dygert (2000) concurred by maintaining that "the decline in the numbers of religious available for schools is due not only to the rapidly declining membership in religious congregations but also to the reality that many religious have committed themselves to other works" (p. 18).

McDonald's (2001b) research cites that in the mid-1950s, 90.1% of Catholic schools' staff were sisters, brothers, or priests. In the 1970s the shift changed to 48.4%; and in the 1990s the laity made up 93% of the Catholic schools' staff. McDonald reiterates Dygert's observations that many of the religious left their congregations, but many others pursued new ministries.

Vatican II also contributed to the structural change of personnel in Catholic schools. *The Religious Dimension of Education in a Catholic School* (Congregation for Catholic Education, 1988) charts new opportunities for the laity in Catholic schools:

The Church, therefore, is willing to give lay people charge of the schools that it has established, and the laity themselves establish schools. The recognition of the school as a Catholic school is, however, always reserved to the competent ecclesiastical authority. When lay people do establish schools, they should be especially concerned with the creation of a community climate permeated by the Gospel spirit of freedom and love, and they should witness to this in their own lives. (#38)

The document clearly gives support and confidence to the laity in their role as voices of the Church. However, it is the formation of the laity that will ultimately reassure us that the gospel values, culture, traditions, and rites of Catholicism are in place for future generations. McBride (1981) contended by citing *Sharing the Light of Faith*: "The Catholic educator must be a person of prayer, one who frequently reflects on the scriptures and whose Christlike living testifies to deep faith. Only men and women of faith can share with others" (p. 24). Catholic schools should call for a formation process for administrators, faculty, and staff in order to retain the Catholic identity and charism that encompassed the school.

Another factor in the reason for the change in the personnel structure of Catholic schools is the lack of religious congregations in the management of Catholic schools, whether parish, diocesan, or private. Mueller (2000) opined:

cultural factors in the United States and in the American Catholic Church, bolstered by new theological and pastoral directions from Vatican II, directions which urged religious congregations to rediscover their original founding charism, which affirmed the role of the laity in ministry, and which invited a reading of the signs of the times, caused religious congregations to reassess their traditional ministries, including Catholic schools. (p. 39)

Vatican II directed religious congregations to review the mission of their founders and foundresses to determine whether their present positions were in alignment with their origins. Arbuckle (1996) explains that this threw religious congregations into chaos and asserts, "Refounding....is a faith-filled collaborative journey of ongoing conversation, whereby we struggle to re-own the mission of Christ to the world by re-identifying with his journey through death into the resurrection" (p. 110). Understandably the effect this had on the management of Catholic schools is doubtlessly more than most realized.

These major reasons for change initiated serious reflection and reassessment of organizational structures for all types of Catholic schools. These changes provide opportunities for development of Catholic schools of the future.

GOVERNANCE AND ADMINISTRATION

It is important to understand Church governance as a ministry (Sheehan, 1990). It serves God's people while it protects and promotes "the rights and obligations needed to carry out the mission Jesus gave to his Church" (p. 51). Church governance includes schools from their earliest beginnings to the present day.

Catholic schools emerged in the United States because the common schools emphasized Protestantism in their classrooms. The early Church in America saw a need to protect children from the Protestant environment and felt an urgency to teach the children about their Catholic faith. In the 1600s in Florida and Louisiana lay people began Catholic schools. Later the laity were replaced by religious congregations of men and women from Europe (Hunt, 2000). Therefore, the presence of laypersons in Catholic schools is not new.

Many Catholic schools started as parish grammar schools. Although he may not have been the head administrator, the pastor was responsible for the school. Sheehan (1994) echoed, "in practice, it is the school principal who functions as the actual administrator of the school and that member of the parish staff who works with the school board/committee and/or other parent groups" (p. 88). Pastors invited religious communities to lead and staff the schools where their charism animated the school (Kelleher, 2000).

Currently the governance and administration of Catholic schools is four pronged: parish, interparish, diocesan, and private. The parish elementary schools have the largest number, 5,475 or 79.1% of Catholic schools in the United States. Some parishes have a high school, although they are becoming fewer in number. The parish high schools number 137 or 11.2%. These figures are reported in *United States Catholic Elementary and Secondary Schools 2000-2001: The Annual Statistical Report on Schools, Enrollment and Staffing* (McDonald, 2001b).

Interparish elementary and middle schools, which may include regional and consolidated ones, are growing in number (Sheehan, 1994). Their principal is accountable to all the pastors involved. School boards or advisory committees provide a vehicle for each parish to be represented, which may cloud the issue of the principal's accountability. Of the elementary and middle interparish schools in the United States, the latest study (McDonald, 2001b) shows 843 or 12.2%; and 138 or 11.3% secondary interparish schools.

Diocesan or central Catholic high schools developed in the 1960s. These schools are under the direct jurisdiction of the bishop of the diocese. They were developed when the need for Catholic high schools increased and the student population was coming from a number of parishes. Religious communities were invited by the bishop to administer and staff these schools; now the lay principal is taking up that role more frequently. The principal of a diocesan school is directly responsible to the bishop through the superintendent. Sheehan (1994) explains that diocesan school principals seek advice from some type of board for financial matters, and in some cases it may be true of policy recommendations. McDonald (2001b) reports that there are 277 or 4% diocesan elementary and middle schools and 436 or 35% diocesan secondary schools in the United States.

Private Catholic schools or academies are established and owned by a religious congregation. Many of these schools are single sex schools, and have been residence schools. The religious order usually owned the property and governed the financial and academic responsibilities of the school. The administrators of private Catholic schools have "unique relationships to the religious congregations and/or boards of trustees responsible for the school" (Sheehan, 1994, p. 89). When the principal was a member of the congregation, appointed by the superior, there was little concern about the roles and responsibilities of the principal by the congregation. When hiring laypersons to fill administrative positions in these schools, it is important that the responsibilities of each party are clearly defined. Private Catholic schools usually adhere to diocesan policies in the implementation of religious education as they acknowledge the bishop as chief catechist (Sheehan, 1994).

In the 1990s, governance and administration in Catholic schools experienced some significant changes. Vatican II in its statement on the new role of the laity in Catholic schools allowed for major changes. An increase of lay teachers and lay administrators developed because of the declining numbers of priests and religious brothers and sisters in Catholic schools (Bryk et al., 1993; Convey, 1992; Dygert, 1998; Hocevar, 1991; Kelleher, 2000; McDonald, 2001b) as well as the directives of Vatican II (Congregation for Catholic Education, 1998; Sacred Congregation, 1982).

In his essay, *Lessons from Catholic High Schools on Renewing our Educational Institutions,* Bryk (1996) speaks about how the decentralization of Catholic high schools depends on the type of school ownership. He says that the "Catholic school system" is a very loose federation and most important decisions are made on site (p. 31).

Innovative planning and dialogue among Catholic educators has produced school boards or advisory committees and boards of trustees, the president-principal model of leadership, and sponsorship and colleagueship of schools by religious congregations. An important factor that most likely contributes to the success in governance of Catholic schools is the delegation of authority to local schools. Most significant issues are managed at the local level with the knowledge that support and assistance can be readily obtained from the diocesan superintendent's office or the religious congregation.

CATHOLIC SCHOOL BOARDS AND BOARDS OF TRUSTEES

Catholic school boards, or advisory committees, and boards of trustees differ in the type of jurisdiction they have over a school. Yet any type of board acts as a support system to the pastor or religious congregation and the principal on matters of philosophy, policy, and supervision of the mission of the school (Curran, 1994). Financial stress puts the schools and the parents in a perilous position of out pricing Catholic education for all who wish to attend. Most parish schools charged little or no tuition in the 1960s. Financial instability was the reason many schools closed in the 1980s. Over the past 10 years professionals involved in Catholic education have labored to find creative means to develop outside financial support and management techniques to stabilize schools and assist parents with the spiraling costs. The need for salaries for laypersons and capital outlay made it necessary to charge tuition for some means of financial stability. Development offices at Catholic schools sprang up in the last two decades to identify ways to head off financial crises. Fund raising became a significant operation for the school community. These offices are quite sophisticated and direct capital campaigns for major repairs and new buildings.

Another major concern to be considered by school boards and boards of trustees is the disrepair of many Catholic school buildings. In addition, installing and purchasing technological equipment usually results in large expenditures and requires considerable staff training. Board members in the business and corporate sector contribute their knowledge and expertise in these matters.

School Boards

Although it may appear that school boards or advisory committees are relatively new to Catholic schools, they are not, but membership of laypersons on the board or advisory committee is the significant change that took place in the mid-1960s. Sheehan (1991) notes that the Third Plenary Council of Baltimore in 1884 called for diocesan school boards. Members were clergy and assisted the bishop with the administration of the schools. Governance was a non-issue when the clergy and religious of the congregations were the school administrators. Sheehan declared, "With few exceptions, these descriptions would have been typical of Catholic school governance through the mid-1960's and Vatican II when the educational board movement, involving more than clergy, was born" (p. 20). Influenced by Vatican II, Catholic school superintendents recommended that the laity become members of the school boards or advisory committees. Originally, the public school board model was used. However, because of the 1983 Revision of Canon Law, it was determined that the public school board model was not appropriate for Catholic schools. The public school board model "was not consistent with how the Church functions" (p. 21). It was decided that Catholic school board models be based on the governance structure which reflects the operation of the Church as a "functional community" (p. 21). Two types of Catholic school boards were recommended by the Chief Administrators of Catholic Education-National Association of Boards, Commissions and Councils of Catholic Education (CACE/NABCCCE) Governance Task Force of NCEA, namely: boards with limited jurisdiction and consultative boards (Sheehan, 1991).

Dygert (1998) observes that Catholic school boards "have the authority to select the principal, set tuition, fix salaries, establish other financial policies, engage in long-range planning and development efforts, and oversee academic, religious and other programs of the school" (pp. 24-25). Basically the exception to this guiding principle is found in diocesan and private Catholic schools where the bishop or the religious congregation are more closely involved.

One difficulty that is prevalent among the laity is that of grasping the term "advisory." Because the popular model is the public school model, laypersons do not have the experience or the knowledge of the advisory capacity. Clearly, the importance of communication and orientation about the role Catholic school advisory members play cannot be stressed too strongly. Sheehan (1990) explains, "In accepting membership on a Catholic school board....Members...understand that as individuals they have no authority. It is only when the board is meeting in formal session that it is authorized to act in accord with its constitution and bylaws" (p. 67).

Shared governance between the principal and the board is key to the successful operation of boards. It is important that this relationship allows the board members "to feel both ownership of and responsibility for the mission" (Curran, 1994, p. 61). With that in mind it is essential that those who sit on boards understand their role. Appointment and election are two common ways of bringing membership to the board. If shared governance is a factor, then it is crucial that people who have commitment to the philosophy and mission of the school as well as an understanding of the governance of the Catholic Church are selected. Curran's article, "The Role of the Principal in Giving Ownership to the Board," implies that appointments are the favored way to select board members. In this way people can be selected who have deep interest in Catholic education as it reaches the spiritual, educational, physical, social, and moral elements of the school community. However, if candidates for board service are elected, Curran suggests they attend an in-service program designed to explain their role and responsibilities. This would be done prior to any election process.

Boards of Trustees

Boards of trustees in Catholic education are generally associated with Catholic schools owned and operated by a particular community. Guerra (1996) maintains, "ownership and trusteeship are not the same" (p. iv). In the non-profit situation "owners hold title to the assets of the institution which is guided by the board of trustees…trustees hold the institution's mission in trust, and employ administrators who are accountable for providing leadership which carries out the institution's mission" (p. iv). Generally, the religious congregations are the owners.

Successful boards of trustees are

fiscally responsible for the life of the school. They are independent; they interact with other boards for guidance. They rely on the provincial and other religious for ideas and dialogue about where the religious order is going and what is happening or not happening in their school. (Magnetti, 1996, pp. 35-36)

Stautberg (1996) defines the role of boards of trustees as "those who have the actual legal responsibility for governance of the institution; they bear fiduciary and statutory responsibility" (p. 28). He cautions that boards of trustees for schools must not follow the corporate model exclusively, but adapt to the "collegial education mode" (p. 28).

EMERGING NEW ADMINISTRATIVE MODELS

There are two prominent administrative models emerging: (1) the president-principal model; and (2) sponsorship and colleagueship. A significant factor in both of these models is the role of lay leadership.

President-Principal Model

Research reveals the importance of the role of principal and its relationship to the success of the school. The position has become more and more demanding. In Catholic schools the principal adds the responsibility of spiritual leader. The workload becomes overwhelming. Thus, the new model of president-principal has emerged.

The president-principal model "features dual or shared authority and a division of administrative responsibility between two people as opposed to the traditional or autonomous model of administration for Catholic high schools where authority and responsibility rest with a single person" (Dygert, 1998, p. 1). Although the model could be used in Catholic elementary schools, it is generally found in Catholic high schools. In this study, Dygert's (1998) operational definitions will be used, namely: president is the chief executive officer and the principal is the chief operating officer.

Thus, the president is responsible for financial management, institutional management, major fund raising, and public relations. The principal is responsible for the academic life of the school, which includes student management, social and athletic activities, and parent relationships. Both chief administrators must work as a team respecting each other's domain, but in open communication about each domain to provide for a smooth running of the school. Collegial collaboration makes the process effective.

Some of the challenges to be faced in this model are the actual governance in light of prior duties and personality conflicts. When adopting the president-principal model, the shift in power cannot be in name only with the person moving to the president position still controlling the academic field. A clear job description, in writing as well as verbal explanation, will help to minimize any misunderstanding in regard to responsibilities. The most important factors contributing to the success of this model are "mutual trust, respect, and support; mutual communication; clarity of expectations and mutual acceptance of the roles; responsibilities, functions, and lines of authority; compatible personalities; common vision; and flexibility" (Dygert, 1998, p. 56).

Dygert (1998) notes that Nick and Doyle maintained that "a basic purpose for using the [principal-president model] is to enable the school to build its future through planning and resource development and to ensure quality Catholic education" (p. 64). The model provides for the transition "from religious to lay leadership while continuing the sponsorship of the founding religious congregation" and the development of "strong governing boards because presidents have had the time to pay attention to board development" (p. 64).

Research on the use of this model (Guerra, 1992; Tracy, 2001) shows that 46% of the leaders in Catholic schools use a title other than principal. However, only 29% actually use the title president-principal. The data demonstrate that models other than just "principal" as school head are growing in acceptance by Catholic school leadership.

Sponsorship and Colleagueship

Sponsorship in Catholic schools reflects the transition of relationships to the school once owned, operated, administered, and staffed to another religious congregation and the laity. Relationships, as defined by Cook (2001a), "provide a unifying theme subsuming many other core values and may even be considered a precondition for community" (p. 20). Sponsorships require that the sense of community be essential to the success of the process. Community is a cornerstone of Catholic education (Bryk et al., 1993; Donovan, 1997; Groome & Corso, 1999; Heft, 1991d). Sponsorship offers an opportunity for religious congregations to continue their influence over their schools while dealing with the decline in their staffing (Mueller, 2000). It establishes new relationships with sponsors whether they are lay or religious.

Sponsorship does not come in a set pattern that can be used for all schools. Sponsorship is better tailored to the needs of the specific community. Yet, as Guerra (1996) aptly points out, the common thread which all Catholic schools must observe, is "the question of whom they teach, what they teach, and how they teach in the context of the Gospel's mandate to teach all nations" (p. v). He also notes that regardless of the religious congregations' gifts to their schools, service is another common thread through which "our work serves God and God's people as [an] integral teaching mission of God's church" (p. v).

When using the word "sponsorship," as it applies to Catholic school governance, what does it mean? In civil or church law there is little consistency in the meaning of sponsorship (Mueller, 2000). Gray (1996) says it "symbolizes the pivotal importance of cultivating and sustaining the relationship between the tradition of the religious community as educators and the evolving reality of a lay-centered Church" (p. 19).

Mueller (2000) comments on the ambiguity of the term, but cites Welch's ideas on the most common meaning of sponsor: "(1) the assumption of responsibilities for mission and identity; (2) the maintaining of communion with the spiritual source; (3) a relationship of benevolence, i.e., a quid pro quo in terms of lending support and receiving some benefit in terms of good will" (p. 42). As it pertains to Catholic schools, sponsorship causes the religious congregations to include the laity in the concept. It is dealing with the world as it is while maintaining the unique characteristics of the religious community.

Partnership (Mueller, 2000) is the key factor in the plan for sponsorship. Gallin maintains that the governance model

must make provision for: a distribution of power, a distribution of responsibility, the implications of those distribution terms of legal accountability and liability, justice in financial arrangements, the ministry goals of individuals and communities, and the various modes of exercise of those goals, and the mission of the institution as acknowledged by the various constituencies. (as cited in Mueller, 2000, p. 49)

In 1995 at the National Catholic Educational Association Convention in Cincinnati, a symposium, "Sponsorship, Colleagueship, and Service: A Conversation about the Future of Religious Communities and American Catholic High Schools," was convened in response to conversations about the future of Catholic high schools owned by religious congregations and the decline in religious personnel to manage these schools. Priests, brothers, and sisters filled the leadership roles in Catholic schools, and in recent years, particularly in private Catholic schools and colleges. This symposium addressed concerns of religious congregations and the laity. How can the transition of relationships of the religious congregation and the sponsors manifest itself in a continuation of the philosophy and charism of the religious community? Can the laity be successful in carrying these qualities to the school community in the future? If so, it appears that laity who will be sponsors, as well as board members, administrators, and teachers working in and for Catholic schools, must be educated in the philosophy and culture of Catholic education as well as in the charism of the religious order. However, the effort is a connection or relationship to the past that will benefit the Catholic school community of the future. The formation gives the laity roots that were planted in the members of religious congregations through their formation processes (Kelleher, 2000).

Gray (1996) states that sponsorship and religious communities symbolize

the pivotal importance of cultivating and sustaining the relationship between the tradition of a religious community as educators and the evolving reality of a lay-centered Church, decreasing religious personnel for educational administration, faculty, and staff, and increasing professional demands in secondary education. (p. 19)

He emphasizes that this relationship can "flourish only in ethical trust and in spiritual growth" (p. 19).

Sponsorship (Mueller, 2000) has evolved from the religious congregations responding to the call of Vatican II and reaction to the present times. Mueller says that rather than closing the schools and hospitals they were no longer able to administer and staff, the religious men and women saw sponsorship as a way to have influence over these institutions that were their ministries.

LAITY IN CATHOLIC SCHOOLS

The laity are the predominant force in administrative and teaching positions in Catholic schools. McDonald's (2001b) 2000-2001 study on Catholic schools in the United States indicates that 93.5% of the full-time professional staff is laypersons and 6.5% religious. While 1.7% of the participants did not respond, of those responding, 84% are Catholic, and 14.3% are non-Catholic. As for the ethnic backgrounds of all faculty, religious and lay, 97% are White, 71% Hispanic, 62% Black, 51% multiracial, 22% Asian, and 4% Native Alaskan.

Will the emerging Catholic schools, led chiefly by laity who lack spiritual formation be able to sustain and cultivate the traditions of the religious orders that founded or staffed them? How can diocesan schools do this? How can the parish school do this? How can the Catholic identity of Catholic schools (teaching, community, and service) be infused into the faculty, students, and parents as the Church document, *To Teach As Jesus Did* (Sacred Congregation, 1972), instructs us? It appears that the lay leadership, whether recent or established, needs the support of a spiritual formation process to prepare them for their role as spiritual leaders of Catholic schools (Kelleher, 2000).

Jacobs (1997) believes a serious threat to the Catholic identity of Catholic schools is "how the laity will receive the formation they need in order to preserve and advance the identity of the Catholic school" (p. vi). Groome and Corso (1999), Gusdane (1999), Hater (1990), O'Brien, (personnel communication, 2000), and Jacobs (1997) "generate a thread of commonality regarding the formation process. They agree that it is an ongoing process that eventually becomes part of oneself. The faith is the gift; the spirituality emerges in the person" (Kelleher, 2000, p. 45).

The emerging lay leadership can be classified into two dominant groups: those who have worked many years with the religious staff and have acquired the charism of the order and the Catholic culture and those with little or no Catholic school experience. Kelleher (2000) identifies the formational experience of the former group as the "osmosis principle." The latter group, however, lacks any spiritual formation processes to prepare them to be witness to the Catholic identity, culture, traditions, and Catholic literacy or knowledge that should be evident in Catholic schools. In referring to Catholic literacy, it will be defined as being "knowledgeable in Church documents pertaining to Catholic education, scriptures, Christology, ecclesiology, moral theology, sacraments, Church history of Catholic schools in America, and the ministry of teaching" (Kelleher, 2000, p. 52). Actually, even those served by the osmosis principle need to have this substantial background. Catholic literacy can be attained through diocesan programs or college courses and completed over a specified time.

The role of the laity in Catholic schools is unique. They are in administrative and teaching positions "carrying out the mission of evangelization for the Church" (Kelleher, 2000, p. 129). While

the unique role of the laity "opens the window" of the Catholic school to a more universal audience, one wider than that of the vowed religious....The great gift that the unique role of the laity gives to the Catholic school and the Church is their personal example of spirituality - a life of living the Gospel values. (p. 130)

It, too, is a vocation; not a career or a job as it demands a higher level of commitment. Fortified by the document *The Religious Dimension of Education in a Catholic School* (Congregation for Catholic Education, 1998) lay leadership is clearly a defining element of today's Catholic schools. It reads:

At the side of the priest and Religious, lay teachers contribute their competence and their faith witness to the Catholic school. Ideally, this lay witness is a concrete example of the lay vocation that most of the students will be called to. The Congregation had devoted a specific document to lay teachers, meant to remind lay people of their apostolic responsibility in the field of education and to summon them to participate in a common mission whose point of convergence is found in the unity of the Church....The Church, therefore, is willing to give lay people charge of the schools it has established, and the laity themselves establish schools. (#37, 38)

Kelleher (2000) advances this notion by stating, "The lay witnesses to faith plant the seeds of the faith in the minds and hearts of those they encounter on a level which others can realistically measure" (p.132).

Hiring Practices

Another consideration in the governance and administration of Catholic schools is hiring practices. It is challenging to find qualified administrators and teachers who understand and are willing to act in accordance with the philosophy of Catholic education. As McBride (1981) asserted, "Hiring a believer does not guarantee the enduring commitment of the believer. The powers of secularization in the culture are sufficiently seductive and enchanting to the point that they may prevail over our Catholic educators and weaken their dedication to Christ" (p. 9).

Although Breslin (2000) refers to Catholic colleges and universities in their efforts to maintain the Catholic philosophy and mission of the institution, his words can be applied to Catholic schools. The hiring process in Catholic elementary and secondary schools is a different process than in colleges and universities. However, at the school level, hiring incompatible personnel can stem from the shortage of teachers and the inability to pay teachers a comparable salary to that of public school teachers and administrators. Breslin recommends that candidates be advised, prior to the appointment, "that the Catholic character of the institution is its defining element" (p. 234). It is crucial that any literature sent to candidates reflect this Catholic character without hesitation. During the interview process it is wise to ask questions that will specifically identify for the interviewer if the candidate's personal philosophy and knowledge of the Catholic faith will be a fit. This does not indicate that only Catholics will be hired. In fact, some Catholics may not be a fit to the mission and philosophy of the school and some non-Catholics may be excellent.

At some time during the hiring process, a candidate's credentials and references must be thoroughly checked before any commitment is made for employment. Many dioceses have screening policies that include checking on any police records or prior problems in school. New candidates out of college or another type of work force present the issue of gathering data from a variety of sources to insure that the school is entrusting the well being of its students to honorable people. This process is crucial to the safety and security of the school. It is easier not to hire someone than to have to remove that person from the institution. It is important that everyone, from the president or principal to the custodial staff and cafeteria employees, be thoroughly reviewed.

Sheehan (1994) states, "the question of who hires is basic to the understanding of accountability" (p. 88). The issue has become more complicated now that laypersons are being selected for administrative positions. When the replacement of an administrator came from within the teaching order, there was usually no question of Catholic identity and culture being sustained.

At the parish level, in accordance with diocesan policy, the pastor and consultative boards now should be involved (Sheehan, 1994). Because the principal works closely with these people, the choice should be compatible to all. Principals conduct interviews when hiring new staff with input from department chairpersons. After the principal consults with the pastor, the pastor interviews the prospective employee. The pastor has the final say as to whether a person will be hired, but after discussion with the principal, will generally agree with the consultative choice.

At the diocesan level a prospective principal is usually first interviewed by the superintendent and present principal. With their approval, additional interviews will take place at the school and will include faculty committees. Then the recommended candidate's credentials are reviewed at the diocesan office before the actual hiring takes place. In the diocesan high school, the principal is responsible to the diocese. "In practice, this usually means that the responsibility is to the bishop through the superintendent of schools and some type of board structure at either the school or diocesan level" (Sheehan, 1994, p. 90).

Another issue is that of hiring public school administrators and teachers who may come to Catholic schools with excellent administrative or pedagogical skills, but are not cognizant of the philosophy and culture of Catholic education. When hiring administrators from public schools, Catholic schools need to employ a shadowing or mentoring program as well as education in Catholic school philosophy and Catholic literacy "because public school personnel bring the culture of the public school with them, in decision-making, relationships, priorities on courses, and so on," (Kelleher, 2000, p. 134). The reasoning behind this notion is "complex, but one factor probably is that these traditions and symbols are not being integrated in their [the candidate's] family life. The rich Catholic culture is the essence of the school's existence. It is developed through knowledgeable spiritual leaders and is the responsibility of the principal" (Kelleher, 2000, p. 26).

A question then is, are Catholic colleges and universities meeting the needs of Catholic schools by forming students in the traditions of Catholic schooling? Or are they meeting the market demands and neglecting their roots? Because of the present lack of administrators and teachers for all schools, it is difficult to address these questions. Thus, some type of formation or mentoring program needs to be in place as an opportunity for such candidates to prepare for Catholic school philosophy and Catholic literacy.

CONCLUSION

Catholic schools of the 21st century are going to be different in outward appearance, but hopefully, the same in the spiritual, community life that they have always offered. Excellence in academics, up-to-date equipment, state of the art technology, and library resources should be considered standard. But will these Catholic schools still exhibit spirituality, traditions of the Church, charism of their founding religious congregations, and the sense of community or "social capital" that sets Catholic schools apart from any other type of school? Or will they become like their Protestant counterparts whose schools have lost the identity of the churches they served?

It appears that the new patterns of governance can assist this effort. The bottom line is accepting the laity into the governing body of the Church. The second issue is the spiritual formation of the laity to insure the continuation of Catholic identity and culture. Third, is there communication among all parties to build trust and confidence in one another as we strive toward the singular goal of spreading the gospel message? Although it is important to plan and design the structural forms of new governance, it is more important to recognize that this is a people-oriented enterprise that will require openness, conversation, consensus, and willingness to focus on the singular goal. Then, the whole school community will engage in the effort. The process must evolve, but cannot be mandated.

The governance of Catholic schools in the United States is changing from a vertical to a collaborative form of jurisdiction, yet ever mindful of the authority and teachings of the Church. School boards and advisory committees, boards of trustees, the president-principal model, and sponsorship are the obvious expressions of this change today.

CHAPTER 14
SCHOOL CHOICE AND VOUCHERS

WILLIAM F. DAVIS, OSFS

As THE NEW CENTURY unfolds, the most controversial issue in American education is the issue of school vouchers. The idea seems simple enough: that the government should expand the choices of parents by providing them with publicly funded grants, or vouchers, that they can apply toward tuition at private schools....The voucher idea, if widely and seriously applied, is capable of transforming the entire education system - perhaps in very good ways, perhaps in very bad ways, depending on which side you listen to. This is what all the fuss is about. The controversy over vouchers is a struggle over America's educational future. (Moe, 2001, p. 1)

INTRODUCTION

Background

With that provocative paragraph, Terry Moe (2001) opens his interesting new book, *Schools, Vouchers, and the American Public,* where he uses a representative sample of 4,700 adults to identify how Americans feel about vouchers and what they think may be the consequences for American education.

At this point in time, we have available to us a significant number of comprehensive, quality works that outline the numerous philosophical, legal, and policy concerns relating to the broad issue of school choice and school vouchers in particular. The earlier works from a variety of contributors, such as Coons and Sugarman (1978), Everhart (1982), Kirkpatrick (1990), and Clune and Witte (1990) provide a solid survey of theory and early but limited practices. More recent publications such as Lieberman (1993), Viteritti (1999), Sugarman and Kemerer (1999), Plank and Sykes (2000), Moe (2001), Goodman and Stieger (2001), and Peterson and Campbell (2001) continue to review theory on issues, but have an increased value because they address a newer and broader variety of functioning programs, current federal and state policy and legal issues, and in many cases, the possibility of both changing legal and policy environments.

The issue of educational choice, not just the question of publicly funded school vouchers, has been with us for a very long time. Kirkpatrick (1990) identifies a rather eclectic group of individuals such as Adam Smith, John Stuart Mill, Tom Paine, and Milton Friedman, as well as Presidents Thomas Jefferson, Ronald Reagan, and George Bush as being supportive of the idea of educational choice. The beginning of the evolution of the modern version of this concept, to expand the number of educational options available to parents, is generally credited to Noble Laureate Milton Friedman (1955, 1962; Friedman & Friedman, 1980) who introduced and advocated for a broad-based free-market voucher proposal that would provide government funding for families to choose where to send their children to school. Chubb and Moe (1990) seem to adhere to Friedman's more free-market approach to school choice and vouchers in *Politics, Markets, & American Schools.* Vitteritti (1999) identifies a number of different voucher proposals whose authors, including Ted Sizer, Christopher Jencks, John Coons, and Stephen Sugarman, begin to shift the emphasis away from Friedman's free-market approach to a voucher that is more focused on groups whose education needs seem to be less adequately served by the existing educational system. In his most recent publication, Moe (2001), has clearly moved away from his earlier free-market voucher position (Chubb & Moe, 1990) and seems to see any voucher success as being linked to proposals that are "going to the center...and targeted...to the neediest kids"(p. 372).

Kirkpatrick (1990) compares school vouchers to the "Serviceman's Readjustment Act of 1944, commonly known as the GI Bill" (p. 1). He also compares the school voucher to existing town wide tuition plans in Vermont, third party social service payments, and food stamps.

Clune and Witte (1990), Monahan (1991), Davis (1997), Sugarman and Kemerer (1999), and Viteritti (1999) provide us with a variety of alternative school choice initiatives beginning in the 1970s and running to the end of the 1990s. They examine options including the Alum Rock voucher demonstration in the 1970s, tuition tax credit proposals in the 1970s and 1980s, public school choice initiatives over this period, and publicly and privately funded school voucher plans. These authors, to varying degrees, look at the legal and political obstacles that publicly funded initiatives have faced and review the reasons why many voucher proposals, especially statewide ballot initiatives, have failed over the years. McDonald (1995) provides a very comprehensive study of the tuition tax credit campaigns that took place in the 1970s and into the early 1990s. Wornsop (1991) covers a variety of choice issues on both the federal and state level up to 1991 and investigates how they might impact public education. McDonald (1999a) and Rees (2000) provide lists of current publicly and privately funded school choice programs. Rees provides a comprehensive state-by-state overview and analysis of what is actually happening with regard to the variety of publicly and privately funded choice options available to parents. This work includes a valuable array of issues, including an overview of home school laws and a listing of school choice resources which help to define the complex issues involved in this area.

Since the early 1990s, we have been provided with a number of conferences that have addressed this issue in some depth. The National Catholic Educational Association (NCEA) has provided three different opportunities to discuss school choice and vouchers. While the Conference on Catholic Schools for the 21st Century was not totally focused on this issue, it was discussed in its public policy sessions. The summary of those discussions and recommendations can be found in the executive summary (Guerra, Haney, & Kealey, 1992). McDonald (1999a) provides us with the deliberations at the second conference, Catholic Schools and School Choice: Partners for Justice, which was co-sponsored by the National Catholic Educational Association and the United States Catholic Conference. The final effort was at the April 2001 NCEA national convention in Milwaukee where delegates spent an entire day discussing the many aspects of school choice and its implications on Catholic schools, their students, and parents. A brief and initial coverage of that meeting is included in the special section of the organization's publication *Momentum* (DeFiore, 2001; Keebler, 2001; McDonald, 2001a).

In March of 2000, Harvard University's Program on Education Policy and Governance and the John F. Kennedy School of Government co-sponsored a comprehensive conference on school vouchers and charter schools. Peterson and Campbell (2001) provide a record of that conference and the numerous policy, legal, and research issues covered during the sessions.

In November of 2000, The Education Policy Center at Michigan State University offered a conference on school choice and vouchers, and those deliberations are covered in Plank and Sykes (2000). The interesting aspect of this conference was that each of the issues was covered from the perspective of both a proponent and opponent of school choice and vouchers.

In 2000, Dr. Howard Fuller reported at the Second Annual Symposium on Educational Options for

African Americans about the continuing struggle poor African Americans face in exercising their right to send their children to the schools they find most appropriate. As the founder of the recently organized Black Alliance for Educational Options, Dr. Fuller is trying to mobilize the African American community in support of school choice and vouchers.

More specific references to details of these conferences will be provided in different sections of this work relating to publicly and privately funded vouchers or scholarships and charter schools.

Almost all commentators, but especially Viteritti (1996), Ravitch (1994), and Fuller (2000), address the impact of school choice and vouchers on inner city children who are generally poor, minorities, and educationally at risk or those who are forced to remain in what parents consider to be unsafe or academically inferior schools.

Finally, Glenn (2000) introduces the issue of vouchers by analyzing the "child care certificates (i.e., vouchers) for low-income parents" (p. 113) of the Child Care and Development Block Grant Act of 1990 which, to this date, have not been challenged in the courts. Glenn's work is especially interesting, in light of President George W. Bush's "Faith-Based Initiative," in that he argues schools and social agencies may play an enlarged role by receiving government funds, still have a good degree of autonomy, and yet remain accountable; two concerns that are often raised by voucher opponents.

Church Documents

The long-standing position of the Catholic Church on the right of parents to choose the education most appropriate for their children is clearly stated in *The Catechism of the Catholic Church*:

> As those first responsible for the education of their children, parents have the right to *choose a school for them* which corresponds to their own convictions. This right is fundamental. As far as possible parents have the duty of choosing the schools that will best help them in their task as Christian educators. Public authorities have the duty of guaranteeing this parental right and of ensuring the concrete conditions for its exercise. (Catholic Church, 1997, #2229)

This position is again articulated in the latest document of the Congregation for Catholic Education, *The Catholic School on the Threshold of the Third Millennium*:

> A correct relationship between state and school, not only the Catholic school, is based not so much on institutional relations as on the right of each person to receive a suitable education of their free choice. This right is acknowledged according to the principle of subsidiarity. For the public authority, therefore, whose duty it is to protect and defend the liberty of the citizens, is bound according to the principle of distributive justice to ensure that public subsidies are so allocated that parents are truly free to select schools for their children in accordance with their conscience. (Congregation, 1997, #17)

This document goes on to recognize that in some countries, the ability of individuals to effectively exercise this very fundamental human right is confronted with the "crucial problem of the juridical and financial recognition of non-state schools" (Congregation, 1997, #17).

These two most recent universal church documents, as well as earlier statements such as *The Catholic School* (Congregation, 1977) and *Lay Catholics in Schools: Witnesses to Faith* (Sacred Congregation, 1982) repeat the need to have a "plurality of school systems" (1977, #13) and state that the idea of "a state monopoly of education is not permissible, and that only a pluralism of school systems will respect the fundamental right and freedom of individuals" (1982, #14).

In 1980, the Synod of Bishops, called to address the theme, "The Role of the Christian Family in the Modern World," requested that the Holy See prepare a *Charter of the Rights of the Family*, and Pope John Paul II accepted the recommendation. In October 1983, the Charter was published. Article 5 of the Charter again addresses the issue of parents having an "original, primary and inalienable right to educate ... their children." The Charter continues by stating that parents "should also receive from society the necessary aid and assistance to perform their educational role properly" (United States Catholic Conference, #5a). The Charter goes on to say:

> Parents have the right to choose freely schools or other means necessary to educate their children in keeping with their convictions. Public authorities must ensure that public subsidies are so allocated that parents are truly free to exercise this right without incurring unjust burdens. Parents should not have to sustain directly or indirectly, extra charges which would deny or unjustly limit the exercise of this freedom. (#5b)

All of these universal church documents draw from, and repeat in a variety of ways, the *Declaration on Christian Education* of the Second Vatican Council (1965/1996), which sets out the basic structure of church teaching on education. Parents have the "primary and inalienable duty and right ... to the education of their children" and "should enjoy the fullest liberty in the choice" of schools, and that government agencies should provide "public subsidies" (#6) so that parents may be free to exercise their right and duty.

The bishops of the United States, over the last decade, have also addressed this fundamental right of parents. In their 1990 statement *In Support of Catholic Elementary and Secondary Schools*, they advocate "that new initiatives will be launched to secure sufficient financial assistance from both private and public sectors for parents to exercise this right" (United States Catholic Conference, p. 6) to send their children to Catholic schools. The bishops went on to say that the Supreme Court, in their 1983 decision in *Mueller v. Allen*, ruled "that states could constitutionally assist parents in defraying costs associated with those educational choices" (p. 8). The bishops called on all citizens to support federal and state efforts to provide assistance so that parents could choose the schools they desired and also encourage Catholic school parents to form diocesan, state, and national groups to assist in pursuing this goal.

In 1995, the bishops joined in the broader debate on education reform in the United States by issuing a statement called *Principles for Educational Reform in the United States*. They addressed a variety of issues affecting all schools including the "inalienable right to a quality education" for all persons (United States Catholic Conference, p. 3). They stressed that "no single model or means of education is appropriate to the needs and desires of all persons" and that our nation should provide "the broadest variety of educational opportunities...including public, private, and religious models" (p. 3). Parents were identified as the "first and foremost educators of their children" and that this right "should not be limited to the economically privileged" (p. 4). They also called on the state and private groups to provide assistance to access these opportunities. Finally, they stated that:

> Since no single educational approach serves all educational needs, policy decisions should allow for the existence of alternative educational systems including but not limited to, charter schools, magnet schools, and public, private and religious school choice programs, provided they offer quality programs and do not teach or practice intolerance or advocate illegal activity. (p. 8)

Finally, in 2000, the bishops issued their regular presidential election year statement, *Faithful Citizenship: Civic Responsibility for a New Millennium* (United States Catholic Conference), which addresses the responsibilities of Catholics in the public life of our society. These key issues relating to education, including the parental right to choose the school for their children, are repeated in this document.

Choice Vocabulary

"'Choice' in schooling means the free, conscious, deliberate selection of a school, program, or set of academic courses, as opposed to involuntary assignment to the same. This means government financial provisions to make this possible" (Buetow, 1988, p. 182). "Vouchers put the decision about which provider to use in the hands of clients rather than government, thus reducing legal as well as administrative entanglements" (Glenn, 2000, p. 129).

While the major debate in the area of educational choice is focused on publicly funded vouchers, we proceed at great risk if we do not consider briefly the many other options available to arrive at the same goal—the freedom to choose and the ability to exercise that freedom. These options include privately funded vouchers or scholarships, tax credits or deductions for tuition and other legitimate education related expenses or for contributions to organizations who provide scholarships to children, educational savings accounts or education IRAs, charter schools, magnet schools, home schooling, tuition towns, and statewide and local inter or intra district public school choice programs.

Detailed and rather easy to understand definitions and descriptions of such options can be found in a variety of sources, such as Viteritti (1999), *Momentum's* special section on school choice (Gray, 2001), Rees (2000), Buetow (1988), Sugarman and Kemerer (1999), and McDonald (1999a).

Legal Considerations

While this researcher is not an attorney and is unable to offer critical evaluation of the legal positions taken by the authors cited, it is impossible to cover the topic of educational choice and vouchers adequately without giving some attention to legal issues that arise on both the federal and state levels. Mark Chopko, the General Counsel for the newly named United States Conference of Catholic Bishops, writes that a "pressing legal issue at the close of the millennium is the use of public tax dollars to assist parents, especially lower income parents, with the rising tuition at private schools. The idea of vouchers...has been argued in legal circles for decades" (1999a, p. 87).

Skillen's work (1993) has chapters that address issues such as neutrality to religion in public schools, Blaine Amendments, the need for courts to re-interpret the First Amendment, and the question of educational pluralism and justice. Ackerman (1997), a worker for the non-partisan Congressional Research Service, outlines the legal standards that apply to aid to religious schools with an emphasis on what he calls, "indirect assistance such as education voucher programs" (p. 1). Chopko (1999a, 1999b, 1999c) covers the legal history, possible changing and more favorable legal environment, and the constitutional validity for vouchers in a clear and easy to read and understand format. His articles in the *Connecticut Law Review* and *Catholic Education: A Journal of Inquiry and Practice* are both especially interesting and informative. Viteritti (1996, 1999) clearly summarizes federal legal questions as well as provides excellent coverage of state issues relating to Blaine Amendments and the hostile, anti-Catholic circumstances surrounding their adoption in many states. Sugarman and Kemerer (1999) provide a number of presentations on this critical issue on both the federal and state levels. This work addresses some interesting issues such as whether choice programs would impose any obligation to recognize the constitutional rights of teachers and students as in public schools as well as what impact they would have on minorities, teachers unions, and children with disabilities. Lewin, in *Policy Review*, (1999), reviews a number of recent federal and state court cases on school choice issues. Goodman and Stieger (2001), Peterson and Campbell (2001), and McGroarty (2001) all touch on the legal issues and cases affecting this topic in understandable language for the legal novices.

In conclusion, it is interesting to note that the Supreme Court thus far has declined to accept either of the two choice cases, the Milwaukee voucher or the Arizona tax credit program, thereby allowing those programs to continue to function. Recently, the Cleveland voucher program has been appealed to the Supreme Court and that appeal will be considered in February 2002. Since the last decision on this program was a negative one, it is possible that the Court will hear the case to resolve the conflict with earlier favorable rulings. The Illinois tax credit program is making its way through the courts but has not yet reached the Supreme Court. All rulings to this point have been favorable to the tax program. Moe (2001) concludes his recent work with a section on what he thinks the Supreme Court might do if it does hear a voucher case. He acknowledges that trying to predict what the Court may do is difficult. But he presents a number of possible results, including allowing the program to stand outright, allowing the program to stand but offering a narrow decision without a "clear and broad precedent" (p. 395), thus creating room for additional court challenges, or rejecting the program outright.

School Vouchers

Publicly funded vouchers

Publicly funded programs of school vouchers, which allow children to attend private and religious schools, currently exist in only three places: Milwaukee since 1990, Cleveland since 1995, and Florida since 1999. The details of the Milwaukee and Cleveland programs are covered in a comprehensive way in Viteritti (1999), McDonald (1999a), Sugarman and Kemerer (1999), Glenn (2000), Moe (2001), Goodman and Stieger (2001), and Peterson and Campbell (2001). The Florida program, due to its short life span, is covered in less detail in most works.

McGroarty (2001) takes a different approach by using anecdotal evaluations of the program through the eyes of six families affected by both publicly (Milwaukee and Cleveland) and privately (San Antonio) funded scholarship programs.

Plank and Sykes (2000) explore many key policy issues relating to the creation of school choice programs and the results obtained by them, including school governance, equity, program innovation, student outcomes, and accountability.

One of the questions that must be carefully examined and resolved with such programs is the actual content of the legislation that creates the program and how the statutory language may impact the unique nature of the private and religious schools accepting the voucher or scholarship students. Since the "devil is in the details," so to speak, it may be helpful to look at the specific voucher proposals developed by Coons and Sugarman (1992, 1999). In both proposed choice programs, there is language that may create a problem for religious schools. For instance, in the 1992 version we find: "scholarship schools may require a curriculum, but no student shall be compelled to profess ideological belief or to participate in ceremony symbolic of belief" (p. 11). In the 1999 proposal, we find the following section: "A participating school may require mastery of a curriculum that includes religious content, but no enrolled pupil shall be compelled to profess belief or to participate in ceremony, or other acts symbolic of belief" (p. 96). The Milwaukee voucher program, since the inclusion of religious schools, contains an "opt out" provision for scholarship children. Parents of scholarship students may ask that they be able to opt out of attending religion classes or religious activities. While the record, so far, indicates that no parent has initiated such a request, clauses like these may cause religiously oriented schools to decline to accept such scholarship children, if they determine this would negatively impact the unique nature and mission of the school.

The Center on Education Policy (n.d.) offers "lessons from other countries" as part of its coverage of the pros and cons of publicly funded vouchers. It seems a rather far reach to accept the Center's conclusion to equate a limited voucher, as currently envisioned here in the United States, with the general educational funding provided to private and religious schools in most countries covered in this study.

Fuller and Caire (2001) offer a detailed, issue by issue response and analysis to most of the key arguments raised by opponents of publicly funded vouchers during the debate around this question.

Privately funded vouchers

Privately funded scholarships or vouchers are available in more than 40 states (McDonald, 1999a), and currently enroll more children than all of the publicly funded voucher programs combined (Sugarman & Kemerer, 1999). The major programs are found in Indianapolis, San Antonio, and New York City. In 1999, financier Ted Forstmann and John Walton of the Wal Mart stores, created the $100 million Children's Scholarship Fund, that offered 43 cities and 3 states the opportunity to apply for 40,000 scholarships. They received 1.25 million applications for the 40,000 scholarships (Rees, 2000). Sugarman and Kemerer point out that these private programs face none of the legal or political problems, but that it is "unimaginable that private charity could sustain a nationwide private scholarship" (p. 28) for all the low-income families wishing to pursue them.

Other Choice Options

Public school choice, charter schools, open enrollment, magnet schools

Rees (2000) provides a clear definition of each option and also gives a state by state review of whether they are permitted in each state. There is limited coverage of charter schools in this work. Peterson and Campbell (2001), Moe (2001), Viteritti (1999), and Sugarman and Kemerer (1999) provide more detail on the variety of options available to parents who desire choice within the public school setting. Peterson and Hassel (1998) and Hassel (1999) provide a more in-depth analysis on charter schools. Hassel covers how charter school laws were adopted and implemented in four states, Colorado, Georgia, Massachusetts, and Michigan, and how they may influence the general educational structure of the nation. The United States Department of Education (2000b, 2001a, 2001b) has produced reports that cover the overall state of charter schools, their impact on public school districts, and how accountable they currently are for the operation of their programs.

Tax credits, deductions, education savings accounts

Minnesota, Iowa, Arizona, and Illinois have some form of tax credit or deduction in place to cover legitimate educational expenses or contributions to scholarship funds. Minnesota led the way and adopted a tax deduction program for parents with children in both public and private schools. The Supreme Court upheld the law in *Mueller v. Allen* in 1983. Iowa followed with a tax credit. Minnesota in the late 1990s expanded its law to provide tax credits for some expenses, but not for private school tuition, which remained covered by the original tax deduction law. Arizona adopted a tax credit for those who donate to groups that use the funds to provide scholarships to children. The Supreme Court refused to hear the case thus upholding the law. Illinois recently adopted a tax credit for educational expenses in public or private schools. During the 2001 legislative session, Pennsylvania passed and the governor signed into law a tax credit program similar to Arizona's. The Federal Congress recently passed legislation, and President Bush signed it into law, extending the higher education savings account program to cover grades K through 12 and increasing the allowable annual contribution from $500 to $2,000. There is some limited research on these programs (Rees, 2000; Viteritti, 1999).

Research Issues

The Center on Education Policy (2000) reports that while there are a number of studies on current voucher programs, the issue is clouded by seemingly conflicting conclusions, in some cases caused by what may seem to be the opposing sides of the issue using selectivity in their studies and then quarreling about the methodology used by people on the other side. This report grew out of a Washington based dialogue, in which this writer participated as a representative of the private and religious school community, that involved an equal number of proponents and opponents of voucher programs and a variety of researchers interested in the voucher issue. The study that was undertaken was limited to existing publicly funded programs in Milwaukee, Cleveland, and Florida. Opponents of voucher programs adamantly refused to include any privately funded voucher programs or any subsequently opened voucher programs. This decision immediately limited the potential for meaningful results, due to the potential for having an insufficient number of students in any actual study. The tone of some of the challenges to already completed research projects caused some of the researcher participants to withdraw from the discussions and planning for any future program evaluations. The end result was to produce a limited set of findings and recommendations for both policymakers and researchers (The Center on Education Policy, 2000).

The trials and conflicts that surround research on vouchers are touched upon by Miller (2001) where he examines three early voucher studies, how they were structured, the potential for distortion in each, and the ultimate findings. The conflict and hostility in this debate on sound and acceptable research seem to be almost unresolvable as the attitudes toward the issue have become more rigid and politicized. Some involved in the dialogue suggested that the only study that would be acceptable to some is the perfect study, which under the current set of circumstances is most unlikely.

Against that background, there are a number of studies of voucher programs by Greene (2000a, 2000c) that cover a variety of publicly funded programs as well as one privately funded program in Charlotte, North Carolina. These reports are all generally supportive of the voucher programs and claim positive academic improvement in voucher students. Greene (2000b) also has developed what he describes as an "education freedom index" and concludes with a ranking of all states as to how much freedom parents have in choosing where to send their children to school. He uses a variety of voucher, charter school, tax benefits, and public school choice options to produce the results shown. Howell, Wolf, Peterson, and Campbell (2000) report on test score effects in Dayton, Ohio, New York City, and Washington, DC. These study results have faced criticism very similar to that encountered by Greene.

Resources

There are numerous groups, educational foundations and organizations, as well as independent public policy think tanks that study and report on the question of school choice, vouchers, and other alternatives to attain the ultimate goal of school choice. Rees (2000) provides a comprehensive list of groups and organizations that are supportive of school choice and vouchers. This publication offers contact information, including web sites. To that list should be added a relatively new, but very interesting organization, the Black Alliance for Educational Options, which is headed by Dr. Howard Fuller of Marquette University and the former Superintendent of public schools in the city of Milwaukee. Some additional agencies that produce studies on both sides of the issue of school choice include the Brookings Institution, the Center for Education Policy, Harvard University's Program on Educational Policy and Governance, and the Education Policy Center at Michigan State University. Organizations generally opposed to school choice and vouchers would include People for the American Way, the National Association for the Advancement of Colored People, Americans United, the two major teachers unions, the National Education Association and the American Federation of Teachers, and almost all of the other public school professional organizations.

CONCLUSION

School choice, publicly funded vouchers, and the other alternatives to providing parents with the ability and freedom to select the school they think best suited for their children will continue to be a major issue on the American educational policy and political agenda on both the federal and state levels. Whether the legislative or judicial branches of government will resolve these issues in the near future, is still an open question. The decision of the Supreme Court to hear the Cleveland voucher case may move this issue forward in late 2001 or 2002. The same might be said for the fate of the Illinois tax credit case as it makes its way through the courts toward the possibility of a Supreme Court review. The question of the fate of sound, quality research on existing or new voucher programs that might produce solid evidence of the long-term effects of the voucher programs, that will be accepted by both sides in the choice debate, by policymakers and parents remains to be seen. Whether lawmakers can formulate legislative proposals that respond to the rights of parents to choose, whether private and religious schools who choose to accept voucher students are able to maintain their unique nature, and whether there is provision of adequate financial assistance and information for parents, and whether proponents of school choice possess the ability to develop an accountability system that is acceptable to all concerned are still open questions. Until these, and any other outstanding issues are resolved, the ongoing debate on school choice will continue. The fact that a wide variety of individuals, policy developers, legislators, and organizations interested in education's future in the United States are producing engaging and compelling publications and discussions on this topic is a positive sign for the future.

CHAPTER 15

FINANCE AND DEVELOPMENT

THEODORE J. WALLACE

While the quality and mission of contemporary Catholic schools provide compelling evidence that Catholic schools play a major role in the education of American youth, an overriding concern about their future overshadows their success. The Catholic school system is severely underfinanced. The number of Catholic schools, teachers, and students in America has decreased dramatically over the past three decades. The primary reason for this decline is finances. The problem of financing Catholic schools has yet to be solved. Unless a viable source of funding is found, the number of Catholic schools will continue to decline. (Hallinan, 2000, p. 216)

This decline is illustrated by the fact that Catholic school enrollment has dropped from 5.46 million students in 1961 to 2.55 million in 1996. The net number of Catholic schools has dropped from 13,208 to 8,250 in the same period. Interestingly, the number of Catholic school age children actually *grew* from 11.45 million in 1961 to 11.75 million in 1991 (Harris, 1996).

This chapter summarizes the research on the important topics of Catholic school finance and development. Suggestions for future research complete the chapter.

Paucity of Research and Available Data

With the echo of Hallinan's words reverberating around us, what does the research of the past decade and quarter century tell us about the important issues of Catholic school finance and development?

Precious little. Only 8 of the 302 dissertations completed on Catholic schools in the United States between 1988-1997 dealt with finance related issues. As for development, there were *no dissertations* during this same period (Hunt, 1998).

A glance further back at the period between 1976-1987 revealed nine dissertations on finance and one on development (Traviss, 1989); thus, since 1976, of the almost 1,800 dissertations on Catholic schools, *only 18* focused on finance or development.

As Joseph Claude Harris discovered while researching his book, *The Cost of Catholic Parishes and Schools* (1996), there is no data clearinghouse and little access to national data on the topic of Catholic school finance, except through purchase of National Catholic Educational Association (NCEA) publications. Harris had to rely on his own negotiated entry to access financial data from several dioceses upon which to make some generalizations.

As for development data on Catholic schools, there also appear to be limited aggregate data and access. The American Association of Fund-Raising Council (AAFRC) Trust for Philanthropy is the primary source of data on philanthropic giving (Pine, 2001). While the Trust has gathered and analyzed data on giving to religion and education for more than 30 years, they do not track philanthropic contributions by individual religions.

The Council for Aid to Education/RAND reports on contributions to independent elementary and secondary education, but does not provide breakdowns for Catholic schools (Pine, 2001). The Council on Foundations and the Foundation Center also do not aggregate philanthropic contributions specifically made to Catholic schools (Pine, 2001).

St. Mary's University in Minnesota, which offers an MA in Philanthropy and Development, has not sought to gather development data specific to Catholic schools. It does not offer courses specific to development issues in Catholic schools (Pine, 2001).

The *Catholic Funding Guide* published by Foundations and Donors Interested in Catholic Activities, Inc. (Robinson, 1998) includes 672 entries from 42 states that identify foundations that provide funding for a full spectrum of Catholic activities. This directory is designed to assist those non-profit Catholic organizations wishing to identify possible funding sources but does not provide researchers trend data aggregated for Catholic schools.

National Catholic Educational Association (NCEA) Data on Catholic School Finance and Development

The National Catholic Educational Association has published statistical reports on Catholic elementary and secondary schools in the United States only since the 1969-1970 school year. And since 1989, NCEA has published reports on elementary school finances in years ending in odd numbers and secondary school finance reports in years ending in even numbers. These reports are random sample surveys that often include data on about 10% of the Catholic schools in the United States (Kealey, 2000).

In 1985, NCEA published *The Catholic High School: A National Portrait* (Yeager, Benson, Guerra, & Manno). Sixty-two percent of the 1,464 Catholic high schools in the United States at that time responded to the survey. *CHS 2000: A First Look* (Guerra, 1998), was a survey of Catholic high schools in 1997. More than 80% of all Catholic high schools responded. Subsequent descriptive reports will be gleaned from the CHS survey and published by NCEA. The first of such, *Mission and Money* (Tracy, 2001) provides descriptive data on high school finance, development, and governance.

Thanks to other NCEA studies and publications, some baseline finance and development data, along with some best practice documentation, are included in such publications as those of: Augenstein and Meitler (2000); Tracy (2000, 2001); Haney and O'Keefe (1999); Collins (1997); Correia (1998); and Kealey and Collins (1994).

Catholic School Finance Data

The average cost to operate a Catholic elementary school increased by $139,721 between 1990-1994; 43% of the increase was due to inflation, 18% related to efforts to reduce teacher-student ratio, 12% due to decreased enrollment, and 27% from a combination of factors including teacher salary increases (Harris, 2000). Tuition covers 78% of the average Catholic high school budget, while in elementary schools tuition represents 59% of cost (Tracy, 2001).

In 1969, 47% of the Catholic school-age population in the United States enrolled in Catholic schools and parishes paid 63% of school costs (Bredeweg, 1980). By 1994, the percentage of Catholic children being educated in Catholic schools had dropped to 18% (Schaub & Baker, 1993) and parish subsidy for schools had similarly declined to 25% (Harris, 2000).

Budgets of parish elementary schools increased by an annual rate of 9.4% between 1980 and 1989 ($184,372 to $420,230) which was twice the rate of inflation during this period. During the 1990s, school costs continued to increase at a rate of 7% annually. During this period, schools raised tuition by an annual average rate of 12.4%. Declining enrollment market share caused by tuition rates growing annually by triple the rate of inflation is considered one of the primary economic factors driving the rate of increase in tuition (Harris, 2000).

The tuition burden for an average Catholic household with one elementary student and one secondary student likely exceeds 11% of household income. Catholic schools succeed for the proportion of the population that can afford the escalating tuition charges. The dilemma lies in the fact that a diminishing portion of the Catholic population can participate in Catholic schools (Harris, 2000).

This reality has placed an enormous burden on schools that wish to serve lower economic students to raise funds for tuition assistance. From 1970-1997, Catholic elementary schools that offer financial aid increased from 11% to 80%. Secondary schools offering tuition aid during the same period went from 8% to 99%. Interestingly, the average elementary tuition rate during this period saw a stunning increase from $60 to $1,499 and from $175 to $4,100 in secondary schools (Guerra, 2000). As Guerra warned and supports Harris's contention, if financial assistance does not escalate with the increase in tuition, the socio-economic profile of Catholic school students may shift upward, leaving many lower and middle class American Catholic families without the ability to send their children to Catholic schools. Guerra suggests that development programs, including endowments, must enable Catholic schools to reduce the operating budget's dependence on tuition or provide increased tuition aid to middle and lower income families (Guerra, 2000).

Catholic School Development Data

In Catholic elementary schools, fundraising income has increased from a per school average of $21,000 in 1980 to an estimated $102,000 in 1998 (Harris, 2000). Various development activities in Catholic elementary schools have increased as recently as between 1997 and 1999. More schools have long-range plans (from 56% of schools in 1997 to 75% in 1999), case statements (9.5% to 13.3%), and an annual appeal (19.3% to 26.2%) (Kealey, 1998a, 2000).

In 1989, 20% of the Catholic elementary schools had endowments and by 1995 that number had grown to 37%. By 1999, 48% of the schools had endowments (Kealey, 2000).

In Catholic high schools, 1% to 5% of the annual operating budget is derived from the annual giving program in 51% of the schools. Nine percent of Catholic high schools derive in excess of 16% of their operating budgets from their annual fund drive (Guerra, 1998).

Seventeen percent of Catholic high schools receive contributions from 26% or more of their graduates. Forty-six percent of the schools receive contributions from 1-15% of their alumni. Twelve percent do not have an annual fund. Only four percent of Catholic high schools have an endowment in excess of $5 million. Seventy percent have an endowment less than $1 million. Fifty-seven percent of Catholic high schools employ a full-time development director and support staff (Guerra, 1998).

The SPICE (Selected Programs for Improving Catholic Education) program was created in 1996 to share best practices in Catholic schools. The 1998 program highlighted 10 schools and dioceses for their successes in funding their schools (Haney & O'Keefe, 1999).

SUMMARY

Assuming that finances will always be a problem for Catholic education, even if some degree of public support is provided, plans for the future direction of Catholic education must take fiscal considerations into account....This planning exercise is salutary, not only to prepare strategies for operating Catholic schools under various financial constraints, but also to force Catholics to identify their preferences and order their priorities for Catholic education under different constraints. (Hallinan, 2000, p. 217)

For such strategizing to be effective, much more research, such as suggested in the following section, will be needed. To make decisions about the future of Catholic schools without a comprehensive understanding of the financial facts would be tantamount to turning our backs on those who have worked in Catholic schools as well as those who have funded them. The declining trend data tell us that if we do not closely examine our history and learn from it in dramatic fashion, we are bound to repeat it.

Suggestions for Future Research

Before any marked increase in research on the topics of Catholic school finance and development occur, some type of comprehensive effort to collect diocesan, parish, and school data must be undertaken. Possibly a Catholic university or some other form of non-profit center could be designated as a data clearinghouse so that collection and access to all relevant data could be made much easier for those wishing to analyze trend data, contribute to policy discussions, and communicate these issues to national Catholic leaders, school practitioners, and families.

Catholic School Finance

• In-depth studies are needed to formally assess such anecdotally regarded school funding ideas as cost-based, need-based tuition programs. This would require a qualitative and quantitative design that would collect historical data on enrollment, cost per pupil, and the number of schools that have begun the program, and for those who have discontinued it, the reasons why. Schools that refused to adopt the program, especially suburban Catholic schools, should be included in such a study.

• Harris has suggested from his study of several dioceses, that Catholic school enrollments have suffered, in part due to tuition rates that have risen faster than the rate of inflation. More analysis is needed to document this (or not) on a national basis.

• Parish subsidy has been a major source of funding for Catholic schools but has been decreasing significantly in recent years. A comprehensive qualitative and quantitative study is needed to further document trends and reasons for such decisions.

• Teacher salaries have increased as the presence of vowed religious has declined since the 1960s. Data need to be collected to help researchers analyze the impact of this trend on Catholic school cost and enrollment. In addition, an analysis is needed to estimate the total cost for Catholic schools to fund more equitable wages for their teachers and staff. This would provide a clearer picture for Catholic school leaders as they attempt to slow the rate of teacher attrition.

• Publicly and privately funded voucher programs have grown since 1990. Catholic schools have benefited by the number of new students and existing students who qualify for funding from these programs. Much research is needed to study the financial impact on Catholic schools from these programs as well as the impact in composite socio-economic levels of the students enrolled in the participating Catholic schools.

• To what degree are long-range plans and budgets used as tools to implement school priorities? If so, in what ways? If not, what types of tools, training, and support for Catholic school leaders are necessary?

• How effectively prepared are Catholic school leaders (pastors and principals) in financial management? What other resources such as additional training, publications, 800-help lines, on-line support, and peer training would help administrators become more effective financial managers?

• Assuming budgeting systems and financial reports are tools to manage schools and implement plans, how well are the systems working that are now used in diocesan schools?

Catholic School Development

• Beyond the baseline development profile data on Catholic schools available from NCEA, data must be collected that document the millions of dollars being raised each year by Catholic schools. Statistics on annual funds, percentage of alumni participation, cost for each dollar raised, including what is spent on consultants, are all needed to properly research this growing field in Catholic education.

• Data are needed on the development expertise required for the professional preparation of development directors and school leaders. Building the capacity of Catholic schools and parishes to raise the amount of money that is needed to sustain an effective Catholic school begins with the people who are responsible for raising the money.

• Millions of dollars are paid each year to consultants who help Catholic schools raise money. A clearinghouse of qualifying data is needed to document the firms that deal with Catholic schools and parishes that would include some criteria to protect Catholic schools as they make this very expensive hiring decision.

• What and where are the best development programs in Catholic schools in the United States? What are the key success measures that make these programs the best?

• In what ways are development programs for schools and dioceses, such as the Bishop's annual appeal, different? the same? Is there a conflict (real or perceived)?

• Can the success story of many Catholic schools and parishes in the Wichita Diocese (time, talent, and treasure that has resulted in free Catholic education for all parish children) be replicated? If so, how would a parish do so?

REFERENCES

Abel, W. A. (1992). Possibilities and risks. *Momentum, 23(1)*, 51-53.

Achilles, C. M., & Finn, J. D. (2000). Should class size be a cornerstone for educational policy? *The CEIC Review, 9(2)*, 15, 23.

Ackerman, D. M. (1997). *Education vouchers: The constitutional standards*. (CRS Report for Congress No. 97-50A) Washington, DC: Library of Congress.

Ackroyd, S., & Thompson, P. (1999). *Organizational misbehaviour*. London: Sage Press.

Adams, N. G. (1997). What does it mean? Exploring the myths of multiculturalism. In K. Lomotey (Ed.), *Sailing against the wind: African Americans and women in U. S. education* (pp. 17-26). Albany, NY: State University of New York Press.

Akerhielm, K. (1993). *Comparing student achievement in public and Catholic schools*. Washington, DC: Association for Public Policy Analysis.

Albertson, J. (1992). Smile – You're on camera! *Momentum, 23(1)*, 65-66.

Alexander, J. (1988). Resource programs for learning disabled students. *Special Education, 10(2)*, 3.

Alexander, K. L., & Pallas, A. M. (1983). Private schools and public policy: New evidence on cognitive achievement. *Sociology of Education, 56*, 170-182.

American Association of University Women. (1998). *Separated by sex: A critical look at single-sex education for girls*. Washington, DC: American Association of University Women Educational Foundation.

Anastasio, P. (1996). *The recruitment, selection and preparation of Catholic school principals in six dioceses in the United States*. Unpublished doctoral dissertation, Fordham University.

Anderson, C. S. (1982). The search for school climate: A review of the research. *Review of Educational Research, 52*, 368-420.

Anderson, C. S. (1985). The investigation of school climate. In G. R. Austin & H. Garber (Eds.), *Research on exemplary schools* (pp. 96-126). New York: Academic Press.

Anderson, G. L. (1990). Toward a critical constructivist approach to school administration: Invisibility, legitimation, and the study of non-events. *Educational Administration Quarterly, 26(1)*, 38-59.

Anderson, G. L., & Grinberg, J. (1998). Educational administration as a disciplinary practice: Appropriating Foucault's view of power, discourse, and method. *Educational Administration Quarterly, 34(3)*, 329-353.

Anderson, G. M. (1999). Small middle schools on the rise. *America, 180(18)*, 16-18.

Anderson, P. (1993). Connecting with the "real" world. *Momentum, 24(1)*, 26-27.

Applefield, J., Huber, R., & Moallem, M. (2001). Constructivism in theory and practice: Toward a better understanding. *The High School Journal, 84(2)*, 35-53.

Arbuckle, G. A. (1996). *From chaos to mission: Refounding religious life formation*. Collegeville, MN: The Liturgical Press.

Archambault, F. X., Jr., Westberg, K. L., & Brown, S. W. (1992, March). Regular classroom practices with gifted students: Findings from the Classroom Practices Survey. *The National Research Center on the Gifted and Talented Newsletter*, 2.

Archer, J. (1997a, February 26). Keeping the faith. *Education Week, 16(22)*, p. 31.

Archer, J. (1997b, February 26). Without abandonment. *Education Week, 16(22)*, pp. 19-22.

Armstrong, T. (1993). *7 kinds of smart.* New York: Penguin Books.

Asante, M. K. (1991). The Afrocentric idea in education. *Journal of Negro Education, 60(2),* 170-180.

Asmussen, L., & Larson, R. (1991). The quality of family time among young adolescents in single-parent and married-parents families. *Journal of Marriage and the Family, 53,* 1021-1030.

Assouline, S. G., Colangelo, N., Lupkowski-Shoplik, A., & Lipscomb, J. (1998). *Iowa Acceleration Scale Manual: A guide for whole-grade acceleration K-8.* Scottsdale, AZ: Gifted Psychology Press.

Assouline, S. G., & Lupkowski-Shoplik, A. (1997). Talent searches: A model for the discovery and development of academic talent. In N. Colangelo & G. A. Davis (Eds.), *Handbook of gifted education* (2nd ed., pp. 170-179). Boston: Allyn & Bacon.

Atkinson, R. C., & Shiffrin, R. M. (1968). Human memory: A proposed system and its control processes. In K. Spence & J. Spence (Eds.), *The psychology of learning and motivation* (Vol. 2., pp. 89-195). New York: Academic Press.

Au, K. H., & Kawakami, A. J. (1991). Culture and ownership. *Childhood Education, 67(5),* 280-284.

Augenstein, J., & Meitler, N. (2000). *Catholic school growth: 1985 to 1999.* Washington, DC: National Catholic Educational Association.

Baddeley, A. D. (1990). *Human memory: Theory and practice.* Boston: Allyn & Bacon.

Bailey, B. (2000). The impact of mandated change on teachers. In A. Hargreaves & N. Bascia (Eds.), *The sharp edge of change: Teaching, leading, and the realities of reform* (pp. 112-128). London: Falmer Press.

Baker, D. P., & Riordan, C. (1998). The "eliting" of the common American Catholic school and the national education crisis. *Phi Delta Kappan, 80(1),* 16-23.

Baptiste, H. P. (1999). The multicultural environment of schools: Implications to leaders. In L. W. Hughes (Ed.), *The principal as leader* (2nd ed., pp. 105-127). Upper Saddle River, NJ: Merrill.

Barber, B. (1997, Spring). Education for democracy. *The Good Society*, 1-7.

Barrett-Jones, K.A. (1993). A study of recruitment and retention among elementary teachers in Catholic schools (Doctoral dissertation, Kansas State University, 1993). *Dissertation Abstracts International, 54-05A,* 1668.

Barth, R. (1990). *Improving schools from within.* San Francisco: Jossey-Bass.

Bashian, K. R. (1991). What's a computer orchestra? *Momentum, 22(4),* 51-53.

Bauch, P. A. (1990). Wanted: Parental involvement. *Momentum, 74,* 74-75.

Bauch, P. A. (1991). Linking parents' reasons for choice and involvement in inner-city Catholic high schools. *International Journal of Educational Research, 15,* 311-322.

Bauch, P. A., & Goldring, E. B. (1996). Parent involvement and teacher decision making in urban high schools of choice. *Urban Education, 31(4),* 403-431.

Bean, R. M., Eichelberger, R. T, Lazar, M., Morris, G. A., & Reed, C. (2000). Listening to students: Voices from the inner city. *Catholic Education: A Journal of Inquiry and Practice, 4(1),* 5-15.

Beatty, A. S., Reese, C. M., Persky, H. R., & Carr, P. (1996). *NAEP 1994 U.S. history report card.* Washington, DC: U.S. Department of Education, Office of Educational Research and Improvement.

Beck, L. G. (1994). *Reclaiming educational administration as a caring profession.* New York: Teachers College Press.

Beecroft, S. A. (1992). "Chimo" to an electronic epistle network. *Momentum, 23(1), 14-16.*

Behrmann, E. H. (Ed.). *(1971). Catholic special education.* St. Louis: B. Herder Book Co.

Bempechat, J., Drago-Severson, E., & Dinndorf, L. (1994). Parents assess Catholic schools: A qualitative study explores the different reasons parents choose Catholic schools. *Momentum, 25(1),* 57-61.

Bempechat, J., Graham, S., & Jimenez, N. (1996). The socialization of achievement in poor and minority children: A comparative study. *Journal of Cross Cultural Psychology, 30(2),* 139-158.

Bempechat, J., Graham, S., & Jimenez, N. (1997). Motivational influences and the achievement of poor minority children. *Journal of Child and Youth Care Work, 11,* 48-60.

Benevento, S. L. (1997). *Parents' and teachers' perceptions of parental involvement and participation in Catholic schools.* Unpublished doctoral dissertation, Fordham University.

Bennett, W. J., Finn, C. E., Jr., & Cribb, J. T. E., Jr. (1999). *The educated child: A parent's guide from preschool through eighth grade.* New York: The Free Press.

Bergan, H. (1997). Getting up to speed. *Momentum, 28(4),* 38-40.

Beuhring, T., Blum, R. W., & Rinehart, P. M. (2000). *Protecting teens: Beyond race, income, and family structure.* Minneapolis, MN: Center for Adolescent Health.

Beyer, L. E. (1991). Teacher education, reflective inquiry and moral action. In B. R. Tabachnich & K. M. Zeichner (Eds.), *Issues and practices in inquiry-oriented teacher education* (pp. 113-129). Bristol, PA: The Falmer Press.

Bianchi, S., & Robinson, J. (1997). What did you do today? Children's use of time, family composition, and the acquisition of social capital. *Journal of Marriage and the Family, 59,* 332-344.

Biddle, J. K. (1997). Peering over the traditional rim: A story from Dayton Catholic Elementary. *Momentum,* 28(14), *71-74.*

Bishop, M. E. (1995). Inclusion: Balancing the ups and downs. *Momentum, 26(3),* 28-30.

Blackmore, J. (1998). The politics of gender and educational change: Managing gender or changing gender relations? In A. Hargreaves, A. Lieberman, M. Fullan, & D. Hopkins (Eds.), *International handbook of educational change* (pp. 460-481). London: Kluwer Academic Publishers.

Blecksmith, L. A. (1996). *Distinguishing characteristics of Catholic identity in Catholic elementary schools.* Unpublished doctoral dissertation, University of San Francisco.

Borras, A. (1994). The canonical limits of Catholic identity: Some problematical situations. In J. Provost & K. Walf (Eds.), *Catholic identity* (pp. 47-59). London: SCM Press.

Bouton, D. A. (1997). Survey research: The effectiveness of the Frontiers program. In R. Haney & A. A. Zukowski (Eds.), *New frontiers: Navigational strategies for integrating technology into the school* (pp. 133-136). Washington, DC: National Catholic Educational Association.

Braun, L. (1992). The worth of a child. *Momentum, 23(1),* 10-13.

Bredekamp, S., & Copple, C. (Eds.). (1997). *Developmentally appropriate practice in early childhood programs* (Rev. ed.). Washington, DC: National Association for the Education of Young Children.

Bredecamp, S., & Rosegrant, T. (Eds.). (1992). *Reaching potentials: Appropriate curriculum and assessment for young children.* Washington, DC: National Association for the Education of Young Children.

Bredeweg, F. (1980). *Catholic elementary schools and their finances-1979.* Washington, DC: National Catholic Educational Association.

Brennan, J. (1997). *Point to the future: A principal's technology planning guide*. Washington, DC: National Catholic Educational Association.

Breslin, R. (2000). Hiring to maintain the mission. *Catholic Education: A Journal of Inquiry and Practice, 4(2)*, 227-238.

Brigham, F. H., Jr. (1990). *United States Catholic elementary and secondary schools 1989-1990*. Washington, DC: National Catholic Educational Association.

Brigham, F. H., Jr. (1991). *United States Catholic elementary and secondary schools 1990-1991*. Washington, DC: National Catholic Educational Association.

Brigham, F. H., Jr. (1992a). The new astronauts. *Momentum, 23(1)*, 8-9.

Brigham, F. H., Jr. (1992b). *United States Catholic elementary and secondary schools 1991-1992*. Washington, DC: National Catholic Educational Association.

Brigham, F. H., Jr. (1993). *United States Catholic elementary and secondary schools 1992-1993*. Washington, DC: National Catholic Educational Association.

Brigham, F. H., Jr. (1994). *United States Catholic elementary and secondary schools 1993-1994*. Washington, DC: National Catholic Educational Association.

Brigham, F. H., Jr. (1995). *United States Catholic elementary and secondary schools 1994-1995*. Washington, DC: National Catholic Educational Association.

Broekman, H. (1997). Education in an age of crisis. *Momentum, 28(1)*, 46-48.

Brookover, W. B., Beady, C., Flood, P., Schweitzer, J., & Wisenbaker, J. (1979). *School social systems and student achievement: Schools can make a difference*. New York: Praeger.

Brooks, J., & Brooks, H. (1993). *The case for constructivist classrooms*. Alexandria, VA: Association for Supervision and Curriculum Development.

Brooks, P. E., Mojica, C. M., & Land, R. E. (1995). *Final evaluation report: Longitudinal study of LA BEST's after-school education and enrichment program, 1992-1994*. Los Angeles: Center for the Study of Evaluation, UCLA.

Brooks, S. (1996). Technology tools for the teacher: Software tools for the teacher. *Today's Catholic Teacher, 30(1)*, 51-53.

Brooks, S. (1997a). Technology in the classroom: Incorporating technology into your teaching. *Today's Catholic Teacher, 31(1)*, 10-12.

Brooks, S. (1997b). Technology in the classroom: Multimedia authoring for teachers and students. *Today's Catholic Teacher, 30(5)*, 50-53.

Brooks, S. (1998). Technology in the classroom: Can the e-rate program benefit our schools? *Today's Catholic Teacher, 32(1)*, 14-16.

Brooks, S. (1999a). Technology in the classroom: Is your technology program girl friendly? *Today's Catholic Teacher, 33(2)*, 10-12.

Brooks, S. (1999b). Technology in the classroom: Teachers keeping up with technology. *Today's Catholic Teacher, 33(1)*, 28-31.

Brooks, S. (2000). Technology in the classroom: Staff development for your instructional program. *Today's Catholic Teacher, 34(1)*, 26-29, 33-34.

Broughman, S. P., & Rollefson, M. R. (2000). *Teacher supply in the United States: Sources of newly hired teachers in public and private schools, 1987-88 to 1993-94*. (NCES 2000-309) Washington, DC: National Center for Education Statistics.

Bryk, A. S. (1996). Lessons from Catholic high schools on renewing our educational institutions. In T. McLaughlin, J. O'Keefe, & B. O'Keeffe (Eds.), *The contemporary Catholic school: Context, identity, and diversity* (pp. 25-41). Washington, DC: Falmer Press.

Bryk, A. S., Bekrig, P. B., Kerbow, D., & Rollow, S. G. (1998). *Charting Chicago school reform.* Boulder, CO: Westview Press.

Bryk, A. S., & Driscoll, M. E. (1988). *The high school as community: Contextual influences and consequences for students and teachers.* Madison, WI: Wisconsin Center for Education Research.

Bryk, A. S., Lee, V. E., & Holland, P. B. (1993). *Catholic schools and the common good.* Cambridge, MA: Harvard University Press.

Buetow, H. A. (1985). *A history of United States Catholic schooling.* Washington, DC: National Catholic Educational Association.

Buetow, H. A. (1988). *The Catholic school: Its roots, identity, and future.* New York: Crossroads.

Bufkin, L., & Bryde, S. (1996). Implementing a constructivist approach in higher education with early childhood educators. *Journal of Early Childhood Teacher Education, 17(2),* 58-65.

Burgoon, R. (1997). Inclusion models: A study of three Catholic elementary schools (Doctoral dissertation, Saint Louis University, 1997). *Dissertation Abstracts International, 58/08,* AAT 9803757.

Burns, T., & Stalker, G. M. (1961*). The management of innovation.* London: Tavistock.

Butler, J. (1997). *The psychic life of power.* Stanford, CA: Stanford University Press.

Butler, S. M. (2000). Catholic schools. *Momentum, 31(1),* 52-53.

Butler, T. M. (1992). An apple core for Catholic schools. *Momentum, 23(1),* 48-50.

Caine, R., & Caine, G. (1991). *Making connections, teaching and the human brain.* Alexandria VA: Association for Supervision and Curriculum Development.

Caine, R., & Caine, G. (1997). *Education on the edge of possibility.* Alexandria, VA: Association for Supervision and Curriculum Development.

Campbell, B. (1994). *The multiple intelligences handbook.* Stanwood, WA: Campbell and Associates, Inc.

Campbell, J. P. (1996). Some cautions about visual learning and religious education. *Momentum, 27(2),* 29-30.

Campbell, J. R., & Carney, T. (1987). The Achilles heel of Catholic education: Why have Catholic schools failed to develop programs for the gifted and talented? *Momentum, 18(4),* 24-26.

Campbell, J.R., Reese, C.M., O'Sullivan, C., & Dossey, J. (1996). *Trends in Academic achievement, 1994.* Washington, DC: National Center for Education Statistics.

Campbell, L. (1995). *Teaching and learning through multiple intelligences.* Needham Heights, MA: Allyn & Bacon.

Canon Law Society of America. (1983). *Code of canon law.* Washington, DC: Author.

Capper, C. A. (Ed.). (1993). *Educational administration in a pluralistic society.* Albany, NY: State University of New York Press.

Capper, C. A. (1996). We're not housed in an institution, we're housed in the community: Possibilities and consequences of neighborhood-based interagency collaboration. In J. Cibulka & W. Kritek (Eds.), *Coordination among schools, families, and communities: Prospects for educational reform* (pp. 299-322). Albany, NY: State University of New York Press.

Carey, L. (1991). Justice and peace: Constitutive elements of Catholicity. In F. D. Kelly (Ed.), *What makes a school Catholic?* (pp. 41-47). Washington, DC: National Catholic Educational Association.

Carnegie Council on Adolescent Development. (1989). *Turning points: Preparing American youth for the 21st century.* New York: Carnegie Corporation.

Carr, D. (1991). *Educating the virtues: An essay on the philosophical psychology of moral development and education.* New York: Routledge.

Carr, K. (1995). *Catholic elementary school leadership: A study of principals' motivation, efficacy and satisfaction.* Unpublished doctoral dissertation, The Catholic University of America.

Carr, K. (2000). Leadership given to the religious mission of Catholic schools. In J. Youniss, J. Convey, & J. McLellan (Eds.), *The Catholic character of Catholic schools* (pp. 62-81). Notre Dame, IN: University of Notre Dame Press.

Carstensen, K. M. D. (1999). *It's all about the girls: The essence of the single sex school.* Unpublished doctoral dissertation, The University of Nebraska, Lincoln.

Carter, P. (Ed.). (1997). Spirit of full inclusion thrives at Purcell Marian. *NICE Inclusion Quarterly, 1(4),* 3.

The case for an all girls public school. (1997). *America, 177(5),* 3-4.

Casey, L., Casiello, C., Gruca-Peal, B., & Johnson, B. (1995). *Advancing academic achievement in the heterogeneous classroom.* Tinley Park, IL: Saint Xavier University. (ERIC Document Reproduction Service No. ED 400073)

Catholic Church. (1997). *Catechism of the Catholic church* (2nd ed.). Washington, DC: United States Catholic Conference.

Catholic Health Association. (1987). *The dynamics of Catholic identity in health care: A working document.* St. Louis: Author.

Center on Education Policy. (2000). *School vouchers: What we know and don't know...and how we could know more.* Washington, DC: Author.

Center on Education Policy. (n.d.). *Lessons from other countries about private schools.* Washington, DC: Author.

Cerveny, C. (1995). Religious educators confront the electronic age. *Momentum, 26(4),* 30-32.

Charlesworth, R. (1998). Developmentally appropriate practice is for everyone. *Childhood Education, 74(5),* 274-282.

Checkley, K. (1997). The first seven...and the eighth. *Educational Leadership, 55(1),* 8-13.

Chikri, R.C. (2000). The relationship between perceptions of the mission of Catholic schools and job satisfaction among teachers in Catholic elementary schools (Doctoral dissertation, Wayne State University, 2000). *Dissertation Abstracts International, 61-03,* 826.

Chilampikunnel, M. A. (1995). *Parental involvement and students' performance and self-esteem in suburban and city parochial elementary (K-6) schools.* Unpublished doctoral dissertation, Fordham University.

Chilinskas, K. M. (1989). Mainstreaming in the Catholic high school: A program that works. *NAMRP Quarterly, 20(1),* 2-7.

Chin, S. H. (1997). High tech connections. *Momentum, 28(1),* 46-48.

Chopko, M. E. (1999a). A favorable legal environment for voucher programs. *Catholic Education: A Journal of Inquiry and Practice, 3(1),* 87-96.

Chopko, M. E. (1999b). Legal history of vouchers - a federal constitutional review. In D. McDonald (Ed.), *Catholic schools and school choice: Partners for justice* (pp. 141-168). Washington, DC: National Catholic Educational Association.

Chopko, M. E. (1999c). Vouchers can be constitutional. *Connecticut Law Review, 31(3),* 945-976.

Chubb, J. E., & Moe, T. M. (1988). Politics, markets, and the organization of schools. *American Political Science Review, 82,* 1055-1087.

Chubb, J. E., & Moe, T. M. (1990). *Politics, markets, and America's schools.* Washington, DC: The Brookings Institution.

Cibulka, J. G. (1978). Creating a new era for schools and communities. In D. A. Erikson & T. L. Reller (Eds.), *The principal in metropolitan schools* (pp. 78-105). Berkeley, CA: McCutchan Publishing Corporation.

Cibulka, J. G., & Kritek, W. (1996). *Coordination among schools, families, and communities: Prospects for educational reform.* Albany, NY: State University of New York Press.

Cimino, C. (2000a). Model programs. In C. Cimino, R. M. Haney, J. M. O'Keefe, & A. A. Zukowski (Eds.), *Forming innovative learning environments through technology* (pp. 7-36). Washington, DC: National Catholic Educational Association.

Cimino, C. (2000b). Overview of SPICE 1999. In C. Cimino, R. M. Haney, J. M. O'Keefe, & A. A. Zukowski (Eds.), *Forming innovative learning environments through technology* (pp. 1-6). Washington, DC: National Catholic Educational Association.

Cioppi, M. T. (2000). Evangelization in Catholic secondary schools (Doctoral dissertation, Immaculata College, 2000). *Dissertation Abstracts International, 61-02A,* 433.

Cipriani-Sklar, R. (1996). *A quantitative and qualitative examination of the influence of the normative and perceived school environments of a coeducational public school versus a single sex Catholic school on ninth grade girls' science self-concept and anxiety in the area of science education.* Unpublished doctoral dissertation, St. John's University, New York.

Ciriello, M. (1993). *Principal as managerial leader.* Washington, DC: United States Catholic Conference.

Clifford, W. (1998). Updating teachers' technology skills. *Momentum, 29(3),* 34-36.

Clune, W. H., & Witte, J. F. (Eds.). (1990). *Choice and control in American education* (Vols. 1-2). Bristol, PA: The Falmer Press.

Coburn, J. (1992a). Technology for technophobes: A do-it-yourself teacher workshop series. *Today's Catholic Teacher, 25(6),* 64-68.

Coburn, J. (1992b). Technology for technophobes: A do-it-yourself teacher workshop series: Moving software into the classroom. *Today's Catholic Teacher, 26(1),* 36-40, 44.

Coburn, J. (1993). Moving ahead with technology: Is this software any good? How to tell. *Today's Catholic Teacher, 27(1),* 40-42.

Coburn, J. (1994). Technology and Catholic schools: Profiles in success. *Today's Catholic Teacher, 28(1),* 33-36.

Coburn, J. (1995). New frontiers: Technology in Catholic schools. *Today's Catholic Teacher, 29(1),* 40-44, 46.

Cohen, D. K. (1990). Governance and instruction: The promise of decentralization and choice. In W. H. Clune & J. F. Witte (Eds.), *Choice and control in American education* (Vol. 1, pp. 337-386). Philadelphia, PA: The Falmer Press.

Cohen, D. L., McLaughlin, M. W., & Talbert, J. E. (1993). *Teaching for understanding: Challenges for policy and practice.* San Francisco: Jossey-Bass.

Coleman, J. (1988). Social capital and the creation of human capital. *American Sociologist, 94,* 5095-5120.

Coleman, J. S. (1987a, August/September). Families and schools. *Educational Researcher, 6,* 32-38.

Coleman, J. S. (1987b, November). Social capital and the development of youth. *Momentum, 18(19),* 6-8.

Coleman, J. S. (1991). *Parental involvement in education.* Washington, DC: U. S. Department of Education.

Coleman, J. S. (1995). Achievement-oriented school design. In M. T. Hallinan (Ed.), *Restructuring schools: Promising practices and policies* (pp. 11-29). New York: Plenum Press.

Coleman, J. S., & Hoffer, T. (1987). *Public and private high schools: The impact of communities.* New York: Basic Books.

Coleman, J. S., Hoffer, T., & Kilgore, S. (1982*). High school achievement: Public, Catholic and private schools compared.* New York: Basic Books.

The College Board. (1999). *College board reports, 1995-1999.* New York: Author.

Collins, K. (1997). *Getting started: An overview of school development practices.* Washington, DC: National Catholic Educational Association.

Collura, K. (1995). Shopping for software. *Momentum, 26(4),* 33-35.

Compagnone, N. (1999). *Lay Catholic elementary principals in the state of Kansas: Self perceptions of their spiritual leadership and ministerial roles.* Unpublished doctoral dissertation, University of Dayton, Ohio.

Conant, J. (1959). *The American high school today.* New York: McGraw-Hill.

Congregation for Catholic Education. (1977). *The Catholic school.* Washington, DC: United States Catholic Conference.

Congregation for Catholic Education. (1988). *The religious dimension of education in a Catholic school.* Washington, DC: United States Catholic Conference.

Congregation for Catholic Education. (1997). *The Catholic school on the threshold of the third millennium.* Rome: Libreria Editrice Vaticana.

Conley, S. C. (1991). Review of the literature on teacher participation in school decision making. In G. Grant (Ed.), *Review of research in education* (Vol. 17, pp. 225-265). Washington, DC: American Educational Research Association.

Conley, S. C., & Bacharach, S. B. (1990). From school site-management to participatory site-management. *Phi Delta Kappan, 71(7),* 539-544.

Connelly, J. (1997). Imaginative alternatives for funding. *Momentum, 28(4),* 24-26.

Conroy, J. C. (1999). *Catholic education: Inside out, outside in.* Dublin: Veritas Publications.

Convey, J. J. (1991). Catholic schools in a changing society: Past accomplishments and future challenges. *In National Congress on Catholic Schools for the 21ˢᵗ Century: The Catholic School and Society* (pp. 23-45). Washington, DC: National Catholic Educational Association.

Convey, J. J. (1992). *Catholic schools make a difference: Twenty-five years of research.* Washington, DC: National Catholic Educational Association.

Convey, J. J. (2000). Views of bishops and priests concerning Catholic schools. In J. Youniss, J. J. Convey, & J. A. McClellan (Eds.), *The Catholic character of Catholic schools* (pp. 14-37). Notre Dame, IN: University of Notre Dame Press.

Convey, J., & Thompson, A. (1999). *Weaving Christ's seamless garment: Assessment of Catholic religious education.* Washington, DC: National Catholic Educational Association.

Cook, T. J. (1990). A study of the religious literacy of Catholic high school educators (Doctoral dissertation, Boston College, 1990). *Dissertation Abstracts International, 52-01A,* 0123.

Cook, T. J. (2000). The next generation: A study of Catholic high school religion teachers. *Catholic Education: A Journal of Inquiry and Practice, 4(1),* 115-121.

Cook, T. J. (2001a). *Architects of Catholic culture: Designing and building culture in Catholic schools* [Monograph series]. Washington, DC: National Catholic Educational Association.

Cook, T. J. (2001b). Recruitment, preparation, and retention of Catholic high school religion teachers. *Catholic Education: A Journal of Inquiry and Practice, 4(4),* 530-564.

Cookson, P. W. (1994). *School choice: The struggle for the soul of American education.* New Haven: Yale University Press.

Coons, J. E., & Sugarman, S. D. (1978). *Education by choice: The case for family control.* Berkeley, CA: University of California Press.

Coons, J. E., & Sugarman, S. D. (1992). *Scholarships for children.* Berkeley, CA: Institute of Government Studies Press.

Coons, J. E., & Sugarman, S. D. (1999). *Making school choice work for all families: A template for legislative and policy reform.* San Francisco: Pacific Institute for Public Policy.

Cooper, D. B. (1993). An evaluation of the DeBusk Enrichment Center for Academically Talented Students summer enrichment program as perceived by gifted student participants and their parents (Doctoral dissertation, University of San Francisco, 1993). *Dissertation Abstracts International, 54*(09), 3398A.

Cooper, R. (1996). Detracking reform in an urban California high school: Improving the schooling experiences of African American students. *Journal of Negro Education, 65(2),* 190-208.

Copland, M. A. (2001, March). The myth of the superprincipal. *Phi Delta Kappan, 82(7),* 528-533.

Corrado, R. (1997). The challenge of high standards and expectations. *NCEA Notes, 29(4),* 4.

Correia, J. (1998). *Business management in the Catholic school.* Washington, DC: National Catholic Educational Association.

Corson, D. (Ed.). (1995). *Discourse and power in educational organizations.* Cresskill, NJ: Hampton Press, Inc.

Cotton, K. (1996). *Affective and social benefits of small-scale schooling.* Charleston, WV: ERIC Clearinghouse on Rural Education and Small Schools. (ERIC Document Reproduction Service No. ED 401 088)

Cottrill, M. G. (1996). Dreams are free. *Momentum, 27(3),* 62-64.

Cowie, H., Smith, P., Boulton, M., & Laver, R. (1994). *Cooperation in the multi-ethnic classroom.* London: David Fulton Publishers.

Craik, F. I. M. (1979). Human memory. *Annual Review of Psychology, 30,* 63-102.

Craik, F. I. M., & Lockhart, R. S. (1972). Levels of processing: A framework for memory research. *Journal of Verbal Learning and Verbal Behavior, 11(6),* 671-684.

Cremin, L. A. (Ed.). (1957). *The republic and the school: Horace Mann on the education of the free man* (Classics in Education Series, No. 1). New York: Teachers College Press.

Cresci, A. E. (2000). An efficiency study and a proposal for the use of technology in Catholic school administration of the Archdiocese of New York and Diocese of Brooklyn (Doctoral dissertation, Seton Hall University, 2000). *Dissertation Abstracts International,* DA9961384.

Cronin, P. (1999). Character development in the Catholic school. *Momentum, 30(3),* 10-12.

Crowson, R. L., & Boyd, W. L. (1992). Urban schools as organizations: Political perspectives. In J. G. Cibulka, R. J. Reed, & K. K. Wong (Eds.), *The politics of urban education in the United States: The 1991 yearbook of the Politics of Education Association* (pp. 87-103). Washington, DC: Falmer Press.

Crowson, R. L., & Boyd, W. L. (1996). Achieving coordinated school-linked services: Facilitating utilization of the emerging knowledge base. *Educational Policy, 10(2),* 253-272.

Cummins, J. (1997). Cultural and linguist diversity in education: A mainstream issue? *Educational Review, 56(1),* 18-36.

Curran, C. (1997). The Catholic identity of Catholic institutions. *Theological Studies, 58(1),* 90-108.

Curran, M. E. (1994). The role of the principal in giving ownership to the board. In *Preserving our ideals: Papers from the 1993 principals academy* (pp. 59-63). Washington, DC: National Catholic Educational Association.

Curran, T. M. (1984). The incidence of handicapping conditions in the elementary schools of the Archdiocese of Boston (Doctoral dissertation, Boston College, 1984). *Dissertation Abstracts International, 45/04,* AAT 8415996.

Curtin, D. F. (1999). Catholic education: Our story, our heritage. *Momentum, 30(4),* 50-52.

Curtin, D. F. (2001, May). From the executive director: Department of chief administrators of Catholic education. *NCEA Notes,* p.12.

Czarnota, P. A. (1994). Schools yesterday, today, and into the 21st century. In National Catholic Educational Assocation, *Preserving our ideals: Papers from the 1993 principals academy* (pp. 39-41). Washington, DC: National Catholic Educational Association.

Daly, J. G. (1996). Teaching values in everything we do: The nativity experience. *NASSP Bulletin, 80,* 74-78.

Dantley, M. E. (1990). The ineffectiveness of effective schools leadership: An analysis of the effective schools' movement from a critical perspective. *Journal of Negro Education, 59(4),* 585-598.

D'Antonio, W. V., Davidson, J. D., Hoge, D. R., & Wallace, R. A. (1996). *Laity American and Catholic: Transforming the church.* Kansas City, MO: Sheed & Ward.

Darling-Hammond. L. (1996). *What matters most: Teaching for America's future.* New York: National Commission on Teaching and America's Future.

Darling-Hammond, L. (1997a). *The right to learn: A blueprint for creating schools that work.* San Francisco: Jossey-Bass Publishers.

Darling-Hammond, L. (1997b, November). What matters most: 21st century teaching. *Education Digest, 63,* 4-9.

Datnow, A. (1998). *The gender politics of educational change.* London: Falmer Press.

Davis, W. F. (1997). Public policy, religion and education in the United States. In T. C. Hunt & J. C. Carper (Eds.), *Religion and schooling in contemporary America: Confronting our cultural pluralism* (pp. 159-180). New York: Garland Press.

Deal, T. E., & Peterson, K. D. (1994). *The leadership paradox: Balancing logic and artistry in schools.* San Francisco: Jossey-Bass.

Deering, P. D. (1996). An ethnographic study of norms of inclusion and cooperation in a multiethnic middle school. *Urban Review 28(1),* 21-39.

DeFiore, L. (1999, Spring). Special needs students bring gifts to classrooms and catechetical centers. *National Apostolate Quarterly,* 5-6.

DeFiore, L. (2001). Message from the president: School choice: The turned tide. *Momentum, XXXII(2),* 4, 6.

Delcourt, M. A. B., Loyd, B., Cornell, D. G., & Goldberg, M. D. (1994). *Evaluation of the effects of programming arrangements on student learning outcomes* (Research monograph 94108). Storrs, CT: The National Research Center on the Gifted and Talented.

Delpit, L. D. (1995). *Other people's children: Cultural conflict in the classroom.* New York: New Press.

Delpit, L. D. (1996). Act your age not your color. In J. J. Irving & M. Foster (Eds.), *Growing up African American in Catholic schools* (pp. 116-125). New York: Teachers College Press.

Denham, S. (1998). *Emotional development in young children.* New York: The Guilford Press.

Denzer, M. (2000). Special needs inclusion plan "benefits all." *The Catholic Key*. Retrieved November 2, 2001 from www.catholickey.org/item/pages/pastissue.pat?cIssue=archive/20001203

Depp-Blackett, M. E. (1997). An analysis of legal issues affecting the inclusive education of children with special needs in Catholic schools (Doctoral dissertation, University of San Francisco, 1997). *Dissertation Abstracts International, AAT 9726477.*

Derrida, J. (1984). Deconstruction and the other. In R. Kearny (Ed.), *Dialogues with contemporary continental thinkers: The phenomenological heritage* (pp. 107-126). Manchester, UK: Manchester University Press.

DeZarn, P. (1997). Technology planning from the elementary school perspective: Beyond chalk, talk, and textbooks. In R. Haney & A. A. Zukowski (Eds.), *New frontiers: Navigational strategies for integrating technology into the school* (pp. 83-91). Washington, DC: National Catholic Educational Association.

Diamond, D. (1997). *An analysis of leadership behavior and self-efficacy of principals of Catholic secondary schools.* Unpublished doctoral dissertation, The Catholic University of America.

Dillard, C. B. (1995). Leading with her life: An African American feminist (re)interpretation of leadership for an urban high school principal. *Educational Administration Quarterly, 31(4),* 539-563.

Dillon, M. (1999). *Catholic identity: Balancing reason, faith, and power.* New York: Cambridge University Press.

Diocese of Kansas City-St. Joseph. (1998, July). *Inclusive Catholic education handbook.* Kansas City, MO: Author.

DiPaola, L. (1990). A study of a staff development program for Catholic elementary school lay teachers (Doctoral dissertation, Fordham University, 1990). *Dissertation Abstracts International, 51-11A,* 3571.

Dolan, W. P. (1994). *Restructuring our schools.* Kansas City, MO: Systems & Organization.

Donahue, P. L., Finnegan, R. J., Lutkus, A. D., Allen, N. L., & Campbell, J. R. (2001). *The nation's report card: Fourth-grade reading 2000* (NCES Report No.2001-499). Washington, DC: U.S. Department of Education, Office of Educational Research and Improvement.

Donahue, P. L., Voelkl, K. E., Campbell, J. R., & Mazzeo, J. (1999). *The NAEP 1998 reading report card for the nation and the states* (NCES Report No. 1999-500). Washington, DC: U.S. Department of Education, Office of Educational Research and Improvement.

Donovan, A. (1995). The philosophy of moral education and the cultivation of virtue: An inquiry into teachers' perceptions of themselves as moral educators (Doctoral dissertation, University of San Francisco, 1995). *Dissertation Abstracts International, 56-06A,* 2162.

Donovan, D. (1997). *Distinctively Catholic: An exploration of Catholic identity.* New York: Paulist Press.

Donovan, J. A. (1999). A qualitative study of a parental involvement program in a K-8 Catholic elementary school. *Catholic Education: A Journal of Inquiry and Practice*, 3(2), 158-172.

Dorsey, J. H. (1992). The role of the Catholic school elementary teacher as model of gospel values (Doctoral dissertation, University of San Francisco, 1992). *Dissertation Abstracts International 53-04A*, 1113.

Dosen, A. J. (2000). Communicating identity and the challenge of *Ex corde ecclesiae. Catholic Education: A Journal of Inquiry and Practice, 4(2),* 170-204.

Doyle, J. (1998, Feb. 6). Catholic schools – moving into cyberspace. *Catholic Chronicle*, p. 3A.

Drahmann, T. (1984, September). Principal of the future: Would God do? *Momentum*, 70-71.

Drucker, P. F. (1980). *Managing in turbulent times.* New York: Harper & Row.

Dudek, A. (1994, April-May). Diversity: The challenge continues. *Momentum, 25,* 4-5.

Dudek, A. (1996). Evaluating computer software. *NCEA Notes, 29(2)*, 5.

Dudek, A. (1997). Technology and young children. *NCEA Notes, 30(1)*, 5.

Dudek, A. (1998). *Is there room for me*? Washington, DC: National Catholic Educational Association.

Dudek, A. (1999). Special ed on the Web. *NCEA Notes, 31(5)*, 6.

Dudek, A. (2000). We're making room, slowly but surely. *NCEA Notes, 32(4)*, 1.

Dudley, L., & Faricy, A. (1951). *The humanities*. New York: McGraw Hill Book Co.

Duignan, P., & d'Arbon, T. (Eds.). (1998). *Leadership in Catholic education 2000 and beyond*. Strathfield, Australia: Australian Catholic University.

Duke, D. L. (1996). Perception, prescription, and the future of school leadership. In K. Leithwood, J. Chapman, & D. Corson (Eds.), *The international handbook of educational leadership and administration* (pp. 841-872). Dordrecht, The Netherlands: Kluwer Academic Publishers.

Duke, D. L., & Leithwood, K. (1994). *Management and leadership: A comprehensive view of principals' functions*. Toronto: Ontario Institute for the Study of Education.

Duncan, D. (1998). Leadership, Catholic school culture and Catholic identity. In P. Duignan & T. d'Arbon (Eds.), *Leadership in Catholic education 2000 and beyond* (pp. 54-68). Strathfield, Australia: Australian Catholic University.

Dwyer, B. (1993). *Catholic schools: Creating a new culture*. Newton, Australia: E. J. Dwyer Publishing.

Dygert, W. (1998). *A study of the president/principal administrative model in Catholic secondary schools in the United States*. Unpublished doctoral dissertation, University of Dayton, OH.

Eccles, J. S., & Barber, B. (1999). Student council, volunteering, basketball, or marching band: What kind of extra-curricular involvement matters? *Journal of Adolescent Research, 14(1)*, 10-43.

Edmonds, R. (1979a). Effective schools for the urban poor. *Educational Leadership, 36(2)*, 15-18.

Edmonds, R. (1979b, March/April). Some schools work and more can. *Social Policy*, 23-32.

Edmonds, R. (1981, September/October). Making public schools more effective. *Social Policy*, 56-60.

Egleson, P., Harman, P., & Achilles, C. M. (1996). *Does class size make a difference? Recent findings from state and district initiatives*. Greensboro, NC: Southeastern Regional Vision for Education.

Ekert, J., & Drago-Severson, E. (1999). Doing well and being well: Conceptions of well-being among academically successful adolescent girls of color in a Catholic school. *Catholic Education: A Journal of Inquiry and Practice, 3(2)*, 183-201.

Elford, G. (2000). Creating information for Catholic educational leaders. In J. Youniss, J. Convey, & J. McLellan (Eds.), *The Catholic character of Catholic schools* (pp. 142-155). Notre Dame, IN: University of Notre Dame Press.

Elkind, D. (1978). Understanding the young adolescent. *Adolescence, 13(49)*, 127-134.

Elmore, R. F. (1996). Getting to scale with good educational practice. *Harvard Educational Review, 66(1)*, 1-26.

Elmore, R. F., & Sykes, G. (1992). Curriculum policy. In P. Jackson (Ed.), *Handbook of research on curriculum* (pp. 185-215). New York: Macmillan.

Emery, F. E., & Trist, E. L. (1965). The causal texture of organizational environments. *Human Relations, 18*, 21-35.

Epps, E. G. (1994). Radical school reform in Chicago: How is it working? In C. E. Finn & H. Walberg (Eds.), *Radical education reforms* (pp. 95-116). Berkeley, CA: McCutchan.

Epstein, H. (1978). Growth spurts during brain development: Implications for educational policy and practice. In J. Chall & A. Mirsky (Eds.), *Education and the brain: 77ᵗʰ National Society for the Study of Education Yearbook* (Part II, pp. 343-370). Chicago: University of Chicago Press.

Epstein, J. L. (1995). School/family/community partnerships. *Phi Delta Kappan, 76(9),* 701-712.

Epstein, J. L., & Salinas, K. C. (1993). *School and family partnerships: Surveys and summaries. Questionnaires for teachers and parents in elementary and middle grades.* Baltimore, MD: Center on School, Family, and Community Partnerships, Johns Hopkins University.

Erhart, N. (1997). Technology coordinator: Who do they say I am? In R. Haney & A. A. Zukowski (Eds.), *New frontiers: Navigational strategies for integrating technology into the school* (pp. 63-68). Washington, DC: National Catholic Educational Association.

Erikson, E. (1959). Identity and the life cycle: Selected papers. *Psychological Issue Monograph Series, I(1).*

Esposito, M. L. (1993). *Parents' attitudes toward the educational and religious alternatives for their elementary school children: Roman Catholic schools, public schools, and parish-catechetical programs.* Unpublished doctoral dissertation, University of San Francisco.

Evans, W. N., & Schwab, R. M. (1995). Finishing high school and starting college: Do Catholic schools make a difference? *Quarterly Journal of Economics, 10(4),* 941-974.

Everhart, R. B. (Ed.). (1982). *The public school monopoly: A critical analysis of education and the state in American society.* San Francisco: Pacific Institute for Public Policy Research.

Faerber, L. J. (1949). *Provisions for low-ability pupils in Catholic high schools.* Dayton, OH: Marianist Book Service.

Fahey, C. J., & Lewis, M. (Eds.). (1992). *The future of Catholic institutional ministries: A continuing conversation.* New York: Third Age Center, Fordham University.

Fairclough, N. (1995). Critical language awareness and self-identity in education. In D. Corson (Ed.), *Discourse and power in educational organizations* (pp. 257-272). Cresskill, NJ: Hampton Press, Inc.

Feldhusen, J. F., Proctor, T. B., & Black, K. N. (1986). Guidelines for grade advancement of precocious children. *Roeper Review, 9(1),* 25-27.

Feynman, R. (1998). *The meaning of it all.* Reading, MA: Perseus Books.

Fiedler, B. A. (1985). Help for the helpers of special children. *Momentum, 16(4),* 44-45.

Figlio, D. N., & Stone, J. A. (1997). *School choice and student performance: Are private schools really better?* Eugene, OR: University of Oregon Institute for Research on Poverty.

Figlio, D. N., & Stone, J. A. (1999). School choice and student performance: Are private schools really better? *Research in Labor Economics, 18,* 115-140.

Fine, M. (1994). *Chartering urban school reform: Reflections on public high schools in the midst of change.* New York: Teachers College Press.

Flavell, J. (1985). *Cognitive development.* Englewood Cliffs, NJ: Prentice Hall.

Fleming, M. M., & Moeller, J. (1996). We walk by faith, not sight. *Momentum, 27(4),* 40-42.

Foster, M. (1995). African American teachers and culturally relevant pedagogy. In J. A. Banks & C. A. McGee Banks (Eds.), *Handbook of research on multicultural education* (pp. 570-581). New York: Macmillan.

Foucault, M. (1977). *Discipline and punish: The birth of the prison.* New York: Vintage Books.

Foucault, M. (1984). *The Foucault reader.* New York: Pantheon Books.

Fox, M. L. (1993). *A comparison of female student leaders in single gender and coeducational high schools.* Unpublished doctoral dissertation, University of San Francisco.

Fox-Genovese, E. (1994). Save the males? *National Review, XLVI(14),* 1-5.

Fox-Genovese, E., & Podles, L. (1995). Two views: Is there a place for all male schools? *American Enterprise, 6(1),* 21-22.

Frabutt, J. (2001). Parenting and child development: Exploring the links with children's social, moral, and cognitive competence. In T. C. Hunt, E. A. Joseph, & R. J. Nuzzi (Eds.), *Handbook of research on Catholic education* (pp. 183-204). Westport, CT: Greenwood.

Franklin, B., & Crone, L. (1992, November). *School accountability: Predictors and indicators of Louisiana school effectiveness.* Paper presented at the meeting of the Mid-South Educational Research Association, Knoxville, TN.

Freìre, P. (1970). *Pedagogia del oprimido* [Pedagogy of the oppressed]. (M. B. Ramos, Trans.). New York: Continuum. (Original work published 1970).

Frey, M. W. (2000). Implementation of a collaborative problem-solving model in an urban Catholic elementary school: Teacher learning and change (Doctoral dissertation, The University of Dayton, 2000). *Dissertation Abstracts International,* 9975899.

Frey, M. W., Hecker, K., Hardy, D., Herzog, S., Paulette, T., & Robinson, J. (2000). Collaborative problem solving: The journey of Dayton Catholic elementary school. *Catholic Education: A Journal of Inquiry and Practice, 3(3),* 342-354.

Friedman M. (1955). The role of government in education. In R.A. Solo (Ed.), *Economics and the public interest* (pp. 123-144). New Brunswick, NJ: Rutgers University Press.

Friedman, M. (1962). *Capitalism and freedom.* Chicago: University of Chicago Press.

Friedman, M., & Friedman, R. (1980). *Free to choose: A personal statement.* New York: Harcourt Brace Jovanovich.

Froehle, B. T. (Ed.). (1999). Special section on Catholic schools. *The CARA Report, 5(2),* 5-8.

Froman, A. D. (1992). Electronic baby steps. *Computing Teacher, 20(2),* 24-26.

Fullan, M. (1991). *The new meaning of educational change* (2nd ed.). New York: Teachers College Press.

Fullan, M. (2000). The three stories of education reform. *Phi Delta Kappan, 8(8),* 581-584.

Fuller, B., Elmore, R. F., & Orfield, G. (Eds.). (1996). *Who chooses, who loses? Culture, institutions and the unequal effects of school choice.* New York: Teachers College Press.

Fuller, H. L. (2000). *The continuing struggle of African Americans for the power to make real educational choices.* Second Annual Symposium on Educational Options for African Americans. Milwaukee, WI: Marquette University.

Fuller, H. L., & Caire, K. (2001). *Lies and distortions: The campaign against school vouchers.* Milwaukee, WI: Marquette University, Institute for the Transformation of Learning.

Fuller, K. C. A. (1997). *With boys or without them: An exploratory study of mathematics education for girls in single sex and coeducational high schools.* Unpublished doctoral dissertation, Stanford University.

Gage, N. L. (1990). Dealing with the dropout problem. *Phi Delta Kappan 72(4),* 280-285.

Galetto, P.W. (1996). *Building the foundations of faith: The religious knowledge, beliefs, and practices of Catholic elementary school teachers of religion.* Washington, DC: National Catholic Educational Association.

Galetto, P. W. (2000). Religious knowledge and belief of lay religion teachers in Catholic elementary schools. In J. Youniss, J. J. Convey, & J. A. McLellan (Eds.), *The Catholic character of Catholic schools* (pp. 124-141). Notre Dame, IN: University of Notre Dame Press.

Gallanter, L. (1994). *Parent selection factors and school admission factors related to transfer from private elementary schools.* Unpublished doctoral dissertation, University of San Francisco.

Gamoran, A. (1996). Student achievement in public magnet, public comprehensive, and private city high schools. *Educational Evaluation and Policy Analysis, 18(1)*, 1-18.

Garanzini, M. J. (1995). *Child centered, family-sensitive schools: An educator's guide to family dynamics.* Washington, DC: National Catholic Educational Association.

Garanzini, M. J. (2000). Dealing with narcissistic families: Lessons for educational leadership in parent and child guidance. In T. C. Hunt, T. E. Oldenski, & T. J. Wallace (Eds.), *Catholic school leadership: An invitation to lead* (pp. 244-258). London: Falmer Press.

Gardner, H. (1984). *Frames of mind: The theory of multiple intelligences.* New York: Basic Books.

Gardner, H. (1999). *The disciplined mind.* New York: Simon and Schuster.

Garlitz, K. A. (1992). Information technology: A small Catholic school's journey. In R. J. Kealey (Ed.), *Why small Catholic schools succeed* (pp. 51-61). Washington, DC: National Catholic Educational Association.

Gauvin, M. (2001). *The social context of cognitive development.* New York: The Guilford Press.

George, F. (2000). *Ex corde ecclesiae*: Promises and challenges. *Catholic Education: A Journal of Inquiry and Practice, 4(2)*, 239-253.

Gerlach, J. M. (1994). Is this collaboration? *New Directions for Teaching & Learning, 59*, 5-14.

Gerson, M. (1997). *In the classroom: Dispatches from an inner city school that works.* New York: The Free Press.

Gestwicki, C. (1999). *Developmentally appropriate practice: Curriculum and development in early education* (2nd ed.). Albany, NY: Delmar.

Gibson, M. W. (1993). *The motivation of suburban Milwaukee parents in choosing private elementary schools for their children.* Unpublished doctoral dissertation, University of Wisconsin, Madison.

Giroux, H. A. (1992). *Border crossings: Cultural workers and the politics of education.* New York: Routledge.

Gleason, P. (1994). *What made Catholic identity a problem?* Dayton, OH: The University of Dayton Press.

Glenn, C. L. (2000). *The ambiguous embrace: Government and faith based schools and social agencies.* Princeton, NJ: Princeton University Press.

Godwin, K., Ausbrooks, C., & Martinez, V. (2001). Teaching tolerance in public and private schools. *Phi Delta Kappan, 82(7)*, 542-546.

Goldhaber, D. D. (1996). Public and private high schools: Is school choice an answer to the productivity problem? *Economics of Education Review, 15(2)*, 93-109.

Goleman, D. (1995). *Emotional intelligence.* New York: Bantam Books.

Goodlad, J. I., & McMannon, T. (1997). Introduction. In J. I. Goodlad & T. McMannon (Eds.), *The public purpose of education and schooling* (pp. 1-17). San Francisco: Jossey-Bass.

Goodlad, J. I., Soder, R., & Sirotnik, K. A. (Eds.). (1991). *The moral dimensions of teaching.* San Francisco: Jossey-Bass.

Goodman, J. C., & Stieger, F. F. (Eds.). (2001). *An education agenda: Let parents choose their children's school.* Dallas, TX: National Center for Policy Analysis.

Gordon, D. M. (2000). *Mentoring urban Black male students: Implications for academic achievement, ethnic/racial identity development, racial socialization, and academic disidentification.* Unpublished doctoral dissertation, University of South Dakota.

Gorman, E. F. (1996). *Fostering the holistic development of the child through Catholic school parent education programs: Areas of concern to be addressed by parents, administrators, and teachers.* Unpublished doctoral dissertation, University of San Francisco.

Gray, B. E. (Ed.). (2001). School choice: The time is now. [Special section]. *Momentum, XXXII(2),* 10-22, 24-28, 30-37.

Gray, H. (1996). *Religious communities and secondary education: Opportunities in sponsorship and governance.* Proceedings of the symposium, Sponsorship, Colleagueship, and Service: A Conversation about the Future of Religious Communities and American Catholic high schools. Washington, DC: Department of Secondary Schools, National Catholic Educational Association.

Greeley, A. M. (1998). The so-called failure of Catholic schools. *Phi Delta Kappan, 80(1),* 24-25.

Greeley, A. M. (1999). More assertions not backed by data. *Phi Delta Kappan, 80(6),* 463.

Greene, J. P. (2000a). *The education freedom index* (Civic Report NO. 14). New York: Manhattan Institute for Policy Research.

Greene, J. P. (2000b). *The effects of school choice: An evaluation of the Charlotte children's scholarship fund program* (Civic Report NO. 12). New York: Manhattan Institute for Policy Research.

Greene, J. P. (2000c). *A survey of results from voucher experiments: Where we are and what we know* (Civic Report NO. 11). New York: Manhattan Institute for Policy Research.

Greene, J. P., & Peterson, P. E. (1996). *The effectiveness of school choice in Milwaukee: A secondary analysis of data from the program's evaluation.* San Francisco: The American Political Science Association.

Greenfield, W. D. (1991). *Educational leadership: The moral art.* Albany, NY: The State University of New York Press.

Greenlee, M. L. (1995). *Vision, philosophy and mission statement within Catholic secondary schools and the perception of need as addressed by administrators and teachers.* Unpublished doctoral dissertation, Spalding University.

Greeno, J. G., Collins, A. M., & Resnick, L. B. (1996). Cognition and learning. In D. C. Berliner & R. C. Calfee (Eds.), *Handbook of educational psychology* (pp. 15-46). New York: Macmillan.

Greenwald, E.A., Persky, H.R., Campbell, J.R., & Mazzeo, J. (1999). *The NAEP 1998 writing report card for the nation and the states* (NCES Report No. 1999-462). Washington, DC: U.S. Department of Education, Office of Educational Research and Improvement.

Greinacher, N. (1994). Catholic identity in the third epoch of church history. In J. Provost & K. Walf, (Eds.), *Catholic identity* (pp. 3-4). London, SCM Press.

Grissmer, D. (1999). Class size effects: Assessing the evidence, its policy implications, and future research agenda. *Educational Evaluation and Policy Analysis, 21(2),* 231-248.

Groome, T. H. (1996). What makes a school Catholic? In T. McLaughlin, J. O'Keefe, & B. O'Keeffe (Eds.), *The contemporary Catholic school: Context, identity, and diversity* (pp. 107-125). London: Falmer Press.

Groome, T. H. (1998). *Educating for life: A spiritual vision for every child and parent.* Allen, TX: Thomas Moore Press.

Groome, T. H., & Corso, M. J. (Eds.). (1999). *Empowering catechetical leaders.* Washington, DC: National Catholic Educational Association.

Gross, D. J. (1994). *Teachers in Catholic schools: A study of the attributes of teachers that foster the identity of the Catholic elementary schools of the Archdiocese of Omaha.* Unpublished doctoral dissertation, University of Nebraska, Lincoln.

Grubb, W. N. (1995). The old problem of "new students": Purpose, content and pedagogy. In E. Flaxman & A. H. Passow (Eds.), *Changing populations, changing schools: Ninety-fourth yearbook of the National Society for the Study of Education* (pp. 4-29). Chicago: The University of Chicago Press.

Guerra, M. J. (1990). *Dollars and sense: Catholic high schools and their finances 1990*. Washington, DC: National Catholic Educational Association.

Guerra, M. J. (1992). *Dollars and sense: Catholic high schools and their finances 1991*. Washington, DC: National Catholic Educational Association.

Guerra, M. J. (1993). *Dollars and sense: Catholic high schools and their finances 1992*. Washington, DC: National Catholic Educational Association.

Guerra, M. J. (1995). *Dollars and sense: Catholic high schools and their finances 1994*. Washington, DC: National Catholic Educational Association.

Guerra, M. J. (1996). *Introduction.* Proceedings of the symposium, Sponsorship, Colleagueship, and Service: A Conversation about the Future of Religious Communities and American Catholic High Schools. Washington, DC: Department of Secondary Schools National Catholic Educational Association.

Guerra, M. J. (1998*). CHS 2000: A first look.* Washington, DC: National Catholic Educational Association.

Guerra, M. J. (2000). Key issues for the future of Catholic schools. In T. Hunt, T. Oldenski, & T. Wallace (Eds.), *Catholic school leadership: An invitation to lead* (pp.79-90). London: Falmer Press.

Guerra, M. J., Haney, R., & Kealey, R. J. (Eds.). (1992). *Catholic schools for the 21st century: Executive summary*. Washington, DC: National Catholic Educational Association.

Gusdane, J. (1999). Strengthening the school leader's evangelizing role. *Momentum, XXX (2),* 26-28.

Habermas, J. (1987). *The theory of communicative action* (T. McCarthy, Trans., Vol. 2). Cambridge, MA: Polity Press.

Habermas, J. (1990). *Moral consciousness and communicative action* (C. Lenhardt & S. W. Nicholsen, Trans.). Cambridge, MA: MIT Press.

Hall, S. E. (1979). Catholic education becomes special. *Momentum, 10(3),* 18-23.

Hall, S. E. (1981). The parish school as "least restrictive environment." *Momentum, 12(2)*, 40-41.

Hall, S. E. (Ed.). (1985). *Challenging gifted students in the Catholic school.* Washington, DC: National Catholic Educational Association. (ERIC Document Reproduction Service No. 257 292)

Hall, S. E., & Dudek, A. (Eds.). (1986). The bridge program. *Special Education, 8(1),* 1-2.

Hall, S. E., & Dudek, A. (Eds). (1987a). Archbishop Ryan memorial diamond jubilee 1912-1987. *Special Education, 9(2),* 1.

Hall, S. E., & Dudek, A. (Eds.). (1987b). Special education in the future. *Special Education, 8(3),* 1-2.

Hallinan, M. T. (2000). Conclusion: Catholic education at the crossroads. In J. Youniss & J. J. Convey (Eds.), *Catholic schools at the crossroads: Survival and transformation* (pp. 201-220). New York: Teachers College Press.

Hallinger, P. (1992). The evolving role of principals: From managerial to instructional to transformational leaders. *Journal of Educational Administration, 30(3),* 35-48.

Hallinger, P., & McCary, C. E. (1990). Developing the strategic thinking of instructional leaders. *Elementary School Journal, 91,* 89-107.

Halvorsen, A. T., & Nealy, T. (2001). *Building inclusive schools, tools and strategies for success.* Boston: Allyn & Bacon.

Hamilton, L. S., & Klein, S. P. (1998). *Achievement test score gains among participants in the Foundation's School-Age Enrichment Program.* Santa Monica, CA: RAND Corporation.

Haney, R. (1997a). New frontiers. In R. Haney & A. A. Zukowski (Eds.), *New frontiers: Navigational strategies for integrating technology into the school* (pp. 45-47). Washington, DC: National Catholic Educational Association.

Haney, R. (1997b). Producing a technology plan. In R. Haney & A. A. Zukowski (Eds.), *New frontiers: Navigational strategies for integrating technology into the school* (pp. 35-40). Washington, DC: National Catholic Educational Association.

Haney, R., & O'Keefe, J. M. (1999). *Creatively financing and resourcing Catholic schools: Conversations in excellence.* Washington, DC: National Catholic Educational Association.

Hanushek, E. A. (1996). School resources and student performance. In G. Burtless (Ed.), *Does money matter? The effect of school resources on student achievement and adult success* (pp. 43-73). Washington, DC: The Brookings Institution Press.

Hargreaves, A., & Fullan, M. (1998). *What's worth fighting for out there?* New York: Teachers College Press.

Harkins, W. (1993). *Introducing the Catholic elementary school principal: What principals say about themselves, their values, their schools.* Washington, DC: National Catholic Educational Association.

Harris, J. C. (1996). *The cost of Catholic parishes and schools.* Kansas City: Sheed and Ward.

Harris, J. C. (2000). The funding dilemma facing Catholic elementary and secondary schools. In J. Youniss & J. J. Convey (Eds.), *Catholic schools at the crossroads: Survival and transformation* (pp. 55-71). New York: Teachers College Press.

Hart, A. W. (1995). Reconceiving school leadership: Emergent views. *The Elementary School Journal, 96(1),* 9-28.

Hart, A. W., & Bredeson, P. V. (1996). *The principalship: A theory of professional learning and practice.* New York: McGraw-Hill.

Hartocollis, A. (2001, March 22). Public and Catholic schools diverge by grade 8, study says. *New York Times,* p. B6.

Harvard study: School vouchers help D.C. children excel. (2000, March 1). *America, 182(11),* 4.

Hassel, B. C. (1999). *The charter school challenge: Avoiding the pitfalls, fulfilling the promise.* Washington, DC: The Brookings Institution.

Hater, R. J. (1990). *News that is good: Evangelization for Catholics.* Notre Dame, IN: Ave Maria Press.

Hawley, R. (1993). A case for boys' schools. In D. K. Hollinger & R. Adamson (Eds.), *Single sex schooling: Proponents speak* (pp. 11-14). Washington, DC: U.S. Department of Education.

Healey, F. H., & DeStefano, J. (1997). *Education reform support: A framework for scaling up school reform.* Washington, DC: Abel 2 Clearinghouse for Basic Education.

Heaviside, S., & Farris, E. (1997). *Advanced telecommunications in U.S. private schools, K-12, Fall 1995* (NCES Rep. No. 97394). Washington, DC: U.S. Department of Education, National Center for Education Statistics.

Heck, R. H., & Hallinger, P. (1999). Next generation methods for the study of leadership and school improvement. In J. Murphy & K. S. Louis (Eds.), *Handbook of research on educational administration* (2nd ed., pp. 141-162). San Francisco: Jossey-Bass.

Heft, J. L. (1991a). Catholic identity and the Catholic schools. In *Catholic identity and the Catholic schools* (pp. 5-20). Washington, DC: National Catholic Educational Association.

Heft, J. L. (1991b). Catholic identity and the church. In F. D. Kelly (Ed.), *What makes a school Catholic?* (pp. 14-21). Washington, DC: National Catholic Educational Association.

Heft, J. L. (1991c). Catholic identity and the future of Catholic schools. In *The Catholic identity of Catholic schools* (pp. 1-20). Washington, DC: National Catholic Educational Association.

Heft, J. L. (1991d, November). *Catholic schools for the 21st century: The Catholic identity of Catholic schools.* Paper presented at the National Congress on Catholic Schools, Washington, DC.

Hegemann, M. T. (1971). The mentally retarded. In E. H. Behrmann (Ed.), *Catholic special education* (pp. 112-140). St. Louis: B. Herder Book Co.

Helfrich, J. A. (1988). Resource rooms in Catholic schools. *Special Education, 10(2),* 1-3.

Helsby, G. (1999). *Changing teachers' work.* Philadelphia, PA: Open University Press.

Heltsley, C. (1996). A content analysis of the explicit and implicit values implanted in microcomputer software in Catholic elementary schools (Doctoral dissertation, University of San Francisco, 1996). *Dissertation Abstracts International,* DA9708656.

Heltsley, C. (1998). Opening the classroom door to a stranger and leaving the room: The importance of scrutinizing values implanted in computer software. *Momentum, 29(4),* 53-61.

Hess, F. (1999). *Spinning wheels: The politics of urban school reform.* Washington, DC: The Brookings Institution.

Hess, G. A. (1993). Race and the liberal perspective in Chicago school reform. In C. Marshall (Ed.), *The new politics of race and gender: The 1992 yearbook of the Politics of Education Association* (pp. 85-96). Washington, DC: Falmer Press.

Hocevar, R. (1991, November). *Catholic school governance.* Paper presented at the National Congress on Catholic Schools for the 21st Century, Washington, DC.

Hodgkinson, C. (1991). *Educational leadership: The moral art.* Albany, NY: The State University of New York Press.

Hodgkinson, H. (1988). The right schools for the right kids. *Educational Leadership, 45(5),* 10-14.

Hoffer, T. B. (2000). Catholic school attendance and student achievement: A review and extension of research. In J. Youniss & J. J. Convey (Eds.), *Catholic schools at the crossroads: Survival and transformation* (pp. 87-112). New York: Teachers College Press.

Holian, G. C., & Chismar, C. (1991, April). *A different dynamic: The changing role of the teacher in the writing classroom.* Paper presented at the Annual Conference on Computers and English, Old Westbury, NY.

Horrigan, D. C. (1978). *The shaping of NCEA.* Washington, DC: National Catholic Educational Association.

Howell, W. G., Wolf, P. J., Peterson, P. E., & Campbell, D. E. (2000). *Test-score effects on school vouchers in Dayton, Ohio, New York City, and Washington, DC: Evidence from randomized field tests.* Annual meeting of the American Political Science Association. Boston, MA: Harvard University Press, The Program on Education Policy and Governance.

Hughes, L. W. (1999). The leader: Artist? architect? commissar? In L. W. Hughes (Ed.), *The principal as leader* (2nd ed., pp. 3-24). Upper Saddle River, NJ: Prentice-Hall.

Hughes, M. E. (1984). A study of mathematically gifted girls, their math achievement, sex-role stereotyping, and attitudes toward math related careers (Doctoral dissertation, Columbia University Teachers College, 1984). *Dissertation Abstracts International,* 45(08), 2375A.

Hunt, T. C. (1998). *Doctoral dissertations on Catholic schools in the United States, 1988-1997.* Washington, DC: National Center for Research in Catholic Education, Department of Chief Administrators of Catholic Education, National Catholic Educational Association.

Hunt, T. C. (2000). The history of Catholic schools in the United States. In T. C. Hunt, T. E., Oldenski, & T. J. Wallace, (Eds.), *Catholic school leadership: An invitation to lead* (pp. 34-58). London: Falmer Press.

Hunt, T. C., Joseph, E. A., & Nuzzi, R. J. (2001). *Handbook of research on Catholic education*. Westport, CT: Greenwood Press.

Hutchison, J. M. (1998). A diocese's exploration into technology. *Momentum*, 29(3), 20-22.

Indrisano, R. (1989). The excellence ethos and the leadership role. In R. J. Kealey (Ed.), *Reflections on the role of the Catholic school principal* (pp. 6-15). Washington, DC: National Catholic Educational Association.

International Society for Technology in Education. (2000). *National educational technology standards for students: Connecting curriculum and technology*. Eugene, OR: Author.

Iozzio, M. J. (2000). University as church: *Fides et ratio* as a source for ecclesiology. *Catholic Education: A Journal of Inquiry and Practice, 4(2)*, 218-226.

Irvine, J. J., & Foster, M. (1996). *Growing up African American in Catholic schools*. New York: Teachers College Press.

Jackson, A. W., & Davis, G. A. (2000). *Turning points 2000: Educating adolescents in the 21st century*. New York: Teachers College Press.

Jackson, P., Boostrom, R., & Hansen, D. (1993). *The moral life of schools*. San Francisco: Jossey-Bass, Inc.

Jacobs, R. M. (1996). *The vocation of the Catholic educator*. Washington, DC: National Catholic Educational Association.

Jacobs, R. M. (1997). *The grammar of Catholic schooling* [Monograph series]. Washington, DC: The National Catholic Educational Association.

Jacobs, R. M. (2000). Contributions of religious to U.S. Catholic schooling. In J. Youniss, J. J. Convey, & J. A. McLellan (Eds.), *The Catholic character of Catholic schools* (pp. 82-102). Notre Dame, IN: University of Notre Dame Press.

Jencks, C. (1985). How much do high school students learn? *Sociology of Education, 58*, 128-135.

Jenkins, M. (2000). Northside Catholic Academy, St. Gertrude Campus. In C. C. Stabile (Ed.), *Ensuring Catholic identity in Catholic schools* (pp. 76-80). Washington, DC: National Catholic Educational Association.

Jensen, E. (1998). *Teaching with the brain in mind*. Alexandria, VA: Association for Supervision and Curriculum Development.

John Paul II. (1982). *Familiaris consortio* [The role of the Christian family in the modern world]. Boston: St. Paul Editions.

John Paul II. (1992). *The Pope speaks to the American church*. San Francisco: Harper Collins.

John Paul II. (1999). *Ex corde ecclesiae*. [On Catholic universities]. Washington, DC: United States Catholic Conference.

Johnson, D. W., Johnson, R. T., Holubec, E., & Roy, P. (1984). *Circles of learning*. Alexandria, VA: Association for Supervision and Curriculum Development.

Johnson, K. A. (1999). *Comparing math scores of Black students in D.C.'s public and Catholic schools*. Washington DC: Heritage Foundation, Center for Data Analysis.

Johnston, R. (2001). Money matters. *Education Week, XX (35)*, pp. 14-15.

Joller, C. (1995). Professional development defeats dyslexia. *Momentum, 26(2)*, 50-52.

Jones, J. H. (2000). The perceptions of the teacher educators regarding the preparation of elementary school teachers as facilitators of student moral development (Doctoral dissertation, University of San Francisco, 2000). *Dissertation Abstracts International, 61-08*, 3126.

Jones, M. (1997). *Differential effectiveness: Catholic and public fourth graders' performance on the 1992 NAEP mathematics assessment*. Boston: Boston College Press.

Joseph, E. (2001). The philosophy of Catholic education. In T. C. Hunt, E. A. Joseph, & R. J. Nuzzi (Eds.), *Handbook of research on Catholic education* (pp. 27-64). Westport, CT: Greenwood Press.

Kahne, J., & Kelley, C. (1993). Assessing the coordination of children's services. *Education and Urban Society, 25(3)*, 187-200.

Katz, A. (1999, April). *Keepin' it real: Personalizing school experiences for diverse learners to create harmony instead of conflict.* Paper presented at the annual meeting of the American Educational Research Association, Montreal, Canada.

Kealey, R. J. (1992). *United States Catholic elementary schools and their finances 1991.* Washington, DC: National Catholic Educational Association.

Kealey, R. J. (1994). *Balance sheet for Catholic elementary schools: 1993 income and expenses.* Washington, DC: National Catholic Educational Association.

Kealey, R. J. (1996). *Balance sheet for Catholic elementary schools: 1995 income and expenses.* Washington, DC: National Catholic Educational Association.

Kealey, R. J. (1998a). *Balance sheet for Catholic elementary schools: 1997 income and expenses.* Washington, DC: National Catholic Educational Association.

Kealey, R. J. (1998b, April). Spotlighting the mosaic of Catholic education. *Today's Catholic Teacher, 31(6)*, 8.

Kealey, R. J. (2000). *Balance sheet for Catholic elementary schools: 1999 income and expenses.* Washington, DC: National Catholic Educational Association.

Kealey, R. J. (2001a). Making room for me: An inclusion conference for Catholic schools. *NCEA Notes, 33(4)*, 5.

Kealey, R. J. (2001b, April). *State of Catholic elementary schools.* Presentation given at the National Catholic Educational Association Convention, Milwaukee, WI.

Kealey, R. J., & Brennan, J. (2000). Preface. In C. C. Stabile (Ed.), *Ensuring Catholic identity in Catholic schools* (pp. v-vii). Washington, DC: National Catholic Educational Association.

Kealey, R. J., & Collins, K. (1994). *Stewardship and the Catholic school tuition program.* Washington, DC: National Catholic Educational Association.

Keane, R., & Riley, D. (Eds.). (1997). *Quality Catholic schools: Challenges for leadership as Catholic education approaches the third millennium.* Brisbane, Australia: Archdiocese of Brisbane.

Keating, F. (1991). Catholicity: A tradition of contemplation. In F. D. Kelly (Ed.), *What makes a school Catholic?* (pp. 10-13). Washington, DC: National Catholic Educational Association.

Keebler, B. (2001). Message from the communications director: Justice for all God's children. *Momentum, XXXII(2)*, 8.

Kelleher, P. M. (2000). *The faith formation of Catholic high school administrators: The unique role of the laity.* Unpublished doctoral dissertation, University of Dayton, OH.

Keller, F. (1955). The comprehensive high school. New York: Harper Brothers.

Kelly, F. D. (Ed.). (1991). *What makes a school Catholic?* Washington, DC: National Catholic Educational Association.

Kelty, B. J. (1993). *Towards a vision for leadership in Catholic schools.* Unpublished doctoral dissertation, Fordham University.

Kelzenberg, K. J. (1993). Gifted education in the Catholic elementary schools of the Archdiocese of Saint Paul–Minneapolis (Doctoral dissertation, University of St. Thomas, St. Paul, 1993). *Dissertation Abstracts International, 54*(03), 0807A.

Kerr, B. (1997). Developing talents in girls and young women. In N. Colangelo & G. A. Davis (Eds.), *Handbook of gifted education* (2nd ed., pp. 483-497). Boston: Allyn and Bacon.

Keyes, M. W., Hanley-Maxwell, C., & Capper, C. A. (1999). "Spirituality? It's the core of my leadership": Empowering leadership in an inclusive elementary school. *Educational Administration Quarterly, 35(2)*, 203-237.

Kimball, D. (1992). Media and youth evangelization. *Momentum, 23(1)*, 71.

Kinney, B. (1997). Creating a partnership. *Momentum, 28(1)*, 6-10.

Kirkpatrick, D. W. (1990). *Choice in schooling: A case for tuition vouchers.* Chicago, IL: Loyola University Press.

Knowles, T., & Brown, D. (2001). *What every middle school teacher should know.* Portsmouth, NH: Heinemann.

Kosmin, B. A., & Lachman, S. P. (1993). *One nation under God: Religion in contemporary American society.* New York: Harmony Books.

Kosse, S. H. (2001). When the internet becomes x-rated: Creating an ethical climate for technology in Catholic schools. *Catholic Education: A Journal of Inquiry and Practice, 4(4)*, 514-529.

Kretzmann, J. P., & McKnight, J. L. (1993). *Building communities from the inside out: A path toward finding and mobilizing a community's assets.* Chicago: ACTA Publications.

Krupka, N. (1997). Emphasizing the staff development perspective in technology integration. In R. Haney & A. A. Zukowski (Eds.), *New frontiers: Navigational strategies for integrating technology into the school* (pp. 93-99). Washington, DC: National Catholic Educational Association.

Kulik, J. A. (1992). *An analysis of the research on ability grouping: Historical and contemporary perspectives* (Research monograph 9204). Storrs, CT: The National Research Center on the Gifted and Talented.

Kushner, R., & Helbling, M. (1995). *The people who work there: A report of the Catholic elementary school teacher survey.* Washington, DC: National Catholic Educational Association.

Ladd, H. F. (Ed.). (1996). *Holding schools accountable: Performance-based reform in education.* Washington, DC: The Brookings Institution.

Ladson-Billings, G. (1994). *The dreamkeepers: Successful teachers of African American students.* San Francisco: Jossey-Bass.

Laengle, T. M., Redder, D., Somers, W., & Sullivan, K. (2000). Success central: Implementing a program to meet the needs of diverse learners in a Catholic high school. *Catholic Education: A Journal of Inquiry and Practice, 3(3)*, 355-362.

Langman, J., & McLaughlin, M. W. (1993). Collaborate or go it alone? Tough decisions for youth policy. In S. B. Heath & M. W. McLaughlin (Eds.), *Identity and inner city youth: Beyond ethnicity and gender* (pp. 147-175). New York: Teachers College Press.

Larabee, D. (1997). Public goods, private goods: The American struggle over educational goals. *American Educational Research Journal, 34(1)*, 39-81.

Larsen, J. (2000). *Religious education and the brain.* Mahwah, NJ: Paulist Press.

Lasley, T. J., II (1997). The missing ingredient in character education. *Phi Delta Kappan, 78(8)*, 654-655.

Lave, J., & Wenger, E. (1991). *Situated learning: Legitimate peripheral participation.* Cambridge, UK: Cambridge University Press.

Lawrence, P. R., & Lorsch, J. W. (1967). *Organization and environment.* Cambridge, MA: Harvard Graduate School of Business Administration.

Lawrence, S. (2000). "New" immigrants in the Catholic schools: A preliminary assessment. In J. Youniss, J. Convey, & J. McLellan (Eds.), *The Catholic character of Catholic schools* (pp. 178-200). Notre Dame, IN: University of Notre Dame Press.

Lazear, D. (1991). *Seven ways of knowing, teaching for multiple intelligences.* Arlington Heights, IL: Skylight Training & Publishing.

Leach, M., & Borchard, T. (Eds.). (2000). *I like being Catholic: Treasured traditions, rituals, and stories.* New York: Doubleday.

Lee, M. A. (1991). Perceptions of Catholic school teachers in Guam of job factors related to motivation (Doctoral dissertation, University of Oregon, 1991). *Dissertation Abstracts International, 52-10A,* 3492.

Lee, S. J. (1996). *Unraveling the "model minority" stereotype: Listening to Asian American youth.* New York: Teachers College Press.

Lee, V. E., Chow-Hoy, T. K., Burkam, D. T., Geverdt, D., & Smerdon, B. (1998). Sector differences in high school course taking: A private school or Catholic school effect? *Sociology of Education, 71(4),* 314-335.

Lee, V. E., & Loeb, S. (2000, Spring). School size in Chicago elementary schools: Effects on teachers' attitudes and students' achievement. *American Educational Research Journal, 37(1),* 3-31.

Lee, V., & Marks, H. M. (1992). Who goes where? Choice of single sex and coeducational independent secondary schools. *Sociology of Education, 65(3),* 226-253.

Lee, V. E., Marks, H. M., & Byrd, T. (1994). Sexism in single sex and coeducational independent secondary school classrooms. *Sociology of Education, 67(2),* 92-120.

Lee, V. E., & Smith, J. B. (1994). *Effects of high school restructuring and size on gains in achievement and engagement for early secondary school students.* Madison, WI: Center on Organization and Restructuring of Schools.

Lee, V. E., & Smith, J. B. (1997). High school size: Which works best and for whom? *Educational Evaluation and Policy Analysis, 19(3),* 205-227.

Lee, V., Smith, J. B., & Croninger, R. (1997). How high school organization influences the equitable distribution of learning in mathematics and science. *Sociology of Education, 70(2),* 128-150.

Leithwood, K. (1994). Leadership for school restructuring. *Educational Administration Quarterly, 30(4),* 498-518.

Leithwood, K., & Duke, D. L. (1999). A century's quest to understand school leadership. In J. Murphy & K. S. Louis (Eds.), *Handbook of research on educational administration* (2nd ed., pp. 45-72). San Francisco: Jossey-Bass.

Leithwood, K., Leonard, L., & Sharrat, L. (1998). Conditions in fostering organizational learning in schools. *Educational Administration Quarterly, 34(2),* 243-276.

LePore, P. C., & Warren, J. R. (1997). A comparison of single sex and coeducational Catholic secondary schooling: Evidence from the National Educational Longitudinal Study of 1988. *The American Educational Research Journal, 34(3),* 485-511.

Leroux, J. A. (1990). Learning in a new mode. *Momentum, 21(2),* 58-61.

Leroux, J. A. (1992). Stretching the limits of learning: Mentorships for gifted high school students. *The Vocational Aspect of Education, 44(3),* 249-258.

Leroux, J. A. (1997). A secondary school journey: Programming for gifted students at a Catholic high school in Canada. *Gifted Education International, 12(2),* 72-76.

Lester, M. L. (1996). The effects of *The Geometer's Sketchpad* software on achievement of geometric knowledge of high school geometry students (Doctoral dissertation, University of San Francisco, 1996). *Dissertation Abstracts International,* DA9633545.

Levin, H. M. (1991). The economics of educational choice. *Economics of Education Review, 10(2),* 137-158.

Levin, H. M. (1998). Educational vouchers: Effectiveness, choice, and costs. *Journal of Policy Analysis and Management, 17(3),* 373-391.

Lewin, N. (1999, January-February). Are vouchers constitutional? Yes, and here's how to design them. *Policy Review: The Journal of American Citizenship, 93*, 5-9.

Lewis, J. C., & Boudreaux, A. (1992). Success for remedial students. *Momentum, 23(1)*, 20-21.

Lieberman, A. (1990). *Schools as collaborative cultures: Creating the future now.* Bristol, PA: Falmer Press.

Lieberman, M. (1993). *Public education: An autopsy.* Cambridge, MA: Harvard University Press.

Lightfoot, S. L. (1983). *The good high school: Portraits of character and culture.* New York: Basic Books, Inc.

Link, M. (1991). Facilitating the students' self-image. In F. D. Kelly (Ed.), *What makes a school Catholic?* (pp. 30-40). Washington, DC: National Catholic Educational Association.

Little, J. W. (1990). Contradictions of professional development in secondary schools. In M. W. McLaughlin, J. E. Talbert, & N. Bascia (Eds.), *The contexts of teaching in secondary schools: Teachers' realities* (pp. 187-223). New York: Teachers College Press.

Little, J. W. (1993). Teacher development in a climate of school reform. *Educational Evaluation and Policy Analysis, 15(2)*, 129-151.

Lockard, J., & Abrams, P. (2001). *Computers for twenty-first century education* (5th ed.). New York: Longman.

Loughran, E. (1999). Character builders and the catechesis. *Momentum, 30(3)*, 64-65.

Louis, K. S. (1990). Contradictions of professional development in secondary schools. In M. W. McLaughlin, J. E. Talbert, & N. Bascia (Eds.), *The contexts of teaching in secondary schools: Teachers' realities* (pp. 17-39). New York: Teachers College Press.

Louis, K. S., & Kruse, S. D. (1995). *Professionalism and community: Perspectives on reforming urban schools.* Thousand Oaks, CA: Corwin Press.

Louis, K. S., Kruse, S., & Marks, H. M. (1996). Schoolwide professional community. In F. Newmann (Ed.), *Authentic achievement: Restructuring schools for intellectual quality* (pp. 757-797). San Francisco: Jossey-Bass.

Louis, K. S., Marks, H. M., & Kruse, S. (1996). Teachers' professional community in restructuring schools. *American Educational Research Journal, 33(4)*, 757-798.

Lutkus, A. D., Weiss, A .R., Campbell, J. R., Mazzeo, J., & Lazer, S. (1999). *The NAEP 1998 civics report card for the nation* (NCES Report No.2000-457). Washington, DC: U.S. Department of Education, Office of Educational Research and Improvement.

MacKenthun, C. (1992). Linking students in global communication. *Momentum, 23(1)*, 44-46.

MacLean, P. (1978). A mind of three minds: Educating the triune brain. In J. Chall & A. Mirsky (Eds.), *Education and the brain: 77th National Society for the Study of Education Yearbook* (Part II, pp. 308-342). Chicago: University of Chicago Press.

Mael, F. A. (1998). Single sex and coeducational schooling: Relationships to socioemotional and academic development. *Review of Educational Research, 68(2)*, 101-129.

Magnetti, J. (1996). Colleagueship and leadership: Not mine, ours; not they, me. *Proceedings of the Department of Secondary Schools, National Catholic Educational Association*, 33-37.

Malen, B., Ogawa, R. T., & Kranz, J. (1990). What do we know about school-based management? A case study of the literature—a call for research. In W. H. Clune & J. F. Witte (Eds.), *Choice and control in American education* (Vol. 1, pp. 289-342). Philadelphia, PA: The Falmer Press.

Manese, M. (1999, Spring). Soaring to greater heights. *National Apostolate Quarterly*, 20.

Mann, P. (1992). Taming the terminator: The spiritual challenge of technology. *Momentum, 23(1)*, 33-36.

Manning, E. (1994). How does a principal sensitize the faculty to use technology? In National Catholic Educational Association, *Preserving our ideals: Papers from the 1993 principals academy* (pp. 43-46). Washington, DC: National Catholic Educational Association.

Manno, B. (1985). *Those who would be Catholic school principals: Their recruitment, preparation, and evaluation.* Washington, DC: National Catholic Educational Association.

Margrabe, M. (1978). The library media specialist and total curriculum involvement. *Catholic Library World, 49(7),* 283-287.

Marion, K., & Monroe, R. (1992). Camp Tech beats the blues. *Momentum, 23(1),* 29-31.

Marks, H. M., & Louis, K. S. (1997). Does teacher empowerment affect the classroom? The implications of teacher empowerment for instructional practice and student academic performance. *Educational Evaluation and Policy Analysis, 19,* 245-275.

Marshall, C. (1993). The new politics of race and gender. In C. Marshall (Ed.), *The new politics of race and gender: The 1992 yearbook of the Politics of Education Asociation* (pp. 1-6). Washington, DC: The Falmer Press.

Martens, P. F. (1996). *The study of parent-child communication about sexuality as implemented in the "In God's Image" Program.* Unpublished doctoral dissertation, Saint Louis University.

Marx, G. (2000). *Ten trends: Educating children for a profoundly different future.* Arlington, VA: Educational Research Service.

Massucci, J. D. (1993). *The unique identity of Catholic high schools: A comparison of the church's expectations and a school community's experiences and beliefs.* Unpublished doctoral dissertation, University of Dayton, Ohio.

Mastaby, K. A. M. (1993). Parental involvement and the urban parochial school: An analysis of participation and involvement practices. *Private School Monitor, 14(1-2),* 5-9.

Matuszek, K. (1999, April). *Our door is open: A successful journey to include students with developmental disabilities.* Presentation at the NCEA 96th Annual Convention & Exposition, New Orleans, LA.

McBride, A. A. (1981). *The Christian formation of Catholic educators: A CACE monograph.* Washington, DC: National Catholic Educational Association.

McCarthey, S. (1994). Authors, text and talk: The internalization of dialogue from social interaction during writing. *Reading Research Quarterly, 29(3),* 200-231.

McClelland, R. J. (1989). Profiles of underachieving gifted students (Doctoral dissertation, University of Alberta, Canada, 1989). *Dissertation Abstracts International, 50*(07), 1991A.

McCormack, P. M. (1995). *Catholic elementary schools as agents of parent formation needs as perceived by parents.* Unpublished doctoral dissertation, University of San Francisco.

McCormack, P. M. (1998). *Parents and teachers: Partners in whole-person formation.* Champaign, IL: Clearinghouse on Elementary and Early Childhood Education, Children's Research Center.

McCormack, P. M. (1999). Parenting formation and information: The contemporary mission of the Catholic school. *Momentum, 30(3),* 52-57.

McDermott, E. J. (1997). *Distinctive qualities of the Catholic school.* Washington, DC: National Catholic Educational Association.

McDonald, D. (1995). *Towards full and fair choice: An historical analysis of the lobbying efforts of the Catholic school community in pursuing federal tax-supported choice in education, 1972-1992.* Unpublished doctoral dissertation, Boston College.

McDonald, D. (1997a). Educational technology funding. *Momentum, 28(4),* 46-47.

McDonald, D. (1997b). Telecommunications discounts. *NCEA Notes, 30(1),* 2.

McDonald, D. (1998a). E-rate: almost a reality! *NCEA Notes, 30(3),* 1.

McDonald, D. (1998b). E-rate for everyone. *NCEA Notes, 30(4),* 2.

McDonald, D. (1998c). *United States Catholic elementary and secondary schools 1997-1998.* Washington, DC: National Catholic Educational Association.

McDonald, D. (Ed.). (1999a). *Catholic schools and school choice: Partners for justice.* Washington, DC: National Catholic Educational Association.

McDonald, D. (1999b). *United States Catholic elementary and secondary schools 1998-1999: The annual statistical report on schools, enrollment, and staffing.* Washington, DC: National Catholic Educational Association.

McDonald, D. (2000a). Some are more equal. *Momentum, 31(1),* 63-64.

McDonald, D. (2000b). *United States Catholic elementary and secondary schools 1999-2000: The annual statistical report on schools, enrollment, and staffing.* Washington, DC: National Catholic Educational Association.

McDonald, D. (2001a). A chronology of parental choice in education. *Momentum, XXXII(2),* 10-15.

McDonald, D. (2001b). *United States Catholic elementary and secondary schools 2000-2001:The annual statistical report on schools, enrollment, and staffing.* Washington, DC: National Catholic Educational Association.

McGroarty, D. (2001). *Trinnetta gets a chance: Six families and their school choice experiences.* Washington, DC: The Heritage Foundation.

McKillop, B. L. (1971). Teacher preparation: Principles and practices. In E. H. Behrmann (Ed.), *Catholic special education* (pp. 32-50). St. Louis: B. Herder Book Co.

McLaren, P. (1986). Making Catholics: The ritual production of conformity in a Catholic junior high school. *Journal of Education, 168(2),* 55-77.

McLaughlin, D. H. (1997). *Private schools in the United States: A statistical profile, 1993-1994* (NCES 97-459). Washington, DC: National Center for Education Statistics.

McLaughlin, D. H. (1998). Catholic schools for the twenty-first century: Challenges for educational leadership. In P. Duignan & T. D'Arbon (Eds.), *Leadership in Catholic education: 2000 and beyond* (pp. 24-41). Strathfield, NSW: Australian Catholic University.

McLaughlin, M. W., & Talbert, J. E. (1993). How the world of students and teachers challenges policy coherence. In S. H. Furhman (Ed.), *Designing coherent educational policy* (pp. 220-249). San Francisco: Jossey-Bass.

McLaughlin, M. W., Talbert, J. E., & Bascia, N. (Eds.). (1990). *The contexts of teaching in secondary schools: Teachers' realities.* New York: Teachers College Press.

McLaughlin, T. (1999). Distinctiveness and the Catholic school: Balanced judgment and the temptations of commonality. In J. C. Conroy (Ed.), *Catholic education: Inside, out, outside in* (pp. 65-87). Dublin: Veritas.

McNeil, L. (2000). *Contradictions of school reform: Educational costs of standardized testing.* New York: Routledge.

Meece, J. L., & Eccles, J. S. (1993, Fall). Recent trends in research on gender in education. *Educational Psychologist, 28,* 313-319.

Meitler, N. (2001, January). *Educational Management.* [Newsletter]. Hales-Corners, WI: Meitler Consultants.

Merrill, S., Tessarolo, J., & Blessing, M. (1999, Spring). A partnership to create a process for inclusion for all. *National Apostolate Quarterly,* 17-19.

Metzler, M. J. (1998). *United States Catholic elementary and secondary schools 1997-1998*. Washington, DC: National Catholic Educational Association.

Meyer, K. A. (1998). From isolation to inclusion: The metamorphosis of the St. Anthony School programs (Doctoral dissertation, Fordham University, 1998). *Dissertation Abstracts International, 59 (*07), AAT 9839513.

Midgley, C., & Wood, S. (1993). Beyond site-based management: Empowering teachers to reform schools. *Phi Delta Kappan, 75(3),* 245-252.

Miles, R. E., & Snow, C. C. (1978). *Organizational strategy, structure, and process.* New York: McGraw-Hill.

Milks, M. J. (1997). *United States Catholic elementary and secondary schools 1996-1997.* Washington, DC: National Catholic Educational Association.

Miller, B. M. (1995). *Out-of-school time: Effects of learning in the primary grades.* Wellesley, MA: Center for Research on Women, National Institute on Out-of-School Time.

Miller, B. M. (2001). The promise of after-school programs. *Educational Leadership, 58(7),* 6-12.

Miller, B. M., O'Connor, S., Sirignano, S., & Joshi, P. (1996). *I wish the kids didn't watch so much TV: Out-of-school time in three low-income communities* [School-age child care project]. Wellesley, MA: Center for Research on Women.

Miller, D. W. (2001, July 13). The problem with studying vouchers. *The Chronicle of Higher Education,* pp. A14-A15.

Miller, G. A. (1994). The magical number seven, plus or minus two: Some limits on our capacity for processing information. *Psychological Review, 101(2),* 343-352.

Min, M. (1991). *Relative effects of coeducation in single sex schools on students' schooling, affection, and career choice: Exploring conventional and feminist perspectives.* Unpublished doctoral dissertation, University of Illinois at Urbana.

Miron, L. F. (1997). *Resisting discrimination: Affirmative strategies for principals and teachers.* Thousand Oaks, CA: Corwin Press, Inc.

Moe, T. M. (Ed.). (1995). *Private vouchers.* Stanford, CA: Hoover Institution Press.

Moe, T. M. (2001). *Schools, vouchers and the American public.* Washington, DC: Brookings Institution Press.

Molnar, A., Smith, P., Zahorik, J., Palmer, A., Halbach, A., & Ehrle, K. (1999a). Evaluating the SAGE program: A pilot program in targeted pupil-teacher reduction in Wisconsin. *Educational Evaluation and Policy Analysis, 21(2),* 166-177.

Molnar, A., Smith, P., Zahorik, J., Palmer, A., Halbach, A., & Ehrle, K. (1999b). *1998-1999 evaluation results of the student achievement guarantee in education (SAGE) program.* Retrieved August 14, 2001 from http://www.uwm.edu/dept/CERAI/sage.html.

Monahan, F. J. (1991). *Non-public schools and public policy: The past, present, and perhaps, the future.* Washington, DC: National Catholic Educational Association.

Moore, L. (1999). *Personal characteristics and selected educational attainment of Catholic elementary school principals in relation to spiritual formation activities.* Unpublished doctoral dissertation, University of Dayton, Ohio.

Moore, M., Piper, V., & Schaefer, E. (1993). Single sex schooling and educational effectiveness: A research overview. In D. K. Hollinger, & R. Adamson, (Eds.), *Single sex schooling: Perspectives from practice and research* (pp. 7-68). Washington, DC: U.S. Department of Education.

Morganthau, T. (1997, January 27). The face of the future. *Newsweek* [Special issue], 58-60.

Morris, C. G. (1993). *Psychology: An introduction* (8th ed.). Upper Saddle River, NJ: Prentice Hall.

Morse, G. (1997). Technology partnerships. In R. Haney & A. A. Zukowski (Eds.), *New frontiers: Navigational strategies for integrating technology into the school* (pp. 41-47). Washington, DC: National Catholic Educational Association.

Mueller, F. C. (1994). The perceived and preferred goals of principals, De la Salle Christian brother teachers, and lay teachers in Lasallian secondary schools (Doctoral dissertation, Boston College, 1994). *Dissertation Abstracts International, 55-06A*, 1514.

Mueller, F. C. (2000). Sponsorship of Catholic schools: Preserving the tradition. In J. Youniss, J. Convey, & J. McLellan (Eds.), *The Catholic character of Catholic schools* (pp. 38-61). Notre Dame, IN: University of Notre Dame Press.

Muller, C. (1993). Parent involvement in Catholic schools. *Private School Monitor, 14(1-2)*, 14-17.

Mulligan, J. T. (1993). A model of formation for teachers in the Catholic high school (Doctoral dissertation, University of St. Michael's College, Canada, 1993). *Dissertation Abstracts International, 54-12A*, 4400.

Murnane, R. J., Newstead, S., & Olsen, R. J. (1985). Comparing public and private schools: The puzzling role of selection bias. *Journal of Business and Economic Statistics, 3(1)*, 23-35.

Murphy, J., & Beck, L. (1995). *School-based management as school reform.* Thousand Oaks, CA: Corwin Press.

Murphy, J., & Louis, K. S. (1994). *Reshaping the principalship: Insights from transformational reform efforts.* Thousand Oaks, CA: Corwin Press.

Murray, W. (1996, April). Are your students emotionally intelligent? *Instructor*, 52-54.

National Catholic Educational Association. (1991). *The national congress on Catholic schools for the twenty-first century.* Washington, DC.

National Catholic Educational Association. (1993). *Technology and Chapter 1: Solutions for Catholic school participation.* Washington, DC.

National Catholic Educational Association. (1995). Technology on the move. *NCEA Notes, 27(5)*, 13.

National Catholic Educational Association. (1999). *A reflection statement on inclusion.* Washington, DC.

National Catholic Educational Association. (2000). *Lighting new fires: Catholic secondary schools for the 21st century.* Washington, DC.

National Center for Education Statistics. (1998). *Violence and discipline in U. S. public schools: 1996-1997* (NCES 98-030). Washington, DC.

National Center for Education Statistics. (2000a). *Stats in brief: Computer and Internet access in private schools and classrooms: 1995 and 1998.* Washington, DC: United States Department of Education.

National Center for Education Statistics. (2000b). *Teachers' tools for the 21st century.* Washington, DC: U.S. Department of Education.

National Center for Education Statistics. (2001). *NCES projections of education statistics to 2011.* Retrieved August 29, 2001 from http://nces.ed.gov/pubs2001/2001083.pdf

National Conference of Catholic Bishops. (1976). *Teach them.* Washington, DC: United States Catholic Conference.

National Conference of Catholic Bishops. (1979). *Sharing the light of faith: National catechetical directory for Catholics of the United States.* Washington, DC: United States Catholic Conference.

National Conference of Catholic Bishops. (1980). *Catholic higher education and the pastoral mission of the church.* Washington, DC: United States Catholic Conference.

National Conference of Catholic Bishops. (1990). *In support of Catholic elementary and secondary schools.* Washington, DC: United States Catholic Conference.

National Conference of Catholic Bishops. (1994*). Follow the way of love: A pastoral message of the U.S. Catholic bishops to families on the occasion of the United Nations 1994 international year of the family.* Washington, DC: U.S. Catholic Conference.

Natriello, G., McDill, E. L., & Pallas, A. M. (1990). Schooling disadvantaged children: Racing against catastrophe. New York: Teachers College Press.

Neal, D. A. (1997a). The effects of Catholic secondary schooling on educational achievement. *The Journal of Labor Economics, 15(1),* 98-123.

Neal, D. A. (1997b, Spring). Measuring Catholic school performance. *The Public Interest, 127,* 81-87.

Neal, D. A. (1998). What have we learned about the benefits of private schooling? *Federal Reserve Bank of New York Policy Review, 4(1),* 79-86.

Nelson, M. S. (2000). Black Catholic schools in inner-city Chicago: Forging a path to the future. In J. Youniss, J. Convey, & J. McLellan (Eds.), *The Catholic character of Catholic schools* (pp. 157-177). Notre Dame, IN: University of Notre Dame Press.

Neuman, M., & Simmons, W. (2000). Leadership for student learning. *Phi Delta Kappan, 82(1),* 9-12.

Newmann, F. M., & Wehlage, G. (1995). *Successful school restructuring.* Madison, WI: Center on Organization and Restructuring of Schools.

Niebuhr, H. R. (1951). *Christ and culture.* New York: Harper and Row.

Nuzzi, R. (1996). *Gifts of the spirit: Multiple intelligences in religious education* (1st ed.). Washington, DC: National Catholic Educational Association.

Nuzzi, R. (1998). Cooperative learning and Catholic schools: A natural partnership. *Momentum, 29(1),* 70-75.

Nuzzi, R. (1999). *Gifts of the spirit: Multiple intelligences in religious education* (2nd ed.). Washington, DC: National Catholic Educational Association.

Nuzzi, R. (2001). Spirituality and religious education. In T. C. Hunt, E. A. Joseph, & R. J. Nuzzi (Eds.), *Handbook of research on Catholic education* (pp. 65-82). Westport, CT: Greenwood Press.

Nuzzi, R., & Rogus, J. (1993). Cooperative learning in Catholic schools. *Catholic School Studies, 66(1),* 52-53.

Oberlander, J. (2000). Checkpoints for excellence in curricular technology integration. In C. Cimino, R. M. Haney, J. M. O'Keefe, & A. A. Zukowski (Eds.), *Forming innovative learning environments through technology* (pp. 117-126). Washington, DC: National Catholic Educational Association.

O'Brien, J. S. (1987). *Mixed messages: What bishops and priests say about Catholic schools.* Washington, DC: National Catholic Educational Association.

O'Day, J. A., & Smith, M. S. (1993). Systemic school reform and educational opportunity. In S. H. Fuhrman (Ed.), *Designing coherent education policy: Improving the system* (pp. 250-312). San Francisco: Jossey-Bass.

O'Keefe, J. M. (1999). Creative resourcing for Catholic schools: The critical issue of hiring and retaining high-quality teachers. *Momentum, 30(4),* 54-58.

O'Keefe, J. M. (2000). The use of technology in Catholic schools: An overview. In C. Cimino, R. M. Haney, J. M. O'Keefe, & A. A. Zukowski (Eds.), *Forming innovative learning environments through technology* (pp. 139-151). Washington, DC: National Catholic Educational Association.

O'Keefe, J. M., & Murphy, J. (2000). Ethnically diverse Catholic schools: School structure, students, staffing, and finance. In J. Youniss & J. J. Convey (Eds.), *Catholic schools at the crossroads: Survival and transformation* (pp. 117-136). New York: Teachers College Press.

O'Laughlin, J. (1982). Future of Catholic schools: A perception. *Education, 102(4),* 322-325.

Olszewski-Kubilius, P. (1998a). Research evidence regarding the validity and effects of talent search educational programs. *The Journal for Secondary Gifted Education, 9(3),* 134-138.

Olszewski-Kubilius, P. (1998b). Talent search: Purposes, rationale, and role in gifted education. *The Journal for Secondary Gifted Education, 9(3),* 106-113.

O'Malley, W. J. (1991). What makes a school Catholic? In F. D. Kelly (Ed.), *What makes a school Catholic?* (pp. 3-9). Washington, DC: National Catholic Educational Association.

O'Neil, J. (1996). On emotional intelligence: A conversation with Daniel Goleman. *Educational Leadership, 54(1),* 6-11.

O'Sullivan, C. Y., Reese, C. M., & Mazzeo, J. (1997). *NAEP 1996 science report card for the nation and the states.* Washington, DC: National Center for Education Statistics.

Owen, M. J. (1997). Inclusion, the millennium and Catholic education. *Momentum, 28(3),* 48-50.

Parker, L., & Shapiro, J. P. (1993). The context of educational administration and social class. In C. A. Capper (Ed.), *Educational administration in a pluralistic society* (pp. 36-65). Albany, NY: State University of New York Press.

Parsad, B., Skinner, R., & Farris, E. (2001). *Advanced telecommunications in U.S. private schools: 1998-99* (NCES Rep. No. 2001-037). Washington, DC: U.S. Department of Education, National Center for Education Statistics.

Paul VI. (1975). *Evangelii nuntiandi* [On evangelization in the modern world]. Washington, DC: United States Catholic Conference.

Paul VI. (1977). The role of the Catholic teacher. *The Pope Speaks, 3,* 241-242.

Paulino, R. (1990). A comparison of the religious beliefs and values of Catholic school teachers and educational leaders in the Catholic schools in Guam (Doctoral dissertation, University of San Francisco, 1990). *Dissertation Abstracts International, 51-11A,* 3665.

Payne, P. (1989). *Parent perceptions of religions and lay principals.* Unpublished doctoral dissertation, Peabody College for Teachers of Vanderbilt University.

Perez, K. (1997). An analysis of practices used to support new teachers. *Teacher Education Quarterly, 24(2),* 41-52.

Perri, S. (1989). The principal as teacher of teachers. In R. J. Kealey (Ed.), *Reflections on the role of the Catholic school principal* (pp. 67-74). Washington, DC: National Catholic Educational Association.

Perry, G., & Duru, M. (2000). *Resources for developmentally appropriate practice: Recommendations from the profession.* Washington, DC: National Association for the Education of Young Children.

Perry, J. N. (1989). Rights in canon law for persons with mental disabilities. *NAMRP Quarterly, 20(3),* 4-9, 23.

Perry, T., & Fraser, J. W. (1993). Reconstructing schools as multiracial/multicultural democracies: Toward a theoretical perspective. In T. Perry & J. W. Fraser (Eds.), *Freedom's plow: Teaching in the multicultural classroom* (pp. 3-24). New York: Routledge.

Persky, H. R., Reese, C. M., O'Sullivan, C. Y., Lazer, S., Moore, J., & Shakrani, S. (1996). *NAEP 1994 geography report card.* Washington, DC: U.S. Department of Education, Office of Educational Research and Improvement.

Peterson, P. E., & Campbell, D. E. (Eds.). (2001). *Charters, vouchers, and public education.* Washington, DC: The Brookings Institution.

Peterson, P. E., & Hassel, B. C. (Eds.). (1998). *Learning from school choice*. Washington, DC: The Brookings Institution.

Peterson, P. E., Meyers, D. E., Howell, W.G., & Mayer, D. T. (1993). *The effects of school choice in New York City*. Washington, DC: National Catholic Educational Association.

Pfeffer, J., & Salancik, G. R. (1978). *The external control of organizations: A resource dependence perspective*. New York: Harper & Row.

Phan, P. C. (1998). "To be Catholic or not to be: Is it still the question?" Catholic identity and religious education today. *Horizons, 25(2),* 159-180.

Piaget, J. (1974). *Understanding causality*. (D. Miles & M. Miles, Trans.). New York: Norton.

Pieper, J. (1954). *The end of time*. New York: Pantheon Books Inc.

Pierce, K. M., Hamm, J. V., & Vandell, D. L. (1994). Experiences in after-school programs and children's adjustment in first-grade classrooms. *Child Development, 65,* 440-456.

Pilarczyk, D. (1982). What makes a Catholic school Catholic? In National Catholic Educational Association (Eds.), *Catholic secondary education: Now and in the future* (pp. 16-22). Dayton, OH: University of Dayton Press.

Pilarczyk, D. (1998). What is a Catholic school? *Origins, 28(23),* 405-408.

Pine, L. (2001). *The Philanthropic Institute study*. Unpublished study. Boston: The Philanthropic Institute.

Plank, D. N., & Sykes, G. (2000). *The school choice debate: Framing the issues*. East Lansing, MI: Michigan State University, The Education Policy Center.

Poe, E. (1948). The philosophy of composition. In J. L. Davis, J. T. Frederick, & F. L. Mott, (Eds.), *American literature: An anthology and critical survey* (p. 478). New York: Charles Scribner's Sons.

Polite, V. C. (2000). Cornerstones: Catholic high schools that serve predominantly African American populations. In J. Youniss, J. Convey, & J. McLellan (Eds.), *The Catholic character of Catholic schools* (pp. 137-156). Notre Dame, IN: University of Notre Dame Press.

Popham, W. J. (2000, April). *Teaching to the test?* Paper presented at the annual meeting of the American Educational Research Association, New Orleans, LA.

Popkewitz, T. S. (1996). Rethinking decentralization and state/civil society distinctions: The state as a problematic of governing. *Journal of Education Policy, 11(1),* 27-51.

Porath, J. (2000). The academic character of Catholic schools. In J. Youniss, J. J. Convey, & J. A. McLellan (Eds.), *The Catholic character of Catholic schools* (pp. 219-240). Notre Dame, IN: University of Notre Dame Press.

Posner, J. K., & Vandell, D. L. (1994). After-school activities and the development of low-income urban children: A longitudinal study. *Child Development, 65,* 756-767.

Potyrala, L. (1993). Free to learn and to love. *NAPMR Quarterly, 24(3),* 10-15.

Power, C., & Brosnan, T. (1992). The future is now! *Momentum, 23(1),* 42- 43.

Prehn, J. S. (2000). The motivational factors of recently hired lay teachers in the secondary schools of the Detroit province of the Society of Jesus (Doctoral dissertation, University of San Francisco, 2000). *Dissertation Abstracts International, 61-03A,* 841.

Prendergast, J. (1998). A welcomed blessing. *Momentum, 29(1),* 16-18.

Pressley, M. (Ed.). (in press). *Alternative teacher education: Notre Dame's alliance for Catholic education*. Notre Dame, IN: University of Notre Dame Press.

Proctor, T. B., Black, K. N., & Feldhusen, J. F. (1986). Early admission of selected children to elementary school: A review of the research literature. *Journal of Educational Research, 80(2),* 70-76.

Provost, J., & Walf, K. (Eds.). (1994). *Catholic identity.* London: SCM Press.

Purkey, S. C., & Smith, M. S. (1983). Effective schools: A review. *Elementary School Journal, 84(4),* 427-452.

Purkey, S. C., & Smith, M. S. (1985). Educational policy and school effectiveness. In G. R. Austin & H. Garber (Eds.), *Research on exemplary schools* (pp. 181-200). New York: Academic Press.

Quirin, L. (2001, February 9). What makes a school Catholic? *The Messenger* (Suppl.), p. 1.

Rahner, K. (1981). *Concern for the church.* New York: Crossroads.

Rallis, S. F. (1990). Professional teachers and restructured schools: Leadership challenges. In B. Mitchell & L. L. Cunningham (Eds.), *Educational leadership and changing contexts of families, communities, and schools: Eighty-ninth yearbook of the National Society for the Study of Education, Part II* (pp. 184-209). Chicago: University of Chicago Press.

Ramirez, K. M. (1996). *A service delivery model for students with special needs in the Catholic elementary school system.* Oakland, CA: Dominican Sisters.

Ravitch, D. (1994, Fall). *Somebody's children: Expanding educational opportunity for all American children.* Paper presented at a conference at Princeton University, NJ.

Ravitch, D. (1996, October 1). Testing Catholic schools. *Wall Street Journal,* p. A-22.

Raywid, M. A. (1997-1998). Small schools: A reform that works. *Educational Leadership, 5(4),* 34-39.

Raywid, M. A. (1999). *Current literature on small schools.* Charleston, WV: ERIC Clearinghouse on Rural Education and Small Schools. (ERIC Document Reproduction Service No. ED 425 049)

Reck, C. (1991). Catholic identity. In *The Catholic identity of Catholic schools* (pp. 21-38). Washington, DC: National Catholic Educational Association.

Rees, N. S. (2000). *School choice: What's happening in the states, 2000.* Washington, DC: The Heritage Foundation.

Reese, C. M., Miller, K. E., Mazzeo, J., & Dossey, J. A. (1997). *NAEP 1996 mathematics report card for the nation and the states.* Washington, DC: National Center for Education Statistics.

Reese, S., & Corrin, D. (1995). *Single sex classrooms in the twenty-first century: Defying the stereotypes.* ISACS Monographs.

Reichel, C. (1999). *Distinctively Marianist: Developing an instrument to identify cultural characteristics in a Marianist high school.* Unpublished doctoral dissertation, University of Dayton, Ohio.

Reil, M., & Fulton, K. (2001). The role of technology in supporting learning communities. *Phi Delta Kappan, 82(7),* 518-523.

Reis, S. M. (1992, March). The curriculum compacting study. *The National Research Center on the Gifted and Talented Newsletter,* 4.

Reis, S. M., Burns, D. E., & Renzulli, J. S. (1992). *Curriculum compacting: The complete guide to modifying the regular curriculum for high ability students.* Mansfield Center, CT: Creative Learning Press, Inc.

Reissman, R. (1999). Emotional intelligence. *Mailbox Teacher, 28(1),* 34-37.

Richardson, V. (Ed.). (1997). *Constructivist teacher education: Building a world of new understandings.* Washington, DC: Falmer Press.

Riley, R. W. (1994). Families come first: Renewed emphasis on parent and community involvement is critical to the success of Goals 2000. *Principal*, 74(2), 30-32.

Rimm, S. (1999). *See Jane win: The Rimm report on how 1,000 girls became successful women.* New York: Crown Publishers.

Rinehart, J. S., & Short, P. M. (1991, October). Viewing reading recovery as restructuring phenomenon. *Journal of School Leadership, 1,* 370-399.

Rinehart, J. S., & Short, P. M. (1994). Job satisfaction and empowerment among teacher leaders, reading recovery teachers, and regular classroom teachers. *Education, 114,* 570-580.

Rinehart, J. S., Short, P. M., & Johnson, P. E. (1997). Empowerment and conflict at school-based and non-school-based sites in the United States. *Journal of International Studies in Educational Administration, 25,* 77-87.

Rinehart, J. S., Short, P. M., Short, R. J., & Eckley, M. (1998). Teacher empowerment and principal leadership: Understanding the influence process. *Educational Administration Quarterly, 34,* 608-630.

Riordan, C. (1993). The case for single sex schools. In D. K. Hollinger, & R. Adamson, (Eds.), *Single sex schooling: Proponents speak* (pp. 47-53). Washington, DC: United States Department of Education.

Riordan, C. (1994). Single gender schools: Outcomes for African and Hispanic Americans. *Journal of Research and Sociology of Education and Socialization, 10,* 177-205.

Riordan, C. (2000). Trends in student demography in Catholic secondary schools, 1972-1992. In J. Youniss & J. J. Convey (Eds.), *Catholic schools at the crossroads* (pp. 33-54). New York: Teachers College Press.

Ristau, K. (1991). The challenge: To provide leadership within Catholic schools. In *Leadership of and on behalf of Catholic schools* (pp. 5-17). Washington, DC: National Catholic Educational Association.

Ristow, R. S., & Wieser, M. (2000). *Bringing special education services to parochial and religious education: A collaborative effort.* Davenport, IA: Davenport Diocese.

Ritzel, J. (1995). A cyberspace odyssey. *Momentum, 26(4),* 20-22.

Rizza, M. G. (1997). Exploring successful learning with talented female adolescents (girls) (Doctoral dissertation, University of Connecticut, 1997). *Dissertation Abstracts International, 58(08),* 3003A.

Robinson, K. A. (1998). *The Catholic funding guide: A directory of resources for Catholic activities.* Washington, DC: Foundations and Donors Interested in Catholic Activities (FADICA).

Robinson, V. M. J. (1995). The identification and evaluation of power in discourse. In D. Corson (Ed.), *Discourse and power in educational organizations* (pp. 111-130). Cresskill, NJ: Hampton Press, Inc.

Rogers, K. B. (1991a). *A best-evidence synthesis of the research on accelerative options for gifted students.* Unpublished doctoral dissertation, University of Minnesota, Minneapolis.

Rogers, K. B. (1991b). *The relationship of grouping practices to the education of the gifted and talented learner* (Research monograph 9102). Storrs, CT: The National Research Center on the Gifted and Talented, University of Connecticut.

Rogus, J. (1991). Strengthening preparation and support for leadership in Catholic schools. In *Leadership of and on behalf of Catholic schools* (pp. 19-39). Washington, DC: National Catholic Educational Association.

Rollow, S. G., & Bryk, A. S. (1993). Democratic politics and school improvement: The potential of Chicago school reform. In C. Marshall (Ed.), *The new politics of race and gender: The 1992 yearbook of the Politics of Education Association* (pp. 97-106). Washington, DC: Falmer Press.

Rose, L. C., Gallup, A. M., & Elam, S. M. (1997). The 29th annual Phi Delta Kappa/Gallup poll of the public's attitudes toward the public schools. *Phi Delta Kappan, 78(1),* 41-56.

Rosenholtz, S. J. (1985). Effective schools: Interpreting the evidence. *American Journal of Education, 93(3),* 352-388.

Rossi, R. J. (Ed.). (1994). *Schools and students at risk: Context and framework for positive change.* New York: Teachers College Press.

Rouse, C. E. (1998a). Private school vouchers and student achievement: An evaluation of the Milwaukee parental choice program. *Quarterly Journal of Economics, 111(2),* 553-602.

Rouse, C. E. (1998b). Schools and student achievement: More evidence from the Milwaukee parental choice program. *Federal Reserve Bank of New York Economic Policy Review, 4(1),* 61-76.

Rusch, E. A. (1998). Leadership in evolving democratic school communities. *Journal of School Leadership, 8(3),* 214-250.

Rutter, M., Maughan, B., Mortimore, P., Ouston, J., & Smith, A. (1979). *Fifteen thousand hours: Secondary schools and their effects on children.* Cambridge, MA: Harvard University Press.

Ryan, C. (1988). One parent's experience with integrated education. *NAMRP Quarterly, 19(3),* 14-18.

Ryan, K., & Bohlin, K. (1999). *Building character in schools: Practical ways to bring moral instruction to life.* San Francisco: Jossey-Bass.

Ryan, M. (1964). *Are parochial schools the answer?* New York: Holt, Rinehart and Winston.

Sacred Congregation. (1972). *To teach as Jesus did: A pastoral message on Catholic education.* Washington, DC: United States Catholic Conference.

Sacred Congregation. (1982). *Lay Catholics in schools: Witnesses to faith.* Washington, DC: United States Catholic Conference.

Samaras, A. P., & Wilson, J. C. (1998, April). *Am I invited? Perspectives of family involvement with technology in inner-city schools.* Paper presented at the annual meeting of the American Educational Research Association, San Diego, CA.

Sander, W. (1996). Catholic grade schools and academic achievement. *The Journal of Human Resources, 31(3),* 540-548.

Sander, W. (1999). Private schools and public school achievement. *The Journal of Human Resources, 34(4),* 697-709.

Sander, W., & Krautmann, A. C. (1995). Catholic schools, dropout rates and educational attainment. *Economic Inquiry, 33(2),* 217-233.

Sandhu, D. S. (July, 1996). A review of the Handbook of Cooperative Learning Methods. *Journal for a Just and Caring Education, 2(3),* 336-338.

Sarason, S. B. (1993). *The case for change: Rethinking the preparation of educators.* San Francisco: Jossey-Bass.

Sarason, S. B. (1995). *Parental involvement and the political principle.* San Francisco: Jossey-Bass.

Sarason, S. B. (1996). *Revisiting "The culture of the school and the problem of change."* New York: Teachers College Press.

Sarason, S. B. (1999). *Teaching as a performing art.* New York: Teachers College Press.

Sares, T. (1992, April). *School size effects on educational attainment and ability.* Paper presented at the meeting of the American Educational Research Association, San Francisco, CA.

Sather, S. E. (1999, April). *Leading, lauding, and learning: Leadership in diverse secondary schools.* Paper presented at the annual meeting of the American Educational Research Association, Montreal, Canada.

Saunders, W. P. (1992). *The impact of the family's social capital on the religious outcomes of eighth-grade students in Catholic elementary schools*. Unpublished doctoral dissertation, The Catholic University of America.

Savage, F. X., & Milks, M. J. (1996). *United States Catholic elementary and secondary schools 1995-1996*. Washington, DC: National Catholic Educational Association.

Schaub, M. (2000). A faculty at a crossroads: A profile of American Catholic school teachers. In J. Youniss & J. J. Convey (Eds.), *Catholic schools at the crossroads: Survival and transformation* (pp. 72-86). New York: Teachers College Press.

Schaub, M., & Baker, D. (1993). *Serving American Catholic children and youth*. Washington, DC: Department of Education, United States Catholic Conference.

Schein, E. H. (1992). *Organizational culture and leadership* (2nd ed.). San Francisco: Jossey-Bass.

Scheinfeld, D. R. (1993). *New beginnings: A guide to designing parenting programs for refugee and immigrant parents*. New York: International Catholic Child Bureau.

Scherer, M. (1999). The understanding pathway: A conversation with Howard Gardner. *Educational Leadership, 57(3)*, 12-16.

Schermerhorn, J. R., Hunt, J. G., & Osborn, R. N. (1994). *Managing organizational behavior*. New York: Wiley.

Schiller, K. (1994, August). *When do Catholic schools have effects?* Paper presented at the annual meeting of the American Sociological Association, Los Angeles, CA.

Schindler, T. F. (1995, June). What makes Catholic managed care Catholic? *Health Progress*, 52-54.

Schinke, S., Cole, K. C., & Poulin, S. R. (1998). *Evaluation of educational enhancement program of Boys and Girls Clubs of America*. New York: Columbia University School of Social Work.

Schön, D. A. (1991). *Educating the reflective practitioner*. San Francisco: Jossey-Bass.

Schuttloffel, M. J. (2000). Promises and possibilities: The Catholic elementary school curriculum. In J. Youniss, J. Convey, & J. McLellan (Eds.), *The Catholic character of Catholic schools* (pp. 103-123). Notre Dame, IN: University of Notre Dame Press.

Schwartz, D. (1992). From wonder to work. *Momentum, 23(1)*, 18-22.

Scott, C. E. (1999). *Self-esteem and reading growth in African American adolescent males: Single sex versus coeducational education*. Unpublished doctoral dissertation, University of San Francisco.

Sears, J. T. (1993). Responding to the sexual diversity of faculty and students: Sexual praxis and the critically reflective administrator. In C. A. Capper (Ed.), *Educational administration in a pluralistic society* (pp. 110-172). Albany, NY: State University of New York Press.

Sebring, P. A., & Camburn, E. M. (1992). *A profile of eighth graders in Catholic schools*. Washington, DC: National Catholic Educational Association.

Second Vatican Council. (1965/1996). The declaration on Christian education [Gravissimum educationis]. In A. Flannery (Ed.), *Vatican Council II: The basic sixteen documents* (pp. 575-591). Northport, NY: Costello Publishing.

Sergiovanni, T. J. (1992). *Moral leadership*. San Francisco: Jossey-Bass.

Sergiovanni, T. J. (1994). *Building community in schools*. San Francisco: Jossey-Bass.

Sergiovanni, T. J. (1996). *Leadership for the schoolhouse*. San Francisco: Jossey-Bass.

Sexton, C. M. (1991). *Gender differences and attitudes toward science: A multiple regression analysis creating a profile of the female most likely to participate in science*. Unpublished doctoral dissertation, Ohio University.

Shaner, L. (1992). PACT: The 21-hour success story. *Momentum, 23(1),* 56-58.

Shaughnessy, M. A. (1995). Ethical and legal challenges of technology. *Momentum, 26(4),* 16-18.

Shaughnessy, M. A. (1997). Ethical and legal challenges of technology. In R. Haney & A. A. Zukowski (Eds.), *New frontiers: Navigational strategies for integrating technology into the school* (pp. 69-72). Washington, DC: National Catholic Educational Association.

Sheehan, L. (1990). *Building better boards: A handbook for board members in Catholic education.* Washington, DC: National Catholic Educational Association.

Sheehan, L. (1991, November). *Governance.* Theme paper presented at the National Congress on Catholic Schools for the 21st Century. Washington, DC: National Catholic Educational Association.

Sheehan, L. (1994). The Catholic school principal's role: Church governance and structures. In M. Ciriello (Ed.), *Formation and development for Catholic school leaders* (Vol. 3, pp. 87-92). Washington, DC: United States Catholic Conference.

Sheehan, L. (1999). Internal issues in private education. *Catholic Education: A Journal of Inquiry and Practice, 2(4),* 444-453.

Sherman, D. (1994). Sleepless in DC: Late-night ramblings on space technology. In National Catholic Educational Association, *Preserving our ideals: Papers from the 1993 principals academy* (pp. 31-38). Washington, DC: National Catholic Educational Association.

Sherman, M. (1984). A biochemistry course for high-ability secondary students. *Journal of Chemical Education, 61(10),* 902-903.

Shimabukuro, V. H. (1993). Profile of an ideal Catholic school teacher: Content analysis of Roman and American documents, 1965 to 1990 (Doctoral dissertation, University of San Francisco, 1993). *Dissertation Abstracts International, 54-04A,* 1280.

Shimabukuro, V. H. (1998). *A call to reflection: A teacher's guide to Catholic identity for the 21st century.* Washington, DC: National Catholic Educational Association.

Shore, B. M., Cornell, D. G., Robinson, A., & Ward, V. S. (1991). *Recommended practices in gifted education: A critical analysis.* New York: Teachers College Press.

Sikes, P. J. (1992). Imposed change and the experienced teacher. In M. Fullan & A. Hargreaves (Eds.), *Teacher development and educational change* (pp. 36-55). London: Falmer Press.

Sileo, J. R., & Allen, P. M. (1999, Summer). *National Apostolate Quarterly, 10,* 13-14.

Simon, K. (1997). *The place of meaning: A study of the moral, existential, and intellectual in American high schools.* Unpublished doctoral dissertation, Stanford University.

Sine, J. E. (1994). In your spare time. In National Catholic Educational Association, *Preserving our ideals: Papers from the 1993 principals academy* (pp. 25-30). Washington, DC: National Catholic Educational Association.

Siskin, L. S. (1994a). Is the school the unit of change? Internal and external contexts of restructuring. In P. Grimmett & J. Neufeld (Eds.), *Teacher development and the struggle for authenticity* (pp. 121-140). New York: Teachers College Press.

Siskin, L. S. (1994b). *Realms of knowledge: Academic departments in secondary schools.* London: Falmer Press.

Six ways to build character in the classroom. (2001). *Curriculum Review, 49(6),* 6.

Sizer, T. (1984). *Horace's compromise: The dilemma of the American high school.* Boston: Houghton Mifflin.

Sizer, T. (1992). *Horace's school: Redesigning the American high school.* Boston: Houghton Mifflin.

Sizer, T. (1996). *Horace's hope: What works for the American high school.* Boston: Houghton Mifflin.

Skillen, J. W. (Ed.). (1993). *The school-choice controversy: What is constitutional?* Grand Rapids, MI: Baker Books.

Slavin, R. E. (1995). *Cooperative learning, theory, research and practice* (2nd ed.). Boston: Allyn & Bacon.

Slavin, R. E. (2000). *Educational psychology: Theory and practice.* Needham Heights, MA: Allyn & Bacon.

Smith, J. K., & Blase, J. (1991). From empiricism to hermeneutics: Educational leadership as a practical and moral activity. *Journal of Educational Administration, 29(1),* 6-21.

Smith, P. R. (1995). Character formation in computer-driven education. *Momentum, 26(4),* 14-15.

Smith-Maddox, R. P. (1994). *African American eighth graders: Factors affecting their educational and occupational aspirations.* Unpublished doctoral dissertation, Brandeis University.

Smrekar, C. E. (1994). *Building community: The influence of school organization on family-school interactions.* Unpublished doctoral dissertation, Stanford University.

Smrekar, C. E. (1996). *The impact of school choice and community: In the interest of families and schools.* State University of New York Series, Youth Social Services, Schooling, and Public Policy. Albany, NY: State University of New York Press.

Smrekar, C. E., & Mawhiney, H. E. (1999). Integrated services: Challenges in linking schools, families, and communities. In J. Murphy & K. S. Louis (Eds.), *Handbook of research on educational administration* (2nd ed., pp. 443-461). San Francisco: Jossey-Bass.

Smylie, M. A. (1994). Redesigning teachers' work: Connections to the classroom. In L. Darling-Hamond (Ed.), *Review of educational research* (Vol. 20, pp. 129-177). Washington, DC: American Educational Research Association.

Snyder, J., Bolin, F., & Zumwalt, K. (1992). Curriculum implementation. In P. Jackson (Ed.), *Handbook of research on curriculum* (pp. 402-435). New York: Macmillan.

Sommerfield, M. (1994, August 3). Study compares religious education of parish programs, Catholic schools. *Education Week, 13,* p. 13.

Southern, W. T., & Jones, E. D. (Eds.). (1991). *The academic acceleration of gifted children.* New York: Teachers College Press.

Sparapani, E. F., Abel, F. J., Easton, S. E., Edwards, P., & Herbster, D. L. (1997, Winter). Cooperative learning: An investigation of the knowledge and classroom practice of middle grade teachers. *Education, 118(2),* 251-258.

Sperry, R. (1968). Hemisphere disconnection and unity in conscious awareness. *American Psychologist, 23,* 723-733.

Sprenger, M. (1999). *Learning and memory, the brain in action.* Alexandria, VA: Association for Supervision and Curriculum Development.

Squillini, C. A. (1999). Motivators of commitment and longevity: A study of the characteristics of job satisfaction that influence Catholic elementary school lay teachers (Doctoral dissertation, Walden University, 1999). *Dissertation Abstracts International, 60-06A,* 1861.

Squillini, C. A. (2001). Teacher commitment and longevity in Catholic schools. *Catholic Education: A Journal of Inquiry and Practice, 4(3),* 335-354.

Squire, L. R., Knowlton, B., & Musen, G. (1993). The structure and organization of memory. *Annual Review of Psychology, 44,* 453-495.

Stabile, C. C. (Ed.) (2000). *Ensuring Catholic identity in Catholic schools.* Washington, DC: National Catholic Educational Association.

Staponska, C. R. (1999). *Effects of single sex education on the mathematics achievement of secondary school females.* Unpublished doctoral dissertation, Central Missouri State University.

Starratt, R. J. (1994). *Building an ethical school: A practical response to the moral crisis in schools.* Bristol, PA: The Falmer Press.

Stautberg, R. (1996). Response. *Proceedings of a symposium sponsored by the Department of Secondary Schools, National Catholic Educational Association*, 28-29.

Stegall, P. (1998, April). *The principal – Key to technology integration.* Paper presented at the Annual Meeting of the National Catholic Educational Association, Los Angeles, CA.

Steinbrecher, M. J. (1991). *A comparison between female graduates of single sex and coeducational Catholic high schools and the attainment of career leadership positions.* Unpublished doctoral dissertation, University of San Francisco.

Stevenson, C. (1998). *Teaching ten to fourteen year olds.* New York: Longman.

Stockton, B. J., & DuChateau, M. C. (1984). Working with gifted and talented children. *Catholic Library World, 55(8),* 346-351.

Strike, K. A. (1993). Professionalism, democracy, and discursive communities: Normative reflections on restructuring. *American Educational Research Journal, 30(2),* 255-275.

Stuckey, M. (1995). Schools working together – It just makes sense. *Momentum, 26(4),* 8-10.

Stuckey, M. (1997a). *From the chalkboard to the chatroom...and how to get there from here: A model for developing and using a diocesan and school site educational technology plan.* Washington, DC: National Catholic Educational Association.

Stuckey, M. (1997b). Planning from the diocesan perspective. In R. Haney & A. A. Zukowski (Eds.), *New frontiers: Navigational strategies for integrating technology into the school* (pp. 73-82). Washington, DC: National Catholic Educational Association.

Sugarman, S. D., & Kemerer, F. R. (Eds.). (1999). *School choice and social controversy: Politics, policy, and law.* Washington, DC: Brookings Institution Press.

Sullivan, H. C. (1995). *Parents' perceptions of quality and staff composition in the Catholic schools of the diocese of Fall River.* Unpublished doctoral dissertation, Boston College.

Sumarah, J. (1993). Exceptionality and service delivery: A critical juncture. *NAMRP Quarterly, 24(1),* 22-25.

Sweller, J., van Merrienboer, J. J. G., & Paas, F. G. W. C. (1998). Cognitive architecture and instructional design. *Educational Psychology Review, 10(3),* 251-296.

Swinburne, R. (1996). *Is there a God?* New York: Oxford University Press.

Sylwester, R. (1995). *A celebration of neurons: An educator's guide to the human brain.* Alexandria, VA: Association for Supervision and Curriculum Development.

Talbert, J. E. (1996). Primacy and promise of professional development in the nation's education reform agenda: Sociological views. In K. M. Borman, P. W. Cookson, A. R. Sadovnik, & J. Z. Spade (Eds.), *Implementing educational reform: Sociological perspectives on educational policy* (pp. 283-311). Norwood, NJ: Ablex Publishing Corporation.

Tamara, H. (1998, February 2). Plan takes aim at Hispanic dropouts. *USA Today,* p. 6-D.

Tarr, H. C. (1992). The commitment and satisfaction of Catholic school teachers (Doctoral dissertation, The Catholic University of America, 1992). *Dissertation Abstracts International, 53-03A,* 684.

Taylor, R. J. K. (1996). *Variables motivating parents to choose a specific type of private school.* Unpublished doctoral dissertation, Florida International University.

Teachman, J. D., Paasch, C., & Carver, K. (1996). Social capital and dropping out of school early. *Journal of Marriage and the Family, 58(3),* 773-783.

Theodore, M. (1959). *The challenge of the retarded child.* Milwaukee, WI: The Bruce Publishing Company.

Thibeau, M. J. (1999). Character development is nonnegotiable. *Momentum, 30(3),* 14-16.

Thornburg, D. D. (1997). 2020 visions for the future of education. In R. Haney & A. A. Zukowski (Eds.), *New frontiers: Navigational strategies for integrating technology into the school* (pp. 13-18). Washington, DC: National Catholic Educational Association.

Thornburg, D. D. (2000). Technologies of liberation: Education in the new century. In C. Cimino, R. M. Haney, J. M. O'Keefe, & A. A. Zukowski (Eds.), *Forming innovative learning environments through technology* (pp. 37-57). Washington, DC: National Catholic Educational Association.

Tomasiello, L. A. (1993). *Catholic school leadership in a time of crisis.* Unpublished doctoral dissertation, Fordham University.

Tracy, M. E. (1996). Small is beautiful – and technological. *Momentum, 27(3),* 66-67.

Tracy, M. E. (2000). *Gateway to the future: Selected essays on institutional advancement.* Washington, DC: National Catholic Educational Association.

Tracy, M. E. (2001). *Mission and money: A CHS 2000 report on finance, advancement, and governance.* Washington, DC: National Catholic Educational Association.

Trafford L. (1993). What makes a Catholic school Catholic? *Grail, 9,* 27-49.

Trampiets, F. (1995). Media literacy is the message. *Momentum, 26(4),* 8-10.

Trampiets, F. (1997). Media literacy. In R. Haney & A. A. Zukowski (Eds.), *New frontiers: Navigational strategies for integrating technology into the school* (pp. 53-61). Washington, DC: National Catholic Educational Association.

Trampiets, F. (2000). Computer literacy-media literacy: What's the connection? In C. Cimino, R. M. Haney, J. M. O'Keefe, & A. A. Zukowski (Eds.), *Forming innovative learning environments through technology* (pp. 101-115). Washington, DC: National Catholic Educational Association.

Traviss, M. P. (1989). *Doctoral dissertations on Catholic schools, K-12, 1976-1987.* Washington, DC: National Center for Research in Total Catholic Education, Chief Administrators of Catholic Education, National Catholic Educational Association.

Traviss, M. P. (1997). Computers, software, and Catholic schools. *NCEA Notes,* 29(5), 15.

Traviss, M.P. (2000). Preparation of teachers for the Catholic schools. In T. C. Hunt, T. E. Oldenski, & T. J. Wallace (Eds.), *Catholic school leadership: An invitation to lead* (pp. 141-156). London: Falmer.

Traviss, M. P. (2001). *Catholic educational leaders prepare for their successors: A conversation.* San Francisco: University of San Francisco Institute for Catholic Educational Leadership.

Treston, K. (1997). Ethos and identity: Foundational concerns for Catholic schools. In R. Keane & D. Riley (Eds.), *Quality Catholic schools: Challenges for leadership as Catholic education approaches the third millennium* (pp. 9-18). Brisbane, Australia: Archdiocese of Brisbane.

Trice, H., & Beyer, J. (1993). *The cultures of work organizations.* Englewood Cliffs, NJ: Prentice Hall.

Tulving, E. (1993). What is episodic memory? *Current Directions in Psychological Science, 2,* 67-70.

Tyack, D., & Cuban, L. (1995). *Tinkering toward Utopia: A century of public school reform.* Cambridge, MA: Harvard University Press.

Tyre, T. (1998). *The state of technology in Catholic schools, 1998.* Dayton, OH: Peter Li, Inc.

Tyre, T. (2000). *The state of technology in Catholic schools, 2000.* Dayton, OH: Peter Li, Inc.

Uderos-Blackburn, G. (1996). Should parents be involved in all school decisions? *NEA Today, 14(8),* 31.

Uline, C. L., Miller, D. M., & Tschannen-Moran, M. (1998). School effectiveness: The underlying dimensions. *Educational Administration Quarterly, 34,* 462-484.

United States Catholic Conference. (1978). *Pastoral statement of the United States Catholic bishops on handicapped people.* Washington, DC: Author.

United States Catholic Conference. (1983a). *Charter of the rights of families.* Washington, DC: Author.

United States Catholic Conference. (1983b). Statement on Catholic schools. In H. J. Nolan (Ed.), *Pastoral letters of the United States Catholic bishops volume III 1962-1974* (pp. 93-97). Washington, DC: Author.

United States Catholic Conference. (1990). *In support of Catholic elementary and secondary schools.* Washington, DC: Author.

United States Catholic Conference. (1995). *Principles for educational reform in the United States.* Washington, DC: Author.

United States Catholic Conference. (2000). *Faithful citizenship: Civic responsibility for a new millennium.* Washington, DC: Author.

United States Department of Education. (1998). *To assure the free appropriate public education of all children with disabilities: Twentieth annual report to Congress on the implementation of the Individuals With Disabilities Education Act.* Washington, DC: U. S. Government Printing Office.

United States Department of Education. (2000a). *The class-size reduction program: Boosting student achievement in schools across the nation.* Washington, DC: U.S. Government Printing Office.

United States Department of Education. (2000b). *The state of charter schools - 2000.* Washington, DC: Author.

United States Department of Education. (2001a). *Challenge and opportunity: The impact of charter schools on school districts.* Washington, DC: Author.

United States Department of Education. (2001b). *The study of charter school accountability.* Washington, DC: Author.

United States Department of Education, Office of Educational Research and Improvement. (1997). *Private schools in the United States: A statistical profile, 1993-94.* Washington, DC: Author.

Valenzuela, A. (1999). *Subtractive schooling: U.S.-Mexican youth and the politics of caring.* Albany, NY: State University of New York Press.

Vatterott, C. (1995). Student-focused instruction: Balancing limits with freedom in the middle grades. *Middle School Journal, 27(2),* 28-38.

Vaughan, K. (1978). Catholicity and goal agreement in Catholic elementary schools having lay faculties and lay principals (Doctoral dissertation, University of California). *University Microfilms International, 78-13, 957.*

Vessels, G. G. (1998). *Character and community development.* Westport, CT: Praiger.

Veverka, F. (1993, Spring). Re-imagining Catholic identity: Toward an analogical paradigm of religious education. *Religious Education, 88,* 238-254.

Viadero, D. (1998, February 18). Small classes: Popular, but still unproven. *Education Week*. Retrieved August 24, 2001 from http://www.edweek.org/ew/1998/23class.h17

Viteritti, J. P. (1996, Summer). Stacking the deck for the poor: The new politics of school choice. *The Brookings Review, 10-13.*

Viteritti, J. P. (1999). *Choosing equality: School choice, the Constitution, and civil society.* Washington, DC: Brookings Institution Press.

Vygotsky, L. S. (1962). *Thought and language.* (E. Hanfmann & G. Vakar, Trans.). Cambridge, MA: The M.I.T. Press.

Wagganer, K., & Standhardt, R. T. (1987). Biblical attitudes toward disabled persons. *NAMRP Quarterly, 17(4),* 2-4.

Waggenspack, D. V. (1997). Planning from a total parish perspective. In R. Haney & A. A. Zukowski (Eds.), *New frontiers: Navigational strategies for integrating technology into the school* (pp. 101-114). Washington, DC: National Catholic Educational Association.

Walch, T. (1996). *Parish school: American Catholic parochial education from colonial times to the present.* New York: Crossroad Herder.

Walker, H. (1999, Spring). Inclusion in elementary school. *National Apostolate Quarterly,* 7-9.

Wall, R., & Rinehart, J. S. (1998, January). School-based decision making and the empowerment of secondary school teachers. *Journal of School Leadership, 8,* 49-64.

Wallace, T. J. (1995). *Assessment of the preparedness of lay Catholic high school principals to be faith leaders.* Unpublished doctoral dissertation, University of Dayton, Ohio.

Ward, C. (2001). Under construction: On becoming a constructivist in view of the standards. *Mathematics Teacher, 94(2),* 94-96.

Wasley, P. A., Fine, M., Gladden, M., Holland, N. F., King, S. P., Mosak, E., & Powell, L. C. (2000). *Small schools: Great strides—A study of new small schools in Chicago.* New York: Bank Street College of Education.

Watson, B. C. (1978). The principal against the system. In D. A. Erikson & T. L. Reller (Eds.), *The principal in metropolitan schools* (pp. 40-54). Berkeley, CA: McCutchan Publishing.

Weaver, H. R., & Landers, M. F. (Guest Eds.). (2000). Focus section. *Catholic Education: A Journal of Inquiry and Practice, 3(3),* 325-396.

Wells, A. S. (1993). *Time to choose: American at the crossroads of school choice policy.* New York: Hill and Wang.

Wells, A. S., & Oakes, J. (1996). Potential pitfalls of systemic reform: Early issues from research on detracking. *Sociology of Education, 69* (Suppl.), 135-143.

Wells, A. S., & Serna, I. (1996). The politics of culture: Understanding local political resistance to detracking in racially mixed schools. *Harvard Educational Review, 66(1),* 93-118.

White, C. E. (1995). Expectations for the beginning Catholic elementary school teacher held by Catholic school principals and Catholic college/university teacher educators (Doctoral dissertation, University of San Francisco, 1995). *Dissertation Abstracts International, 57-06A,* 2446.

White, J. A., & Wehlage, G. (1995). Community collaboration: If it is such a good idea, why is it so hard to do? *Educational Evaluation and Policy Analysis, 17(1),* 23-38.

Whitehead, B. D. (1994). The failure of sex education. *The Atlantic Monthly, 274(4),* 55-77.

Whitton, D. (1997). Regular classroom practices with gifted students in grades 3 and 4 in New South Wales, Australia. *Gifted Education International, 12(1),* 34-38.

Wiles, J., & Bondi, J. (2001). *The new American middle school* (3rd ed.). Upper Saddle River, NJ: Merrill Prentice Hall.

Wilkinson, V. (1996). A walk through the school of the future. *Thrust for Educational Leadership, 25,* 37-39.

Winfield, L. F., Johnson, R., & Manning, J. B. (1993). Managing instructional diversity. In P. B. Forsyth & M. Tallerico (Eds.), *City schools: Leading the way* (pp. 97-130). Newbury Park, CA: Corwin Press.

Wirth, E. (1996). Challenge them and they will come. *Momentum, 27(4),* 28-30.

Witt, P., & Baker, D. (1997). Developing after-school programs for youth in high risk environments. *Journal of Physical Education, Recreation and Dance, 68(9),* 18-20.

Witte, J. F. (1992). Private school versus public school achievement: Are there findings that should affect the educational choice debate? *Economics of Education Review, 11(4),* 371-394.

Witte, J. F. (1996). School choice and student performance. In H. F. Ladd (Ed.), *Holding schools accountable: Performance-based reform in education* (pp. 149-176). Washington, DC: The Brookings Institution.

Wojcikewych, J. H. (1996). Blessed with the brightest. *Momentum, 27(3),* 68-70.

Woodward, J. (1965). *Industrial organization: Theory and practice.* London: Oxford University Press.

Wornsop, R. L. (1991, May). School choice: Would it strengthen or weaken public education in America? *CQ Researcher, 1(1),* 253-276.

Wright, P. B., & Leroux, J. A. (1997). The self-concept of gifted adolescents in a congregated program. *Gifted Child Quarterly, 41(3),* 83-94.

Wynne, E. A. (1980). *Looking at schools: Good, bad, and indifferent.* Lexington, MA: D. C. Heath.

Yeager, R., Benson, P., Guerra, M. J., & Manno, B. (1985). *The Catholic high school: A national portrait.* Washington, DC: National Catholic Educational Association.

Youniss, J., & Convey, J. J. (Eds.). (2000). *Catholic schools at the crossroads: Survival and transformation.* New York: Teachers College Press.

Youniss, J., & McLellan, J. A. (1999). Catholic schools in perspective: Religious identity, achievement, and citizenship. *Phi Delta Kappan, 81(2),* 104-113.

Yowell, C. M. (1996). Youth empowerment and human service institutions. *Journal of Negro Education, 65(1),* 19-29.

Zajac, M. B. (1995). High-tech high schools. *Momentum, 26(4),* 52-54.

Zane, N. (1994). When "discipline problems" recede: Democracy and intimacy in urban charters. In M. Fine (Ed.), *Chartering urban school reform* (pp. 122-135). New York: Teachers College Press.

Zanzig, T. (1991). Building a religious curriculum. In F. D. Kelly (Ed.), *What makes a school Catholic?* (pp. 22-29). Washington, DC: National Catholic Educational Association.

Zarra, E. J., III. (2000). Pinning down character education. *Kappa Delta Pi Record, 36(4),* 154-157.

Zemelman, S., Daniels, H., & Hyde, A. (1998). *Best practice for teaching and learning in America's schools.* Portsmouth, NH: Heinemann.

Zigarelli, M. M. (1996). An empirical test of conclusions from effective schools research. *Journal of Educational Research, 90(2),* 103-110.

Zill, N., Nord, C. W., & Loomis, L. S. (1995). *Adolescent time use, risky behavior, and outcomes: An analysis of national data.* Rockville, MD: Westat.

Zukowski, A. A. (1992). Rethinking Catholic education: A dialogue. *Momentum, 23(1),* 24-27.

Zukowski, A. A. (1995). Seize the day. *Momentum, 26(4),* 4-7.

Zukowski, A. A. (1997a). Artisans of faith: A new renaissance. In R. Haney & A. A. Zukowski (Eds.), *New frontiers: Navigational strategies for integrating technology into the school* (pp. 115-121). Washington, DC: National Catholic Educational Association.

Zukowski, A. A. (1997b). New learning paradigms for Catholic education. *Catholic Education: A Journal of Inquiry and Practice*, 1(1), 51-56.

Zukowski, A. A. (1997c). Paradigms of innovation and criteria. In R. Haney & A. A. Zukowski (Eds.), *New frontiers: Navigational strategies for integrating technology into the school* (pp. 19-26). Washington, DC: National Catholic Educational Association.

Zukowski, A. A. (1997d). A pastoral perspective: Theology and communication. In R. Haney & A. A. Zukowski (Eds.), *New frontiers: Navigational strategies for integrating technology into the school* (pp. 5-11). Washington, DC: National Catholic Educational Association.

Zukowski, A. A. (1999). Does technology nurture community? *Momentum, 30(2),* 88-89.

Author Index

ABOUT THE AUTHORS

THOMAS C. HUNT currently holds the position of professor of foundations in the Department of Teacher Education in the School of Education and Allied Professions at The University of Dayton. His major career interest has been the history of American education, with an emphasis on religion and schooling, especially with Catholic schooling. He has authored or edited 11 books on religion and schooling in the past 20 years, the most recent being *Handbook of Research on Catholic Education*, published by Greenwood Press in 2001. His articles have appeared in many educational and religious education journals. A past president of the Associates for Research on Private Education, Professor Hunt was the editor of *The Private School Monitor* from 1998-2000 and has served as co-editor of *Catholic Education: A Journal of Inquiry and Practice* since 1998.

ELLIS A. JOSEPH joined the University of Dayton School of Education faculty in 1961, after receiving his A.B., M.A., and Ph.D. degrees from the University of Notre Dame. He was named chairperson of the Department of Secondary Education in 1964. In 1972, he became Dean of the School of Education and served in that capacity for 23 years. He was named Distinguished Service Professor and Dean Emeritus in 1995. Joseph was named professor of the year twice, and in 1997 he received the Lackner Award from the University. He chaired the Ohio Teacher Education and Certification Advisory Commission and served as president of the Ohio Association of Colleges for Teacher Education. He was awarded an honorary doctorate by the College of Mt. St. Joseph. Joseph is the author of approximately 76 publications and is currently chairing the Ohio Department of Education's Task Force on Preparing Special Education Personnel for the Handicapped.

RONALD J. NUZZI is a priest of the Diocese of Youngstown, Ohio, and is an associate professor in the Department of Educational Leadership and Higher Education at Saint Louis University. He serves as co-editor of the research journal, *Catholic Education: A Journal of Inquiry and Practice*. In June 2002, he will become the Director of Catholic Leadership at the University of Notre Dame.

RICHARD M. JACOBS, OSA is an associate professor of Educational Administration at Villanova University. Fr. Jacobs is editor of the NCEA's monograph series, *Catholic Educational Leadership*, and has served as guest editor of the *Journal of Management Systems*. A former member of the USCCB Committee on Education, Fr. Jacobs was the USCCB's 12th Seton-Neumann laureate.

JAMES B. CARROLL is an assistant professor in the School of Education at the University of Portland. Carroll teaches technology and statistical research. His major area of research is the infusion of technology in teaching.

MARIA J. CIRIELLO, OP, is the Dean of the School of Education at the University of Portland. Sister Maria is well known as a writer and speaker in the areas of planning and leadership in Catholic education.

ELIZABETH A. MEEGAN, OP, served one year as assistant professor in the School of Education at the University of Portland. She was named Superintendent of Schools for the Diocese of Rochester, New York, in July 2001.

TIMOTHY J. COOK is assistant professor and Director of Secondary Education at Creighton University in Omaha, Nebraska. His research interests include Catholic school culture and identity, Catholic teacher preparation, and the spirituality of leadership and teaching. Cook is the author of *Architects of Catholic Culture: Designing & Building Catholic Culture in Catholic Schools* and the chief investigator for the national survey research project, *The Next Generation: A Study of Catholic High School Religion Teachers.*

JAMES M. FRABUTT, received his doctorate in Human Development and Family Studies from The University of North Carolina at Greensboro. He is currently Director of the Division for the Prevention of Youth Violence and Aggression at the Center for the Study of Social Issues at UNC-Greensboro. His primary research interests center on children's social development, parenting, and family development in racial and ethnic minority families. Recently, Frabutt has co-directed a collaborative community-university partnership featuring the involvement of school personnel, parents, law enforcement, mental health practitioners, the faith community, and juvenile justice professionals. Together, this partnership has developed a comprehensive youth violence prevention and intervention program targeted at middle school and high school youth.

RICHARD J. McGRATH, OSA, has been president and principal of Providence Catholic High School in New Lenox, Illinois for 16 years. His previous experiences include teaching, coaching, and athletic administration. Fr. McGrath holds advanced degrees in Theology, School Administration, and English. A past member of the executive committee of the NCEA Secondary School Department, he has authored articles for *NCEA Notes* and *Momentum*. He has presented at NCEA conventions.

LESLIE S. REBHORN, is a consultant in private practice in St. Louis, Missouri, and a licensed school psychological examiner. She works with families and schools on issues concerning education of the gifted, particularly the highly gifted and gifted girls. She is a frequent presenter at workshops and conferences in the Midwest. Two of her most recent works include an examination of the relationship between risk-taking and cognitive ability, and a synthesis of information about the childhoods and early educational experiences of women who have won the Nobel Prize.

H. ROBERTA WEAVER, is an Assistant Dean in the School of Education and Allied Professions at The University of Dayton. She is a career urban educator and special educator. Her experiences include teaching at the secondary level prior to coming to the university, service on a number of local, state, and national boards, numerous presentations, and publications. She is a recognized leader in teacher education and in the area of special education.

MARY F. LANDERS, is the Director of Accreditation at The University of Dayton in the School of Education and Allied Professions. She taught at the elementary level in both the general education and special education fields prior to becoming a university professor in special education. For the past 10 years, she has headed grant activities, spoken, and written on the inclusion of all students in our schools based on the gifts each has to offer.

LINDA J. BUFKIN, is an associate professor at Saint Louis University where she teaches courses in Early Childhood and Special Education as well as coordinates the partnership with the Professional Development School. She received her doctorate in Special Education/Child and Family Studies from the University of Missouri-Columbia. She has published several articles on Constructivist teaching methods. In the past, she taught children with special needs ages preschool through high school.

ANN M. RULE, is an associate professor at Saint Louis University in the Department of Educational Studies, where she serves as the Chairperson. Rule also teaches Elementary, Middle, Secondary, and Remedial Mathematics Methods courses and a variety of middle and secondary curriculum and instruction classes. She has been a middle and secondary school teacher. She has published several articles and given local, state, and national presentations on how to teach mathematics to children.

DORTHY D. MILES, is an associate professor at Saint Louis University where she teaches courses in Educational Psychology, Special Education, and Research and Statistics, and also serves as the Associate Chair of the Department of Educational Studies. She received her doctorate from the University of Connecticut and has been a teacher, counselor, and school psychologist before teaching at the university level. She has published several articles and presented papers at state and national conferences.

JEANNE L. HAGELSKAMP, SP, received her doctorate in Catholic Educational Leadership from the University of San Francisco, where she has been an assistant professor in the Institute for Catholic Educational Leadership (ICEL). In addition to teaching courses in Catholic educational leadership and technology, she has also designed course modules in a distance learning format for the ICEL program. She has also been a Catholic school administrator and has taught math, physics, and computer classes in Catholic schools.

FRANK X. SAVAGE, is a professional, Catholic educator with over 25 years of experience. He has worked with a variety of learners, from young children to older adults, in diverse parish and school settings. In recent years, he has devoted himself to educational and catechetical leadership development at the diocesan and national levels.

From 1992-1996, Savage served as Executive Director of the Chief Administrators of Catholic Education Department of the National Catholic Educational Association (NCEA). In this position, he worked with superintendents, diocesan directors of religious education, and national leaders to plan and implement national initiatives in support of the Church's educational and catechetical ministries. Prior to work at NCEA, Savage served 11 years as Executive Director of Catholic Education for the Archdiocese of Indianapolis. This diocese was a pioneer in developing organizational structures and strategies supporting a comprehensive, integrated vision for the Church's educational catechetical and formational ministries. Savage is currently the Director of Catholic Education and Lifelong Formation for the Diocese of Birmingham, Alabama. Savage holds graduate degrees in education and theology and has received specialized training in communications, group dynamics, and creative problem solving.

PATRICIA M. KELLEHER, is a native of Massachusetts, presently living in Ohio. She spent 22 years in public education with teaching experience in elementary and middle school grades as well as guidance counselor at the high school level. In the Catholic schools, she served in administrative positions for most of the next 13 years. Kelleher completed her doctorate in Educational Leadership in Catholic Schools at The University of Dayton.

WILLIAM F. DAVIS, OSFS, has been the Assistant Secretary for Catholic Schools and Public Policy at the United States Conference of Catholic Bishops (USCCB) since 1990. From January to September 2001, he also served as the Interim Secretary for Education. Before coming to USCCB, Fr. Davis served as the Director of Personnel and Education for the Wilmington-Philadelphia Province of the Oblates of St. Francis de Sales for four years, as the Superintendent of Schools for the Diocese of Arlington, Virginia, for eight years, and as a high school teacher administrator for 18 years. Fr. Davis received a bachelor's degree in Philosophy from Catholic University, a master's degree in History from Villanova University, and a doctorate in Educational Administration from Catholic University.

THEODORE J. WALLACE, served as a Catholic educator for 20 years. He was the first director of the Center for Catholic Education at The University of Dayton, during which time the Lalanne Program, which places teachers in underresourced Catholic schools, was established. Wallace is the program director for education and children for The Mathile Family Foundation in Dayton, Ohio. He has helped schools and parishes develop strategic plans in the Archdioceses of Cincinnati, Baltimore, Indianapolis, and the Dioceses of Toledo and Columbus. He was co-editor and a chapter author of *Catholic School Leadership: An Invitation to Lead*, published by Falmer Press in 2000.